D0681900

Jesus

Last of the Pharaohs

Jesus

Last of the Pharaohs

The true history of religion revealed

Ralph Ellis

Edfu Books

First published in 1998 by Edfu Books
PO Box 3223
Dorset
BH31 6FJ
edfu.books@virgin.net

First Limited Edition 1998
revised
Second Edition 1999

Hardback ISBN 0-9531913-1-1
Printed in the United Kingdom by T.J. International, Padstow.

Muse

By the rivers of Babylon,
there we sat down,
yea we wept,
when we remembered Zion.

Carry me away captivity,
requires from us a song.
But how can we sing the Lord's song,
in a strange land?

Popular 1980s song by 'Boney M'
Taken from Psalms 137:1.

Dedication

To my children, that they may know the truth

Acknowledgements

First and foremost I would like to thank Linda Doeser, my editor-cum-researcher, who put a great deal of time into this project at a time when its publication was by no means certain. Her tireless efforts in checking the material and adding the classical theories on theology and history has enabled this book to stand up in the presence of scholars as a work to be taken seriously. I admire her professionalism and I am deeply grateful for her assistance.

In addition, I have to acknowledge the other authors who have trodden this same road before me and have both influenced and eased my task. I cannot thank Ahmed Osman enough for his promotion of the concept of Moses and the Pharaoh Akhenaton being somehow linked. The minute I saw this, I knew it had to be so; thus the trilogy of books by Ahmed have had the deepest influence on my thinking. Christopher Knight and Robert Lomas also had a profound influence on this work, but in a peculiar fashion. Their simple observation that the title 'Nazarene' for Jesus could be translated as 'fish' generated two whole chapters and has potentially rewritten much of the New Testament. It will be interesting to see what theological scholars make of the radical assertions in chapters VIII & IX. Michael Baigent, Richard Leigh and Henry Lincoln have also had a great influence, and the thesis I wrote to them after the publication of their best-seller *Holy Blood Holy Grail*, forms all of chapters VI & VII. It is virtually unchanged despite the intervening 17 years.

Thanks are also due to all those who have read and enjoyed my previous work *Thoth, Architect of the Universe*, it was entirely due to the support and encouragement of these readers that I had the confidence to continue in this search for the historical truth. Finally a special thank-you is due to Chris Ogilvie-Herald, who remained a tower of strength even when the literary world was threatening to overwhelm us. With patience, persistence and much support, we won through.

Ralph Ellis
March '99
Dorset.

Contents

Prologue

Promised Land

It was a hot and dusty road back to Ein Zivan in the summer of '78. I had secured a lift in a battered old Land Rover, but the driver had dropped me off at the foot of the Golan Heights and I was faced with the prospect of a roasting trek back to the kibbutz. I thanked the driver, placed my trusty wide-brimmed hat firmly in position and set off for my temporary home. To save time, I cut the corners of the road where possible, striking out across the rocky terrain, dodging the tangled masses of the prickly pear cacti, climbing all the while to the upper plain. It was hard work and my legs began to feel like jelly. The crickets called incessantly, the sweat dripped from my brow and the intense sun threatened to burn my back through my shirt. At last I reached the upper plain and there was a chance to survey my progress. I stopped for another water break, blinked as the salty perspiration stung my eyes, wiped my brow and surveyed the scene below. There, shimmering in the heat of the afternoon, was Yam Kinneret, the Sea of Galilee, surrounded by the green blanket of the irrigated valley of the River Jordan.

Far below, an army convoy was winding its way up the hillside. Three tank transporters, two open lorries with machine guns mounted on top and a few Jeeps. The growl of their engines on full power waxed and waned as the transporters alternately appeared and disappeared from view on the snake-like ribbon of tarmac below. It was some time before they finally reached the top of the pass and as they thundered past, the ground perceptibly trembled. The last jeep in the convoy stopped and the driver offered a lift which I gratefully accepted. He looked like a grizzled professional from the front line – tanned and muscular with a healing wound winding its way up his right forearm.

We set off across the Golan, the transporters kicking up such a cloud of dust and debris in front that we had to trail some way behind in order to be able to see anything. The driver seemed more amiable than his appearance suggested and we struck up a conversation. He spoke good English and it turned out that he was a geography teacher from Haifa, on a month's obligatory army service and that the ugly scar was inflicted by nothing more aggressive than a rogue oil drum. However, the threats he was facing were real enough; the convoy was escorting reinforcements up into the Golan because of rocket attacks on Quiriat Shamona a few days earlier. This had heightened the tensions all along this northern border, so these tanks were not there for their annual manoeuvres.

We sped on across the plain, the trails of dust now being blown to the south of us on a stiff breeze. It was one of those intolerable desert winds that do not cool you down, but make you feel as if you were in a fan oven. Sand was crossing the road in snaking rivers and small, parched bushes rolled across the landscape as we lurched from pothole to pothole in the narrow, winding road. I held onto my hat and squinted against the sting of the sand.

Finally, Ein Zivan came into view, a small cluster of flat-roofed buildings in a splash of green – the only irrigated land for miles around. Just beyond the kibbutz, the land sloped down through rows of fruit trees that seemed to spring magically from the desert. At the bottom of the orchard, watched over by two gun emplacements, was the 1974 ceasefire line. This was a strip of no-man's land, a double row of electric fences that ran the entire length of the Golan Heights. This fence not only separated Israel from Syria, but also encircled the ghost town of El Qunaytirah, a place left abandoned since the Six Day War in 1967.

This was the closest I had come to armed conflict; I found it to be a surreal place, far removed from the reality of my usual suburban existence. Not so long ago I had been on the commuter run into London; now I picked apples with a machine-gun escort. Not so long ago the local London pub had been in a quaint cellar, now the kibbutznic bar and disco was in a working nuclear bunker.

This, and the valley of Galilee that I had just left behind, was the 'promised land'. In reality it was a hard and inhospitable place – both physically and politically – to have been chosen as the cradle for three of the world's great religions. It is a small strip of land, no bigger than Wales, that seemed to mimic in miniature the topography of the great Nile valley to the south west. Palestine is an arid land crossed by a valuable source of water for irrigation, in this case, the River Jordan. It is hardly prime real estate, yet this is a strip of land that has rarely seen peace over the last 3,500 years. It has been fought over by armies from all possible points of the compass: Egypt, Persia, Rome, Arabia, France, Germany and Britain. Some had conquered, others had been vanquished, but always there was conflict. It is curious why this should be so because it would appear that there is so little to be gained in the conquest of Palestine. What did the invading armies really want, besides a barren conduit that ran between the great empires of Egypt and Persia?

As is often the case, the answer to this question is not always the most obvious one. Perhaps it is not the physical land that is the problem here, perhaps the fact that Palestine is the renowned center for both Western and Middle Eastern religions is the cause of this strife. These continual clashes do not seem to be just the usual conflicts caused by disputes over which religion is the more authoritative, they appear to be more like crusades in the pursuit of knowledge. Josephus Flavius, the first-century Jewish historian, seems to have agree with this when he described his religion thus:

> ...a scheme, under which religion is the end aim of the training of the entire community, and the priests are entrusted with the special charge of it, and the whole administration of the state resembles some sacred ceremony. Practices which, under the name of mysteries and rites of initiation, other nations are unable to observe for but a few days, we maintain with delight and unflinching determination all our lives. [J1]

Quite obviously, the Jewish nation considered themselves to be the holders of a great and ancient tradition; there was sacred knowledge to be found in Palestine. This was the knowledge that, according to Josephus, Solomon traded with King Hirom in return for raw materials with which to build his great temple [J2] and that the crusader knights also fought for many centuries later.

Whether real or not, this tradition of a sacred knowledge being held in this area has attracted kings and potentates from around the globe and it has caused the region much strife. Yet the root source of this knowledge would appear to be religious. What could there possibly be in a religion to attract a neighbouring civilization in such a manner? It is an interesting question and the answer to all these conundrums has to lie in the sacred books.

* * *

0. *Promised Land*

The Creed

Religion is a curious subject. It is probably one of the first subjects we learn in the western world, yet it is probably one of the worst-taught and least understood subjects of all. Christians are taught that family life is central to the creed, yet I was fifteen years old before I discovered for myself that Jesus had brothers and sisters. [B3] It is implied that numerous calamities will befall us if we do not go to church, yet I was seventeen before I discovered that Jesus said we should not go to church. [B4] These glaring gaps in our education exist because the texts do not agree with the creed and in order to bridge these great theological chasms, the more contentious sections of the text are glossed over.

This book aims to provoke thoughts and discussions about the concepts of the four western religions, to reveal the dark corners of the Bible where the professionals dare not tread, the explosive secrets that they dare not mention. In addition I aim to explore how these texts evolved, what they are for and, indeed, in what way are they relevant to the modern world. Is it possible for us to unearth the real history of religion, to uncover why it become such a central theme in the human psyche? Why, for instance, did a particular nation think that it was uniquely called upon to keep this tradition?

In fact the origins of western religions are more focused than just a particular nation, the history of Judaism revolves around the patriarchal family, that of Abraham, Joseph and Moses, but these figures are also central to the Christian, Islamic and Masonic faiths. Why has this particular family line been picked out from among the countless millions of families as being so special in the history of mankind?

This book came into being, because the research undertaken for my first book, *Thoth, Architect of the Universe,* strongly suggested that there was a secret tradition wrapped up somewhere within the upper echelons of society in the ancient world. The obvious place to begin looking for that ancient tradition was Egypt, the mother of all civilizations. The subject matter was, therefore, to be the pharaohs of Egypt and the religion that was the foundation of that ancient and majestic empire. Could any links be found within that sphere that pointed towards a secret tradition? During the initial background research, I was browsing through the book *Act of God* by Graham Phillips. On page 194, I came across some interesting information; there was a two-line observation that simply said:

> Remarkably, one of the sixteenth-dynasty Hyksos pharaohs was

> called Yacobaam, a name in which a number of Biblical scholars have seen a striking similarity to the Hebrew name Jacob. [5]

My heart raced for a minute, expecting that something dramatic and earth-shattering was about to be disclosed; the discovery of a lifetime, the sensation of the millennium was imminent. But the moment quickly passed, the text continued into the Amarna Dynasty. Yacobaam was not to be heard of again, the moment was lost. Like so many scholars before, including Josephus, Graham Phillips had probably thought this association was an impossibility and he sped onto other topics. This door onto history had been missed, the link had not been made, the pharaoh Yacobaam still rested in peace and the secret tradition remained just so.

But the links are so obvious that I cannot believe that these traditions have not been seen before. Perhaps one or two historians in the past *have* seen the link, but maybe looked again and, not liking the consequences of such a discovery, they moved onto less controversial topics. On the other hand, perhaps this particular door has never been opened – who knows? The important thing is that *Jesus, Last of the Pharaohs* will uncover all these missing links in our history and more besides.

To make this transition we must once more cleanse our minds of the baggage of orthodox history and to question the veracity of every last snippet of information we are given. I began this process myself at the tender age of seven, while sitting in front of a roaring coal fire one Christmas Eve. The discussion turned to the expected arrival of Father Christmas and as the conversation continued, it transpired that Father Christmas did not exist. I was mortified, not so much that the expected hero figure was not going to pay a visit, but that I had been lied to by the people I trusted most – my parents.

It may seem to be a trivial event in the fullness of one's life, but it has forced me to question everything I have been taught ever since. The inference was clear: those in positions of power and influence were able to fabricate history to suit their own personal goals. Father Christmas may be a lie of no consequence, but if this had been done on one occasion, it was likely to be repeated. How many more Father Christmases can we find in our history?

Notes to the reader

Some explanation is required of the layout of this book, to explain some of the conventions that I have used and the difficulties I have tried to bridge.

a. Many historical texts have been used in the compilation of this work. Those texts often disagree on the spelling of a particular name, I have tried to standardize spellings, so the references in the particular texts used may disagree with my standardized spelling. Some of the different spellings have been used in this work to illustrate certain points, so names can sometimes change subtly.

b. The references in the text are numerous. To ease the problem of continuously referring to the reference section at the back of the book, some references have been prefixed. Prefixes are as follows:
B = Bible, K = Koran, J = Josephus and T = Talmud, N = Nag Hammadi.

c. Due to the radical nature of this enquiry, some well-known historical characters appear under other appellations, Akhenaton, for instance, becomes the biblical Aaron. It is not always possible to refer to both names and so, in general, only one name is used.

d. The biblical quotes may not always concur with your particular Bible. Unfortunately, the later editions of the Bible have been over-enthusiastically translated into modern English and where the modern translators have come across biblical nonsense, they have used modern idioms to make sense of the text. These amendments have often distorted the original import of the text. For example, Genesis 31:12 talks of 'sheep mating with cattle', which appears to be utter nonsense to most readers and so the Gideons Bible, for instance, has translated this as 'goats mating with the flocks'.

The Gideons, however, have inadvertently altered the true meaning of the text, for the original story was not of real sheep and cattle – it was of the stellar constellations of Aries and Taurus, the stellar sheep and cattle. The original text did make sense if one knew how to interpret it. To overcome this problem, the more reliable King James Bible has been used throughout, with some amendments to reduce the number of thee's and thy's.

e. Two terms often cause confusion in Egyptology, as they seem to be counter-intuitive. Lower Egypt refers to the northern half of the country, including the Nile Delta. Upper Egypt refers to the south of the country and Thebes (modern Luxor). The terms are actually quite logical, in that the Nile flows *downhill* through the country into Lower Egypt.

Chapter I

King Jacob

The pharaoh alighted from the boat on the river Nile and stepped up on to the rear of his golden chariot. Buglers barked their staccato welcome to the king, the crowds cheered and the two white stallions in their jewelled finery jostled with each other in slight surprise at the tumult. The musicians, dancers, priests and dignitaries at the head of the procession took this as their cue and moved on. In turn, the chief charioteer brandished his whip cautiously and the team eased its way up the processional road to the great temple of Heliopolis. At the front of the procession there were cymbals, music and dancing, next came the priests who maintained a restrained solemnity, then the dazzling display of the pharaoh in his finery and, finally, at the rear, was the royal guard; their scarlet and white uniforms flowing beneath gleaming bronze.

The great temple stood in front of them. The walls of its outer pylons were as high as the east-bank cliffs and painted in brilliant white, embossed with battle scenes picked out in a glorious kaleidoscope of colours that gleamed in the bright winter sun. The four enormous flagpoles of Lebanon cedar wood rose up higher than any ship's mast, daring to reach towards the gods, the white and gold flags on their tops fluttering in the morning breeze. The jostling crowds lining the route cheered, sang and threw palm fronds on to the road, the carpet of green being symbolic of the king's dominion over the bounty of the Nile. They fell silent and to their knees as the pharaoh passed them by, for here was their only chance to be in the presence of the gods. The pharaoh was not just the king, but the Son of God himself, the world of the spirits made into flesh and blood for the benefit of mankind.

As the procession approached the towering golden gates that

sealed the entrance to the temple, the king's bejewelled chariot made its way to the front. The pharaoh stepped down on to a lush red carpet, strode up to the gates and ceremonially struck them with his bronze, serpent topped rod of office. Slowly and silently, the great doors were opened for the king, an ancient tradition designed to demonstrate the pharaoh's power over everything in the land – no door was barred to him. A small bier was made available for the king and he was transported to the more sober atmosphere of the temple's outer courtyard, lined with all the dignitaries in the land of Lower Egypt.

After the procession had made its entry and arranged themselves at the far end of the courtyard, the main doors were shut again. A deathly hush descended over the common people outside: the gods were about to be in communion with each other. The chief priest of Heliopolis approached the king, pausing and bowing at every second step. As he knelt down on a small stool, the audience, too, knelt down. There was a rustle of movement around the courtyard and then silence fell once more. The priest made a short speech of welcome to his humble temple, his voice echoing around the great stone pillars that surrounded the cloister. The pharaoh made a small gesture to indicate that he might rise once more and, as he did so, the temple's master of ceremonies cried out aloud "Long live the pharaoh". The assembled lords and ladies rose to their feet en masse and chanted in return, "Long live King Abraham, father of the nation".

Fantasy?

If I suggested that the scene above referred to the biblical Abraham, would it appear to be an utterly absurd figment of a deranged mind? Initially, that may seem so, but only because we have grown so used to the orthodox ecclesiastical creed that we have forgotten that the biblical Abraham was, in fact, a king. The image I have portrayed is not quite so absurd; at the most, it is just an embellishment on what the texts say. This grandiose image of King Abraham and his grandson Jacob is one that I want to inspect in minute detail, for it holds within it the key to the fundamentals of modern theology and these are far removed from the Christmas card images with which we are so familiar.

Is this quest of any relevance today? Indeed, some may even be tempted to say that none of religion has any relevance in the modern world; it is something that society has largely outgrown. But look around the world, see the fervour with which it is followed in some quarters and observe the consequences of the conflicts that occur in its name. Religion is still very important to us all, it is a subject that we must look to, learn from and, most importantly, learn about. A religious person has to be in command of all the facts in order to make an informed decision on his/her beliefs. Even an atheist or an agnostic must know religion just as intimately, for how can you reject what you do not understand?

The first task, therefore, is to lay bare the true foundations of our religious world here in the West. For the clergy, whom we entrust to educate us on religious matters, often tell the biblical stories to us without highlighting their ramifications. We, in our ignorance, listen to their sermons but do not understand their meaning. The most fundamental thing to underline from the beginning is a little truth that gets rather forgotten about in clerical circles. What the priests forget to tell their flocks is that the Bible, the Koran and the Torah are all based on the same events; they all tell the same tale about the family history of Abraham, his forefathers and his descendants.

Many people, even today, may be tempted to look at one of these 'other' religions and think that it is quite alien to their own and that its followers are somehow misguided. 'We' are somehow quite civilized to have a particular religion, on the other hand, 'they' are barbarians. It is a common failing to attach such labels and it is caused by a failure in our education. We are not taught in our religious instruction that Muslims, Christians, Jews and even Freemasons are all religious cousins. Indeed, the relationship is closer even than that; they are religious brothers, born from the same rootstock.

The Jewish Torah, the older sections of the Islamic Koran and the Christian Old Testament are all based upon the same story, that of Abraham and his family. The five books of Moses, as these texts are sometimes known, are simply the story of a royal bloodline, but it is a story that has branched off in different eras and into slightly different sects. This most ancient of stories first divided in Babylon in about the 6th century BC and the Torah was founded. The story divided again in the first century AD, forming the Bible, and it branched off once more in the sixth century AD and the Koran evolved. Nevertheless the basic message remains the same, no matter how it is delivered.

One other religion has held the traditions of this sacred family, Freemasonry. In some respects, Masonry appears to have preserved an even older version of the history of this holy family than that even in the Torah, but much of this is still held in an oral tradition. In support of this notion, it is apparent that Masonry appears to keep many of the original cosmological and mathematical tenets that this biblical family was teaching – evidence for which will be presented later – whereas the other religions tend now to regard astrology as merely a heresy. But until Masonry becomes more open, we cannot tell how close to the original teachings of Abraham Masonry's 'theology' really is or, indeed, how much it has been corrupted down the years. It would be interesting to compare the two and it is a shame we are denied the opportunity of further research in this field.

Nevertheless the basic story remains the same in each of these religions. With some additions and some deletions, it is just the history of the family of Abraham and their descendents. Why was this family so special that millions of books have been written about it and billions of people have believed in it and often laid down their lives for it? Just what was it about this particular family that made it so important in the world? Clearly, something momentous must have happened in the distant past that led a particular family to believe that it was somehow very special and blessed by the gods, something that convinced their followers likewise. This event, if we can trace any evidence of it, may be the basis for much of our religious beliefs.

In order to understand these religious texts, though, it is necessary to adjust our general perceptions of our theology. The first adjustment is to our time scale. Many people take history to be something very distant, with no connection and no influence on the present. They are wrong. History *is* relevant and the major upheavals that happened some 3,000 years ago still rumble on and are affecting our lives to this day, even if we do not realize it.

Ancient Egypt, however, was quite adept at thinking in vast time spans and it will be shown why this is important later. Manetho (Syncellus quoting Manetho), the Egyptian priest and historian, points to traditions that record the 'flood' in the year 5500 BC. The Egyptians also appear to have recorded the precession of the axis of the Earth, the wobbling motion of the Earth, with records (extrapolations) going back some 36,000 years. [1] Manetho quotes the precessional cycle of the Earth's axis as being some 36,000 years long, a vast span of time, and he is nearly right too, for the real cycle is about 25,700 years long.

This is a long tradition indeed, but the Egyptians were not so bold as to say that this marked the beginning of the world; it was just the beginning of Egyptian recorded history. Even if the Egyptians managed to conceptualize the aeons with ease, it is still difficult, perhaps, for us to make these readjustments to our time frame. Another illustration may help.

The Family

The Jewish people do not have a faith as such; they have a complete way of life. When a Jew learns of the lives of Abraham and Joseph, it is not a story in a book or a history lesson, it is not even a religious instruction to be slavishly learned and believed without understanding the text or the principles involved. The tales of the patriarchs in the Torah are more a part of his/her own family. These are not hazy figures from the distant past, but more a 'grandfather' and, perhaps, a 'cousin' or two. The lives of the patriarchs become a part of the modern Jew's life and they are very real, even in today's frenetic world.

This is the kind of image that one needs to grasp in order to understand this book and wider concepts of theological and world history. For it would appear that this is how history works in the real world. It would seem that there are some families that take religion so seriously that they will hold a grudge for 2,000 years or more, and then still try to win over their mortal enemies. This concept, that of the royal bloodline, is to be the central theme in this book.

So what is the fundamental meaning of religion in the three main Judaic religions, Judaism, Islam and Christianity? Are we to believe the orthodox ecclesiastical dogma that it is really a tale of a few shepherds, a carpenter and a tent maker? Are such people able to transform the world and lives of millions of people through a history of 3,500 years or more? Would the diaries of such people have been written and preserved through the long unstable epochs of the ancient world, when the written word itself was sacred, exclusive and very expensive? Words were considered so magical in these eras that we still 'spell' them even to this day. Would a shepherd have had access to such sacred knowledge? One would think not. A lonely shepherd on a barren hilltop does not set about rewriting the entire history of the world and, even if he did, nobody would believe or follow him. The truth is that religion has become divorced from its real roots, we have lost its real history and this is to be the first task in this quest; to try and find the true social status of the biblical patriarchs.

This process of obfuscation has not been some unguided, random transition from a tale of important people to mere shepherds wandering the deserts. It appears to be more of a designed and orchestrated program by the religious authorities to divorce our daily usage beliefs from their real roots and there is good reason for them to do this. The majority of people are too busy in the secular world to worry too deeply about theology, so what the authorities wanted was a simple tale to give to simple people. The formula has worked as planned and the folk-tale of simple shepherds with a divine message has permeated every household throughout the western world, but the reality of the real story was very different. Just looking at a few of the ancient texts shows the truth in this matter. Josephus, for instance, says of Abraham:

> Pharaoh Necho, King of Egypt at the time, descended on this land with an immense army and seized Sarah the Princess, mother of our nation. And what did our forefather Abraham do? Did he avenge the insult by force of arms? Yet he had three hundred and eighteen officers under him, with unlimited manpower at his disposal! [J2]

Some people may dismiss the works of Josephus as being unreliable fabrications, but time after time his writings can be verified within other texts. For instance the extract above is confirmed for us in the Bible, but the text there tries to obfuscate the inconsistency in Abraham's social status by calling the officers involved 'servants'.

> When Abraham heard that his brother was taken captive, he armed his trained servants, born in his own house, three hundred and eighteen, and pursued them unto Dan. [B3]

That these were really soldiers and not servants is confirmed in the Bible by the subsequent battle for Abraham's brother and the slaughter of all those in Chedorlaomer. Indeed, when looking at the two texts, it would appear that Josephus's version of the Old Testament holds the more reliable account; he is not to be dismissed so lightly. If each officer under Abraham commanded just 30 men, then it would appear that Abraham had an army of over 11,000 strong. This is not only quite a force for the era, but it also reinforces the idea that Abraham was more powerful than the texts like to admit. He was, indeed, powerful enough for his wife Sarah to be a royal princess. In a similar vein the Bible also says of a later character, Joseph:

> And [pharaoh] made [Joseph] to ride in the second chariot which

> he had. And they cried before him. Bow the knee: and [pharaoh] made [Joseph] ruler of all the land of Egypt. [B4]

The historian Manetho, equally upbeat about Joseph's position in Egypt, says:

> ...it was in their time * that Joseph appears to have ruled in Egypt. [5]

So what are we to make of this? The religious authorities say that these men were nearly beggars in the streets; poor farmers grazing a few miserable sheep in the wastelands of the Negev desert. The texts, however, say that they were powerful men and rulers of vast nations. Joseph was the chief vizier to the pharaoh of Egypt and therefore the second most powerful man in the world after him. Here was a man who controlled the lives of an entire nation, one that was the most powerful in the world at the time. Abraham was also not a poor shepherd, of that we can be certain. He was the leader of an army of 'unlimited manpower', an army with three hundred and eighteen officers. Nevertheless the religious authorities try to infer that both patriarchs were just poor shepherds! Why?

There would appear to be a huge dichotomy in the texts: just what is the truth between these two disparate positions? Moreover, if the biblical patriarchs were, indeed, powerful men, what is the purpose of this obfuscation by the religious authorities? The inescapable conclusion is that there has been a cover-up at some point in our history. Nobody in his right mind would turn heroes from the position of kings and chief viziers into poor shepherds, if there were not something to hide. But what is being hidden?

Pesher Prose

Barbara Thiering in her two books on the same topic proposes a possible solution to the problem. She says that the biblical texts were really meant for two or more audiences and were composed in a form of Judaic writing known as the Pesher technique. [6] Ordinary people would see and hear only the simple pastoral tales and believe in a picture postcard life of farmers, families and the ways of leading a moral life. Yet the inner circle of initiates, those who had 'ears to hear', could read between the lines in

* It was in the time of the Hyksos kings of Egypt, a subject covered in full in later chapters.

the text and follow the real agenda. This is a logical deduction, but why the two classes of follower?

Part of Barbara Thiering's thesis is that the texts themselves held the secrets of the Jewish freedom fighters who were pursuing a campaign against the Roman occupation of Israel. It is true that, at the turn of the first century, there were many fundamentalist Jewish factions who were fighting tooth and nail for independence from Rome. This was a course of action which eventually resulted in the sacking of Jerusalem by the Romans, the total loss of the Jewish homeland and the exile of much of the Jewish population. This was the fourth great exodus of the Jews, the one that most heavily reinforced the foundations of the Diaspora, the modern day expatriate Jewish population. It is quite reasonable to expect that any freedom fighters in that era, whose lives must have been in constant danger, would have wanted to keep their intentions secret. It is quite possible, therefore, that the religious texts they were writing may have held within them two layers of information, one for the laity and one for the rebels.

Unfortunately for the rebellion against Rome theory, Abraham's demotion in these religious texts from great military leader to lowly shepherd occurred well before any problems with Rome. The circumstances of Abraham's life in Egypt were very different from the later struggle with Rome for a homeland. The Jewish nation was not even supposed to have a homeland during Abraham's time, yet even in the Old Testament there is much deliberate obfuscation of the historical facts.

So why did the story of Abraham have to be altered so radically? Why should any nation wish to say that one of its greatest military leaders was a mere shepherd? It was not as if Abraham had fallen from grace among his people, for he is still revered as the patriarch. He is the founding father of the Jewish nation and ultimately the founder of Christianity and Islam too; he is a pivotal figure in all three of these religions. We can start to get closer to the truth by looking deeper into the texts, without trying to see so much that it obscures our vision. There are two parallel stories in these religious texts, but perhaps they are not the nationalistic taunts of Rome by the rebel forces in Jerusalem, but something more subtle and more ancient.

The process of double meanings can be demonstrated by a rather nice example from the New Testament. Jesus himself confirmed that there are two meanings in the biblical stories. His disciples asked him why he always spoke to the common people in parables and the answer to this simple question is quite peculiar:

> Because it is given unto you [the disciples] to know the secrets of the kingdom of heaven, but unto them [the people] it is not given. [B7]

The import of this comment is startling: the church withholds secrets from the people. This line of reasoning is made even clearer in the Gospel of Philip from the Nag Hammadi scrolls. These scrolls comprise 52 manuscripts in Coptic script, found in Nag Hammadi in east central Egypt. They are thought to be fourth-century copies of texts written in the first and second century. In these, Jesus said:

> Now [the farmer] was a sensible fellow, and he knew what the food of each of them was. He served the children bread, he served the servants meal, barley and grass to the cattle, bones to the dogs and slops to the pigs. Compare the disciple of God, if he is a sensible fellow, the bodily forms will not deceive him ... There are many animals in the world which are in human form ... to the swine he will throw slops, to the cattle grass and barley, to the dogs he will throw bones, to the slaves he will give elementary lessons, and to the children he will give the complete instruction. [8]

This source may be disputed because it is not from the central cannon of the church. However, compare the sentiments given in that paragraph with the way Jesus treated the Greek woman in the Gospels of Matthew and Mark. The two paragraphs dovetail exactly:

> But Jesus said unto her, Let the children first be filled, for it is not [right] to take the children's bread and cast it unto the dogs. And she answered him and said unto him, Yes Lord, yet the dogs under the table eat of the children's crumbs. [B9]

There can be no doubt that the paragraph from the Gospel of Philip is taken from the teachings of Jesus and, at the same time, it is a further verification that the Nag Hammadi scrolls are as authoritative in these matters as are the texts that were chosen to go into the Bible. The more complete text from these valuable Nag Hammadi scrolls, now makes it perfectly clear why Jesus was calling this woman a dog.

It was not a simple racist rebuke just because she was a Greek. It was more because she was not of his religion and she certainly was not an initiate into the secrets of the church. Therefore, she was not entitled to the bread (the secrets) that was given to the children (the disciples).

Such is the double talk and the double meanings that can be found in the Bible.

The Bible

It must be pointed out that using the Bible for reference and quoting from it is not entirely straightforward, as there are any number of different 'Bibles' in circulation. The Jewish Bible, known to Christians as the Old Testament, consists of 39 books, mostly written in Hebrew, although a few were written in Aramaic, between about 1000 BC and AD 100. The Christian Bible includes these Jewish books of the Old Testament, plus the 27 books of the New Testament, the latter written mostly in Greek.

The world Bible is derived, via Latin, from the Greek *biblia*, meaning books. This is an appropriate appellation, as the Old Testament is not a book as such, in terms of authorship or date of composition. Rather, it is a kind of library, including an extensive range of literary styles – narrative, law, history, prophecy and poetry – put together over period of more than a thousand years. The process of writing the Old Testament could more accurately be described as editing. Older material, both oral and written and from different sources, was collected, interpreted and collated over a prolonged period by a sizeable number of people with varying abilities and viewpoints. Stories are often duplicated, even within one narrative, with changes, modifications and with many contradictions.

Tradition ascribes authorship of the Torah or Pentateuch – from Genesis to the end of Deuteronomy – to Moses, although no such claim is made in the text. Not only is there such variation in style, detail and approach that composite authorship is the only explanation, but also Deuteronomy ends with the death of Moses, something he would have found quite hard to write about after the event. There is, therefore, really no such thing as a definitive Old Testament and to make the processes of scholarship and research more complicated, there is no extant version of the original Hebrew canon.

Early copies of some individual books of the Old Testament, in Hebrew and dating from the sixth century AD, were discovered stored in the Cairo synagogue during the late nineteenth century. The earliest complete Hebrew manuscript still in existence, the Aleppo Codex, dates from the first half of the tenth century AD, more than a thousand years after the last books of the Old Testament were written and perhaps two thousand years after the earliest. The standard Hebrew Bible today is based on a manuscript dating from AD 1088 that is now in the St Petersburg Library. Both manuscripts are in codex or book form rather than the traditional scroll form and are known as Massoretic texts. [10]

Matters are no easier for scholars and researchers when they are tackling the New Testament, although the problems here are rather different. To begin with, early Christian writers did not expect their work to carry the same Scriptural authority as the Jewish Bible. Rather, it was intended as instruction to the newly emerging Christian congregations. It was not until the second century that the idea of a Christian canon equal to the Jewish Bible began to emerge.

The first 'New Testament', consisting only of Luke's Gospel and heavily edited versions of ten of Saul's (Paul's) Epistles, was collated in the second century by Marcion. Subsequently, the mainstream Christian Church asserted the authority of all four Gospels and 13 Pauline Epistles in their entirety. This established the framework of what ultimately became the Christian canon. It was not until AD 325 at the council of Nicaea, convened by the Roman emperor Constantine I, that a consensus as to the content of the Bible began to emerge. This was ratified in AD 367, and the 27 books of the New Testament were eventually canonized by Athanasius of Alexandria. Acceptance of this Christian Scripture followed in the Western Churches. [11]

The final difficulty with both Old and New Testaments is that most people read them translated into their own language, which adds a further level of interpretation. In some instances, they will be reading a translation of a translation and a text written in an old-fashioned format. For example, the Authorized or 'King James' Bible, first published in 1611, remains much loved for its beautiful language and is widely known in the English-speaking world. Yet the meanings of some English words have changed since the seventeenth century and others have become archaic and obsolete or, at least, are not exactly easy for the modern reader to understand.

Despite this I have used the Authorized version throughout this book, as the translation was made as verbatim as possible from the Old Testament Massoretic texts and the sixteenth century Tindale New Testament. In addition, the revised Authorized of 1885 took great pains to revise the texts based on the earliest first millennium vellum copies of the New Testament available. These included the Sinaitic text from St. Petersburg, the Beza in the Cambridge Library and the Laudian in the Bodlean Library Oxford. During this revision, many translation errors were found in the contemporary editions of the Bible and duly corrected.

Because of this, many of the Bibles available to this day still disagree on important sections of their text. In addition some modern Bibles, such as those distributed by the Gideons, have attempted to interpret the meanings of these texts in modern terms and in the process they have lost much of the original import.

Royal Blood

These are some of the many and varied problems that scholars have to deal with when interpreting these texts, but perhaps the largest of them all is the deliberate changing of the texts many centuries ago to suit the creed that was current at those times. It is quite apparent from the duplicated stories that some of the scribes were happy to change the texts in order to portray their heroes in a more favourable light. This was also done in order to change more ancient beliefs and practices into more acceptable 'modern' formats.

Despite these problems, there is nevertheless good evidence in the accounts of Abraham, Joseph and Jesus, to be found in the Nag Hammadi scrolls, Josephus and the Old Testament that there is indeed an underlying agenda in these religious texts. But if it was not the war with Rome that was being covered up, what was the big secret? What is there to hide and why does the subterfuge appear to continue to this day? For that, we have to come back to the true identity of Abraham, Isaac, Jacob and Joseph, the patriarchs from the Torah. Exactly who were these people in reality? Why cannot we spot these important characters in the secular historical world? How did such important people evade the historians?

The Graeco/Egyptian historian Manetho's texts have been lost to history and his writings arrive by way of quotes from other historians, Eusebius and Africanus; these are in turn quoted by Josephus. Manetho, as quoted by Josephus, says that the patriarchs of the Jewish people were both shepherds and captives. [J12, M12] This is the basis of the standard biblical story-line with which we are all familiar. It is from these roots quoted from Manetho, that we now have the folk-tale of the poor Jewish shepherds being captives in a foreign land, where they had to make bricks as slaves for the nasty and brutal Egyptians. Finally, after many generations, their great leader Moses comes to the rescue and initiates the great exodus of the Jewish nation, from slavery in Egypt to their promised land – Israel. Northwards and eastwards they fled as poor and starving wretches, up into Israel and the city of Jerusalem. That is nonsense; just a story for children. The real biblical story is far more interesting, much more subtle and a lot more important than that.

Hyksos

The ancient historian Josephus told a very interesting story of the origins of this 'captive' theory for the Jews, a story which he again took from the historian Manetho. Josephus described the Jews as being captives in Egypt, as does the Bible. He then gave the derivation of the Egyptian word for this term, although it seems that he missed some huge ramifications in doing so, for he made no mention of the following coincidence.

The Egyptian word from which 'captive' is derived is known as 'Hyk'. However, Manetho, through Josephus, explained that 'Hyk' has two meanings in Egyptian, depending on how it was pronounced. [J13, M13] If the word is aspirated as the rapid sounding word 'Hik' (as in tick), the result is the traditional word '*captive*'. But if the word is given a longer more rounded sound, the resulting word 'Hyk' (as in bike) means '*king*' instead. This is confirmed by modern translations of Egyptian, in which the word 'h´k' can be seen either as being a 'ruler of a pastoral people' or a 'prisoner of war'.

The inference is quite plain; there are two meanings to this word and they have been interpreted quite differently in the disparate disciplines of history and theology, each to suit their own story. The historians choose the term 'Shepherd King', because they are dealing with a lineage of pharaohs and the word 'king' fits their story rather well. The religious texts are not so comfortable with this notion. They wish to portray a pastoral tale of simple folk, so they chose the term 'captive shepherds'.

Even if the Old Testament had taken up the term 'ruler of a pastoral people' this would not have assisted their cause in the portrayal of a tribal people. For the term 'Hyksos' does not refer to any old tribal leader, but to a very specific line of kings. In this new interpretation, Abraham would not just have been a minor Asiatic king controlling some of the wastelands bordering the Negev desert, with a couple of thousand subjects and a few starving sheep. No, the problem with this alternative interpretation, is that the word 'Hyk' is associated with a specific line of kings, the Hyksos or the Shepherd Kings; pharaohs of Egypt.

Historians usually describe the Hyksos as Semitic invaders from

Palestine and Syria who conquered Egypt in the early seventeenth century BC. They are said to have taken Memphis at first and then established a capital at Avaris, a place historians tentatively identify as the city later known as Tanis. This, in turn, is identified as the biblical city of Zoan. [B14] The military superiority of the Hyksos and their followers can in part be attributed to their use of cavalry, the horse having been previously unknown in Egypt. They are said to have established a kingdom on the north-east border of the Nile delta, leaving the territory to the north of Memphis to the remaining nobility of the indigenous sixteenth dynasty. It is thought that these northern princes were probably subservient to the Hyksos. To the south, an independent Egyptian seventeenth dynasty ruled the territory between Elephantine and Abydos, with their capital at Thebes.

The Hyksos are said to have ruled their northern Egyptian kingdom (Lower Egypt) from 1680s BC until 1590s BC. They were finally driven out of the country by a nationalistic revolt by the vassal princes of the Nile delta and Upper Egypt under Ahmose I, who was the founder of the eighteenth dynasty. Little archaeological evidence of the Hyksos kingdom has been found, but fragments of pottery and sculpture dating from this period suggests that the Hyksos kings used Egyptian customs and names. As I have indicated, Egyptologists originally interpreted the word Hyksos as meaning 'Shepherd Kings', but it has also been suggested that, in fact, it means 'Foreign Rulers'. As the former appellation seems to be meaningless, while the latter apparently has obvious relevance, historians have tended to opt for 'Foreign Rulers'. However, it is quite possible that they are mistaken, as we have already seen, and the significance of the title 'Shepherd Kings' is discussed more fully in Chapter II.

The Hyksos, then, were nothing less than the pharaohs of Egypt during the fifteenth and sixteenth dynasties of Egypt. This is a period, under the classical dating of Egypt, that equates very well with the projected lifetime of the biblical Abraham. In this case, Abraham was not only a military leader, but he was quite possibly a pharaoh of Egypt as well. This is the reason he and his family were known as shepherds: he was not a poor farmer in a barren field, but a 'Shepherd King', a pharaoh, and that designation of shepherd is crucial to my theory, for there is a rationale to the term and it is the root cause of the great biblical exodus.

This is the essential core conundrum of the three Judaic religions. These religions wanted to project a new, fresh image of a religion that was descended directly from 'God'. However, the history of their peoples indicated strongly that they were descended from the pharaohs of Egypt, a nation that they had begun to despise because of the later treatment of the Israelites at the time of the exodus. What were they to do? If they admitted that their patriarch was a pharaoh, they admitted that they were part of the very regime that had rejected them and sent them into exile and which they now hated with an unbelievable passion. That was utterly unacceptable. The alternative was to continue a process of parallel histories. This process had always been present in the Egyptian religion, from which Judaism and eventually Christianity emerged.

The Temples

In Egypt, the core of religion was always somewhat separate from the laity; it was not something that they were deeply involved with. Certainly, they would have had a shrine in their houses and would have joined in the annual celebrations and festivals, but the core of the religion was always separate from the main population. The temples of Egypt may have been great meeting places for the people, but only the outer courts were available for the common man. Only important people would have been admitted to the courtyard inside the great pylons that flanked the entrance. It was in this inner courtyard that a great square rock crystal altar was placed, its upper surface unwrought and untouched by any tool, just as can be seen in the Great Crystal Altar at Karnak in ancient Thebes. In mirror fashion, the Bible describes how altars should be fabricated:

> And thou wilt make me an altar of stone, thou shalt not build it of hewn stone: for if thou lift thy tool upon it, thou has polluted it. [B15]

According to the plan laid down in the scriptures, the altar in the inner court of the temple at Jerusalem was constructed in just the same fashion as the one at Karnak in Egypt:

> Within this enclosure is a square altar, built of heaped stones, unhewn and unwrought. [J16]

But, of course, the Bible is following the ancient Egyptian tradition, not the other way round. Further inside the Egyptian temples lie the great hypostyle halls (from the Greek, meaning resting on pillars). These form a fantastic forest of pillars, a sacred grove carved in stone. Only the priesthood and the nobles would be admitted this far into the complex and, even then, only after ritual cleansing. Yet further on through the length of the temple, we finally come to the Shrine, the Holy of Holies. Officiating here would be only the chief priests and the pharaoh himself, as is depicted on the walls of the Shrine itself. The Holy of Holies was both sacred and secret, a place where the priests and the pharaohs kept the order of the cosmos intact by making offerings to the gods. It is a Shrine that is littered with cosmological rather than orthodox theological connotations.

Egyptologists may call the figures inside these Shrines 'gods' and perhaps the people thought so too, but these characters, such as Osiris and Thoth, were more like administrators than 'gods'. The real deity was always the deep workings of the cosmos, the wheels of which had to be greased with offerings and ceremonies to ensure that the stars continued their annual foxtrot and their millennial waltz.

The laity in Egypt would, therefore, have no concept of the inner working of the temple. They were happy that the gods had been appeased, the harvest for next year would be propitious and, perhaps if they had a minor ailment or two, they would pray at their personal shrine to a minor god. What is important is the separation of the functions of the priesthood and the general population, a process seen equally in the Temple of Solomon at Jerusalem, the Temple of the Jews. There will be a fuller exploration of this temple in later chapters, for as the description above and in later chapters indicates, the temples in Egypt and Jerusalem were very much the same.

That the upper echelons of the priesthood and the royalty were separated from the laity is often the way, but in this case, we can also speculate that their religion was separate as well, for this was part of the source of the religious divide that resulted in the biblical exodus, a subject covered in detail later. The laity believed in Osiris and Seth, Isis and Nephthys, Sekhmet, Nut and Horus; there were any number of gods depending on your town, social position and predicament. Some of the priesthood, however, had a different agenda. These priests held the Secrets of the Universe and they were not about to let these slip out of their reach, for this knowledge was the source of both their secular and theological power.

With this ancient tradition of dual meanings to their religion, it was quite easy for the Jewish authorities to cover up the true history of their peoples. History is quickly lost without history teachers and, as the history of the Soviet Union has recently shown, it is just as easy to twist and

bend your history until it fits the story-line that you wish tell. It all depends on what the history teachers are allowed to say.

Biblical Kings

So the evolving theory here is that Abraham, Isaac and Jacob were not a family of poor, captive, downtrodden shepherds at all. They were nothing less than the Hyksos, the 'Shepherd Kings', pharaohs of Egypt. This why these stories from the Bible have been told and retold, written and translated into every language on this planet. Far from being poor vagabonds from the desert, they were the most important and most powerful men in their time, controlling most of the known world and its wealth, and this is why their story is important. It is an ancient history where some of the protagonists could trace their royal lineage back through 73 generations, as could Jesus. How many royal families, let alone carpenters' families, can do that? [B17] This idea may seem to be a staggering reversal of biblical history, one evolved out of a vivid imagination, but it is also a concept that can be supported with plenty of evidence.

As a starting point, take a look at an encyclopaedia of the pharaohs of Egypt and flick through the pages until you reach the sixteenth dynasty, the period that covers the last of the Hyksos pharaohs. The last pharaoh listed, as mentioned in the prologue, is Yacobaam, the pharaoh that started this quest. [18] But there is more here than just the similarity of this name to the biblical Jacob. Evidence of a direct link to the Hyksos pharaohs has already been presented and that link can now be proved quite firmly, for there is also a clue to this particular pharaoh's beliefs.

Judaism, Christianity and even the early Essene cult of Israel all have an initiation process that involves immersion in water. In Egypt, the body of the great God of Osiris was floated down the Nile in a casket prior to his resurrection and this is possibly based on a similar Sumerian tradition of great leaders being 'taken from the water'. Moses, too, was apparently named because he was a prince that had been cast upon the Nile in a basket and 'taken from the water'. [19] Whatever the origins of this tradition, it is clear, that water was central to the Israelite faith; it could even be considered to be their shibboleth or marker. This is very important when looking at the name of the pharaoh Yacobaam.

Pharaonic names are always presented in a cartouche, a more or less oval or oblong figure, which is read from the rounded end to the flat end. The cartouche was actually supposed to represent a coil of rope around the name and it gave the name and its owner symbolic protection. There is a curious coincidence in the cartouche of the pharaoh Yacobaam in that the final glyph in the name is 𓈗 (a glyph is most often a symbolic character, but it can also represent an alphabetic letter). The glyph has the phonetic value 'mw' and when used as a complete word, it also means water, as might be expected from its shape.

Fig 1. The cartouche for Yacobaam

However, Egyptology is just guessing in many respects, for we do not know the phonetic value of any of the vowels in these names. The vowels of each word are not given in any of the hieroglyphs; as in many ancient languages, they were simply not written down and had to be remembered, but the spoken language of the Egyptians died out about a millennium ago. In the absence of any firm data on how these names are to be pronounced and in a somewhat cavalier fashion, Egyptology simply states that where a vowel sound is unknown, an 'e' should be inserted into the word. Take a look at the Egyptian names; there are an awful lot of e's around. This convention has also hit long-established pharaonic names, so that Akhenaton has become Akhenaten in many texts. However, it is only a convention, there is no etymological reason for this change in pronunciation and in Arabic the name is still known as Akhenaton.

We are not entirely certain of the phonetic value of each of the consonants in these Egyptian names either. The Greeks came to Egypt in the centuries before the Christian era, when the Egyptians were still speaking their original language. Yet the Greeks sometimes tended to give very different sounds to the Egyptian names. They often differ considerably from what has been teased out of the texts by modern comparisons with the Coptic language. For instance, modern

Egyptologists will read some of the New Kingdom pharaohs as being Amenhotep, but the Greeks translated the same glyphs as being pronounced Amenophis. Were the Greeks just cavalier in their translations? They did, after all, have a habit of placing a suffix of 'is', 'es' or 'us' on the end of each name, whether or not the text called for it. Nevertheless, it is a possibility that some of the translations that have come down to us through Greek and through Aramaic, still contain good representations of the original names, such as Yacobaam.

All in all, the translation of Egyptian texts is not an exact science. Very little is known of the real spoken language and if a modern Egyptologist met an ancient Egyptian, it is highly likely that they would be able to communicate only in the most staccato of speech, comparing each word and debating its meaning. 'Oh!' the former would exclaim. 'Is that how you pronounce it? We thought for some reason it should be like this.' What is required in the Egyptological world is a precise guide to how these names were actually pronounced, a list of these names in another language, a Rosetta stone of pharaohs.

It is becoming possible that we may have just that in the biblical genealogies, but the matter is far from straightforward. In Greek translations, according to Plato, the meaning of the word governed the translation, only if the name had no specific meaning was the vocalization used as a basis for transliteration. Is this the reason why we find little or no similarity with the proposed equivalents in the Bible or Torah? This may be so, but equally, the problem may be more to do with our lack of knowledge of the precise phonetic value of the Egyptian texts, than with translation errors or any lack of pharaonic patriarchs. This is probably one reason why this area of investigation has not previously been much pursued; there appear to be no connections to be made here. However, knowing that some of the pharaonic names really *are* in the Bible is a distinct advantage, for the pronunciation of the biblical names is fairly well known and perhaps these names have altered only slightly down the years. We can then tease out the real pharaonic names, using the biblical names as our guide.

Name or Title

In addition to all these problems, not all the Egyptian glyphs are actually vocal sounds; some are what are known as determinatives. A determinative is a glyph that makes sure there is no confusion about what you are referring to. If you are talking about the sky, say, you may finish your word with the determinative glyph , for sky. On the other hand, if you are talking about a god, you might finish the word with , the determinative for gods. It reinforces your point and indicates that you are not using the glyph as a phonetic letter; you are, instead, using it to denote the actual name of that god.

A good example that encompasses many of these concepts is the name of the God Ra (Re). There are many ways of writing this god-name; it can either be seen as a seated priest-figure, or as the Sun-disk . Alternatively, the name could be spelt using the phonetic alphabet , the smile glyph being 'r' and the arm denoting 'a'. But this word could possibly be confused with another, so to be sure about what is being said, the god-flag is added and the word becomes . Clearly, there are many variables in this game of ancient name reading, so it is only through knowing what the pharaonic name 'should' be that we can read the name in its final form. Only then can we see where there should be vowels of a particular sound, where there should be none at all, and where some of the letters are really determinatives. [20]

Returning to the cartouche of Yacobaam, firstly we know that the 'J' and the 'Y' are interchangeable in Hebrew, so Yacobaam can equally be Jacobaam. The final glyph in this name is , which has the phonetic value of 'mw'; this gives the traditional 'm' sound at the end of the pharaonic name. However, if this glyph is taken instead as being a determinative for water (a determinative is always at the end of the word) and not the phonetic glyph 'mw', we can delete this letter and the name of this pharaoh suddenly changes to Jacoba. The determinative at the end adds meaning to the name by indicating the person's function or title, thus we derive Jacoba (who is from the water) or, perhaps, Jacoba (who baptizes).

Equally, the Hebrew translation of Jacob is 'to follow' and this pharaoh's cartouche contains the 'foot' glyph; the leg glyphs are all concerned with movement and journeys. Simply knowing the phonetic value and meaning of the name can change the entire perception of the word. Suddenly, the biblical Jacob, father of Joseph, becomes the historical Jacoba, a Hyksos Egyptian pharaoh. This is a revolution in theology, but it is only a small step in a long process of uncovering the truth. The biblical family is about to be transformed in terms of its political and secular importance. We have found the first bunch of grapes on this ancient royal vine.

This is the theory that underpins the following chapters in this book. It is a real story, constantly backed up by the ancient texts themselves. The first step towards this transformation is to readjust our perceptions of the past. Throw out the years of established dogma that clouds our normally rational and critical analysis of the world and look at history anew. See the incredible tale of a ruling dynasty that has managed to cling to the greasy pole of history, despite the millennia of misunderstandings and persecutions, a family that is not even recognized by the faithful that worship it to this day. The Torah and Old Testament were never intended to be simple tales of Asiatic tribes and sheep herders. The true story is a complete history of the ruling family of Egypt, the 'royal bloodline'. It is a history that can both solve the mysteries of our dim and distant past and also tell us something of our destiny.

Chapter II

Genesis

In the subsequent chapters it will be necessary to include a large amount of explanatory material setting out where the data has come from and how it has been reinterpreted. I have decided that if this information is in the general text, it will break up the story and make it difficult to follow. However, if all this data is consigned to the references section, much of this very interesting material may not be read. I have, therefore, decided to place much of the research into the first part of each chapter, and the resulting narrative, the new history of the ancient world and theology, will be in the second. In Part 2 of each chapter, there will be a biblical narrative that may be rather surprising in classical terms, but one that is supported by the texts themselves. If the traditional biblical story is unfamiliar or if it has been so long since it has been studied that much has been forgotten, it should be pointed out that this new narrative follows the biblical one very closely indeed. Even so, the resulting account is radically different from the established dogma.

What I have attempted to achieve in the second part of each chapter is to get back to the original import of the biblical texts. They had a message of important people and important events in human history. It is not only the important people that have been changed into poor shepherds, the events of the era have suffered the same fate too. It is only through a radical and lateral rethink of the origins and meaning of religion that the new history can come to light. The only major difference between these two histories is a change to the pastoral allusions that occur in the traditional texts. It is my assertion that the allusions to sheep and cattle are not agricultural, but astrological. Thus, I have changed the word 'cattle' to 'followers of Taurus', and the word 'sheep' to 'followers of Aries'. It is a relatively small change, but one that makes a huge difference to the biblical texts.

Surprisingly enough, after this radical change has been made, many of the texts make much more sense than they did before. It is my contention that these astrological connotations within the Bible were an essential part of the story. The Egyptian heritage of these religions dictated that there would be many such allusions; astrology and astronomy were central to the Egyptian faiths. As the centuries rolled on, however, such things were no longer in vogue. Egypt had become a distant and embarrassing memory to the Jews in Jerusalem, the story had to be changed and the constellations in the heavens were now translated into real animals. It was a small change, but one that suited the climate of the times very well.

2. *Genesis*

Part 1

Jacoba, pharaoh of Egypt was master of all he surveyed and the most powerful man in the world. Now this is a real story to set the scribes scribbling, the story of his sons, his parents, his mighty works and deeds. As with the tales of all kings, each and every schoolchild would be forced to learn by rote the names and accomplishments of the royal family; it would be engrained into the national psyche. This is the kind of family that could trace its history back through more than 70 generations and would spawn a billion books. Jacoba has been identified with the biblical Jacob, but what of the rest of the family? There was also an allusion to the royal position of Abraham, Jacob's grandfather; the texts indicate that he too was a king, but a king of what land and of which people? Was Jacob the most successful in the family, or could it be that Abraham was a pharaoh as well? It is a topic that deserves more attention, so the task was to find more evidence of this royal lineage in the religious and historical texts.

The question has been posed as to whether the standard doctrines of the church are in any way based in fact. Is the Bible an authoritative historical guide that can be used with any confidence? I think many people today are so wary of the historical value of the Bible that they probably even underestimate its worth. On the other hand, if you use the Pesher technique to the full, you can read more or less anything you like into these texts and so not be able to draw any valid conclusions. There is a comfortable median in this approach; there is historical information in the Bible that is verifiable, if we understand what it is trying to say. Of course, the Bible has gathered its fair share of mistakes and deliberate misinformation over the years, yet there are ways of seeing through the translators' errors, down to the core of the story and the true text.

Fortunately, there were many contributors to the Bible and not all agree with each other, so we can often see the deliberate mistakes. In the New Testament, for instance, no fewer than five authors provide much the same information. Reading five versions of the same event and comparing them one to another, gives us a good perception of what really happened. In the Old Testament, the different contributors are less obvious. But there are often repetitions in the text, areas where the same story is repeated, often with different characters playing the same roles.

Not all of this is disinformation; probably these stories arrived at the compiler's desk from widely different sources and traditions and down the years each tribe or faction has remembered the story slightly differently. The scribe has merely written down what he has been told and so the rather confusing narrative that is the Old Testament has emerged. It is from these repetitions in the text that we can pass through the veil of obfuscation and approach the truth, for each version holds a different viewpoint of the same events.

We have already seen the evidence that Abraham may have been a king rather than a poor shepherd, but can we build on this evidence? What more can be found to support this concept? As is often the case, not all of the texts could be changed and much of the original material has survived the censor. So, despite what one might think, in reality the texts are full of grand allusions to the status of Abraham. For instance, Abraham has three wives, this is not too bad for a shepherd, but it also happens that one of these wives, Hagar, was an Egyptian slave. How and why did Abraham become bethrothed to an Egyptian slave. [B1] Does this not tend to confirm his royal status? What of the marriage of Isaac, Abraham's son, who described his father as being well blessed:

> The Lord has blessed my father greatly, and he has become great: and he has given him flocks, and herds, and silver, and gold, and menservants, and maidservants, and camels, and asses. [B2]

Abraham rises once more beyond the level of mere shepherd, into the realms of the aristocracy. How far can this be taken, was Abraham really of royal blood and if so, from which country did he originate? The story-line is tortuous in places, but I think a compelling case can be made that Abraham was not just a Semitic king, but an Egyptian pharaoh and for this, we must look at his travels in Egypt. The biblical Genesis, for example, includes a tale of Abraham going down into Egypt to buy grain, as there was a famine in his land. [B3] In his travels, Abraham meets a pharaoh who comes from the south of Abraham's land.

However, if Abraham were just a minor king from Palestine or from the Sinai, he would have had to travel more to the west than south to go into Egypt and meet a pharaoh. Yet on each occasion this event takes place, it is reported that he travelled to the south. There is no kingdom to the south of Palestine to travel to and, equally, there is no land to the north of Egypt that Abraham could travel from. The texts seem to be unanimous on this point, so does this preclude Abraham from being an Egyptian? Are the texts confused and unreliable?

The ancients were well aware what south meant. There seems little reason to change the texts and the Bible seems to be quite specific, as this section is repeated more than once. Yet this strongly indicates that Abraham was not in Egypt at the time, so how does this square with the hypothesis that Abraham was in fact a northern Hyksos pharaoh, living in Egypt? This argument has been used on numerous occasions by the orthodoxy to indicate that Abraham was based in Judaea and that he travelled 'down' (south-west) into Egypt. But the Bible may not be quite so mistaken about the compass direction of Egypt from Palestine. This may just be a cartographical misunderstanding, the ancient definition of Egypt may not be the same as ours. The historian Josephus confirms this when he says of the Jewish Sicarii sect of Jerusalem that:

> ...six hundred of them were caught immediately; but as to all those that fled into Egypt, and to the Egyptian Thebes, it was not long ere they were caught also... [J4]

But these Sicarii were based in Alexandria, in the Nile delta, the land of the Hyksos, and yet they fled *south* into Egypt. Clearly, the boundaries of 'Egypt' had a different terminology from that of today. William Whiston, the compiler of the works of Josephus notes:

> Since Josephus informs us that some of these Sicarii went from Alexandria into Egypt and Thebes, Relland well observes, from Vossius, that Egypt sometimes denotes 'Proper' or Upper Egypt, as distinct from the Delta and the lower parts near Palestine. Accordingly, as he adds, those that say it never rains in Egypt, must mean Proper or Upper Egypt, because it does sometimes rain in the other parts. [J5]

In this case, the Bible is not wrong, the texts ring clear and true, if we know how to interpret them correctly. Abraham *was* travelling south, from the lands of the Hyksos in the Nile delta, which is known as *Lower Egypt* and lies in the north of the country, and down into 'Egypt' proper, to Thebes in the south, which is known as *Upper Egypt*. Many hundreds of years later, the Sicarii were following the same path as Abraham into Egypt.

Indeed, as Josephus's '*Antiquities of the Jews*' represents a complete (but slightly different) version of the Old Testament, one might speculate that the same scholarly and scribal lineage that would have been responsible for Josephus's texts, were also responsible for rewriting the real Old Testament texts. It is not hard to see how the same terminology to describe Egypt was used in both books. Once more, the texts are not necessarily wrong; it is simply necessary to know the local politics of the era in order to make sense of the situation.

This strange terminology may have resulted from the Hyksos period in Egyptian history, as discussed in chapter I; it so happens that the era of Abraham is roughly coincident with the era of the Hyksos. So during the second intermediate period of Egypt, that is from roughly 1680s BC to 1590s BC, Egypt was split into two nations, north and south. There was a southern pharaoh with a capital at Thebes and a northern pharaoh based at Avaris in the Nile delta.

The northern pharaoh would have been the Hyksos, the Shepherd King and they clearly saw themselves as being a separate nation. Consequently, there was a historical occasion when you could have travelled south into 'Egypt' to meet a pharaoh and purchase grain - the Hyksos pharaoh in the north could have done this. So is the Bible describing the period when Egypt was divided? Was Abraham travelling from Avaris in Lower Egypt to Thebes in Upper Egypt to purchase grain? Was the pharaoh he met a Theban pharaoh?

There is more to this concept than immediately meets the eye, for if Abraham was from the era of the Hyksos, it could transform classical theology. During the Hyksos period, there were two pharaohs, one in each half of the country, so although Abraham was meeting a pharaoh in the south, there was still another pharaoh who ruled in the north. Abraham is described in the historical texts as being a king with an army of unlimited manpower. Historically, the Hyksos army was the most powerful in the world at the time. It had access to the new technology of composite bows, horses and chariots and it was quite a formidable force that threatened the southern pharaoh at Thebes. In that case, was Abraham the northern pharaoh, the Hyksos pharaoh?

Sarah

As Abraham entered the south and met the pharaoh, a strange event occurred. He was forced to tell the southern pharaoh that his wife, Sarah, was his sister and *not* his wife. In the biblical texts, Sarah was given two possible places within the family. She was initially described as being the young niece of Abraham, but later she was described as being his half-sister:

> And yet indeed she is my sister, she is the daughter of my father, but not the daughter of my mother; and she became my wife. [B6]

The explanation for Abraham's strange denial of his wife and her promotion to the position of full sister is quite odd. It is said that because Sarah was so beautiful, Abraham's life would be in danger if the pharaoh found out that she was his wife. This explanation makes no sense. It is not as if this pharaoh was in the habit of taking other people's beautiful wives. It is clearly stated in the texts that the southern pharaoh was subsequently horrified to find out that Sarah was already married and, therefore, he was nearly made into a unintentional adulterer by Abraham's actions. Subsequently, Abraham had to make a hasty retreat from Thebes, as the situation was getting out of control.

This is a prime example of the way in which the texts have been altered to cover up a small embarrassment. The event cannot be deleted from the texts, for it was quite important and everyone knew of it. But a subtle change can often entirely alter the meaning and import of the event. The true explanation of this strange story is more likely to be that Sarah was not just beautiful, but that she also looked very similar to Abraham, for she was his full sister. If Abraham were the northern pharaoh, the Hyksos pharaoh, he would have married his sister, according to the pharaonic tradition. This likeness between Abraham and his sister-wife would have made the southern pharaoh angry: marrying a sister was primarily a pharaonic tradition, so the royal status of Abraham would have been obvious. The Theban pharaoh would have been very upset suddenly to discover that he was not dealing with a rich northern merchant and priest purchasing a few sacks of grain, but, instead, with a northern 'rebel' pharaoh that had taken control of 'his' northern lands.

This is a much more plausible story, given the politics and technology of the day. It would have been difficult for this southern pharaoh to obtain a true likeness of the northern Hyksos pharaoh, so he and his advisors would not necessarily have known with whom they were dealing. In this case, the subterfuge could have worked, Abraham could easily have disguised himself as a wealthy trader and physically met his southern foe. This is precisely the sort of tale that would have been talked and laughed about for centuries over frothing casks of beer. Just imagine the wealth of tales that would have erupted if Winston Churchill had gained an audience with Hitler in Berlin, disguised as an Italian Mafia mogul, and obtained sensitive information on the Third Reich. This analogy is not so wild as it may seem, for Abraham was not in the south to purchase grain; there was a much more important mission afoot.

An alternative and more interesting explanation for this trip is given in Josephus's *Antiquities*, which again has more than an air of plausibility about it. Josephus says that the trip was actually made in order to spy on the southern priests and to find out what they were saying about the gods. [J7] This is just the sort of action that might be expected if Abraham was a northern pharaoh. It is my contention, which will be developed fully later, that this split between northern and southern Egypt had nothing to do with an invasion by a people from Palestine, but was a religious divide within the same nation. It was an ancient precursor of the situation found today in Northern Ireland: two identical peoples from the same Celtic stock, irrevocably split into two nations by what, in effect, is a common religion. Indeed, later in the book I will argue that the modern divide in Ireland was caused by the shock waves that emanated from this ancient Egyptian dispute; this is why religion is relevant to the modern situation.

Back in Egypt, Abraham was also deeply concerned about a divisive religious dispute that had split the country into two and had simmered for generations. Josephus makes it clear that the intention in his spying mission was to see what the southern priests were saying about the gods. His political goal was to solve this theological dispute at its source, within the priesthood, and, perhaps, to persuade the southern priests of the errors of their ways. On this quest into the enemy territory of Upper Egypt, Abraham would have been forced to keep secret the status of his wife Sarah to protect his identity. It is a good question as to why Sarah was there at all, but perhaps with the journey times involved, successful traders in those days travelled with a complete retinue. Whatever the case, if Abraham had successfully employed this deception on the southern pharaoh, it would undoubtedly have been talked about for centuries within every Judaic tribe and it *was* talked about, again and again.

Indeed, it must have been quite a remarkable event in the annals of the Hyksos, for this same episode is described on no less than three occasions within the Bible. Of course, it is not possible that exactly the same event occurred three times; the scribes were simply being over enthusiastic and wrote down everything they heard or read. We can even see how this interlay of the same story must have been written by different scribes at different desks, because the complete text makes no sense. The second story is placed further on in the texts, so that when Abraham made his next journey down into Egypt, Sarah was over 90 years old and yet still the southern pharaoh found her attractive! [B8] The Bible does not explain why the Theban pharaoh should want a 90-year-old wife. On the third occasion, the couple involved have turned into Isaac and Rebecca, Abraham's son and daughter-in-law. [B9] Quite clearly, this same peculiar event could not have happened three times – the separate traditions that evolved into the story known as 'Genesis' are simply confused about when it really happened. In fact, some of these changes to the text may have occurred relatively recently, for Josephus makes no mention of the third occasion, but the rest of his narrative follows the Old Testament very closely.

The changes made in the telling of the duplicated stories are illuminating. Instead of journeying south into Egypt and meeting a pharaoh, on the second and third occasion, they journey south and arrive in Gerar, instead, and meet a Philistine king called Abimalech. This story makes no historical sense: the Philistine nation had not been founded in this era and, in addition, the king Abimilichi was a Phoenician king from Tyre in the era of Akhenaton, a later pharaoh. It is quite apparent that 'Egypt' has been changed to 'Gerar', perhaps to distance these events from Egypt herself. To match this change, the Egyptian pharaoh has been changed into a minor king, thus confusing the Egyptians with the Philistines and Phoenicians. Are there any similarities in these peoples? Interestingly enough, the Greek historian Herodotus does seem to confirm this idea. He mentions a tribe of 'Shepherd Philitis'; this short reference does tend to link the term Philistine with the Shepherd Kings and with Lower Egypt. [10] This confusion of the Philistine, Phoenician and Egyptian peoples will become important in chapter 10, for these three races may be related in some respects.

Abimalech is not a familiar appellation in the historical record among the Theban pharaohs of the seventeenth dynasty, hence the assumption that this is a simple confusion with the Phoenician king. This appears to lead us into a cul-de-sac, clearly not all the biblical references will translate into pharaohs of Egypt. But by using this technique of name comparison, can any more kings be found within the biblical texts? There are no obvious pharaohs in the narrative, for wherever there is a reference to Egypt within the Bible or if a pharaoh is mentioned, the king concerned is just called 'pharaoh'. This is strange, for within the Bible nearly every prince, priest, follower, family member, publican, beggar and whore is named. Yet the most important and powerful men in the world at that time, the pharaohs of Egypt, who affected Jewish destiny at every twist and turn of history, appear never to be named – why? There is a good reason for this, however, and it is related to the arguments and antipathy between Egypt and the Jews that eventually led to the great exodus of Moses.

But if we look more closely, it would appear that some pharaohs have missed this censorship and their names were passed on in other texts. Josephus preserves one of them and he does so within a biblical context, so perhaps this particular connection between Egypt and the Bible can be dated. This is crucially important, for many scholars have tried, often unsuccessfully, to date biblical events, such as the exodus. To do so requires these datable connections between the two records of history and Bible and having just one connection is somewhat frustrating. Nevertheless, this one link can fix a date and we can subsequently build upon it, pharaoh after pharaoh, until an entirely new history evolves from the texts. The link that Josephus mentions concerns the story just described of Sarah being taken by the pharaoh, who subsequently found out that she was already married. The pharaoh concerned in this dispute is now named as Necho.

> Pharaoh Necho, king of Egypt at the time, descended on this land with an immense army and seized Sarah the princess, mother of our nation. And what did her husband, our forefather Abraham do? Did he avenge the insult by force of arms? Yet he had three hundred and eighteen officers under him... [J11]

This is clearly a reference to the Sarah dispute mentioned earlier and a search of the historical record for an equivalent pharaoh reveals that the closest match to this name in the correct era is Nehesy, a fifteenth dynasty pharaoh. This may not seem totally convincing at this stage, but Nehesy will later be identified as being the patriarch Nachor, the father (or grandfather) of Abraham. This slip in pronunciation from Nehesy to Necho may have been influenced by the history contemporary to the era in which this record was written, for at about that time, in the Egyptian twenty-sixth dynasty, there was a pharaoh named Necho.

This particular pharaoh was a thousand years later than the incident mentioned, but perhaps a scribe, being used to this name, thought that this was the correct pronunciation for Nehesy. In the same fashion, the influential author Ahmed Osman says that Egyptian priest Panhesey, became the biblical character Pinhas, a similar transformation. This identification of the pharaoh Nehesy/Necho, if we can confirm it, places a definite link between the late fourteenth dynasty (*c.* 1700 BC) and

Abraham, the most famous of the patriarchs, the man who essentially founded the biblical family.

Even if this scenario of a biblical pharaoh called Necho is accepted, the circumstances may seem strange at first, with the historical record now seeming to indicate that Abraham was fighting his father. However, this is an event that has recurred throughout history and is enshrined in numerous mythologies, with royal princes in many countries often being at odds with the king, so it should not be too surprising that this should have happened. If this were the case, it would also have been another reason for keeping secret the marital status of Sarah. Consider the position that would have arisen if Abraham had married the royal princess, his sister, without permission. Pharaoh Nehesy, father of Abraham, now wished to marry his daughter, as was often the tradition in pharaonic times. For Abraham to have married without Nehesy's permission may have been a treasonable offence; he was usurping the authority of the pharaoh and the possible punishment may have been severe.

If this were the case, something important must have been happening for the son to undermine the authority of his father in this fashion and I propose that this was essentially a religious dispute. This is the reason for Abraham becoming the primary biblical patriarch, the father of a new religion and the 'Father of the Nation'. He made a significant break with tradition at this point, effectively starting a new dynasty, and it was a divergence that would prove to be fatally divisive; it would result in civil war.

It is strange that this little theory built on fresh air turns out to have some historical validity. Although the historical record of Egypt is rather uncertain in this period, it would seem that the pharaoh Nehesy was the last pharaoh in his era. The next pharaoh to take the throne was Sheshi and he was the first of the Hyksos pharaohs in the north. The hazy apparition known as history is slowly beginning to coalesce into something more tangible.

Royal Bloodline

Two pharaohs, however, do not make a bloodline. Without further evidence, this is still a rather weak position for a royal bloodline theory concerning the biblical patriarchs and it was clear that further research was necessary. The results were not long in coming, for there is some further evidence to be found by comparing the other biblical names of the family of Adam, which extended through Noah (Noe) and up to Abraham. These names, like Jacob, do not necessarily sound like pharaohs, but they can be compared directly to them using careful scrutiny. It is important to be cautious when doing this because it is easy to become carried away with phonetic similarities. In addition, it is obvious that some of the names have altered slightly down the years and the order of inheritance has changed slightly, so direct comparisons are not exactly straightforward.

That some of the names have altered over the years can be seen within the Bible itself, for some Old Testament names are not quite the same as their New Testament versions. This is probably because the Old Testament was written in Aramaic, Coptic or Hebrew and then translated into Greek and, then, English. Instead, the New Testament went straight from its original Greek to English. In comparing with other religious texts, the Koran obviously involved a translation into Arabic, and the Torah into Hebrew. Inevitably, some of the names in these texts will have a slightly different pronunciation.

The ancestors of Abraham provide a good example of how much these names have altered just within the same traditions. In the book of Genesis, two of Abraham's forefathers are called Elber and Reu. [B12] Moving forward a few centuries and into the New Testament, the same characters are now called Heber and Ragau. [B13] The problem is obvious, in that names do subtly change in the Bible, so identifying other pharaohs in this royal lineage will not be an easy task. Fortunately, there are many texts to choose from and compare, so the ranges of pronunciation will be clearly understood. There are Egyptian records inscribed on clay tablets, the writings of Manetho, the Egyptian historian whose quotations have come to us through Josephus, other Greek historians and, finally, the three religious texts of the Bible, Torah and Koran.

The Bible is a good starting place for this process. Here, Abraham's father is called Terah and his father is called Nachor (or Nahor, the spelling varies in the texts). Nahor we have already provisionally aligned with the pharaoh Nehesy, but Terah is more uncertain, as no pharaohs with this name appear in the Egyptian record. Looking at the historical list of Hyksos kings shows that the pharaoh Nehesy also had a throne name of Aasehre. Nehesy, Nahor and Nachor look very much like the same sort of names, and Terah is equally similar to Aasehre.

Remember that Egyptologists are uncertain of the exact pronunciation here, so the name Nehesy could also be seen as being pronounced as Nehosy, each is a valid transliteration. It is also significant that the name of Abraham's wife was Sarah, which is quite possibly a derivation from the pharaonic name Aasehre, the wife taking the king's name. Another valid transliteration of this pharaoh's throne name could be Aasahra and because of the following reasoning this is the spelling that I shall use.

The name Sarah means princess in the Semitic languages, so Sarah was obviously quite an important person. Josephus confirms this when he calls her a princess and mother of the nation in the quote above. But the name Sarah is not just a female appellation, nor did it originate with the pharaoh Aasahra. Aasahra has been translated as meaning 'as powerful as the gods', certainly a name fit for a king, but the name Sarah has an even older source than this.

Sarah was a very important name and it has had a long and illustrious history. The male gender equivalent of Sarah is Sah, meaning king, and if anyone was to be 'as powerful as the gods', it would have to be the king. But Sah was not a reference to any old god. In the Egyptian language, Sah is a direct reference to the constellation of Orion and Orion has always been identified with the Egyptian God Osiris. [14] Osiris was one of the founding fathers of the Egyptian gods and eventually became the most influential deity in Egypt. Because Osiris was so important in Egyptian theology and because his role was central to the resurrection of the dead pharaoh, over the centuries, the name Sah became intimately linked with the name of the king himself. Indeed, the Egyptians believed that the recently deceased king would become an incarnation of Osiris – he would become Sah himself. He would then depart on a spiritual journey to the constellation Orion to become a new star.

As a result of this intimate association between the pharaoh and Sah (Osiris), the name Sah has become a royal appellation, not just in Egypt, but all over the world. It has been transliterated into nearly every language in the western world and used as the title of nearly all our kings. Sah was seen as a sacred title by the Magi and used in Persia, where it became the royal title Shah. Further eastwards, in India, it became Sahib. In the greatest of all the ancient empires, Rome, they chose the appellation Caesar. In the frozen wastes of the north, in Russia, they inherited the same tradition and the title became Tsar. Word of the power of such a sacred name spread far and wide and so in the damp north-west of Europe, in Britain, the royal appellation became Sire. For the lesser nobles here, the title became Sir, but in the military world the tradition remains and this is always pronounced as 'Sar!' Such was the power and influence of ancient Egypt.

King List

There is an additional problem in looking at these ancient records. We have only a limited knowledge of the Hyksos kings, the line of pharaohs that we need to study, making the task very difficult. After the Hyksos exodus, many of the Egyptian records of Lower Egypt were deliberately destroyed, leaving little for modern Egyptologists to use in order to date and name the Hyksos pharaohs. However, Josephus provides a list of pharaohs taken from Manetho. His king list does not entirely tally with the established chronology of Egypt, but, while there are some peculiarities, some of it does make sense.

Where he lists a pharaoh, for instance, by the names of Harmesses Miamoun, [J15] we find that there is a pharaoh by the name of Ramesses II Meryamun. [16] Manetho also lists three pharaohs by the name of Akencheres, following the reign of Amenophis (Amenhotep III). These pharaohs do not appear in the historical records, but it is believed that Amenhotep III had at least four male children, Tuthmoses, Akhenaton, Smenkhkare and Tutankhaton (Tutankhamen). All four of these brothers were unique in being ardent believers in the God known as the Aten (Aton), [17] a belief that divided the nation of Egypt and precipitated a civil war.

It seems likely that Manetho has used the prenomen of Aken on the names of three of these brothers because they worshipped this god (although Manetho says one of these pharaohs was female, there is no historical evidence of a female pharaoh at this time). In addition, the Hebrew word for the Sun is Achares, which appears to be a direct derivation of the name Akencheres given to these sons of Amenhotep III in the Greek translation. The Aton was principally a Sun deity, in which case the name being given is something akin to Aton-achares. In which case it is abundantly clear as to which family the name Akencheres is being applied and to which locations in the world the name eventually travelled.

The pharaoh in the middle of these three brothers in the list of Manetho (in the correct position chronologically) is said to be Rathothis. Once more this is not initially very helpful, for we would have expected the pharaoh in this position to be Amenhotep IV, the second of the four brothers. Amenhotep IV was possibly treated differently in this translation because he was the most infamous of all these brothers and he had already changed his name to reflect the new belief in the Aton, calling himself Akhenaton. This change in name does not appear to be very helpful in this quest, as the names Akhenaton and Rathothis do not appear to match whatsoever, that is, until we take a look at the hieroglyphs and the politics involved in the name of this pharaoh.

The name Akhenaton was spelled backwards, with the god-name (Aton) at the beginning of the cartouche, thus the name is read phonetically as being Aton-akhen. A short explanation as to why this has been done is necessary here. There seems to have been an Egyptian convention that gods were so important that they must be written at the beginning of the name, even if the name is pronounced with the god-name at the end. Thus, Akhen-aton is spelt Aton-akhen. The same happens with the pharaohs Wadjkara, Merykara, Kanefera and Djedefra; the God Ra is always written at the beginning of the cartouche, even if the pronunciation places his name at the end. However, like all good linguistic rules, there are some exceptions.

Fig 2. The cartouche of Akhenaton

Ramesses is pronounced with the god-name at the beginning, just as it is spelt, as is Amenhotep. This presents us with a problem in translation and even Egyptologists are not entirely certain of the rules here. Take the pharaoh Khafre, traditionally ascribed as the builder of the second largest pyramid in Egypt. In nearly every text on the subject, this pharaoh is called Khafre, but George Hart, staff lecturer on the Egyptian collection in the British Museum, calls this pharaoh Rakhaf. [18] He has simply placed the god-name at the beginning of the word instead of the end. In view of the confusion in this matter, either pronunciation is a possibility that must be considered.

In addition to this little problem, the god-name of Aton is often simplified to a simple sun-disk, which could be mistranslated as being Re or Ra, the Sun-God. [19] Instead of reading Akhenaton, a translator might therefore read Akhen-ra. The simplified cartouche is more interesting here because it shows to what Manetho was alluding. The god-name could be rendered as being Ra and it could be read as being at the beginning of the name, as not all god-names are shunted to the end. Thus we read the name as being Ra-akhen. The second part of the name can also have another rendering, bearing in mind the political climate of the era. The pharaoh Akhenaton became a non-person because of his attempt to change the theology of Egypt and his name was not to be uttered by anyone. It is hardly surprising, therefore, that the precise pronunciation of his name has been lost to history.

Bear in mind that Manetho was writing about 1,000 years after these texts were first written down. If, therefore, the readers Egyptian were a little rusty or if one did not want to mention the forbidden name Akhenaton, the Ibis in the name could always be read as the god-name Thoth. In reality the Ibis in the name 'Thoth' is standing on a stick, but the pictograms are very much the same. Thus the name Akhenaton can be read in some circumstances as being **Rathothen** – is this Manetho's **Rathothis**?

Manetho is often nearly right – correct enough to be taken seriously, if cautiously. Manetho has produced for us a long list of Hyksos kings and these, in tandem with the Egyptian record, can now to be matched with the names of their biblical counterparts. Three or four more pharaonic names suddenly seem to be identifiable in the Bible. When listing the names I have kept to the biblical order; in this case, some of the historical pharaohs jump a few places within the fourteenth to seventeenth dynasties. Remarkably though, most of the pharaohs are in chronological order. The resulting table looks like this:

* * *

Table of pharaohs taken from the following records:

Manetho	**Bible**	**Egyptian history** [20]
Salitis	Sem	
Apachnat	Arphaxad	
[Cian] Jannus	Cainan (Cain)	[Ciiaan] Khyan (Seuserenre)
Apophis	Salah	
		Apopis II (Aqenenre)
Bnon	Heber	[Eecbher] Yakubher (Meruserre)
	Peleg	
	Ragau	[Raqu] (Aquenre) Apopis II
	Seruch	
	Nachor (Nahor)	Nehesy (Aaserra)
Assis	Thara (Terah, Azar)	(Aa**sahra**) Nehesy [Assii]
	Abraham	Sheshi
	Isaac	Anather
	Jacob	[Jacoba] Jacobaam
	Joseph (Sothom Phanech)	Sobekemsaf II

Entries in square brackets [ ] are my altered names. Those in curved brackets ( ) are throne names or, for the biblical names, they represent alternative spellings in other texts.

Just prior to this table, the throne name of Ramesses II was mentioned, or Meryamun. Notice here the occurrence of another famous biblical name, Miriamme. (The word meri in Egyptian means much the same as it does now - happy or loved by). In its short form, the resulting historic name is Mary; this will be very important later in the unfolding story. As with the name Sarah, the throne name of a pharaoh, Ramesses Meryamun, has come down through history as a biblical female name.

Some entries in this table may appear to be pure guesswork, but others are already looking quite positive. For instance, Apachnat and Arphaxad are almost a perfect match, and Josephus, when quoting Manetho, indicates that Apachnat is a real pharaoh, even if he has not yet been found in the Egyptian record. Salah and Aasahra (Apopis I) also look fairly positive, especially as the chronological order in following Cain gives a match with Manetho's Apophis. (The match between Cain and Khyan will become one of the most positive associations.) We also have the first of our finds, Jacob and Jacoba. The rest of the table may look ragged in comparison and further explanation is required as to why they have been placed in this order.

This is not simply a case of making the names fit. Remember that Egyptologists do not know how these names were pronounced; these names in the historical texts are only guesses taken from comparisons with other languages. The Rosetta Stone is a good guide, but is by no means a complete dictionary and, besides, the Greek pronunciation of Egyptian words is still suspect in places, so any translation taken from the Greek is not guaranteed to be accurate. Think of the confusion that can be caused if the proper pronunciation of a modern name is not known. Take Stephen, for example; is it pronounced Steven or Step-hen? Such a minor alteration can make a big difference to the name and, without a native speaker to provide a definitive answer, the task of deciding the correct pronunciation becomes almost impossible. This confusion has caused a wide spectrum of possible English transliterations for these names, so I must apologize if there is occasionally some differences in spelling in this book, but every Egyptological work and every biblical text carries with it a different spelling.

However, most of the resulting phonetic sounds to the names are broadly similar, and when deciding the correct pronunciation, the Bible will be used as our 'native speaker', to guide us in the right direction. This is not a perfect solution, but with this assistance on how the names should be pronounced, progress can be made. All I have done in the table above is to change the pronunciation of the names very slightly, following the standard Egyptian rules, to produce some of these alternative names that now match the biblical record.

Cain

Take a look at the three Cains in the table. With a subtle change to the traditional transliteration of the Egyptian name, the comparisons look very good. This name is often identified as having a hard 'k', as in 'key', at the beginning. The second letter is then said to be pronounced as 'y', as in 'why', giving the conventional historical record of the pharaoh Kyan, pronounced 'Kh-y-an'. However, according to Professor Karl-Theodor Zauzich, a respected Egyptologist, the first glyph in the name, , can be read as a soft 'k' projected from the back of the throat, as in the German 'ich'. [21] This results in the name Cyan or 'Cian'. The second letter is written as a double reed or rush , which can either be read as a short 'i', as in' it', or a longer 'ee' as in 'we'. The latter is more likely, as a single reed , is pronounced 'i'.

When these small changes are taken into account, the resulting pharaonic name sounds more like the name Ian or, if the first letter is included, Cii-an (Cee-an, with the 'c' pronounced like the 'ch' in the Scottish 'loch'). This pronunciation makes more sense in this quest, so I have equated this particular pharaoh with the biblical patriarch Cain. (This is a another biblical Cain, not as in Cain and Abel.)

But these changes we have just made to Cain (Kyan) do not help this name to fit any better with the equivalent pharaoh in Josephus's list, Jannus, the only likely looking candidate. However, in the original Manetho document from which Josephus was copying, there is another spelling of this pharaoh's name, Iannus (Eeannus). Manetho wrote in Greek and the 'us' on the end of a name is a typically Greek suffix to a name. This should be deleted, producing the simpler name Iaan (Eann), which is virtually the same as pharaonic name Cii-an that has been teased from the historical record. In Manetho's version, it would appear that the initial 'c' has been dropped from the name and the standard Greek suffix 'us' has been added, but essentially the names are the same. Perhaps the rendering of the name with the 'J' at the beginning is hinting that there should be a soft 'c' as in lo**ch** at the beginning. Whatever the case, it would appear that there is full agreement in all three of the ancient records, the biblical Cain was indeed a Hyksos pharaoh.

Fig 3. Cartouche of the biblical Cain

The biblical Elber was another interesting conundrum, for it did not seem to fit any pharaohs from either the Manetho or Egyptian records. However, the New Testament provides another pronunciation of the same name, Heber. While that did not fit well with Josephus's version of the name, there was something in the Egyptian records that could help, the pharaoh

Yakubher. At the front of the hieroglyphs for the cartouche of Yakubher, there are the double reeds 𓇌. This glyph can be transliterated as 'ye', producing the Egyptologists' version, Yakubher. It could equally be translated as the longer 'ee', as we have just seen, resulting in the name Eekubher.

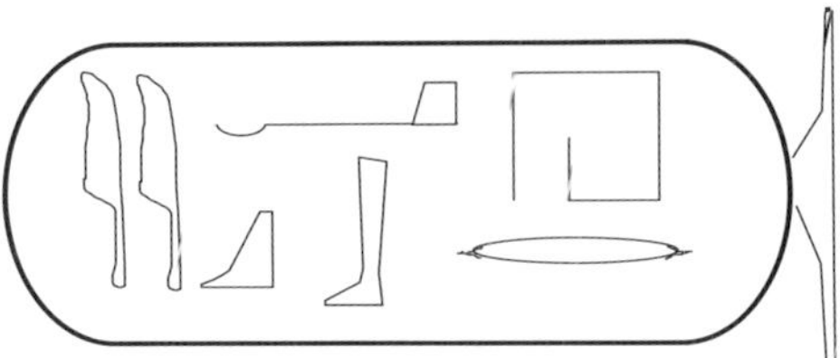

Fig 4. Cartouche of the biblical Heber

In the middle of the name is the glyph 𓈎, which sounds like 'k'. Someone has placed a 'u' after the 'k', but vowels are not given in hieroglyphs, so this insertion is probably pure guesswork and based on a nice-sounding English pronunciation. The Egyptian language, according to Masonic tradition, seems to have an unusual staccato pronunciation, so that this additional vowel may not originally have been used at all. [22] With these two small changes, the name Yakubher becomes Eekbher, just a step away from Heber (Eeber). Once again, to match the names exactly, a 'k' must be changed into a soft 'c', like lo**ch**.

Another pharaoh seems to be visible in these texts if we take a look at the name Aqenenre, the throne name of Apopis II. The 're' at the end of the name is taken from the God Ra (Re), and Ra is a glyph at the beginning of this name, not at the end. Once more we have that peculiar situation where the name of the god can be read either as being at the beginning or at the end of the name and once more we shall look at the alternative option. So it is not beyond the realms of possibility that the name Aqenenre should be read as Raqenen, which is similar, although not identical, to the biblical name Ragu. But what about the last glyph in the name? Is that the letter 'n' twice or is it the determinative for water, as in the case of the pharaoh Jacoba. If the biblical translator read it as a determinative, even incorrectly, then Raqenen changes to Raqu. This is why Aqenenre has been placed alongside the biblical Ragu. Raqu and Ragu are virtually identical.

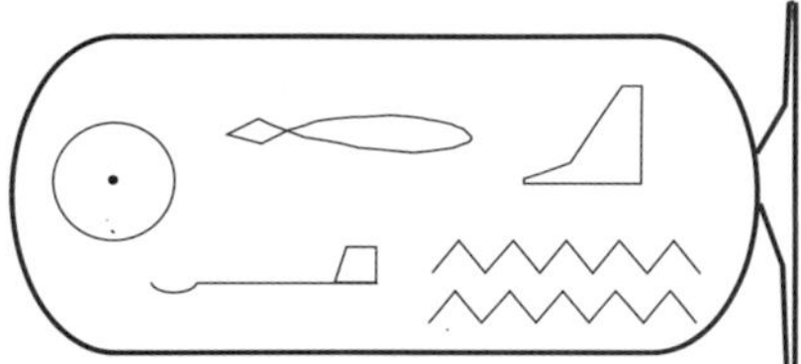

Fig 5. Cartouche of the biblical Ragu

Just another incidental observation on this name, the name of Apopis can also be given as Apapi and the original sixth dynasty version of this name was Papi or Popi. Can we see here the root of papa – meaning father? Papa is an archaic name of uncertain origins, but it may be central to the later arguments in this book, as it also means Pope, the leader of the Catholic church. I shall be arguing for Christianity being derived from the Hyksos beliefs in later chapters and so it is worth noting that Apopis was a Hyksos king. There are many ancient Egyptian words that have found their way into Semitic, Latin, Greek and thence to English, so this would not be unusual. Nob, for instance is Egyptian for Nobility, desert means desert, it is not beyond the realms of possibility that Papi or Popi is akin to Pope.

Abraham

Coming, once more, to the father of Abraham, Thara, again there is no such pharaoh and there is a need to look at alternative texts. The possibly surprising name taken from the Egyptian record is the pharaoh Nehesy. As I indicated previously, I have made this assumption because Thara may be just a form of the throne name of this king, Aasahra. But Josephus gives us another version, that of a pharaoh called Assis. This also likely to be linked to the first name of this pharaoh, Nehesy and this change in pronunciation could easily have resulted from a simple mistranslation of the hieroglyphs in ancient times.

The ‘ne’ in Nehesy comes from the glyph , a guinea fowl, which has the phonetic value of ‘neh’. However, if the reader’s Egyptian were a little rusty or the text were faded, it would be easy to mistake a guinea fowl for an Egyptian vulture, which looks like this .

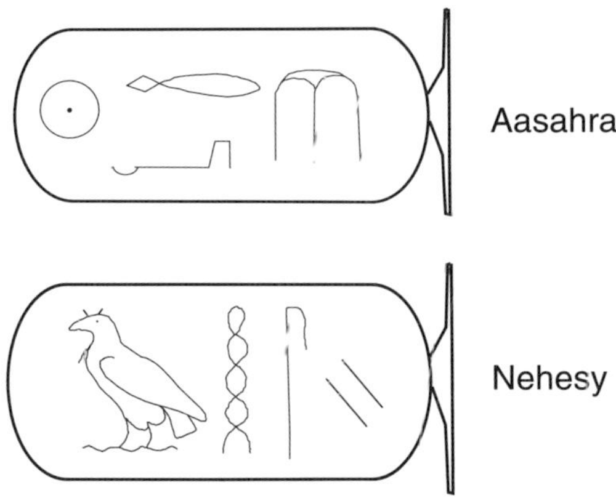

Fig 6. Cartouches of Aasahra - Nehesy

While the Egyptian vulture and the guinea fowl look very much the same, the only obvious difference being the wattles on the latter, the sounds they represent are very different. The vulture has the phonetic value ‘aa’, instead of the guinea fowl’s ‘neh’. If such a simple error had been made by the rather poor translator who was all Manetho could afford, the name in the Egyptian texts, Aasahra Nehesy, would have become Aasahra Aassii. The name ‘Aassii’ is more than just close to Manetho’s pharaoh Assis, so is the pharaoh (Aasahra) Aassii really the identity of Abraham’s father?

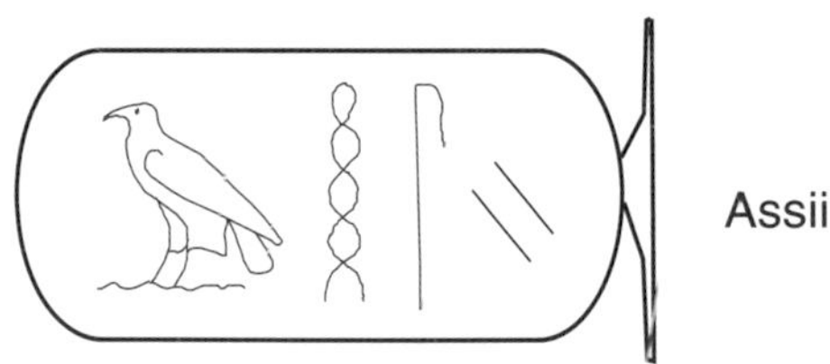

Fig 7. Cartouche of Assii, throne name of the father of Abraham

It should be noted that all of these pharaohs had at least two names and sometimes many more; at the very least, each pharaoh had a birth name and a throne name. It is possible, therefore, that the biblical record might be registering the two names of a pharaoh as being separate and additional patriarchs. With this in mind, some further progress can be made.

In the Egyptological record, against the son of Aasahra (Nehesy) I have inserted the incongruous name of Sheshi, who is being matched with the biblical Abraham. Why should this be? The answer goes back to the quotation from Josephus that indicated that the biblical Abraham and the pharaoh Necho were squared up to each other, ready for battle. Josephus's pharaoh called Necho was identified as being the historical pharaoh Nehesy and, at the same time, he is also being equated with the biblical patriarch Nahor, Abraham's grandfather (also the name of Abraham's brother). It is at this point that we seem to have one of these surpluses of biblical names in comparison to Egyptian pharaohs from the historical record, yet this surfeit can be adjusted if the biblical Nachor and his son Thara are amalgamated into one individual – Nachor Thara.

Nachor and Nehesy, I have indicated, were different renditions of the first name of this pharaoh and Josephus gave us the third translation, that of Necho. The throne name of the pharaoh Nehesy is Aasahra and this seems to equate very nicely with the biblical Thara (Terah). It looks as if the Bible has simply dropped the initial 'A' in the name. The fact that there was an original 'A' attached to this biblical name is confirmed in the same stories in the Koran, where the same individual is called Azar. [23] The Koran seems to have lost the suffix of this name instead, but if we conjoin the two names Thara and Azar, we either derive the name **Aathara** or **Azarah**. All in all, it would appear that the pharaonic name of **Aasahra** has been preserved rather well over the years in these religious texts.

What we now have is the father and grandfather of Abraham being joined into just one individual and in the historical record he is listed under the two names of the pharaoh Nehesy. If we quite legitimately change the second vowel in the name Nehesy to an 'o', we thus derive:

Pharaoh:	Nehosy	(Aasahra)
Patriarch:	Nachor	(Azarah)

This is a very satisfying arrangement. However, the whole edifice seems to fall down on the count of one glaring error – the royal inheritance. Nachor Azarah fathered Abraham himself, yet if we look at the historical record, the son of Nehesy is the pharaoh called Sheshi. This is truly unsatisfactory and it seems to undermine all the progress that has been made so far.

Actually this is not so, it was just the result that was needed to convince me, and perhaps the reader, that this was not all wishful thinking, that this line of biblical pharaohs is a historical reality. Why? Because the throne name of the pharaoh Sheshi is none other than Mayebre or Mayebra. This name not only sounds like Abraham, with the 'M' displaced to the end, it is quite possibly another very simple mistranslation of it. The cartouche of Mayebra looks like this:

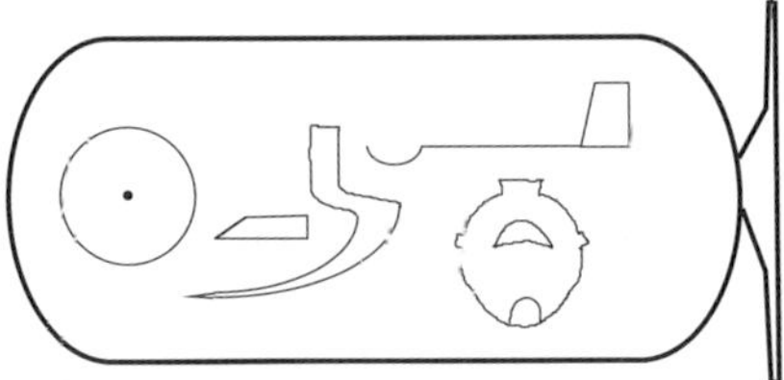

Fig 8. Cartouche of Mayebra

The name 'Mayebra' is even closer to the name 'Abraham' than one might initially expect, because this biblical character is actually called 'Abram' throughout the early sections of Genesis. Mayebra is a perfect phonetic match for Abram, again with the 'M' being displaced. Only later was his name changed to Abraham.

> Neither shall thy name be called Abram, but your name shall be called Abraham; for a father of many nations I have made thee. And I shall make thee exceedingly fruitful ... and kings shall come out of thee. B24

Once more, the true status of Abraham can bee seen: it is just as the texts tell us, "... and kings shall come out of thee." This was a promise from the gods to Abram because it was by no means certain that he would inherit the pharaonic throne of Egypt. Abram had two brothers, one of whom carried their father's name of Nahor. Was he an elder brother that should have taken the throne? This happens time and again in these texts, with the younger brother taking the birthright from the rightful heir. It looks as though Abram had to fight for his inheritance, so that he could establish this famous line of kings. But the message is clear: the pharaoh Abram was to establish a new pharaonic dynasty and to this day, in the guise of the pharaoh Sheshi, he is known as the first of the Hyksos dynasty of pharaohs.

At the same time, the name of his wife was changed from Sarai to Sarah. Something peculiar is going on here. Was this just a problem in the translation, with some poor scribe suddenly being told not to use the nickname of Abraham, but to use the full royal title? There are many possibilities, but it is odd that modern Egyptologists seem to be having the same problem all over again. The sickle glyph is being interpreted in the Egyptological world as giving the vocalization of 'ma', but once more the text books disagree on such subtleties. Karl Zauzich says that this design is actually a compound of two glyphs, just as it appears to be drawn, giving the glyph the sound 'mam'. This makes an equivalent difference to the name of this pharaoh, who now becomes Mamayebra. This 'mam' glyph is very similar to the suffix 'ham' that was given to Abram later on in the Bible, and I think that all the required syllables to make the new name of Abraham are now quite plainly visible in this pharaonic name.

Mam-aye-bra ~ Ay-bra-ham.

This problem with the sickle glyph has obviously taxed many minds, both ancient and modern. But despite overcoming this error, the syllables in the name Abraham still appear to be reversed from their pharaonic cousin. Quite plainly there has either been a mistranslation or there has been a little sleight of hand by a biblical translator. All through the bible, the names of the pharaohs have been either deleted or tampered with in order to obfuscate the truth that the biblical patriarchs were pharaohs of Egypt.

But the translator in the Bible was obviously proud of the great founding father's name and he did not want to delete it entirely. What better way to hide the truth than simply moving the first syllable to the end of the name? So subtle and yet so effective was the ploy, that the truth lay hidden for thousands of years. But now the ma'at, the truth, can be told and the cartouche of Abraham can be shown in the form that the priests have decreed. Here is the pharaoh Abraham, known also as Sheshi, pharaoh of Egypt, master of all he surveys. The biblical patriarchs were indeed powerful people.

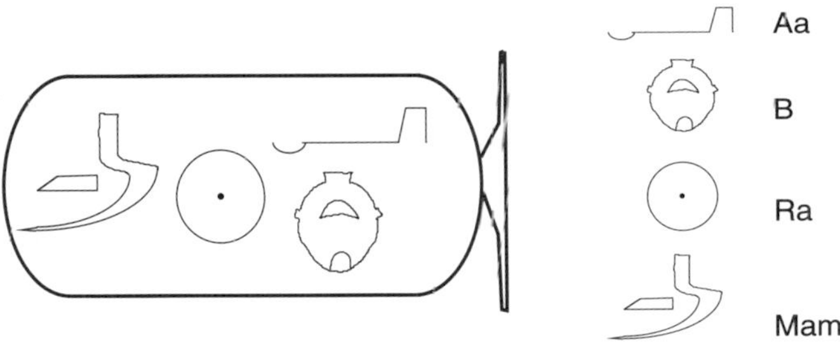

Fig 9. The cartouche of Abraham (reading backwards)

After that climax, there are only a few more intriguing similarities to highlight. The final entries that this technique unveils in the table are guesses in comparison to what we have just seen, but the chronology of these pharaohs is interesting enough to warrant mention. I have placed Isaac alongside the pharaoh Anather, simply on the basis that the final glyph in Anather is the 'smile' glyph and Isaac means 'laughter'. [J25] But chronologically this makes sense. In the biblical record, Isaac was the father of Jacob and in the historical record Anather was the father of Yakoba, the two happen to fit exactly.

Finally, Joseph is tentatively linked to Sobekemsaf II (or Sobemsaf, as there is no evidence of a 'k' in the glyphs) through Josephus's other list, his version of the biblical family tree. In this list, Josephus says that Joseph took on the Egyptian name [p]Sothom Phanech, (whereas the Bible gives Zaphenath Paneah) which sounds extremely similar to Sobemsaf. [J26] It also happens that Sobemsaf II was the son of the pharaoh Jacoba and, in turn, Joseph was the son of Jacob. These similarities just keep on flowing.

There are some problems with this association, however. Firstly, there is the fact that the biblical record indicates that Joseph did not become king. However, he did become the vizier, the second most powerful man in Egypt and the world at the time. Secondly, although the pharaoh Sobemsaf is placed in the right sequence chronologically for my later arguments, in being the son of the pharaoh Jacoba, Egyptologists have identified him as being a Theban pharaoh, not a Hyksos pharaoh. In addition, he appears just before the Hyksos expulsion, whereas in my adjusted history he should appear just after. If the latter were correct, it would diminish any significance in the similarity of the names, but it has to be remembered that the exact chronology of the pharaohs in this era is uncertain. The former is not quite such a problem, for even if Joseph was only vizier to the pharaoh Sobemsaf, it would not be unexpected for his followers to call Joseph privately by the name of the pharaoh himself; for in their eyes *he* was pharaoh.

The Shepherds

What is to be made of this table of pharaohs? Considering the difficulties in translation and the time that has elapsed since these events happened, there still seems to be a very good comparison in some places. Is this the beginning of the royal bloodline – a line of biblical pharaohs? If so, why has it not been seen before? Biblical scholars have been poring over these texts for millennia, so why did they not see – or not want to see – the similarities? Another question that has to be answered is why was this line of kings known as the 'Shepherd Kings'? Why was this appellation so important to them? The answer is simple, but requires another major change of viewpoint.

Christianity and Judaism insist that their religions are new, supplied by 'God' to the fathers of the religion in various meetings with the deity. The Jewish people were then charged with keeping these rules and customs through the ages, to uphold the Judaic laws, and they seem to have done this with remarkable tenacity. However, with all respect to the Judaic religion, the Jewish people are upholding only one part of it, the religion of the laity or ordinary people.

As previously discussed, there were two layers of religion – the priesthood's version and the laity's version – and they were substantially different. We are all familiar with the laity's religion: it is about personal morality, veneration of the biblical family and veneration of the deity. The original priesthood's version, however, was more cosmological. It looked at the universe and the galaxies, the stars and their motions, the Earth and its form, matter and its component atoms. It was very much more akin to the Hermetic principles, the teachings of the Egyptian God Thoth. As Josephus says of the Jewish ancestry:

> God afforded them [the patriarchs] a great number of years of life on account of their virtue and the good use they made of it in astronomical and geometrical discoveries. [J27]
> In the tenth generation after the flood, there was among the Chaldeans a man righteous and great [Abraham] and skilful in celestial science. [J28]

Again, when talking of Abraham, it is said that in discourse with the Egyptians, Abraham:

> Communicated to them arithmetic, and delivered to them the science of astronomy, for before Abraham came into Egypt, they were unacquainted with those parts of learning. [J29]

So while the populace of Egypt was praying to the various local gods, the priesthood looked to the Sun and the stars and contemplated the cosmos. Traditionally, this religion was based around the sacred city of Heliopolis, the city of the Sun, the biblical city of On. Heliopolis was not only central to Egyptian religion, but it was also sacred to the Jewish religion, a notion which will be further explored later. So the Heliopolian priests surveyed the skies, looking for omens, both good and bad, and as they did so a momentous event was about to unfold there.

Apis Bulls

Egypt has been worshipping the sacred Apis Bull for millennia. The Apis was the most sacred of all the bull cults in Egypt and it became assimilated into worship of both the gods Ptah and Osiris. There was only one physical Apis Bull at any one time and, upon its death, it was buried with great ceremony in the large underground vaults known as the Serapeum. Manetho says that Egypt had been worshipping the bull since the second dynasty, but other sources indicate that this worship was even older, pre-dating dynastic Egypt. That would date the cult back to 3500 BC; in other words, Egypt had worshipped the Apis Bull for more than 2,000 years. [30]

I am tempted to agree with the second assumption because, from the cosmological point of view, worshipping the Apis Bull stemmed directly from the rising of the Sun and the stellar constellations. In many recent books, it has been argued that the constellation that rises with the Sun at the spring equinox has been known as the ruling constellation. [31] That may sound complicated, but it is not really. As the Sun rises into the sky each morning, a certain group of stars will rise with it, although the intensity of the Sun will drown out the faint stars very quickly.

The established date for looking at this phenomena is the Spring Equinox, or March 23rd. In our current era, the rising constellation on March 23rd is Pisces and very soon it will become Aquarius. It is because of this movement in the stars, that our era is sometimes known as the 'Dawn of the age of Aquarius'. However, for much of dynastic Egypt, that ruling constellation was not Pisces, not Aries, but Taurus, the Bull. Hence, the veneration of the Apis Bulls throughout the first half of dynastic Egypt and also, no doubt, in the ancient Minoan civilization. This cult has stagnated in some outlying regions, where the true purpose of this worship was unknown, thus the bull is still venerated in modern Spain and India. In Egypt, the Apis Bull cult was represented by a bull with the sun-disk between its horns – the Sun was seen to be rising and setting in the sky whilst superimposed upon the outline of the constellation of Taurus, the Bull.

But the stars are not static in the sky because the Earth wobbles and this small wobble causes the rising constellation slowly to change. The constellations slowly drift around the sky, completing one circuit of the Earth every 26,000 years or so. Egyptian priests were well trained and very patient. Eventually they became aware that Taurus was slowly drifting away from the rising Sun at springtime – a new age was dawning. A momentous event in the theology of Egypt was about to unfold: finally the priests declared that the era of Taurus the Bull was over, the constellation of Aries was now the stars rising with the Sun. The era of Aries, the Ram, had begun.

Unfortunately for Egyptian religion, Taurus is physically a big constellation and so its rising in the spring equinox had continued from 4500 BC to 1850 BC. [32] During this vast length of time, the people had grown used to their Apis Bulls and they were not about to change their entire religion for the sake of a few priests and their incomprehensible predictions. In addition, the priesthood that had been patiently observing the skies for thousands of years was based in Heliopolis. This city was one of the most important cult centers in ancient Egypt, dedicated to the worship of the Sun (or more fully, perhaps, the cosmos), and it lies on the Nile Delta, in Lower Egypt near the Giza pyramids. While it remained a very important and influential religious center throughout Egyptian history, by this time, it was no longer the sole source of theological learning. In Thebes, in Upper Egypt, a new center of learning had emerged and they had different ideas in the south.

Try to imagine the turmoil that the priests of Heliopolis had started with their proclamation and the size of the Pandora's box that they had just opened. The people had been worshipping the Apis Bull for 2,600 years, that is nearly as long as the Jews have been Jewish, and suddenly some religious authority says that everything they believed in must change:

> "I know you must feel a little peeved about this", says the priest cautiously, "but we have been watching the stars for a few thousand years, and it is time now for you to start worshipping... er... sheep... er... I know we did not tell you exactly what we have been doing all this time, and I cannot tell you exactly why you should worship sheep, but take it from me, the gods have ordained it long ago and this is what you should do."

Despair

For the majority of people, this massive change to their daily lives must have been devastating. Just try to imagine the fuss that would be made today if a senior rabbi stood up and said that all the basic tenets of Judaism have to change. If that senior rabbi also managed to get high-level backing from the civil service and even the 'king' of the country, the result might well be civil war. This is exactly what happened in ancient Egypt. The Heliopolian priests said the religion must change, the people were devastated by this enormous change to their lives and they turned to see who would support their position. It was Thebes that eventually gave the people the theological reassurance they craved.

It would appear that even at the great religious center of Thebes and the Temple of Karnak the priests did not have access to all the secrets of Heliopolis; these matters may have been as much a shock to them as they were to the general public. Or perhaps Thebes was just a little more commercial in its enterprise. After all, each temple of Egypt depended on the lands and tithes that were granted to them by the nobles in the land; then as now, these aristocratic nobles could be of great influence behind the scenes.

Thebes backed the common people in this dispute and so the people rallied around Thebes; the country was in turmoil. The people were split down the middle, southerners against northerners, Upper Egypt against Lower. Upper Egypt declared the northerners heretics and made itself an independent state with its own pharaoh in Thebes. Lower Egypt declared the southerners uneducated plebeians and crowned their own pharaoh in Avaris – a Hyksos pharaoh, a Shepherd King, a follower of Aries.

Siwa

There was another religious center in Egypt that had come to the same conclusion, The Temple of Amun at Siwa. Siwa is a remote oasis town on the far western borders of Egypt and Libya, 700 km from the Nile. It is dominated by the Temple of Amun, poised precariously on the top of a sandy knoll that rises majestically from the oasis in the same fashion as Ayres Rock rises from the deserts of Australia. Herodotus says that the priests there:

> ... took a dislike to the religious usages of the country concerning sacrificial animals, and wished no longer to be restricted from eating the flesh of cows. [33]

It would appear that here also the priests had ceased to worship the Apis Bull; they, too, must have been in tune with the cosmos. The demands of the priests were denied; it was claimed that the laws of Egypt applied to remote Siwa as well. With this decree, the origins of a great religious dispute that would eventually grow into a world-shattering event were beginning to surface. Did Siwa really listen to 'Egypt', that is, the priests of Thebes, or did they listen more to the priests of Heliopolis?

I believe that the traditions of Heliopolis must have been well established at Siwa and that they remained there into more recent history. I say this with confidence because these traditions endured at Siwa until the coming of Alexander the Great, more than 1,500 years later. Alexander was a man who was posturing for his place alongside the gods as much as he was engaged in the conquest of the world and accordingly he took time off from his campaigns to visit Siwa. This was no passing interest; Alexander and a few chosen men deliberately made the 1500 km round trip across the inhospitable and sometimes deadly Es Sahre'el Gharbiya in the Western Desert. The purpose of this trip to Siwa was to consult the priests at the Temple of Amun who had held tenaciously to their sacred knowledge.

Would Alexander have understood the deep implications of the priests' knowledge? Alexander was primarily a man driven by a desire to emulate the power of the gods through secular and physical means, to dominate and control the world. Yet he not only wanted the power of the ancient pharaohs, but also the divine knowledge that was located in these sacred lands, he wanted to be nothing less than the Son of God himself, a pharaoh.

The wise oracles of Siwa looked at this new conqueror of their lands, they might not have liked what they saw, but they were sensible enough to comply with his demands to some degree; he may even have been a useful tool for the priests, an ally against Thebes. They imparted some of their divine wisdom of the cosmos to the conqueror, they pronounced Alexander to be the 'Son of the Sun God'. Alexander left Siwa as pharaoh of all Egypt and from then on he would be known throughout the world as the 'two horned one' and he would be henceforth portrayed with the *two horns of a ram*. He had understood and accepted the changing of the constellations, he openly endorsed the cult of Aries.

Part 2

And Nachor Thara fathered Abraham, the first of the Shepherd Kings who lived in Avaris in Lower Egypt, close to the Nile delta. This was in the northern nome (county) that came under the jurisdiction of Heliopolis. It happened that there was slight 'famine' in the north of Egypt and Abraham, the pharaoh of Lower Egypt, thought to use this excuse to travel south into enemy territory. [B34] So Abraham journeyed south into Upper Egypt, [B35] not only to purchase grain, but also to spy on their priests and to find out what they said of the recent change in stars from Taurus to Aries. [J36] As he was nearing Upper Egypt, he said to his wife Sarah,

> "If the pharaoh of Upper Egypt understands that you are my sister as well as my wife, [he will know that I am pharaoh of Lower Egypt]. I beg you to say that you are just my sister and all will be well." [B37]

Abraham's mission went very well indeed and he sowed the seeds of discontent among the southern priests and by:

> ... confuting their reasonings [in still venerating Taurus] ... he demonstrated that such reasonings were vain and void of truth. [J38]

While Abraham was spying on the priests, the pharaoh of Upper Egypt took a fancy to young Sarah and he took her into his harem. [B39] But the weather took a turn for the worse and the southern pharaoh took this as a bad omen that something was amiss with Sarah. When he found out the truth about her marital status, it confirmed his suspicions of Abraham's social status, so he threw Abraham out of his lands for nearly making him an adulterer and for spying on his people. Abraham retreated with many cattle for food (Taurus worshippers for conversion?), as the southerners would still not eat cattle for religious reasons and there was lots of surplus livestock to be had cheaply. So in addition to a successful political sortie, he had saved much of his gold as well, in fact it is said that he was now:

> very rich in cattle, in silver and in gold. [B40]

Even when he was back in Avaris, the religious troubles did not end. Lot, his nephew, was still unhappy with some aspects of worshipping Aries the Ram. There were many things that he could put up with, but slaughtering sacred cattle for food was going too far; the bull was sacred, just is it is in India to this day. Not surprisingly, there was strife between Abraham's Taurus worshippers in the north and Lot's Taurus worshippers.

> There was strife between the herdsmen of Abraham's cattle and the Herdsmen of Lot's cattle. [B41]

It is clear that even those who still venerated Taurus in the north were beginning to be more liberal in their interpretation of the faith. Finally, Lot could bear the changes no more and he left with his family and his Taurus worshippers (cattle) to the cities in the plain, Sodom and Gomorrah. [B42] After Lot had left, Abraham looked in every direction and, at last, all the land he could see was his to govern; there was now only the far south, Upper Egypt, to conquer. Then, at last, people would believe [that the cosmos had changed and that Aries was now the dominant constellation]. [B43]

But Lot and his people were still a thorn in Abraham's side. The pharaoh of Thebes was using the towns of Sodom and Gomorrah as a base for launching attacks on Abraham because they still worshipped the Apis Bull there. Lot had even gone to the assistance of the Sodomites when they fought the Assyrians. The priesthood at Heliopolis and the people of the north were in favour of destroying Sodom, but Abraham, knowing that his nephew Lot and his family lived there, asked the priests at Heliopolis:

> Would they consider sacking a town if one true believer [in Aries] lived there?

After much discussion, it was decided that Sodom would be spared if one believer (in Aries) could be found in the town. [B44] In his alarm at the rapidly escalating situation, Abraham sent messengers to Lot to warn him of the crisis and the impending attack on the town. [B45] But the townspeople of Sodom heard of the secret visit and crowded around Lot's house, demanding that Lot send out these nice young boys so that they could bugger them. [B46, J46] In desperation, Lot presented the people with his two virgin daughters for them to rape instead, if only they would spare his important visitors such degradation. [B47] This was to no avail and a fight ensued, but Lot, his wife and daughters made a hasty escape and left the town. [B48] Abraham, who was outside the city with the whole Hyksos army, descended on it and burned it to the ground, as he had done to the Assyrians a little earlier. [B49]

> When Abraham heard of their calamity [at Sodom] he was at once afraid for Lot his kinsmen, and pitied the Sodomites ... to afford them assistance, he did not delay, but marched hastily on the Assyrians ... and before they could arm themselves, he slew some as they were in their beds, before they could suspect any harm; and others who were not yet asleep, but were so drunk they could not fight, ran away. [J50]

Lot, with his life spared by Abraham, returned to the town of Avaris, married his own two daughters, as was the pharaonic tradition, and had two children by them. [B51] (See fig 14, family tree of Abraham.)

Abraham at last had a son, Isaac, by Sarah, even though Sarah was 90 years old by this time. [J52] But still the dispute with the south raged over whether his people (the sheep) or the southern people (the cattle) should drink from a particular well, [B53] and for some time Abraham's people (shepherds) gained the upper hand over Abimalech. Abraham then set seven followers of Aries (the seven sheep) to be witnesses to the agreement he was about to make with Abimalech, [B54] that the well belonged to Abraham. [B55] Abraham found his conscience tested by these religious struggles and made ready to sacrifice his only true son to the gods. He was quite prepared to do so, [B56] but just in time he saw a ram caught by its horns in a thicket * and took this as a prophesy that Aries would eventually win the battle with Taurus. [B57]

But the future of his dynasty was still not secure, so Abraham said to his chief vizier, guardian of all the vast lands he ruled:

> Promise that you will not let my son (Isaac) marry a daughter [princess] from [Upper Egypt]. [B58]

* This incident must have a greater theological meaning than the biblical interpretation, as the royal tombs at Ur, Sumer, contained a statue depicting exactly this event. This artifact possibly dates from the same era as Abraham. Bearing in mind the arguments on Sumer to follow in chapter III, I would propose the following: the bush is a representation of the Sumerian seven-branched tree of knowledge, a concept that eventually metamorphosed into the Israeli sacred seven-branched candlestick (they look very similar). Thus the image of the ram caught in the tree becomes the concept 'the knowledge of the era of Aries'. Both of these Sumerian artifacts can be seen in the British Museum.

And the servant swore. So Isaac met and fell in love with Rebecca, the daughter of Abraham's nephew, and married her. [B59] Rebecca was just a child and unable to conceive, [B60] but finally, she was able to have twins. Again, like his father before him, the pharaoh Isaac went down to Upper Egypt. (This is the same tale again of the wife being the sister; it is more likely that this is an account of a military expedition into Upper Egypt.) [B61] Once again, various calamities befell the king of Upper Egypt and Isaac gained much more land in the south. [B62] In his turn, Isaac forbade his son Jacob to take a wife from among those that believed in the old ways, [B63] and told him to take a wife from the daughters of his mother's brother. He also hoped that the sons of this union would once more rule southern Egypt:

> May he give you and your descendents the blessing given to Abraham, so that you may take possession of the land where you now live as an alien, the land God gave to Abraham. [B64]

So Jacob was sent to Padam-aram on the eastern delta to seek his wife. On his travels, Jacob had a premonition and, to mark the event, he sett up a large pillar, as is the tradition in Heliopolis. [B65]

Jacob met, fell in love with and proposed to Rachel, the daughter of his uncle Laban. But Rachel was not a worshipper of Aries and kept her images of the old gods to the very end, despite Jacob having instructed her to despise them. [J66] Laban promised that Jacob could lead all his sheep (believers in Aries) as chief shepherd [J67] and if he worked for seven years, he could marry Rachel. Jacob served his time, but on the wedding night, when Jacob was drunk, Laban put his elder daughter Leah into bed with Jacob instead. [J68]

Jacob was unhappy with this double-dealing, but agreed to serve more time to win the hand of Rachel once more. They married, but their son, Joseph, was not born until after his first wife, Leah, had had many children. Jacob eventually had 12 sons who formed the 12 tribes of Israel and each of them was educated to become kings.

> ... it not being possible that a private man should produce so many sons ... such an education of so many children not being easily obtained by kings themselves. [J69]

But Jacob was still unhappy that some of Laban's people were not followers of Aries, so he evangelized among Laban's own people. Jacob showed the people (the cattle and sheep) the striped rods, the blue and gold striped Sceptre in the shape of a shepherds crook that denoted the authority of the pharaoh. [B70] Then Jacob separated those who followed Aries (the sheep) from those who followed Taurus (the cattle):

> And Jacob did separate the lambs ... and he put all his flocks by themselves, and put them not unto Laban's cattle. [B71]

Whenever the dominant citizens among them had children, Jacob taught the strongest and the most influential of them the ways of Aries, so that their following would become more powerful with each generation. But when the citizens were weak and ineffectual, he did not teach them and left them to follow Taurus, so Laban's followers became poorer and poorer. [B72] (This technique of evangelizing only among the rich and powerful is practised even to this day by one surviving sect from Egypt). Finally, Jacob heard Laban's sad cry that everything his father had believed in was now ruined; the people now worshipped Aries. [B73] Jacob said to his wife:

> I know your father is distraught, but it is God that has given your father's followers of Taurus (the cattle) unto me. [B74] I saw it in a dream that when the followers of Taurus had children (cattle conceived) Aries (the rams) would convert (jump upon the backs of) [literally meaning mating] the followers of Taurus (the cattle). Lift up your eyes and see the followers of Aries (the rams) winning converts from the Taureans (on the backs of the cattle) [mating with the cattle]. [B75] *

Jacob's father was growing old and so the elder son was invited into a co-regency with the pharaoh. This privilege should have been given to Esau, the elder brother, but he was not a true follower of Aries and had, therefore, forfeited his birthright. Accordingly, it was now the younger brother, Jacob, who was pronounced as the 'Prince that has power with the pharaoh' (with God), and he was given the throne name of Israel. [B76] But Esau was not at all happy with this situation and enlisted the assistance

* This passage is interesting, for in pastoral terms rams mating with cows does not make sense, but in terms of two religious sects it makes every sense, especially if one reads the 'mating' as being in the vernacular. The Gideon Bible translated this as being 'male goats mating with their flocks', this makes every sense in the physical world of today, but totally destroys the original import of the text.

of the pharaoh of Upper Egypt to regain his throne. At Jacob's coronation, Esau arrived with an entire army. Jacob was:

> Jacob was greatly afraid ... and considered how, in his present circumstances, he might preserve himself and those that were with him, and overcome his enemies if they attacked him injuriously. [J77]

Jacob sent emissaries to his brother, who try to explain why Jacob and his people had to live separately from him. The emissaries return and indicate that Esau will meet Jacob in no-mans-land with a token guard of 400 men each. [J78, B78] Jacob saw Esau and bowed to the floor, as did his wives and servants, bowing a total of seven times as they approached. Esau was initially pleased to see Jacob, but then turned on his brother and said: [B79]

> "What do you mean by bringing all these men here? [Jacob's army]"

A major battle was about to ensue, which might result in the loss of all Jacob's lands. (Esau is conforming to the historical record which indicates that vassal princes in the north helped the southern pharaoh Ahmose I to evict the Hyksos.) As an alternative to war, Jacob sent tributes to pacify Esau, including all his cattle (Taurus believers?). These were rejected out of hand:

> "I have enough my brother; keep what you have for yourself." [B80]

The meeting did not go well and the brothers retired back to their respective forces. Jacob stood his wives on the brow of a hill to watch the coming battle, if that was what Esau desired. [J81] Jacob then lined up his soldiers in three parts, a small vanguard, the major force in the middle and some in reserve, so that:

> If the first were overpowered when his brother attacked them, they might have those that followed as a refuge to fly (retreat) into. [J82]

Faced with such a powerful force, Jacob was now compromised. His people were torn with theological disputes and were not united in the rightness of the cause. Aries had not put down strong enough roots in Lower Egypt and the Taureans, the bull worshippers, were always in the background, demanding a restoration of the traditional beliefs. Now the people had a real choice – Esau and the old ways or Jacob and the new – and they were making that choice with their feet, moving over into Esau's camp. The Talmud is quite specific on this, the choice the brothers had was between ruling the land they were in (Egypt) or the land of Canaan. [83] Jacob could see that he did not have the full support of his people, even the powerful Hyksos army was divided and the situation looked lost.

Eventually, he had no real choice. The army of Upper Egypt was advancing to aid Esau and Esau had the upper hand. The only recourse for Jacob was exile; he chose to rule the land of Canaan. The first and greatest of the exoduses had begun.

Chapter III

Exodus

Part 1

The biblical exodus has had a profound effect on the history of the Western hemisphere. The events of those times have been minutely pored over, word by word, for thousands of years. Although it occurred some 3,500 years ago, for some it is as real now as it was then. It can be visualized as being a deep scar that runs throughout Christianity and Islam, while for the Jews, the injury has not even begun to heal; it is more like a festering wound. Of all the historic events that have happened in this world, why should this be so? The orthodox version of events is well known, even if its incongruous beginnings are somewhat glossed over by the clergy.

In the Bible, the last pages at the end of the book of Genesis describe Joseph and his descendents as being among the most powerful people in the world: Joseph had risen to the rank of vizier to the pharaoh, second only to pharaoh himself. As we shall see later, the historical record also seems to confirm that Joseph reached this exalted position and then went on to establish a line of royal viziers that maintained their elite position for many generations. Turning the page in the Bible, we now enter the book of exodus. Suddenly in the space of two pages, the Jewish people are poor starving slaves working in the stone quarries of the pharaoh! What terrible calamity overcame these people to be demoted in such a tragic fashion is not mentioned. Quite plainly, the biblical texts are not to be trusted in the finer detail of this story, the circumstances are simply too bizarre.

The book of Exodus is centered on the hero Moses, who was

born to lead the Israelite people out of this new-found misery in Egypt to the promised land of Israel. But the evil pharaoh would not let the people go and Moses had to resort to sending the seven plagues onto the people of Egypt in order to persuade pharaoh to release the Jewish people. Thus began the biblical exodus, the flight of the Jewish nation. A flight is what it eventually became, because pharaoh had second thoughts about letting Moses and the Israelites go and they were forced to make a midnight dash for freedom, taking with them the morning's bread that had not even had the time to rise (hence the feast of the unleavened bread). [B1] Pharaoh pursued them with his vast army. With a little more help from 'God', in trapping the Egyptian cavalry in the Red (Reed) Sea, the Israelite people migrated en-masse to the promised land and to the city of Jerusalem. All of this is a part of our common heritage and culture in the Western and Middle Eastern world, even if it has faded in recent generations.

But what of the rest of the story – the hidden story? Something else happened during the exodus that is never openly discussed. This was no flight of slaves under the Egyptian yoke; it was more like a major military engagement. The biblical texts are quite clear as to what happened during that fateful episode: there was firstly the mass slaughter of the Egyptian children by the Israelites, the widespread looting of the town before they left and the eventual defeat of the Egyptian army. Finally, the departing Israelites emigrated to the promised land. The image that is often given of this new land is of an uninhabited paradise, in reality, Palestine was already quite densely populated. Settling here demanded the destruction of tens if not hundreds of towns and cities across this 'new' land, culminating with the sacking of Jerusalem itself.

Exodus Era

So when did all this happen? The story unfolding so far is still in the reign of Jacob and yet already there are the beginnings of a biblical exodus. In fact, it is said in the Bible that Jacob departed for Canaan, where he and his sons sacked Jerusalem. [B2] It sounds very much like a re-run of the great exodus, so was Jacob involved in the 'real' exodus? Quite possibly so, but that is certainly not the orthodox view of the traditional exodus, where the hero of the day was the much later figure of Moses. Historically, Egyptologists have placed the exodus at the time of Ramesses II (*c.* 1280 BC), that is some 400 years later than the era of Jacob described above. This traditional chronology is based on some circumstantial biblical evidence identifying the cities the Israelite slaves were building as being Pithom and Raameses, which were built in the time of Ramesses II. [B3]

Sigmund Freud, in the 1940s, in his book *Moses and Monotheism*, alluded to a more controversial theory. This idea was eventually taken up by Ahmed Osman in his book, *Moses, Pharaoh of Egypt*. Ahmed undertook a very serious and scholarly study into the biblical and Egyptian texts and propounded persuasive arguments that the biblical Moses was, in fact, the Egyptian pharaoh Akhenaton. This may be correct in some respects and this theory will be more fully explored later. However, the reign of Akhenaton (*c.* 1350 BC) was still 300 years later than the reign of the pharaoh Jacoba, so why are we looking at the era of Jacoba/Jacob?

Historically, there is a very good reason, for there is not only a documented biblical exodus, there is also a documented historical exodus from Egypt – the Hyksos exodus. This was a huge event at the time, with some 240,000 people fleeing Egypt, according to Manetho (possibly 240,000 *families,* depending on which interpretation is placed on the style of the text). This is certainly the sort of event that was likely to become ingrained in the human psyche, rather than the flight of a few slaves from captivity. This was an entire nation on the move, involving the relocation of at least a quarter of a million people at a time when the world may have held only a few million in total. It was a colossal event. [4] Josephus, quoting Manetho, says of these fleeing Shepherd Kings:

> It is clear that the so-called Shepherds, *our ancestors*, quitted Egypt and settled in our land 393 years before the coming of Danaus to Argos. [5] (my italics).

There is a great deal of confusion in the works of Manetho at this point. Firstly the identification of Danaus is unclear. His other name is given as Armais and he is described as the 'brother of Ramesses' (the second). A possible identification has been proposed as Horemheb, the ex-military commander, but I think Seti I is more likely. This would make Seti I the equivalent of Manetho's Sethos, and, therefore, Seti I was the brother of Ramesses I, not the son.

Further confusion is evident in these texts by the indication that there were two exoduses. Thus when Josephus, Africanus and

Theophilus quote Manetho, they say that Moses left Egypt at the time of the Hyksos exodus. Eusebius, however, when quoting the same text by Manetho, says that Moses left in the reign of Rathotis, whom I have already equated with the pharaoh Akhenaton. It is clear that there were two events being described here and Josephus confirms this. His list of kings clearly places the Moses exodus at the time of Tuthmoses (the first), who is elsewhere identified as Amos. This makes historical sense as the Hyksos exodus was in the reign of Amose I (co-regent with Jacoba). Later Josephus states that:

> After citing King Amenophis, a fictitious person – for which reason he did not venture to define the length of his reign – Manetho attaches to him certain legends, having doubtless forgotten that according to his own chronicle ... the exodus of Shepherds to Jerusalem took place 518 years earlier. [6]

The Amenophis to which he refers is presumably Amenhotep III, the father of Akhenaton, who incidentally does have a reign length. It is abundantly clear that there are two events being talked about, that is why Eusebius and the Bible indicate that there was a later exodus and this is the source of information that has infuriated Josephus. In this case, the larger exodus of a multitude of people from Egypt took place at the time the Hyksos were expelled and a later, smaller, exodus took place at about the time of Amenhotep III. It is also clear that the Shepherd Kings and their people in the first great exodus (the Arians), were the primary ancestors of the Jewish nation. As does Josephus before me, I am equating the Hyksos exodus with the great biblical exodus. The tradition of a later exodus of important people out of Egypt is in addition to the real exodus, and the two traditions have now become intertwined and inseparable. Both the Bible, Josephus's version of the Old Testament and Manetho support this hypothesis.

The Bible supports this notion by describing the exodus during the time of Jacob, that has been explored in chapter II, and also the exodus of Moses. In the same fashion, Manetho alludes strongly to the same possibility, in describing the exodus of the Shepherd Kings and also the exodus of the '*lepers and cripples*'. These two events were separated by 500 years, according to Josephus, [J7] but Manetho makes little of it in the theological debate. Josephus, on the other hand, was outraged at these suggestions and hotly disputes the possibility of a second exodus, an attitude which clearly demonstrates the tensions

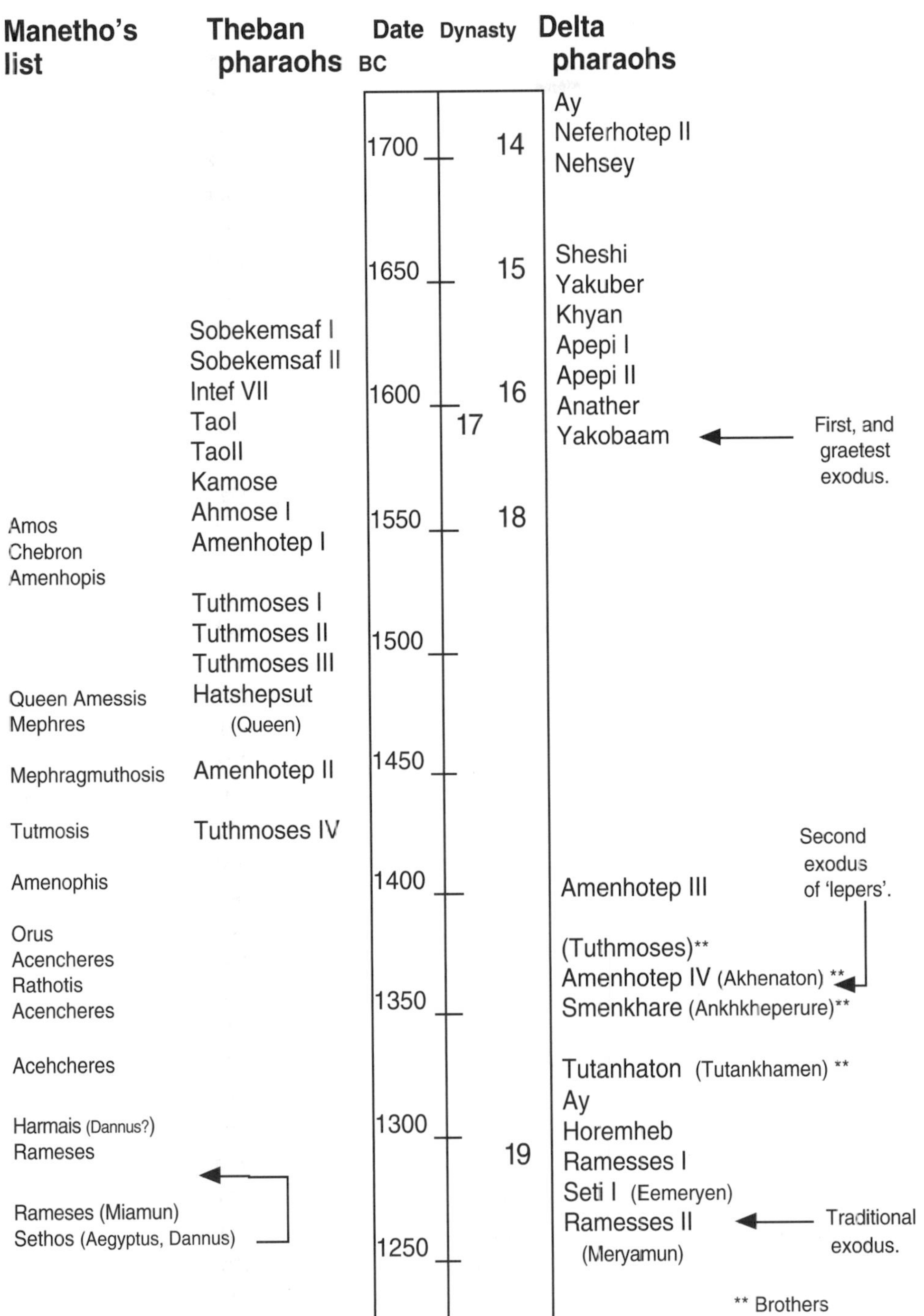

Fig 10. Chronology of the pharaohs

created by such a theory. It is quite apparent that Josephus did not wish to be associated with the Egyptians at all. He says of them:

> These frivolous and utterly senseless specimens of humanity, accustomed from the first to erroneous ideas about the gods, were incapable of imitating the solemnity of our theology, and the sight of our numerous admirers filled them with envy. [J8]

Cripples

It seems that Josephus did not like the Egyptians in the slightest. This is a recurring theme in this story, for the Egyptian civil war and the resulting exodus caused an open wound in the Jewish psyche. Besides defending the Jewish nation, perhaps Josephus was also concerned with his Levite ancestry and did not wish to be associated with this second exodus of what Manetho called the 'lepers, cripples and maimed priests'. Moses was also a Levite, a descendant of Jacob's son Levi, founder of one of the twelve tribes of Israel, and until the advent of Jesus, this was traditionally the tribe that controlled the Jewish priesthood. Moses is traditionally thought of as being the author of the biblical account of exodus, but historians prefer to ascribe this to the later Levite priesthood in approximately 550 BC. This is not only a long time after the events, but also the Levite viewpoint of these events was likely be quite different to Manetho's. Manetho was, after all, a Greek speaking Egyptian priest living in Egypt and educated from the Egyptian perspective.

Manetho's identification of the second exodus as being composed of 'lepers and cripples' was bound to cause offence: he is effectively calling Moses a cripple. Not surprisingly, Josephus was upset by this. (Incidentally, Manetho was right, but not in the way that Josephus has interpreted this, see chapter V.) To overcome this inconvenient history of the Levites, Josephus has placed both the Levite exodus of priests and the great exodus of the people back to the time of the Hyksos exodus. To distance his ancestry even further from Egypt, he also claimed that the Hyksos, the ancestors of the Jews as Josephus claims, were invaders of Egypt and not Egyptians themselves. This idea of the Hyksos being invaders from the East is the line taken by classical Egyptology as well.

This earlier chronology for the exodus is why Josephus states that the Jews were in Egypt for only 215 years and the other 215 years were spent in Canaan (Palestine). The Bible, of course, disagrees with Josephus on this point. Here the exodus is placed at a much later date, hence the Bible says that the Jews spent the full 430 years in Egypt. [J9] The are two differing opinions here. The biblical account of the Israelites spending 430 years in Egypt would equate reasonably well with an exodus at the time of Amenophis IV (Akhenaton), but not so well with the Hyksos' expulsion. Josephus's theory, that the Jews spent only 215 years in Egypt, equates well with the Hyksos expulsion, but not with the biblical exodus of Moses. What is the truth between these two different viewpoints of the same history? I believe that both Josephus and the biblical account are right in some respects, and if we amalgamate the two stories, we end up with something like the account of Manetho. There *were* two exoduses.

Gilgamesh

Historically the Hyksos period started in about 1670 BC, but to equate to the biblical 430 years that the Israelites spent in Egypt we should start the Hyksos period much earlier, in 1780 BC. This is in the reign of the pharaoh Wegaf, which will become important later. I believe that the priesthood would have been 'Hyksos' in his reign even if the pharaoh and the population were not. The theory evolving here is that the Hyksos dispute started with the changing of the constellations, a change in the stars from Taurus to Aries, bulls to sheep. The northerners and the southerners in Egypt were very much the same peoples; it was the change in religion that divided them, not the invasion of the country by a nation from the east. The Hyksos were native Egyptians, separated by a religious divide that was founded on a difference of opinion over a common religion.

If this theory is correct, then the era in which the Hyksos should have become the Hyksos – when the Shepherds became the Shepherds – can be accurately dated. The changing of the constellations is eminently predictable and a computer planisphere program can run the movements of the constellations with great accuracy. [10] The change between Taurus and Aries occurred at about 1850 BC. Of course, this date does depend slightly on where the dividing line between the two pictograms of the constellations is drawn, but by the 1780s BC and the reign of the pharaoh Wegaf, the picture is definitely skewed in favour of Aries. By this time, the priests of Heliopolis should have declared a change in the religion.

The theory is further enhanced by the history of Sumer. The historical record of Sumer runs substantially parallel to that of Egypt, dating back to some 3000 BC, with king lists, much the same as to be found in Egypt. Historically, it would appear that at some point in history, elements of the Sumerian culture sailed across to Egypt and that the first dynasty kings of Egypt, therefore, had much in common with the Sumerian peoples. David Rohl goes as far as to indicate that the history of these two lands and peoples can be taken much as the Bible tells the story, with the sons of Noah originating in Sumer and travelling out and populating the world, with his son Shem remaining in Sumer. This will become a more reasoned argument later in the book, but for now it was more than interesting to find that two of the Sumerian kings were known as 'Shepherd Kings' in the historical king list. This is exactly the same designation as is found with the Egyptian Hyksos kings and given the close links between these two cultures, it deserves further study.

The two kings concerned were called Lugulbanda and Dumuzi, from the Uruk dynasty of kings who reigned from very roughly 2400 BC. [11] Even more interesting is the fact that the king who is supposed to follow them in the king list, is the more famous Gilgamesh, of whom the fantastic legends of the Sumerian flood and the epic quest into the mystical forests of cedar is told. The epic of Gilgamesh is thought to be the earliest heroic story ever written in the world, but the historians may be up to 600 years adrift in this calculation, as their chronology is founded on a gross misinterpretation of what the story is really about. Historians have translated the tale as being a heroic epic of a Sumerian king making his mark on the world, as Gilgamesh himself says:

> I have not established my name, stamped on bricks as destiny decreed; therefore ... I will set up my name in the place where the names of famous men are written. [M12]

On the simplistic level, therefore, the tale can be seen as a standard rendition of heroic deeds by a royal prince, but it is not that at all. Ancient heroes are invariably legends pertaining to the gods, not men, the Gilgamesh epic is no different. It is first and foremost a story of stars and constellations and the allusions are so strong that it is amazing that this has not been commented on previously. The first clue is that Gilgamesh's companion, Enkidu, is described as being a meteor:

> This star of heaven which descended like a meteor from the sky; which you tried to lift, but found too heavy ... This is the strong comrade, the one who brings help to his friend in need. [M13]

The texts go on to describe the Enkidu in great detail. The allusion is quite obvious: Enkidu is a stellar object. Gilgamesh, in turn, is described as arming himself for the coming quest and battle in the following fashion:

> Gilgamesh took the *axe*, he slung the quiver from his shoulder, and the *bow* of Anshan, and buckled the *sword* to his *belt*; and so they were armed and ready for the journey. [M14] (my italics.)

In stellar terms, the allusion is again quite plain: the axe in the right hand, the bow in the left hand, the sword hanging from his belt – Gilgamesh is simply the Sumerian term for the constellation of Orion. This is an epic of the skies, an impending battle of the constellations and the greatest of all the constellations, Orion, is arming himself to do battle with the cosmos. But Gilgamesh (Orion) does not know the way, so it is only fitting that he needs Enkidu (the meteor) to lead him:

> Let Enkidu lead the way, he knows the road to the forest [of stars] ... the mountain of cedars, the dwelling place of the gods. [M15]

It is at this point that the correlations with the Egyptian history already outlined become obvious, for the purpose of Gilgamesh's (Orion's) quest is to slay the constellation of Taurus the Bull and see in the era of the new constellation of Aries the Ram. In stellar terms, it is the constellation of Orion who is armed with the axe, the bow and has a sword hanging from his belt. It is Orion who had drawn his bow and has aimed it at the adjacent constellation of Taurus. This same change in the heavens is about to unfold once more, but here in Sumer it is the hero Gilgamesh, in the guise of Orion, who is reported as killing the Bull of Heaven, the constellation of Taurus. But first Gilgamesh has to seek out the watcher of the forest [the stars], a fearsome beast called the Humbaba:

> The watchman ... has put on the first of his *seven splendours* but not yet the other six, let us trap him before he is armed ... At the first stroke Humbaba blazed out, but still they advanced ... and

> *seven times* Humbaba loosed his glory upon them ... At the third blow Humbaba fell ... Now the mountains were moved and all the hills, for the guardian of the forest was killed ... the *seven splendours* of Humbaba were extinguished. [M16] (my italics.)

For a 4000 year old story, the prose is still as clear today as when it was written, if you know the subject matter. There is only one guardian of Taurus and that is the Pleiades, the constellation known as the '*seven sisters*', a small group of seven stars that are visible to the naked eye and resides on the back of Taurus. From this elevated position, the Humbaba (Pleiades) could watch over the constellation of Taurus and protect it. Thus, if Taurus were to be attacked, the Humbaba had to be dealt with first. With the Humbaba 'extinguished', Taurus's back was exposed and vulnerable; here was the weak-spot for the hero, Gilgamesh (Orion) could close in for the kill.

> 'Now thrust in your sword between the nape and the horns.' So Gilgamesh followed the Bull, he seized the thick of its tail, he thrust the sword between the nape and the horns and slew the Bull. When they had killed the *Bull of Heaven* they cut out its heart and gave it to Shamash (the Sun), and the brothers rested. [M17] (my italics).

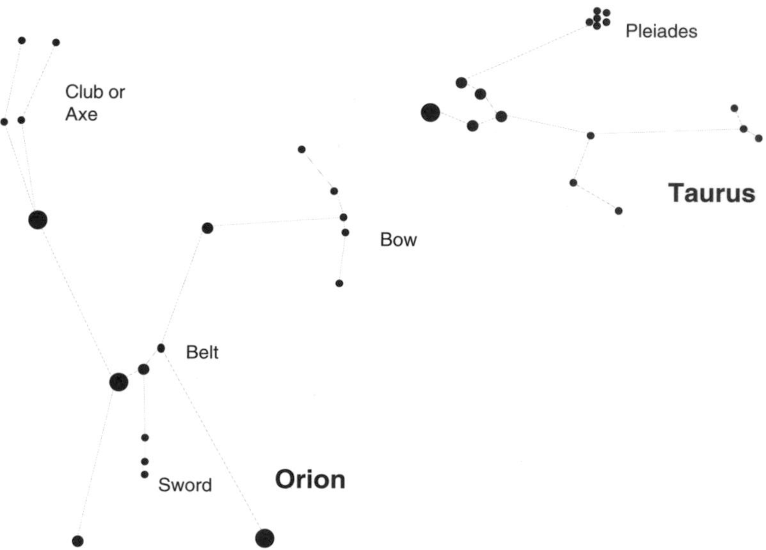

Fig 11. Gilgamesh (Orion) attacks Taurus

Gilgamesh had ended the reign of the constellation of Taurus, just as Abraham had achieved in Egypt. But some of the gods were angry with this:

> Ishtar ... uttered a curse: 'Woe to Gilgamesh, for he has scorned me in killing the Bull of Heaven'. When Enkidu heard these words he tore out the bull's right thigh and tossed it in her face saying, 'If I could lay my hands on you, it is this I should do to you ...' [M17]

Thus, we find that the Egyptian zodiac of the heavens showed a bull's thigh as depicting what we would now call the constellation of Lynx. This is a northern constellation close to Ursa Major, the Great Bear (which is depicted as the Great Hippo in the Dendera zodiac of Egypt).

Fig 12. Zodiac of Dendera, from ancient Egypt

The similarities with Egypt do not end here, for the name of the hero was not simply Gilgamesh. It is clear that the Gilgamesh epic is referring to a god, but like the Egyptian pharaohs, the gods of Sumer were also associated with mortal men, the kings of the land. Thus Gilgamesh was somehow related to King Lugulbanda. The pharaohs of Egypt were not simply men, they were also manifestations of the gods, physical incarnations of the god Horus and then, after death, they became Osiris. It is probable, therefore, that King Lugulbanda was not only related to Gilgamesh, he was the same individual. (When making this connection, remember that Osiris was also associated with the constellation of Orion.) As confirmation, Enkidu (the meteor) says to Gilgamesh (Orion):

> The one who gave water from his water-skin (Aquarius), that is your own God who cares for your good name, your Lugulbanda. [M18]

It is clear that Gilgamesh was the god-name to which this king was associated. His royal appellation, however, was Lugulbanda. To take the similarities with Egypt one stage further, Abraham was the first recorded Shepherd King of Egypt and, in turn, the Sumerian king lists say that Lugulbanda was the first of the Shepherd Kings of Sumer. It was King Lugulbanda in his dual role as the god Gilgamesh (Orion) who fought the Sumerian theological battle with the followers of Taurus and became the Shepherd King, the first Sumerian follower of the new era of Aries. This is why the epic of Gilgamesh was written: it was not an epic tale of a king as such, but an ancient bi-millennial celebration of the movement of the stars. The peoples of Egypt and Sumer were inextricably linked by their religion, but perhaps the transition period between the constellations went a little smoother in Sumer than in Egypt.

This simple observation provides another invaluable historical tool, a cast-iron peg that historians can hang the rest of Sumerian history upon. Sumerian history is notoriously imprecise, the kings are reported as having individual reign lengths ranging from six to 43,000 years. It is because of this unreliable reporting that the precise chronology and dating of the Sumerian historical record has varied enormously between individual scholars. Now there is at least one concrete, astronomically datable era that historians can work with, and it lies right in the middle of the Sumerian record. Gilgamesh - Lugulbanda and the King Dumuzi reigned at the turn of the constellations from Taurus to Aries, between 1900 and 1800 BC.

Before Abraham

Back in the Egyptian record, this precise date means that, according to the astronomical record, most of the thirteenth dynasty of Egypt should have been Hyksos as well. If they were not openly so, then we can speculate that there must have been resistance to this change within the administration or among the population, another cosmic battle, fought not only in the stars, but in the hearts and minds of the common people. In fact, there is evidence, within the Old Testament of Josephus, which seems to indicate that this change in belief *was* actually forced upon the population at a late stage. This event is contained in the section where the pharaoh Abraham (Sheshi) met his father Nehesy Aasahra, each prepared for battle. The outcome of this dispute is only inferred, yet Abraham must have been the victor because he went on in the historical record of Egypt to become the first of the Hyksos pharaohs, the first of the Shepherd Kings. Equally, in the biblical record, Abraham went on to become the 'great patriarch' of the Jewish people. He was the first in a new era of kings, whichever ancient record is followed.

Something must have happened at this point to force this change in the administration and create a new dynasty. I propose that this new dynasty of Abraham was founded on this evolution in the stellar constellations and its equivalent change to the theology of Egypt. It was another Gilgamesh epic and both these stories have survived into the modern era. Abraham was not the first of the Shepherd Kings, only the first to declare himself so.

Egyptologists are highly uncertain about both the chronology and politics of this era in Egypt, as the historical record is not well documented during this time, and:

> Our knowledge of the first few monarchs (of the thirteenth dynasty) is rather scanty. [19]

However, if the dynasty were also potentially Hyksos, it may be possible to find some more biblical pharaohs. Even if the pharaohs before Abraham were not truly Hyksos, they *are* mentioned in the biblical record. The new biblical pharaohs that this freedom unveils are highlighted below:

* * *

Table of pharaohs from:

Manetho	**Bible**	**Egyptian History**
	Noah	
Salitis	Sem	**Senusret III (Sesostris III)**
Apachnat -		
(**Arphaxad**)	Arphaxad	**Amenemhat VI**
[Cian] Jannus	Cainan (Cain)	[Ciiaan] Khyan (Seuserenre)
	Salah	
Bnon	Heber (Elber)	[Eecbher] Yakubher (Meruserre)
Phaleg[20]	Peleg (Phalac)	**Wegaf** [Faweg]
Apophis	Ragau	[Raqu] (Aqenenre) Apepi
	Seruch	[**Serrau**] (Auserre) Apepi
	Nachor (Nahor)	Nehesy (Aaserra)
Assis	Thara (Terah, Azar)	(Aasahra) Nehesy [Assii]
	Abraham	Sheshi (Mayebra) [Ayebramam]
	Isaac	Anather
	Jacob	[Jacoba] Jacobaam
	Joseph (Sothom Phanech)	Sobekemsaf II

Entries in square brackets [ ] are my altered names. Those in curved brackets ( ) are either throne names or they represent alternative spellings in other texts.

These are only tentative identifications, but worth looking into. The new entries in Manetho's list are especially interesting, as the translator of Manetho has immediately assumed that the pharaohs Arphaxad and Phalec were the biblical patriarchs Arphaxad and Peleg, yet having identified them as such, he makes no further comment. This is a good illustration of how blinkered one can become by the doctrines of our religious authorities. Manetho is quite explicit: these characters appear in the middle of a chronicle of Egyptian pharaohs; the kings both before and after the entries for Arphaxad and Phalec are all pharaohs of Egypt. Yet the translator has assumed that these two people are just biblical patriarchs and he makes no further links between the two. This is despite the fact that Manetho states that both Arphaxad and Phalec *ruled*. Shepherds do not *rule,* unless they are Shepherd Kings – the Hyksos pharaohs. [21]

As counterparts to Phalec and Arphaxad, taking into account that the thirteenth dynasty pharaohs are now available for this association of names, I have pencilled in the names Amenemhat VI and Wegaf. Firstly, the name Amenemhat seems to have some similarities to

Arphaxad. Secondly, in the case of Wegaf, it happens that if exactly the same glyph swap is performed as was applied to the name of Abraham, the result is '**Faweg**'. Faweg has great similarities to the biblical **Phalec** – was the same scribe at work in these translations? This odd little association produces another coincidence, for the pharaoh Wegaf is the first pharaoh in the thirteenth dynasty, the exact era during which the constellations should have changed to Aries. Such a cosmic event may have been recorded in the biblical record; if this were so, it would lend vital support to this association.

Josephus's history of the Old Testament provides a clue. He says that Phalec was given this name because it means 'dispersal', the era when many of the sons of Phalec were dispersed among neighbouring civilizations. But Josephus must be a little confused in this, because the great 'dispersal' of the sons was primarily the sons of Noah, that is Shem, Ham, and Japheth. It is the descendants of these patriarchs that are supposed to have journeyed out to the corners of the known world and populated them, not the sons of Phalec.

The texts of Manetho, however, seem to agree with Josephus in some respects, but Manetho increases the time period for the 'dispersal' by saying that it was in the thirty-fourth year of the reign of Arphaxad and the fifth year of Phalec. This time span is odd, as there are two pharaohs that lie in between the two mentioned. In that case the 'dispersal' must have been a protracted affair over many years. But perhaps we are not talking of a 'dispersal' of a family as such, for the dispersal had already occurred four generations before. Perhaps this is a poor translation of another kind of 'emigration', one that does indeed take a long time to complete – the movement of the stars from one astrological 'house' to another. This change in the constellations is one such event that could easily span itself over three or four generations, from Arphaxad all the way through to Phalec. Was this the 'dispersal' or the change that is being mentioned? The Bible seems to support the latter interpretation, for it says that this event was less to do with divisions of people and more to do with the wider cosmos:

> And unto Eber were born two sons: the name of one was Peleg (Phalec); for in his days was the *Earth* divided. [B22] (my italics.)

The texts are not clear about what this means and in what way was the 'Earth divided'. It could be saying that the land of Egypt was divided, or perhaps it is obliquely saying that the Earth itself was 'divided' and its cosmic position was now precisely on the cusp between two constellations, those of Taurus and Aries. Evidently the priests understood the changes that were happening in the cosmos, even if it took another four generations until the pharaoh Abraham fully implemented this change in the religion of Egypt. Once more, the historical record confirms that this concept is entirely plausible. The throne name of this pharaoh, Wegaf, is Khutawyre and the cartouche of the throne name is as follows:

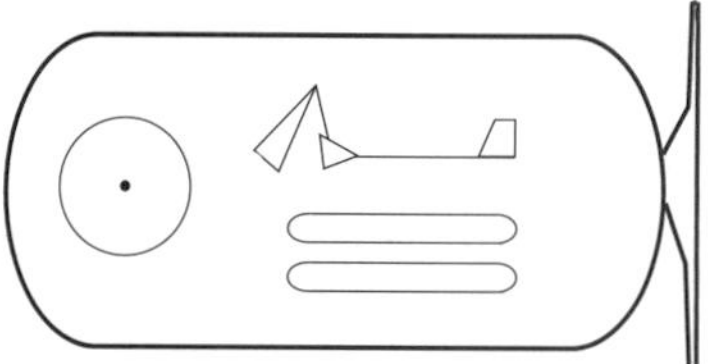

Fig 13. Cartouche of Khutawyre

This name has been interpreted as meaning 'Ra protects the two lands'. The God, Ra, is denoted by the sun-disk ☉ and the two lands are indicated by the two oblong shapes ═, leaving the arm, which has been interpreted as being the idiogram 'to protect'. This interpretation is presumably because hieroglyphs of an arm holding an object are 'generally an expression of aggression in the hieroglyphic code' and, in addition, the resulting name or title makes historical sense: the mighty pharaoh is presented as protecting his two lands. [23]

However, all good linguistic rules have exceptions and this is no different. The glyph, for example, means 'to give', a concept far removed from aggression. Take a close look at the arm glyph in the cartouche: the Egyptologists call this a 'whip', but quite plainly this arm is carrying a flail, the sacred emblem of the pharaohs traditionally held across the chest with the blue and gold striped Sceptre. Both the whip and the flail can be seen as offensive weapons, but the primary function of a flail is not for defence. The flail was not originally designed to *protect*, it was designed instead for the process of threshing, for *separating* or *dividing* the corn from the husks.

Using this new interpretation of the ancient texts, there is now a new name for this pharaoh, one that would have made little sense to Egyptologists. 'Ra *divides* the two lands'. No historian would countenance such an appellation for a pharaoh, for how could a king be named as presiding over the division of his lands? Understandably, this version of the name was dismissed, but in the biblical and astrological world, the name makes every sense. The pharaoh was called Wegaf (Faweg) and his throne name of Khutawyre was given to him because in his day 'Ra *divided* the two lands'. In the Bible the same pharaoh is known as Phalec and '*in his days the Earth was divided*'.

Manetho indicated that the 'dispersal' or division of the lands occurred between the reigns of Arphaxad and Phalec. I identified Arphaxad with Amenemhat VI primarily because of the similarity in the names. In the historical record the division of the stars started during the reign of Wegaf and it ended just two generations later with the reign of Sobekhotep II, this pharaoh being the only other to receive the designation of Khutawyre, divider of the lands. It was pleasing to later find that this pharaoh Sobekhotep II and Amenemhat VI, are exactly the same person. Thus both Wegaf and Amenemhat VI are known as Khutawyre, dividers of the land. In the biblical record and that of Manetho they are known as Phalec and Arphaxad and they are also known as dividers of the land.

New Chronology

This new technique of pharaonic anagrams, provides the last in the line of biblical pharaohs and note that the pharaoh Auserra now appears in substantially the correct chronological order.

Pharaonic name	**Revised name**	**biblical name**
Auserra (Apepi I)	Serrau	Seruch
Auyibre (Hor)	Eebreau	Hebrew

Josephus says that the term Hebrew was derived from the patriarch Heber, whom I have identified with the pharaoh Eekber. But the pharaoh Auyibre (Eebreau), in following the pharaoh Faweg, follows a closer chronological order.

Having made this historical/biblical association, I was interested subsequently to find that David Rohl in his controversial book *Legend* has made exactly the same observation of the more ancient patriarchs. He has found evidence that the patriarchs from Adam to Noah can be found in the Sumerian king lists by exactly the same method as I have independently applied to the later patriarchs, the technique of syllable swapping. The early patriarchs were of royal Sumerian stock and they emigrated to Egypt, just as the historical record indicates. The later patriarchs from Noah onwards then became pharaohs of Egypt.

With these bold new comparisons with the pharaonic record, we are now in a position to draw up an alternative family tree for the pharaonic dynasties, that takes into account the available biblical data. This provides new details on the names of the wives and offspring of the pharaohs, and their family connections. This information is not available in the historical record for these Hyksos dynasties and it would be more than interesting if some were unearthed in the future.

Hyksos exodus

The expulsion of the Hyksos is traditionally set in the 1570s BC, the era immediately following the pharaoh Jacoba and that is why I have placed the first exodus at this time. There is also the biblical evidence of an exodus at this point in the record: the often overlooked battle between Jacob and Esau and Jacob's subsequent flight to Jerusalem. This was not just the wanderings of some shepherds through the Sinai and into Palestine, it was a major biblical event because, on reaching Palestine, Jacob sacked Jerusalem. Jerusalem, even at that time, was a major fortified city and its sacking could have been brought about only by a large military force. If proof were required of the status of Jacob, this is it: he was the commander of a mighty military force, a Hyksos pharaoh in retreat. [B24]

In brief, there are two exoduses from Egypt in both the historical and biblical records. The historical record (through Manetho) says that the first exodus was the bigger of the two; the biblical record says the second was. They cannot both be right, so a choice must be made. I shall surmise that the first exodus was the bigger; it is just that some of the texts concerning this incident have been shunted through the Bible from the story of Genesis into the book of Exodus. The original compilers or perhaps the translators, were either confused by the two exoduses or they had ulterior motives for concentrating on the second exodus.

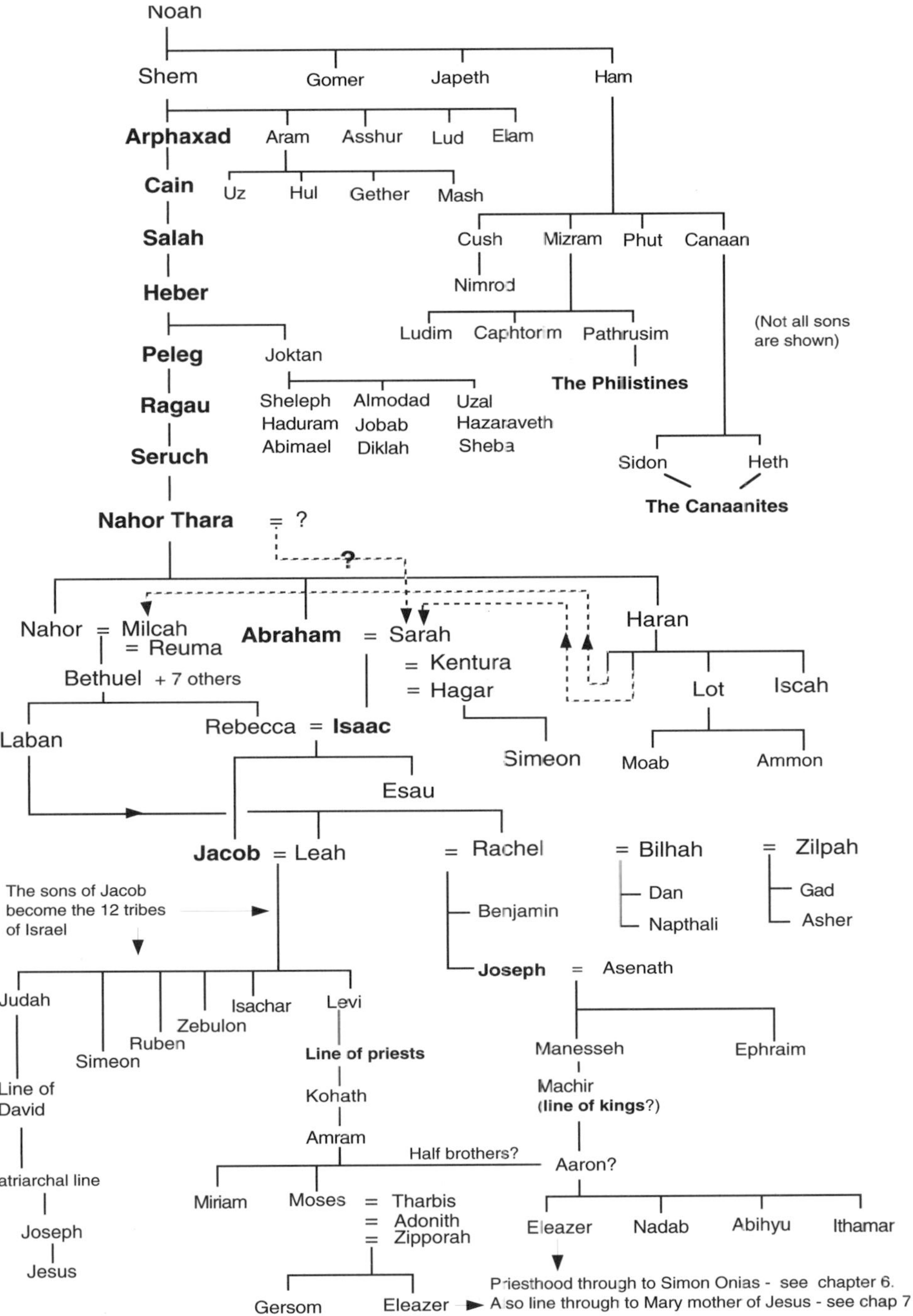

Fig 14. Pharaonic family tree from the biblical viewpoint

Comparisons between the biblical and historical records seem to confirm this. Ahmed Osman in his book *Out of Egypt* highlights the curious fact that the biblical exodus cannot be verified historically. The book of Judges mentions many cities destroyed by the retreating Israelites, yet in the historical record these towns seem to have been destroyed either before or after the date currently assumed for the exodus. Jericho, for instance, appears to have been destroyed in the fifteenth century BC and there is no evidence of it having ever been re-occupied. Indeed, the evidence confirms that the destruction was most probably at the hands of the retreating Hyksos army.

This evidence is treated as a problem for the biblical story, but it is not – it is an answer. The fact remains that the rump of a story of an earlier exodus at the time of Jacob still appears in the Bible and if we bring the exodus back in time by two or three hundred years, the events start to match. This earlier event was the true exodus, the Hyksos exodus. Seemingly in confirmation of this, the Bible records that a curse was placed on the ruins of Jericho and it was not rebuilt, just as the historical record shows.

Even Josephus, despite his repudiation of Manetho's two-exodus idea, preserves a record of the earlier exodus of Jacob to Jerusalem. [J25] In backing this double exodus concept, with the expulsion of 240,000 Hyksos families in the first exodus being the major event, I shall be bringing some of the later exodus story in the Bible back in time by 230 years, from the time of Moses and Akhenaton to the time of Jacob. This is not an adjustment made without reason and it does sort out another thorny problem – the plagues of Egypt.

In his best-seller *Act of God*, Graham Philips makes out a good case for the plagues of Egypt having been caused by the eruption of the volcanic island of Thera. Indeed, the plagues, which he lists and discusses one by one, are just the sort of result to be expected from the fallout of a major volcanic eruption. The sacred life-giving river Nile turned red and bitter, the fish died, the frogs came out and the hot ash caused boils on the skin and the crops to die. Vast thunderstorms poured hail on the land, the dead fish and frogs caused a plague of flies and finally the lack of predators in the river caused a plague of gnats or mosquitoes.

Once more, this is just the sort of major cataclysm that might be expected to have become ingrained in the cultural psyche of the Egyptians; it must have been an awesome and terrible event to witness and experience. Yet this *was* a real event: it is known that Thera suffered a devastating volcanic eruption at some time, what is not certain is the precise date and the effects that it produced.

During such a cataclysm, any theological nation would have had cause to think that the gods were angry with them. If, at the same time, that terrible event happened to coincide with a cultural and theological shift, might not the population think that the 'new ways' were the cause of the gods' anger? It does all seem to fit, as Graham Philips suggests, even if the pillars of fire and the clouds by which the people of the exodus navigated are easily explained. However, the exact dating of this great eruption is unclear. In his investigations, Graham Philips reports that, in 1990:

> A Danish team from the National Museum of Denmark in Copenhagen attempted to date the Thera eruption by radiocarbon dating organic remains from within the ancient volcanic crater. Inside once molten rock, they found charcoal deposits thought to be from trees that had perished in the eruption ... Using this procedure, the team arrived at a date two centuries earlier than anyone had previously considered Thera to have erupted – around 1650 BC. If the Danish team were right, then the archaeologists had been completely wrong. [26]

This presented a problem, for if the Danish team were correct, then the Thera eruption could not have been responsible for the biblical plagues, as the date is far too early. Consequently, many arguments have been put forward as to why the radiocarbon data was incorrect in order to justify the biblical hypothesis. The data was being amended to fit the biblical story. However, there is a simple solution to this problem. If the great exodus is taken as being in the reign of Jacob, the Hyksos expulsion, then there is no disagreement with the carbon-dating results; the dates tie in very nicely.

There is still another problem with this early date for the eruption of Thera and this concerns the demise of the Minoan empire. Although the Minoan economy and civilization appears to have waxed and waned over the centuries, the eventual collapse of the Minoan empire seems to have occurred much later than this carbon-dating era for the Thera eruption. Yet the location of the island of Crete, being so close to Thera, would indicate that the Minoans should have been affected even more than the Egyptians. However, it is possible that the Minoans could have survived the eruption in better shape than the Egyptians, for a number of reasons:

a. The shape of the island of Thera could well have shielded the island of Crete from the main effects of a tidal wave. The main thrust of the wave may have been out to the west.

b. The deep water off the Cretan coast would have helped them as well. Tsunamis grow to their full extent only on meeting a shelving sea floor, whereas a deep-water cliff tends to reflect tidal energy back into the sea. Perhaps this moderated tidal wave caused only relatively minor disruption to the island. In addition, it is evident that Egypt was not devastated by a tsunami; it may have caused the rivers of the Nile delta to recede and flood, according to the biblical story of the exodus, but it was the ash cloud that caused the biblical plagues and the majority of the devastation.

c. Egypt depended on agriculture and the Nile. If the ash cloud had devastated the ripening crops and polluted the river, Egypt would have had to survive without food for at least a year, devastating the economy. In contrast, the Minoan civilization depended more on the sea, yet any ships at sea would have easily survived the tsunami. After the ash fall, they could have ranged as far as they liked across the Mediterranean in search of fresh fish for the population; the people could be fed with ease.

In addition, the ash fall would have poisoned the sea around Crete. The resulting mass of dead marine life in the coastal waters may have given the islanders an unexpected boost, if the fish were still edible and could be salted or dried quickly. Such a destruction of marine life and this unexpected abundance of food, would have most certainly been recorded in Minoan history as a gift from the gods. Was this the influence behind Minoan type-1b pottery, which displays a plethora of marine life and is peculiar to this era?

Jacob's Flight

We left off some while ago with Jacob beginning his exodus out of Egypt. In order to complete this story a look at the unmentionable aspects of the exodus are required. As already hinted, the exodus was not just a story of a few escaping slaves. Even before the Israelites had left Egypt, it would appear that some of their number went around the town, indeed around much of Lower Egypt, slaughtering 'children', and specifically the 'children of the cattle'. [B27] The text is quite specific: only young cattle were killed, not other young animals. The reason why the text was written in this format is now clear. As previously suggested, this episode was a memory of a divisive religious civil war, finally fought between Jacob (the pharaoh Jacoba) in Lower Egypt, who worshipped the rising of Aries, and Esau with his allies in Upper Egypt, who worshipped the rising of Taurus. The country was divided. Jacob was faced with either a major military engagement or certain exile; he was about to choose the latter. However, he was not going down without a fight, so platoons of his men went around Lower Egypt slaughtering all the children of the Taurus worshippers (the young cattle) so that:

> ... there was a great cry in Egypt; for there was not a house where there was not one dead. [B28]

Then Jacob's cohorts went to each house of the Taurus worshippers and plundered them for every piece of gold and silver to be had; there was wholesale looting and the country was in turmoil. [B29] In addition to all this occurring in Egypt, Jacob's retreating forces also moved up into Palestine and wreaked even greater havoc, with whole cities being burned to the ground. It is quite obvious that this was not the work of a small band of slaves who had given the Egyptians the slip. It could only have been the work of a retreating army, the Hyksos army and the most powerful in the world at the time. It had the finest and most technical military equipment available and was invincible. In which case, the question arises – why on Earth was it retreating?

Civil War

Wars are not always won by soldiers or weapons; more often than not, they are won by the hearts and minds of the people and the discipline of the army. Julius Caesar's account of the war with Gaul shows exactly what can be done in the most dire of circumstances if commanders retain the trust of their men and inspire enough respect to maintain discipline. Even taking into account the inevitable exaggeration of Caesar's accounts, it is apparent that the Roman legions faced the most terrible odds on many occasions, with vast hoards of bloodthirsty natives wielding huge axes and screaming terrible curses at them.

The discipline of the Roman army was absolute; the men were convinced of their superiority in tactics, skills and weaponry. The officers kept their cool and cunning, when the opposing forces had lost theirs. The Romans held their ground while this terrifying hoard, outnumbering them by five or six to one, advanced. Any other army would have fled in sheer terror, but not the Romans. The adrenaline flowed, but the neat ranks held their line. Finally, in the heat of the battle, the rabble were defeated by superior tactics, communications, discipline and armament. There was no contest.

Jacob's problems were different: some of the forces he faced were from within his own ranks. The dispute had festered for generations, but flared up once more because the plagues that had descended on the country. This caused a dispute between two brother princes, each blaming the others desertion of the gods for the calamity. Each of these princes would have had the support and following of his own group of priests, civil servants and commanding officers and once the dispute was in the open, each senior priest and commanding officer would have had to have made his own judgement. Would they follow the elder brother, the rightful pharaoh of the land and his continued support of the long-established worship of Taurus? Or would they follow the younger brother, who had 'cheated' Esau out of his birthright and who now followed this new strange worship of Aries? There was no contest for many in the population. Esau had arrived at the coronation with a huge army; perhaps more than half of the entire military had backed him.

Jacob had no alternative; he had been wrong-footed and must flee. (Wrong-footed is an apt description, as it is a particularly Egyptian phrase. All the statues of the pharaohs of Egypt are depicted with their left foot first, for strength and victory. All the armies of the world start marching with the left foot for the same reason.) Jacob was in retreat, but, on the other hand, Esau knew that Jacob was not only family – his twin brother – but that he also still had a sizeable army of his own. It would be folly to attack if there were another way out of the situation, so Esau offered safe passage if Jacob would leave the country. The Bible and the history by Manetho are in complete agreement about this. Manetho says that '[Jacob] was allowed to retreat unmolested', and the Bible in both the account of the exodus under Moses and the exodus under Jacob indicates that the Israelites were initially allowed to depart unmolested under some sort of treaty. Only later did the trouble begin ...

This is the outline of the first exodus: it was a huge and organized flight of the rump of the Hyksos army escorting the Shepherd nation. These were native Egyptians, who had converted to Aries and who were being thrown out of their native lands into exile in Palestine, just as Manetho indicated. Relocating the first exodus into the era of Jacob has meant that in part 2 of this story, some of the references to Moses have been changed back to Jacob. However, this does not mean that Moses was not a real character or that he was any less important in the unfolding story, for his time will come in what Manetho described as the 'exodus of lepers and cripples'. Moses was the leading character in the second of the two great exoduses.

Part 2

Dark foreboding clouds rolled in from the north, the clear blue skies of Egypt were darkened for the first time in living memory. The sky frothed and boiled, the rain and hail fell in great sheets hammering the crops to the ground. Seven terrible plagues descended on the lands of Egypt and the people were very frightened; never in the history of their lands had such a calamity happened to them. [B30] The gods were angry and there had to be a reason why. The people of Upper Egypt pointed at Jacoba and his royal line for changing the old ways. Surely if proof were needed that it was the bull that was sacred and the rams were an evil heresy, this was it – the judgement of the gods. Even the faithful in Lower Egypt were cautious; indeed, it did seem that the gods were angry with them. However, Jacob appealed to their common sense – the gods were not saying that Taurus was still sacred, otherwise why have all the cattle in Upper Egypt died, when not one of ours has? [B31]

But the people were torn with doubt and many turned to Esau. His army swelled in number until Jacob was forced to retreat. But Jacob was determined to retreat in good order and with maximum damage to his enemies. Consequently, he sent word to his faithful followers that they should hang the skin of a lamb (blood of a lamb) on their front doors to identify themselves as followers of Aries so that his soldiers would pass them by. [B32]

> 'For on the fourteenth day of this month I shall order my troops to go around all of Lower Egypt at night to kill all the children of those who believe in Taurus, (the first-born of the cattle). [B33] Then they shall loot all their property, taking all their gold, silver and precious jewels and they will loot everything that belongs to (devastate) those that worshipped Taurus, (the Egyptians).' [B34]

On the fateful day when this had been accomplished, there was not a Taurean house without someone dead, and a great cry erupted throughout Egypt. The Taureans fought back and attempted to throw the Arians out of Egypt. The Arians were forced to retreat towards the north-east of the Nile delta, to an area know as Avaris, where Manetho explains what happened.

> The Shepherds ... were defeated, driven out of all the rest of Egypt and confined in a region measuring within its circumference 10,000 arurae, by the name of Avaris. [35] The Shepherds enclosed this whole area with a high, strong wall to safeguard all their possessions and spoils [taken from the Taureans]. The pharaoh [Esau] besieged the fortress with an army of 480,000 men in an attempt to force them to surrender.
>
> Finally, giving up the siege in despair, he concluded a treaty by which they should all depart from Egypt and go unmolested where they pleased. On these terms, the Shepherds, with their possessions and households complete, no fewer than 240,000 persons (families?), left Egypt and travelled over the deserts into Syria. [J36]

The departing Hyksos (600,000 according to the Bible) took all the wealth of Lower Egypt with them. It was a victory for Esau, but in some respects a hollow one, for the entire region had been stripped clean, looted for every last coin. Esau visited the town of Avaris, and on seeing the devastation and wanton greed for riches, he declared that this terrible deed should be called from henceforth, *Avarice*!

After seeing the destruction of Avaris and the entire area, Esau changed his mind and, instead of letting the Hyksos go unmolested as agreed, he decided to pursue them to teach them a lesson. Pharaoh [Esau?] set out with a huge army with 600 chariots and chased the Hyksos towards Canaan, navigating, as Jacob had previously, by the sight of the vast plume of ash that still poured periodically from the volcano of Thera. But Jacob sent a few of his most trusted soldiers into Esau's camp by night and they took out all the locking pins on the wheels of their enemy's chariots. During the day, as Jacob watched, the charioteers charged across a ford on the river Nile. As planned, all the wheels fell off the chariots, making it look as though the river had flooded and swallowed them up. [B37]

On seeing this, Esau's troops retreated, afraid that they were not only fighting Jacob, but the gods as well. [B38, J38] So the army withdrew to Memphis, and to reinstate the worship of the Apis Bull there, idols were brought from the south. [J39] This was much to the disgust of the remaining priests in Memphis and Heliopolis, who were ordered not to venerate Aries and were forced to turn their sanctuaries into kitchens for roasting the sacred lambs. [J40]

* * *

Promised Land

Jacob and his army moved up into Canaan, but there was to be no peace for him and his people yet, for they met armed resistance at every twist and turn of their long journey. When they reached the land of Kedemoth, he sent messengers to Sihon, King of Heshbon, with words of peace. Jacob appealed to King Sihon:

> Let me pass through your lands and I will take the main road, neither turning left nor right; I will give you money for food and water. [B41]

However, the king would not let them through, instead, he attacked them. Jacob killed them all. After this victory, he went into their towns and cities unopposed, killed every woman and child to be seen and took what spoils could be found. [B42] Further on in their journey, King Og and his people attacked him and Jacob destroyed his towns until nothing remained; no fewer than 60 cities were taken and destroyed. [B43] These lands were given to certain of Jacob's people. Presently, they came to Jericho, but the city gates were closed to keep them out, so they laid siege to the city. They sent spies into the city to see how it could be taken. The spies took up lodgings in a brothel run by the prostitute Rahab and bided their time.

Trumpets and parades were used to create a six-day diversion outside the city walls so that the spies could continue their work. On the seventh day, the guards' attention was diverted by the Hyksos army shouting outside the city. The prostitute Rahab and the spies took their chance: suddenly the gates were opened, the siege had ended and the Hyksos flooded in. Their first action was to bring out Rahab with her family, keeping them safe as a reward for their assistance in opening the gates. Her family lives in Israel 'to this day'. [B44] Then they killed every man, woman, pensioner, child and animal that they could find with the edge of the sword, and destroyed them all. [B45] Finally, they took all the silver and gold to be found and set fire to the city. Jacob declared that anyone who dared rebuild Jericho would be cursed and so it remains deserted to this day. [B46] (Even into the modern era.)

Finally, they came to Jerusalem. [B47] But Dinah, Jacob's daughter, was raped by Shechem, one of the princes of the city, so Jacob laid siege to Jerusalem as well. [B48] He was deeply distressed by this, as Jerusalem was a formidable fortress, so he proposed a compromise to the King of Jerusalem. If the men of Jerusalem were circumcized as he was (circumcision was an Egyptian tradition) and took on his religion, then Dinah could marry Shechem and all would be forgiven. Hamor, the king agreed and opened the city gates for his sons to go out and be circumcized. However, when the sons of Hamor were still sore from the circumcision and unable to defend themselves, Jacob's army rushed through the gates and killed all the men of the city. He took the women and animals captive. [B49]

Jacob was worried about waging war on this land, for other nations were beginning to oppose him. He was especially afraid that 'the Perizzites (Persians?) may gather forces to destroy us', so he travelled to the area around Bethlehem to settle and secure his northern border with Assyria. [B50] As Manetho says:

> There (in Canaan), dreading the power of the Assyrians who were at that time masters of Asia, they built in the land now called Judaea a city large enough to hold all those thousands of people, and gave it the name of Jerusalem. [J51]

Jacob considered the position of his people carefully. Finally, he decided that they should give themselves a separate identity from the people remaining in Egypt. Esau and the Upper Egyptians were fools not to have seen the significance in the changing of the constellations and they were evil in having thrown them, the Hyksos, out of Egypt. Did they understand only the workings of the world and not the deeper workings of the cosmos? The people and the priesthood, he decided, had been misled by the plethora of gods that had been the basis of the public's perception of religion in Egypt; a confusion that had been caused by the innumerable tales of Horus, Seth, Isis and Osiris. Their vision had been clouded and the underlying concepts of religion had been usurped. The solution was simple: Jacob commanded the people to give up all of their old gods, from now on there would be just one God. It was to be an intangible, unnameable, unknowable entity, with no visible countenance that could be copied and worshipped. It was, in essence, the power behind the Sun, the workings of the cosmos.

At the same time, Jacob was also planning for the future once more. His son Joseph's destiny lay in Egypt still, but here in Judaea was a new land full of new opportunities for the rest of his offspring. Here in these new lands they might carve new kingdoms for themselves, new dynasties and royal lines. As a symbol of this new covenant, this break with the traditions of Egypt, he made his other sons take out their earrings and he buried them all in the ground. [B52] These earrings had been a symbol of the lesser princes in Egypt, sons of the pharaoh who did not carry the bloodline and could not rule, but here in this land of new opportunity, each could be king. These sons would not be known as Egyptians any more, they would be the twelve tribes of Israel and their people would take the name of his sons. They would become the Levites from Levi, the Danites from Dan, the Jews from Judah.

Chapter IV

Joseph

Part 1

Jacob and his family were now safely ensconced in Jerusalem; the great exodus was over and the Hyksos peoples had left Egypt. This creates a problem with the chronology because this was far too early for the biblical exodus, so how can the two be reconciled? The fact that the texts indicate that there were two exoduses has already been mentioned. However, if the second one involved the same peoples, how did it occur? For there to have been another exodus requires a scenario whereby some of the Hyksos peoples remained in or returned to Egypt and it is to the Bible that we must turn for this information.

Joseph, the biblical character famed for his 'coat of many colours',* was one of Jacob's sons. The Bible tells the story of Joseph being sold by his brothers to some merchants, who finally sold him on to a highly placed individual in Egypt. There, Joseph proved his worth as a fortune-teller and from these 'humble' beginnings he rose to be the most powerful man in the country, apart from the pharaoh. It is from his descendants and those of his brothers, who later returned to Egypt, that the 'Hebrew slaves' of the exodus were eventually descended. Moses himself, the great hero who orchestrated the second exodus of 'cripples', as Manetho described it, was also descended from Jacob.

This tale is a little sugary for a real history of those times. It is more likely to be the narrator's attempt to place a gloss on history to

* Coat with many ornaments. From the descriptions in the Bible and from modern-day observations this was quite obviously a priests stole or tunic.

obscure the real facts. The key to the true story is to be found in the New Testament, of all places. After the birth of Jesus, it is reported that Herod decided to kill all boys under the age of two in order to prevent Jesus from growing up and claiming to be the rightful heir to the throne. This, incidentally, is a good indication of Jesus' true social status. To prevent his death, Mary was instructed to take her son to Egypt for safekeeping. Why was the country that the Jews supposedly despised chosen? Perhaps Herod was really after Jesus' blood, but it is also likely that there is a link between Joseph having been sent off to Egypt and Jesus being sent there many centuries later. Both these children were the elder sons in a royal line of priest-kings and were to inherit the royal title on maturity.

Joseph was technically not the first-born, of course, but he was the first born of the favourite wife Rachel, the Chief Wife of Jacob. In Egyptian terms the pharaoh often had many wives, as did Jacob, but, to maintain a pure matriarchal bloodline, the royal line only flowed through the Chief Wife. In the Bible it is made abundantly clear that both Joseph and Benjamin, Rachel's sons, were the favourite sons of Jacob, the royal princes. Joseph was the favourite son and his brothers were continually jealous of his status in the family. Benjamin likewise was the primary concern of their father Jacob during their journey to 'purchase grain' in Egypt. The Bible does not explain the background to Jacob's great concern, but it is entirely understandable in the new context. Of all his sons, Jacob had just two royal sons that carried the bloodline, Joseph and Benjamin. Joseph was presumed dead in Egypt and no king can contemplate the loss of his only true heir.

Therein lies another question. If the preservation of the bloodline was so important, why did Jacob sanction the sending of his eldest heir on such a hazardous trip into enemy-held Egypt? What was so important there? Both Joseph and Jesus were to inherit the royal titles of their fathers, but why did each have to make such a perilous journey? What would Egypt have to offer such individuals? Josephus, once more, provides a possible reason:

> Onias, the son of Simon, fled from ... Antiochus the king of Syria when he made war with the Jews, and came to Alexandria; and as Ptolemy received him very favourably on account of his hatred of Antiochus ... he assured him he would give the Jews every assistance. [Onias] decided to build a temple somewhere in Egypt, and to worship God according to the customs of his own

> country ... So Ptolemy ... gave him a place one hundred and eighty furlongs from Memphis. That Nome was called the Nome of Heliopolis where Onias built a fortress and a temple ... such as resembled a tower. [J1]

Onias was a Jewish priest, who had fled Israel because of the 'oppression by the Macedonians and their kings'. It seems that Heliopolis was deserted at this time and he wished to restore the temple there in the fashion of the temple at Jerusalem. Onias the priest was known as the 'son of Onias', so it looks as if this is another hereditary title, especially as the new temple was built at Heliopolis, a city that the Bible names as On. So the Jews and their priesthood have had a distinct and verifiable association with Heliopolis in Egypt and the reason for this is inescapable.

The center of Celestial understanding in Egypt had traditionally been at Heliopolis for thousands of years. Heliopolis was the first of the Sun temples, dating back at least as far as the third dynasty of the Old Kingdom and the fact that the temple was to be rebuilt at On by a priest called Onias shows the depth of the association between Heliopolis and the biblical story. The city was the center of learning for the priesthood and for many of the pharaohs. It was Heliopolian priests who had set this whole dispute in motion by adhering to the most ancient of Celestial laws and declaring that the age of Taurus was finished and that of Aries had begun. We can postulate that during the exile of Jacoba in Jerusalem, some Heliopolian priests stayed in Heliopolis, for they did not consider their lives nearly as important as their work in tracing the motions of the cosmos. They were treated badly by the victorious Esau and the southern pharaoh, but while you can change what a person says and does, you cannot necessarily change what he thinks. So the ancient traditions remained in the great temple and were passed on to the next generation.

Now we come to the reason behind these two young princes journeying to Egypt in this long and ancient tradition. Both Joseph and Jesus were heirs to the Shepherd pharaohs, having descended from Abraham and Jacoba, both were the elder sons of the Chief Wife. They were heirs to the ancient Heliopolian tradition of observing the stars and to the belief in the revolution of the stars to the new constellation of Aries. This was their royal heritage: they had to travel to Egypt to be educated in the ancient ways of Heliopolis, the biblical On. This is known to be true of Joseph because he married the daughter of a priest of On, Asenath (Asnath, a Phoenician god); in other words, the daughter of one of the high priests in the ancient temple of Heliopolis. [B2,J2] In addition, his family was given land in Heliopolis in which to live. [J3] The message is inescapable: Joseph was of the royal bloodline and his destiny lay in Egypt, in Heliopolis. This explains the great interest of the northern pharaohs in this temple: it held the secrets of Egypt and educated the royal sons.

However, all this happened so soon after Jacoba's exile that Joseph could not possibly go straight to Egypt and declare his royal status; he would probably have been murdered. The strategy was more subtle than that. Despite the exile of the Arians, Joseph would not have been without supporters in Egypt. Throughout history, kings have been deposed and some have been driven into exile with thousands of their supporters. For example, Tsar Nicholas II of Russia was deposed by an alliance of the Petrograd Soviet of Workers' Deputies and the new Russian parliament, the Duma, in 1917. This hastily convened government was as ineffectual as the Tsar had been and the resulting civil war between 1918 and 1921 saw the Red army victorious, the Tsar killed and the emigration of millions of Russians from their homeland. Yet despite all this, plus the power and brutality of seven decades of Soviet rule, there are still many supporters of the Romanoff family in Russia. A true heir to the throne would not be short of somewhere to stay if he or she should return to Russia today.

Similarly, Joseph would have had the support of the priesthood in Heliopolis and also the loyalty of a royalist supporter, Potiphar, a captain of the royal guard. Potiphar held high office and secured a key position for Joseph in the royal court. Again, there is a direct parallel with much more recent history. The Scottish royal line of Stewarts many thousands of years later found themselves in the same position. The ancestors of the Stewart line forfeited the throne on the death of Lady Macbeth of Shakespearean fame. It took the family another three generations to manoeuvre themselves back into the royal court as stewards to the king. (The similar name and profession of steward and Stewart is not a coincidence; the surname is derived from the earlier title.)

This may seem like a digression, but the Stewart kings are more closely involved in this story than one might think. Back in Egypt, Joseph was luckier than the Stewarts in this respect: his supporters had managed to place the very next generation back into the royal court of Egypt, where he could bide his time as royal vizier (steward) to the pharaoh. Later on we shall see evidence that his name too is derived from the position of Joseph within the royal court. From this exalted position Joseph controlled the people and the nation of Egypt; he was pharaoh in everything but name.

To maintain his status as vizier, Joseph had to convince the people that he was a follower of Taurus to avoid giving away his true position. Many years later, when his family joined him in Egypt, he advised his brothers not to mention the cult of Aries to avoid alerting the pharaoh to their true status as exiled royals. It may seem incredible, but this statement by Joseph still exists in the Bible (see part 2). The only important alteration that the scribes seem to have made is that the word 'religion' has been turned into 'occupation'. Of course, there are also the standard changes that have already been noted in these texts: 'follower of Aries' being changed to 'shepherd' and 'follower of Taurus' into the word 'cattle'. Other than this, the statement is virtually unchanged. This interpretation is utterly convincing, as the statement makes absolutely no sense in terms of agriculture, but it makes every sense in terms of theology. This statement alone is proof that the dispute between the exiled Egyptian Hyksos (the Israelites) and the remaining Egyptians was a religious one – a dispute between Aries and Taurus.

Although Joseph made a fortune beyond imagination in Egypt, he was not lucky enough to see his descendants become pharaoh. The political machinations were to take far longer than one generation to achieve. The same ponderous process was also at work in medieval Scotland, where, with a little help from a few supporters, it was eventually possible for the loyal stewards of the Scottish kings to become the Stewart kings and regain the throne. This was not the work of one ambitious man, but the patient plotting of a royal dynasty that kept its allegiances and goals a secret for generation after generation. This game of maintaining the royal bloodline transcends such secular trivialities as normal lifetimes and ambitions.

The Stewart line took no less than seven generations and 230 years from Walter Fitz Alan, the first High Steward, to Robert Stewart, who was crowned Robert II in 1371. [4] In Egypt, the royal line of Joseph used the same strategy, serving as loyal viziers to the pharaoh and manipulating the royal allegiances and alliances to suit their goal. They eventually achieved their objective, the pharaonic throne, and, in a similar fashion, it took nearly 200 years for the right time to come for Joseph's descendants. History constantly repeats itself.

Part 2

Joseph always knew his destiny, as the elder son of the Chief Wife of Jacoba. The dispute with Egypt rumbled on and the time was not right for him to return to Egypt; his father simply asked for a sign to be given when he thought the time had come. Eventually, after a few years, Joseph dipped his coat in the blood of a lamb and presented it to his father – a sign of the exodus. It was time to go back to Egypt to learn again the old ways. [B5]

Joseph was delivered safely across the dangerous border regions with Egypt by nomadic traders. They told the border guards a tall story of a son being sold into slavery by poor shepherds in order to pass through the outposts of the Egyptian guard with their precious cargo. The ruse worked as planned and the guards let them through. Everyone laughed so much about such a simple strategy that the tale eventually became enshrined in folklore – the royal prince Joseph being sold to traders. Once in Egypt, the young boy was delivered safely to Potiphar, an old ally of the family and captain of the guard (chief cook according to Josephus), who installed Joseph in some luxury in his house. [J6]

Joseph was educated by the priests of Heliopolis. It was a long and demanding scholarship and on his graduation, he married the daughter of the chief priest, who was of the royal bloodline. To further their goals, the priests of Heliopolis used their great influence upon the reigning pharaoh, recommending Joseph as a great prophet, who could divine the future of Egypt. After making some astute observations about the Egyptian nation to pharaoh, Joseph rose to the exalted rank of chief vizier. In recognition of his invaluable assistance to the royal household, pharaoh said to Joseph:

> ... thou shalt be over my house and according to thy word shall all my people be ruled; only in the throne will I be greater than thou ... [and he made Joseph] ride in the second chariot which he had; and they cried before him. Bow the knee; and he made him ruler over all the land of Egypt. And pharaoh said unto Joseph, I am pharaoh, and without thee no man shall lift up his hand or foot in all the land of Egypt. [B7]

* * *

Plate 1. Thoth, the god of knowledge, inscribing symbols of knowledge on the fruits of a tree. The Queen Hatshepsut is shown taking the knowledge from the tree. Quite plainly, this is the origin of the Eve story in the Bible.

Plate 2. *The finding of Moses*, by Nicolas Poussin (1594-1665). The background owes more to Greece and Rome than anything to be found in Egypt. The Biblical story is based on the Egyptian myth of Osiris, who was found drifting on the Nile in a sarcophagus, before being raised from the dead by Isis

Plate 3. *The adoration of the Golden Calf*, Nicolas Poussin. Moses is to be seen returning from Mount Sinai on the far left of the painting, while the people worship the Apis Bull of Egypt. In his rage at this, Moses murders 3,000 of his followers.

Plate 4. Akhenaton. Note the distorted head, wide hips, slight bust and lack of genitalia.

Plate 5. Nefertiti, Chief Wife of Akhenaton. Clearly the artists could produce anatomically precise work when required.

Plate 6. Akhenaton - Aaron, the heretic pharaoh and brother of Moses. Akhenaton is portraying himself here in the physical form of the gods, with wide temples, a narrow jaw and almond shaped eyes. All that is needed to complete the picture is grey skin.

Plate 7. The plain of Akhetaton - or Amarna. It was on this small barren plateau that Akhenaton built his new city. To the Theban priests, it became known as the **'Stone Quarry on the east bank of the Nile'.** (Quote from Manetho).

Plate 8. One of the boundary stele, carved into the eastern rock-face at Amarna. It proclaims the various evils that befell Akhenaton and his family.

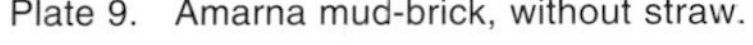

Plate 9. Amarna mud-brick, without straw.

Plate 10. Later mud-brick restoration, with straw.

Plate 11. The mud-brick palace of Akhenaton at Amarna.

Plate 12. Temple of the Aton at Amarna. Only the pillars were made of stone, the rest of the temple was fabricated in mud-brick with plaster linings. The pillars seen in the picture are reproductions, as the entire site was cleared in pharaonic times.

Plate 13. Michaelangelo's *Pieta* in St. Peter's Cathedral, Vatican city. A portrayal of Jesus and his wife, Mary Magdelene.

Plate 14. The rock crystal altar at Karnak. "And thou wilt make me an altar of stone, thou shalt not build it of hewn stone: for if thou lift thy tool upon it, thou has polluted it". (Exodus 20:25).

Plate 15. The Dome on the Rock, Jerusalem. The sacred city and the sacred rock of Judaism, Christianity and Islam.

Plate 16. *The dead Christ mourned*, by Annibale Carracci, also titled "The three (4) Maries". This is a good illustration of the deliberate obfuscation generated by the new Testament writers. All four women present are called Mary, there is Mary (mother of Jesus), Mary (Magdelene), Mary (Salome) and Mary (mother of James).

Plate 17. The Holy of Holies at the temple of Edfu, Egypt. The granite shrine, although an unusual addition to the room, is actually older than the temple.

Plate 18. Sun imagery, St. Mark's Cathedral, Venice.

Jacoba's long-term planning was bearing fruit: his son, the true royal prince, was now the most powerful man in Egypt and little did pharaoh (a Theban pharaoh, no doubt) realize that he had a cuckoo in the nest. Joseph and the priests would now have to be patient and await the right moment to make a bid for the throne.

In addition to this exalted position, Joseph had also been made royal keeper of the grain stores. [J8] This was a fortuitous appointment and Joseph planned to use this to his family's advantage. There was a famine in Canaan, a periodic problem in such an arid area, and Joseph's brothers, dressed as merchants, came to Egypt to buy grain. Joseph, in order to help his family, ordered that they should be given the grain and their money should be placed back in the tops of their sacks. [B9]

It was a kind gesture, but, unfortunately, when their father, Jacob, found the money in the sacks, he was afraid. He did not realize that this was his son's doing and he thought that the Egyptians might accuse them of theft, so blocking any further trade. Jacob knew that they might need more grain in the near future and sought to resolve the situation quickly. [B10] He declared that they should pay double the money next time, so the brothers went to Egypt to purchase grain once again. Joseph did the same again and placed all the money back into the sacks of grain. He had heard of the family's distress about the money last time, so he placed his personal silver cup in the top of Benjamin's sack, so that Jacob might know the truth.

The ruse worked: Jacob understood that his favourite son was behind the gifts of grain and it was only at this point that his brothers were told the truth about him. They were delighted with his success back in the old lands of their fathers and the whole family decided to join him in Egypt. Jacob and a retinue of nearly 70 followers made the long trek down into Egypt and they went straight to meet Joseph in Heliopolis, the sacred city of the royal line. [J11] Joseph was not only educated in the secret ways of the Heliopolian priesthood, but he lived there with his Egyptian wife. When his extended family arrived, he used his new power to grant them further tracts of land in Heliopolis to live. [J12]

Despite his great influence in Egypt, Joseph was still worried about these new arrivals, for they were not being very diplomatic at times. They were followers of Aries, and Egypt worshipped Taurus once more. The exodus was less than a generation ago and, in effect, they were living in enemy territory. Joseph had words with his extended family and warned them about the ways of Egypt and how to deal with the pharaoh to cover their true identity:

> (Paraphrased) You are Arians (shepherds) as you know, and your duty is to convert (feed) the followers of Taurus (the cattle) ... And it shall come to pass that pharaoh will call you, and shall say 'what is your religion' (occupation). You must say in return that your religion has been Taurean (trade has been cattle) from our youth even until now, both we and also our fathers. Otherwise you will not be allowed to stay in the land of Egypt, for we Arians (shepherds) are an abomination to the Egyptians. [B13]

But Joseph's brothers were both bold and foolish. When they were presented to the pharaoh, he said to them:

> (Paraphrased) What is your religion (occupation). And they said unto pharaoh; Thy servants are *Arians* (shepherds) both we and also our fathers. Moreover they said unto pharaoh we are looking for more lands to preach the word of Aries in (for our sheep), so pray thee let thy servants dwell in the land of Heliopolis. [B14]

There was a pregnant pause, for Joseph was not expecting his brothers to be so foolhardy. Pharaoh looked at Joseph and remembered all the wisdom he had imparted. He had expected as much in his dealings with Joseph and he was not entirely sure now just who was right in this theological debate. Pharaoh thought long and hard about the situation and finally he said to Joseph:

> The land of Egypt is before thee, in the best of the land make thy father dwell: and if thou knowest any evangelists (men of activity) amongst them, then make them rulers over my Taurus worshippers (cattle). [B15]

The family now had the royal blessing, not only to stay in Egypt, but also to practise the ways of Aries. The Heliopolian priests must have pulled some very influential strings to have persuaded the pharaoh to grant this freedom and in their moment of triumph they nick named Joseph 'Sobemsaf', the title of the pharaoh himself. They had succeeded beyond their wildest dreams: Joseph was but one step away from becoming pharaoh.

There were other concerns now, for the Nile did not flood so high as usual and the famine had now spread to Egypt. Luckily, Joseph had warned pharaoh of this calamity and he had been stockpiling grain for years. As the famine worsened, he began to sell this grain back to the people for the profit of the pharaoh. After a while, people had no more money to buy grain, so they sold their sacred cattle that they would not eat. Joseph bought them all and fed his people well. Next, the people of Egypt came to Joseph and sold their land to him to pay for grain until all the land of Egypt belonged to pharaoh and Joseph. When the floods at last returned to the land, Joseph said to the people:

> Here is seed corn for you, and ye shall sow the land. But in return you shall give one fifth part unto pharaoh and keep four fifths for your family. And they said; Thou hast saved our lives: let us find grace in your sight, and we will be pharaoh's servants. [B16]

And Joseph smiled, knowing that he was the saviour of all of Egypt and, in addition, he would receive a 20 per cent return on all his investments and become the richest man in the world.

As the years passed, Jacob their father, became infirm and died. Joseph had his father embalmed in the Egyptian manner. The Arian Egyptians mourned for 40 days, as was their new custom, and the Taurean Egyptians for 70 days, as was their custom. [B17] Joseph had permission from pharaoh to bury Jacob back in Canaan, so the cortege left Egypt in grand style, with all the elders of Egypt in attendance, and Jacob was buried in Canaan. Joseph himself lived long and his family prospered, but the years were rolling by and Joseph too died. Because of his royal connections and his high office, they *embalmed him in the Egyptian manner*, placed him in a sarcophagus and laid him in a tomb in Egypt. [B18]

Chapter V

Moses

Part 1

The Hyksos people now had two strongholds: both Jerusalem and Egypt were under their control. It must have been a time of great rejoicing, although it has to be said that the rejoicing would be short-lived, as only one and a half centuries into the future, the pharaoh Tuthmoses III would be taking his armies up through Palestine and on to Mesopotamia in search of conquest and territories. Undoubtedly the Hyksos Arians in Jerusalem would have been a defeated people during this campaign. But for the moment, Joseph controlled Egypt and was the most important man in the world, and his brethren controlled Jerusalem and Palestine. Yet of all the tribes of Israel, it was not the sons of Joseph who would become the most numerous, it was the sons of Judah, the Jews. Why was this?

It is probably as a result of the order in which Jacob's twelve sons were born. Rachel was Jacob's Chief Wife, the one that held the bloodline, but Rachel was not his first wife. Jacob's first wife was Leah, but she had been betrothed to him through deceit. The reason for this intrigue is not explained, but perhaps Leah, Rachel's older sister, was actually a half sister and therefore her six children had a weaker claim to the throne. Certainly, the lesser wives, Billah and Zilpah – respectively Rachel's and Leah's slaves – were not of the bloodline, yet they bore another four of Jacob's sons. None of these children was destined to become Jacob's favourites, only the two from Rachel would bear that mantle; Joseph and Benjamin. Jacob was worried about this lack of a true heir from his favourite wife because, as so often happens in the

Bible, Rachel was found to be 'barren'. This biblical tradition of 'barren' wives who eventually give birth to many children results from another pharaonic convention, the child bride. Such wives are not 'barren', just too young to bear children immediately, accordingly Rachel would at last bear two sons.

In this case, the first of Jacob's children to establish families in Jerusalem came from Leah and the slaves, not Rachel. In order of birth the first three were, Reuben, Levi and then Judah. As they were not directly of the bloodline, they established themselves in other roles in the new society in exile: the sons of Levi became the bloodline of the priesthood and the sons of Judah became the most populous of the tribes and gave their name to the nation, the Jews. The important thing to bear in mind is that these families established themselves in Jerusalem and, no doubt, many of them stayed there instead of migrating back to Egypt with Jacob and Joseph.

Rachel's sons, Joseph and Benjamin, the favourite sons who were destined to rule, were born much later and were still young when they travelled back to Egypt. Their families and descendants were established in Egypt, not Jerusalem, and these descendants were to get caught up in another war. It is logical, therefore, that Judah's descendants were to be the more populous among the Israelites in Palestine, to found the nation and write the history of their people. This is why I think that it is unlikely that King David and eventually Jesus were really of the line of Judah, as the Gospel of Mathew describes; this was perhaps the bias of a Judaic scribe. The favourite sons of the Pharaoh Jacoba were Joseph and Benjamin and it is highly likely that the matriarchal royal line would have flowed through them.

Déjà Vu?

For two centuries Joseph's descendants controlled Egypt as stewards, yet just as they were reaching their long-desired goal, a calamity would once again overtake them. All this intricate long-term planning was about to go wrong and the Egyptian-Israelite tribes would soon be lost in a second exodus – joy would become despair in less than three short centuries. That there was a second exodus from Egypt is indisputable. The Egyptian historian Manetho wrote an account of this second exodus of 'lepers and cripples' and the Bible also confirms this tradition of two exoduses. Its compilers wrote of the exodus of Jacob and of the more popular exodus of Moses. The problem is merely one of sorting out which exodus was which. Indeed, Josephus also knew of this tradition and became quite animated about the 'absurdity' of such a suggestion. It is apparent that a tradition of two exoduses existed in the centuries before Jesus, but it was not necessarily the history that Jewish historians, such as Josephus, wanted to propagate. There was something here that they wished to hide:

> The libels against us originated with the Egyptians. To gratify them, certain authors undertook to distort the facts ... These frivolous and utterly senseless specimens of humanity, accustomed from the first to erroneous ideas about the gods, were incapable of imitating the solemnity of our theology ... [Manetho] took the liberty of introducing some incredible tales, wishing to represent us as mixed up with a crowd of Egyptian lepers and others, who for various maladies were condemned ... to banishment from the country. [J1]

It is clear that the second exodus was the story that Josephus wanted to suppress, but in trying to do so, he inadvertently preserved it for posterity. This second exodus, as mentioned by Manetho, was a much smaller affair than the exodus previously described. It is said to have consisted of a mixture of '*maimed people*' and '*learned priests that were afflicted with leprosy*', numbering some 80,000. Before this exodus started, these people were initially banished to the '*stone quarries*' along the Nile. [J2] Remember these terms as they will become important later. Despite this scene being very similar to the traditional image of the Jewish nation being forced to make bricks for the pharaoh, Josephus ignores this obvious connection and, instead, leaps in with both feet, taking great offence at Manetho's slur on his people. However, in his rage Josephus takes the passage too literally.

It is apparent from the paragraph quoted above that Josephus was aware of the basic problem, as he defined the dispute as being essentially religious: the Egyptians, that is, the Upper Egyptians, had erroneous ideas about the gods. Josephus was so upset that he did not make the logical extrapolation as to how Theban scribes – on the other side of the fence – would have defined this theological dispute. Instead, he rather naively wrote of Jewish laws concerning the treatment of lepers, how they would not have been allowed to become priests and how difficult it would have been to round up 80,000 lepers in one day.

He missed the point entirely, for these people were not physical lepers at all, they were being labelled as *social lepers, theological pariahs.*

Summary

This was simply a religious dispute that has already been defined as being a battle of the Taureans against the new cult of Arians. The change was brought about by the priests of Heliopolis carefully noting the movement of the stars and recognizing that Aries had become the rising constellation. The Arians had, at one point, gained control of Lower Egypt under the rule of the Shepherd Kings. Eventually, the Taureans, under the rule of the Theban pharaohs, gained the upper hand and chased the Shepherds from the land in the first and greatest of the exoduses. Thus, by this time, the majority of Arians were in Jerusalem, licking their wounds and plotting revenge.

However, it would be simple minded to assume that the entire population of Arians had been thrown out of the country. That is not the way of wars. Those against the restored Taurean regime would have had two choices: face the perils of mass migration and the prospect of moving their family and belongings to a new land or keeping their heads down and pretending never to have supported the Arians in the first place, while biding time until conditions in the country changed once again.

The previous chapter contained an allusion to the Russian royal family, but such events have happened time after time throughout history. There are numerous examples: in Asia Minor during the fourth century BC under the brief reign of Alexander the Great, in Russia during the thirteenth century under the rule of Genghis Khan, in India under British administration established in the eighteenth century, and in the European Eastern bloc that survived fifty years of Soviet rule in the twentieth century. In all these cases, the people struggled on somehow; the customs, religion and traditions of the nation may be submerged for a while, but they rarely perish. It is very difficult to cleanse a land of a particular nation, but it is harder still to erase a small sect, especially when there is no physical attribute to distinguish its members from the rest of the population. Recorded history indicates strongly that this is how wars and campaigns are conducted and it would be naïve to think that it was any different in the ancient world.

After the pharaoh Jacoba and his followers had fled from Egypt, there would have been any number of followers left in the countryside, waiting and praying for a restoration of their Shepherd King, just as many other nations have waited and prayed for their exiled leaders to return. In this particular case, the period of waiting was not long, for the son of their beloved leader, Joseph, returned within one generation. Joseph was not yet pharaoh, but his presence in the land must have given great hope to the privileged few who knew the truth. He and his offspring had only to bide their time as viziers of the pharaoh, waiting patiently for an opportunity to take back the throne.

Things went well at first and the descendants of Joseph were closely aligned to the pharaoh, but then after the death of the pharaoh Amenhotep I, there was a break in the succession. A new pharaonic line established itself, a military leader had seized the throne, possibly after a military coup – Tuthmoses I. It was to be the line of Tuthmoside pharaohs that pushed out the boundaries of the Egyptian empire, through to Syria and Persia in the north and east and to Nubia in the south; the Egyptian army conquered all. It is significant that these campaigns across the Arian (also called Hyksos or Jacobite) held territories of Palestine occurred when a line of pharaohs was in power who were definitely not of the bloodline. Josephus also alludes to this change in the pharaonic bloodline in his version of the Old Testament, when he talks of:

> (The Egyptians) having forgotten the benefits they had received from Joseph, particularly the crown being now come into another family, they became very abusive to the Israelites (Arians)... [J3]

That 'other family' was the Tuthmoside kings and perhaps they *were* abusive to the Arians (Israelites), but the situation would change rapidly after a convenient marriage alliance. It would appear that this fresh opportunity for securing power and influence finally presented itself to the line of Joseph either during the reign of Tuthmoses III, or Tuthmoses IV. In the latter case, the vizier Yuya (who will be shortly identified as a descendent of the vizier Joseph) had allied himself so closely with the monarch that the pharaoh's son, the future Amenhotep III, married Yuya's daughter Tiye.

It is probably not a coincidence that the foreign campaigns by the Egyptian military through Palestine only stopped when Amenhotep III, the son of Tuthmoses IV, came to power. At last, the Shepherd Kings had been able to manoeuvre their bloodline back into that of the reigning monarch, at last their influence could halt the devastating attacks on their relatives in Jerusalem and Palestine. Historians record that under the rule of Amenhotep III, Egypt had indeed entered a stable period of power and prosperity. It was also a time of royal and political manoeuvring, with an unusual number of diplomatic marriages to the tribes of Palestine being arranged.

The suggestion here is that the Hyksos kings, the Shepherd Kings, were back in control in Egypt. But historians will say that the last of the Hyksos kings were ejected from Egypt at the time of the Hyksos exodus, under the rule of the pharaoh Jacoba, and were never seen again. This is not the full story. We know that the Hyksos kings regained the throne of Egypt, just as the Bible indicates, because the king lists of Egypt tell us so. These new pharaohs, who were on better terms with their brothers in Palestine, really were Shepherd Kings. Both Amenhotep II and Amenhotep III were called 'hyk' in their royal title – meaning 'Shepherd King'. More interestingly, their origins are also listed in the record and Amenhotep II's full title is the 'Hyksos King of Heliopolis', the sacred temple and university of the Hyksos princes. Egyptologists are strangely silent on this fact.

The Hyksos era in Egypt was one of the great intrigues in the history of this land and yet when a Hyksos pharaoh returned to the throne of Egypt, it barely causes a ripple in Egyptological circles. Why and how did they return? Why did the people of Egypt accept them once more? There are a host of questions to be answered, yet the response is silence. Uncomfortably for the orthodoxy, the answers to these questions are to be found in the Bible, with the story of the return of Joseph to Egypt, his family settling in Heliopolis, his marriage to the daughter of a priest of Heliopolis and the long line of Hyksos viziers to the pharaoh.

The Bible is silent on when the line of Joseph finally regained the throne, but the historical record provides enough clues. It was Amenhotep II who was called the 'Shepherd King of Heliopolis'. Quite obviously the Hyksos kings were back in control at this time, but the family history of this pharaoh is uncertain. The history of Amenhotep III, however, is well documented and so it is to his family that we must turn for further evidence. The intermarriages of Amenhotep III with the family of his vizier Yuya, as we shall see, confirm that the bloodline had returned to the throne.

The image in the historical record is of a period of unparalleled success for the royal bloodline. The Amenhotep pharaohs were

Shepherd Kings, the daughter of Yuya was also of the bloodline, becoming the wife of Amenhotep III, and their son would be ruler of all Egypt. This would consolidate their position, deflect the claims of the Tuthmoside clan and so the Arians would fully control the nation once more, including the turbulent south. Indeed, Amenhotep III called himself 'the Shepherd King of Thebes' a provocative title if ever there was one.

Turning the Page

In the parallel biblical narrative, the story has arrived at the birth of Moses, yet the Bible portrays the infant Moses as being a poor Israelite left in a basket on the banks of the river Nile. Ironically, Moses was destined to be discovered by the pharaohs daughter – so that Moses (who was a Levite and therefore an Arian) arrived in the pharaoh's royal court. In each of these histories, an Arian hero ended up in the royal court, but which version is the more likely, the poor shepherd or the royal prince?

Once more, it is the biblical narrative that makes no sense and a deeper search of the texts produces further evidence of censorship and alterations on the behalf of the biblical scribes. Chapter IV ended with Joseph and his family of the 12 tribes of Israel (including the Levite clan from which Moses was descended), at the admission of the biblical texts, being the most powerful people in the world. Joseph was vizier to the pharaoh, the most powerful man in the world at the time and undoubtedly a little nepotism would have been used to elevate his family into the highest posts in the lands of Egypt and Palestine. The texts admit that Joseph controlled 20 per cent of the gross national product of all Egypt; it is unthinkable that, in this era, some of this wealth did not filter down into the coffers of the 12 tribes. These were truly influential people in the land of Egypt, the new aristocracy.

In the Bible we turn the last page of the narrative of Genesis and arrive in the book of Exodus. Within this short space of time, a few short paragraphs, these same rich and influential tribes of Israel have been reduced to poor foreign natives, at the mercy of the evil Egyptians. No explanation is given of how these members of the Egyptian aristocracy fell from grace so quickly and so totally, but now the Hebrews are presented as being slaves to the Egyptians, with Moses being cast adrift on the Nile to save him from the bloodthirsty persecution of the Hebrew children. How and why did this happen? The texts are silent on the matter, it is simply another biblical mystery.

There is a rational answer to this problem, for the true plight of the Hebrews depends on your viewpoint. The Arian people had many powerful enemies and they did not choose to portray the Arians in a flattering light. Images of the 12 tribes being slaves to the Theban nobility and priests would have been very satisfying to them. The later biblical scribes seem to have been happy to go along with some of these unflattering descriptions, as they portrayed the Hebrews as the victims in this social war and, equally, they implied that the Egyptians were a cruel people. However, to elevate Moses into the royal court , so that he could converse with pharaoh directly, what better method than the use of the old Osirian myth of being cast adrift on the Nile. Egyptian history was eventually defeated by its own propaganda and it would be the Hebrews who would tell this tale to the wider world. History is made by the teachers.

This was an historic moment in both theology and history. In the Bible, Moses was about to embark with the Israelite people and their single omnipotent god who had no physical form, on their trek to the promised lands of Israel. In historical Egypt, the pharaoh Akhenaton, son of Amenhotep III, was about to lead his people into a new world governed by a new, singular god and a new religion without carved images. These events seem to be undeniably similar and inextricably linked, but what is the truth behind them? How do they relate to each other?

The renowned theological author Ahmed Osman has spent a lifetime researching the Amarna age, as this era later became known, and its links with the biblical exodus. In the first book of his Amarna trilogy, he makes a well-argued case for identifying the vizier Yuya with the biblical Joseph. Yuya held the same position as Joseph in the royal court, was designated 'Father to Pharaoh' and, unusually for Egypt, he wore no earrings, as the unpierced ears on his mummy clearly show. This last point is very interesting, for Joseph would not have worn earrings, just as his father Jacob had commanded. [4] Ahmed Osman's well-researched and scholarly thesis could be seen as undermining the theories presented here, for I have placed Joseph nearly three centuries earlier than the Amarna pharaohs. The evidence presented so far places Joseph as following the pharaoh Jacoba during the Hyksos reign.

However, this may not be the full story and the apparent contradiction can be resolved by looking once more at the Scottish Stewart parallel. The stewards to the Scottish kings eventually became the Stewart kings – the professional title became the surname of kings. The same thing could equally have happened in ancient Egypt. Joseph may not have been a name at all, but a title, possibly meaning steward. Ahmed Osman argues that Joseph is derived from Yahweh, the name of the Jewish deity, in which case 'Joseph' could easily have been a title, like Christian.

Josephus, when quoting Manetho, said that Moses was also called O**sar**seph, [M5] which Ahmed Osman admits is likely to be a corruption of the name Joseph, with the inserted 'sar' in the name meaning king or prince. Many of the royal cartouches are written in just this fashion, with the royal title in the name. The cartouche of Amenhotep II, for instance, is actually saying 'Amun is pleased (with) the Shepherd King and ruler of Heliopolis'. Historians have extracted from this long title the section 'Amun is pleased', which sounds like 'Amenhotep', but there is no reason why the name should not include the royal epitaph and be pronounced Amen**hyk**hotep, or Amen**sar**hotep.

On the next page in this book, Josephus, this time quoting a historian known as Chaeremon, offers further evidence. The text here describes Moses as being named Tisithen and it was *his scribe* who was called Joseph, known as Peterseph. It seems that there is a succession of personalities with substantially the same name and the obvious explanation for this is that Joseph (Osarseph, Peterseph) is nothing more than a title. This is a title for a vizier who eventually became known as 'Father to Pharaoh'. It was inherited through the generations and was finally given to Moses; hence Moses was called Osarseph (O...seph). If this is the case, there is no dispute between the thesis here and that of Ahmed Osman; the name or title of 'Joseph' could have been passed down through the family line from Zaphenath-paneah (the first Joseph, son of Jacob) to Moses, the last of the Josephs in Egypt.

Blood Fusion

So after nearly two centuries of waiting, the Arians finally had their chance to regain the throne. We do not have the family history of Amenhotep II, to ascertain how exactly he fits into this picture, but we can follow the family ties of his (son?) Amenhotep III. Tiye, the daughter of the vizier Yuya, whom we can assume to have been a lineal descendant of the vizier Joseph, became the chief wife of Amenhotep

III. The bloodline of Abraham, Jacob and Joseph had married into the pharaonic line once more. This marriage may seem like a minor detail and needs further explanation. Just as in modern Judaism, the lineal descent of pharaonic Egypt was through the *matriarchal* line of the wife, not the patriarchal line of the pharaoh, in this case Amenhotep III. So through this strange marriage, it was Tiye's family line that was being continued, not the bloodline of the pharaoh. Yet it would appear that the family of Yuya held no royal titles, just 'Commander of the Chariotry', [6] and later, the grander title of 'Father to Pharaoh'. [7] With such a lowly background, how did the vizier Yuya persuade the pharaoh to marry his daughter – indeed, to make her his chief wife?

This marriage was, therefore, quite strange. The normal pharaonic marriage alliance was for an immediate betrothal to a sister or half-sister, so that the pharaoh's descendants could perpetuate the *matriarchal* line of the family. Any marriage to a chief wife from outside the family would immediately nullify the pharaonic line completely and confer the kingship on the family of the wife. It would be inconceivable that a pharaoh would want to do this, unless, of course, the 'outsider' wife were a lineal descendant of a former pharaoh and could prove it. There certainly must have been something very special about this line of royal viziers, for Akhenaton, Amenhotep III's son, did exactly the same thing as his father. He married Nefertiti, who was the daughter of Aye, Yuya's son and the next vizier in the family line. This very special family of viziers eventually provided the queens for four or more successive pharaohs, but what made them so special?

There is a reasonable assumption that can be made about this episode. Perhaps Tuthmoses IV, was sympathetic to the plight of the vizier Yuya (the history of Tuthmoses IV is uncertain, but it is thought that he was not related to the Amenhotep pharaohs). It has already been pointed out that there is biblical evidence that Joseph was able to declare his family as being Arian supporters, so, perhaps by the era of Yuya, the atmosphere was friendly enough for him to prove his descent without fear of persecution. This may have been why Yuya was elevated to the high position of 'Father to Pharaoh', apparently the only time this appellation was used in Egypt. This may also be why Yuya and his wife, Tuyu, have the grandest tomb ever found in Egypt, apart from that of Tutankhamen. Perhaps Yuya was raised to the position of 'Father to Pharaoh' because he was just that: he was directly descended from the pharaoh Jacoba and both his son-in-law and his grandson became pharaoh. Yuya *was* of the bloodline.

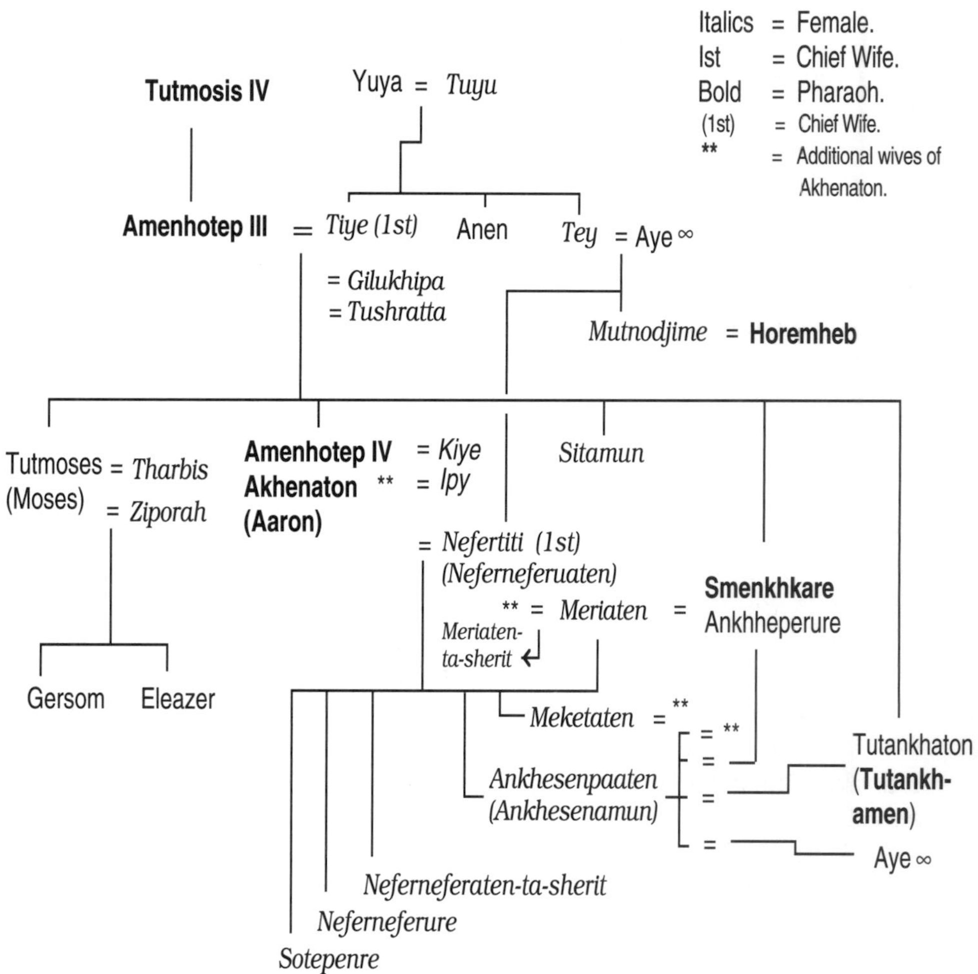

Fig 15 Family tree of the Amarna pharaohs

This is speculative in some respects, but undoubtedly there are a lot of similarities within the biblical story and the Egyptian record and it is an important observation. This episode was to become another turning point in the long history of Egypt and something monumental was brewing once more in this ancient land. In this period, in both the Egyptian and the biblical stories, it is quite apparent that a new culture was emerging. A new line of thought, which had radically different ideas on art, culture and theology, was being established. In each of these separate histories, it can be seen that this new line blossomed briefly and then ended abruptly in either defeat or exile. In the Bible, the story centres on the religious figure of Moses, the great leader of the Israelites. In the Egyptian record, it centres on a pharaoh, Akhenaton, the most radical of all the pharaohs of Egypt.

Akhenaton

Akhenaton was the second son of Amenhotep III. His first son was named Tuthmoses, but he disappeared from the record at an early age and is usually presumed to have died. However, no tomb or inscription has been found that can substantiate this claim of an early death and the discovery of his ivory whip in the tomb of Tutankhamen, for use as commander of the king's chariot forces, would indicate that he did not die young. Amenhotep's second son, Amenhotep IV, was the son who caused all the chaos and changed the religion of an entire nation. Amenhotep IV, who later changed his name to Akhenaton out of his respect to the 'new' deity that he worshipped, was a revolutionary monarch in all respects. Egypt had been a relatively stable society for thousands of years, both before and after this rebel pharaoh, the capital cities, temples, gods, arts, and social graces of the empire had changed little. Akhenaton would change them all. His whole career was out of the ordinary. *This* is the kind of character that millions of books are written about.

This 'new' deity of Akhenaton, the Aton or Aten, initially appears to have been an innovation of Akhenaton, but looking further into the records shows that the Aton was mentioned during the reign of his father, who had a royal barge named 'Aton Gleams'. Further back still, there is a reference in the twelfth dynasty, where Ammenemes I is described as 'dying and flying to heaven to unite with the Aton'. [8]

Significantly in this argument of a longer history to the Aton, Akhenaton was educated at Heliopolis and the traditional worship there was to the Sun god Atum. The name of this god is not only similar to Akhenaton's own deity, the Aton, but its worship was as well. The fundamentals of this Solar cult required temples to be open to the skies, for the sunlight to fall on the sacred obelisks within their courtyards, the Benben stone. Akhenaton's temples were all open to the skies in the same manner. This link with the Benben stone will also become central to this investigation, for the worship of the Benben was the oldest theological creed in Egypt and it spawned the cult of the obelisk. This cult is central to tracing the subsequent dispersal of this religion around Europe after the next great exodus.

There were hundreds of obelisks, both large and small, commissioned by pharaohs in Egypt and Akhenaton was no exception:

> His majesty giving command to the Master of Works ... for mustering a large body of forced labour in order to cut sandstone for the making of the great Benben or Re-Herakhte in his aspect of the Light which is in the Aton, in Karnak. [9]

Classically, the Aton is described as being the first monotheistic religion, one that attempted to do away with the plethora of gods that were then in vogue in Egypt. Like Amun, it was essentially a solar worship, but modified in that it was not the Sun itself that was worshipped, but rather the 'power behind the Sun', as it has been called. This could be thought of as being the worship of the workings of the cosmos itself, the traditional study of the Heliopolian priests. Akhenaton, according to both the revised biblical history and the king lists of Egypt, was a direct descendant of the Hyksos pharaohs, who were so strongly influenced by the priests of Heliopolis. This deity has to be a direct result of their influence: it is simply the Hyksos belief system under another name. Akhenaton's father, Amenhotep III, must have had many sympathies with this belief in the Aton as well, but he never dared openly to promote this 'new' cult. Perhaps he was not so committed to the cause or he may simply have realized the turmoil it would ignite if he did promote it. Nevertheless, he was content to be portrayed at the new city of Amarna (originally named Akhetaton) as receiving blessings from this new deity, the Aton.

It would appear that Akhenaton himself was made of sterner material. His matriarchal descent from Yuya and education at Heliopolis no doubt convinced him that he was born to promote this ancient religion. Although Akhenaton was only promoting a very ancient creed, the teachings of Heliopolis and the veneration of the sacred Benben stone, it was the degree to which he went in his piety that caused all the trouble, the placing of a Benben stone at Karnak, where the priests probably thought this symbol to be heretical and the excision of the name of Amen, the southern gods title. The fact that the 'Mansion of the Benben', constructed at Karnak, was dedicated to and officiated by the queen Nefertiti, must have caused some further divisions in the priesthood there. Whatever the case, it is certain that Akhenaton was not being very diplomatic, his actions were bound to cause trouble. It is well documented that Akhenaton not only changed the theological environment of Egypt, but that he received a great deal of opposition to his reforms, eventually leading to another civil war. History was to repeat itself and, like Jacoba before him, Akhenaton was to see the demise of all he had worked for, the failure of more than two centuries of planning and the end of the entire Amarna regime.

Moses

At this point, it is necessary to return to the dispute that the historian Josephus was having with the ancient texts of Manetho. Manetho said that there were two exoduses from Egypt, the second of which was composed of *maimed people and leprous priests.* To what was Manetho alluding? Some things seem fairly certain. The nature of this dispute, both in the Egyptian record and the biblical record, has been established.

It was a theological struggle between the Taureans and the Arians, but the Arians had redefined themselves in this new era as followers of Aton. It is more than likely that the (eventually) victorious Taurean scribes would have wanted to portray the opposition, the Arians, as being somehow afflicted with disease. Consequently, they described the followers of the Arian (Aton) cult as being physically or socially tainted by this 'new' religion; they were *'maimed people'* and their priests were *'afflicted with leprosy'*. Manetho was, therefore, correct in his assertions of Egyptian history, the texts can be believed, but Manetho was just preaching from a highly biased point of view.

Josephus had just misunderstood what these ancient texts were driving at. He failed to recognize that they were concerned with religion, the most important subject in Egypt. In his rage, he could not see that Manetho was not interested a few people with physical diseases, but was very worried about a theological 'cancer' that was affecting thousands of the Egyptian people and changing the theological environment of the country. That is why we can believe this second exodus was a real event. There *is* evidence, if you read between the lines, that a major crisis was about to happen again in Egypt.

So who was the biblical Moses, the saviour of the Jewish nation, and who were his followers? Ahmed Osman, in the second book of his trilogy, makes a case for Moses being none other than this heretical pharaoh Akhenaton. From the little we have seen already, this is certainly a possibility and Ahmed Osman makes a very good case for this connection, even without the background data on the patriarchal pharaohs previously discussed. With this extra knowledge, the scenario becomes very compelling. Indeed, there are so many similarities between the environment and religion of Akhenaton's Amarna regime and the subsequent religion of the Israelites, that it is worth listing a few of them. Items marked with an asterisk are derived from the works of Ahmed Osman:

a. The god of Akhenaton was called the Aton. The god of the Israelites was called Adonai. As the 't' and the 'd' are interchangeable in Egyptian, the Israelite god could be called Atonai.*

b. In the Talmud, the wife of Moses is called Adonith, which can be translated into Egyptian as Aton-it.* Joseph's wife had a similar name, that of Asenath, a Phoenician god.

c. Akhenaton promoted a single god without an image, as did the Israelites.*

d. The Ark of the Covenant bears more than a striking resemblance to the Ark of Tutankhamen. Tutankhamen was the last of the Amarna pharaohs.

e. The Israelites were commanded to make an altar that was not hewn with any tool, nor had steps leading up to it. (Due to an absence of underwear, this ruling prevented the priests' bottoms from being seen). The great altar of Karnak was made with the upper surface being of unhewn rock crystal and neither it nor the altars in the other temples had steps before them. [B10]

f. The wearing of earrings was common in Egypt and, in the royal family, it designated a prince who was not of the bloodline and could not become pharaoh. Many of the Israelites used to wear earrings, but were commanded not to when they reached Jerusalem. Significantly, this practice was resurrected by seventeenth-century pirates, a group with undoubted Templar affiliations (the role of the Templars is discussed later).

g. The Egyptian priesthood had dietary prohibitions and ritual ablutions that are similar to those of Judaism.

h. The Egyptian priesthood had shaven heads, Christian priests altered this to a tonsure, which is similar to a Jewish yarmulke, or skullcap. Rabbis often sport the shaven forehead. [11]

i. Orthodox Jews often wear long, curled side-locks of hair. In Egypt, exactly this fashion denoted a young man – the uninitiated.

j. The symbol of the cross (in Christianity) is an Egyptian symbol. The Egyptian cross, the Ankh, was promoted by Akhenaton into a major part of his theology, where it symbolized life or the resurrection.

k. Christian churches are orientated towards the east, as was the mobile Israelite temple, the Tabernacle. Similarly, all the temples at Amarna face towards the rising Sun.

l. Circumcision had been an early Egyptian custom and the ceremony is depicted in many Egyptian texts. [J12]

m. The carrying of religious shrines around the town or city was a common festival event in Egypt. For instance, in the era of Tutankhamen, after the restoration of the old deities, the shrine of Amen at Karnak was taken on a barque to visit the southern temple at Luxor. This annual procession can be seen on the carved reliefs in the processional colonnade of the Luxor temple; the outward journey is on the western wall and the return on the eastern. This same rite is still practised in many Catholic countries, when reliquaries are paraded around towns and villages.

n. From Tuthmoses through Yuya to the Ramesside pharaohs of the nineteenth dynasty, the pharaohs typically display the long aquiline nasal phenotype, a feature typical of the Jewish race.

These similarities demonstrate that the Egyptian religions and, specifically, the religion of Akhenaton did not die. They escaped during the exodus and have evolved into the familiar forms of today. Many of our ancient traditions are rooted in the theology of ancient Egypt and further similarities will be discussed later.

But does all this prove that Akhenaton was the biblical Moses? It cannot be said to be definitive proof, but it is apparent that the events of the Amarna regime in Egypt strongly influenced the events leading up to the biblical exodus and that many of the traditions established at Amarna were transferred to Jerusalem. Given the theory outlined in earlier chapters, this is hardly surprising. The descendants of Jacoba were still in Jerusalem and if the Amarna regime was also descended from Jacoba, similarities are to be expected. Accordingly, it can be seen that both Akhenaton and Moses were educated at the temple of Heliopolis. This is not a coincidence, but precisely the education to be expected for an Arian prince. [13]

> It is said that the priest who framed their constitution and their laws was a native of Heliopolis, named Osarseph after the god Osiris, worshipped at Heliopolis; but when he joined his people, he changed his name and was called Moses. [M14]

Moreover, if Akhenaton were the biblical Moses with his regime in tatters and facing exile, he would have been most likely to flee to Jerusalem, the city of his ancestors. Both the Bible and Manetho, in their as yet two separate stories, indicate that this is exactly what happened. However, the links between Moses and Akhenaton are still a little tenuous and more proof is required of their common history.

There is another possibility for the identification of the biblical Moses, which is very similar in concept, but allows more flexibility in the interpretations. This possibility was explored in *Act of God* by Graham Philips and concerns Akhenaton's elder brother, Tuthmoses, who apparently disappeared from the historical record very early in his life. Did Tuthmoses die prematurely? The whip bearing his name was found in the tomb of Tutankhamen and this would seem to indicate that he reached early manhood at least. If this is so, why did Tuthmoses renounce his birthright to become the next pharaoh, just like the biblical Esau, and why did he disappear from the historical record?

I believe that the similarities between the Amarna regime and the family of Moses are strong enough to declare a link, but the problem is identifying which character is which; it is entirely possible that Moses was *Tuthmoses*, rather than Akhenaton. Some scholars believe that the name Moses was derived from the Egyptian word 'son' and this is, in turn, derived from the name Tuthmoses, but such scholars cannot make the next logical deduction – that Moses *was* Tuthmoses. Moses and Tuthmoses not only shared the same name, but the Torah and the Bible also explain exactly why this character was forced to give up his birthright to his brother, Akhenaton.

The first thing to note is the regular pattern in which biblical patriarchs pass on their inheritance to the younger of the bloodline sons. Isaac, Jacob and David all chose the younger sibling and now we see Moses, too, passing up his birthright. Is there a common cause to these stories? In respect of Moses the case is clearer and a clue to his misfortune can be seen in his physical description; it would appear that the pharaoh had to be physically perfect to accept his office:

> ... as for his beauty, there was nobody so impolite as [to say] they were not greatly surprised at the beauty of his countenance; nay, it happened frequently, that those who met him ... were obliged to turn again upon seeing the child; that they left what they were about, and stood still a great while to look on him... [J15]

This is confirmed by the demise of the much later high priest of Jerusalem, Hyrcanus II, who had his ears bitten off to make him 'imperfect' and therefore unable to continue in his office. In a similar vein, according to the Talmud, Moses lost his physical perfection at the hands of the reigning pharaoh (explained in part 2) and perhaps this is the reason for the birthright being passed onto his brother Aaron. If this were the case, it is reasonable to surmise that Aaron was the pharaoh Amenhotep IV, later called Akhenaton. Again, this is a very similar appellation.

Hero or Despot?

There are some basic problems with this identification that need to be overcome. For instance, in the religious texts concerned with this era, all the disasters that befell the Israelites were blamed on the 'pharaoh' and, in addition, both Moses and Aaron occasionally conversed with the 'pharaoh'. The texts, therefore, seem to be at odds with the concept of Aaron's being the pharaoh himself. There is a good reason for these texts that can be gleaned from the historical record. It seems that for much of his reign, Akhenaton (Aaron) shared a co-regency with his father, Amenhotep III. Whatever the reason for the co-regency, there appears to have been two pharaohs at large in Egypt at the time. Ahmed Osman, for instance, gives no fewer than 13 reasons he thinks that there was at least a 12-year co-regency, which also indicate that Amenhotep III was sympathetic to the cult of the Aton.

None of these really explain why this co-regency should have happened. Why should Amenhotep III have crowned his son king, but still retained the throne for himself in the rest of the kingdom? With this theory of Aaron's being Akhenaton himself, a reason becomes clear. The Bible relates that Moses (and most probably Aaron as well) were exiled from Egypt for a while for the murder of a Taurean (an Egyptian). Moses, Aaron and probably some of their followers, whom I have identified as the followers of Aries, were given a period of exile before the main exodus. These biblical princes were exiled to another location, where Aaron could have crowned himself 'king' of his little empire, a temporary co-regency. [B16] The Israelite people, too, were subjected to a period of exclusion; they were given hard labour to perform for the pharaoh in the famous period of brick-making, a form of internal exile in captivity. These are the biblical stories, but can they be verified from the historical point of view? For example, what did Manetho say of the Arians at this time?

This is fertile ground because Manetho also related a tale of the Arians (Israelites) being exiled before the main exodus itself. They were initially exiled with all the 'lepers' of the country to the *stone quarries* on the east bank of the Nile to perform hard labour. Finally, classical Egyptian history also provides another possible case of a pharaoh and a people being exiled – in the strange account of the founding of Akhe**n**aton's remote city called Amarna (Akhe**t**aton).

Did Akhenaton go to Amarna to found his new city there or was he pushed? Either way, it appears that his father, Amenhotep III, was still in power elsewhere and governing the rest of the country for at least a decade after Akhenaton's city of Amarna was founded. This is a very satisfying unanimity among these disparate texts. Aaron and Moses, Akhenaton and Tuthmoses, the Israelite people, plus the 'leper' priests, were all given a period of exile somewhere in Egypt or the surrounding districts. Can these coincidences be linked in any way?

On returning to the biblical stories of Moses, it can now be seen that they are not necessarily at odds with the theory of Aaron's being a pharaoh. Aaron and Moses could easily have conversed with the pharaoh, for their father was a pharaoh, too. Historical records indicate that Amenhotep III visited Amarna at some time, so the pharaoh Akhenaton could easily have spoken to 'pharaoh', his father. In this case, the only changes that the scribes made to the texts is to blame some of the calamities on a generic term 'pharaoh'. They are not being totally deceitful in doing this, for some of the calamities were, indeed, caused by Akhenaton (Aaron). Thus the scribes have saved the reputation of their hero Moses and his family without changing the texts at all. When Aaron (Akhenaton) or his father did something wrong, the name Aaron was deleted and 'pharaoh' was inserted. At the same time, there was no mention of the fact that the pharaoh concerned was Moses' brother. There is no real deceit, just obfuscation.

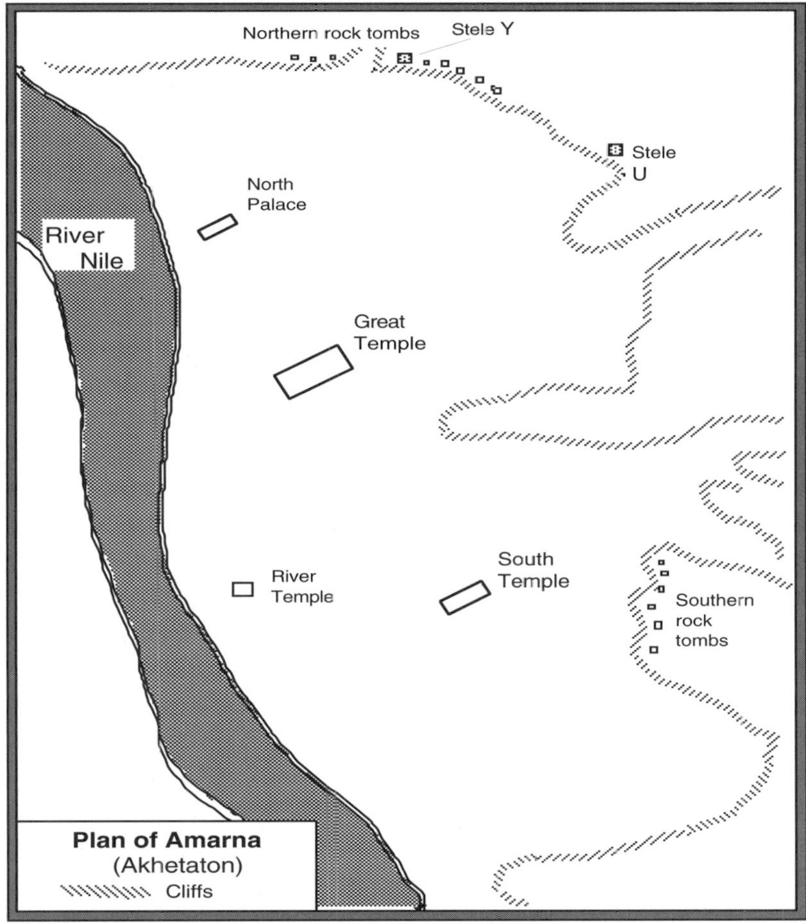

Fig 16. Plan of Amarna

When pharaoh berated the Jewish people for not making bricks when no straw was available, it was simply their own pharaoh urging them on to ever-greater feats. In fact, this is a strange request by the pharaoh because very little of the ancient mud-brick in Egypt contains any straw at all. Having examined every temple in Upper Egypt, I found straw samples in only one small section of the perimeter wall at the temple of Dendra. Other than there, straw was only to be found in the more modern repair work. Certainly, in the temples and palaces at Amarna, there was no straw-binder to be found in any of the brickwork.

Amarna, the city of Akhenaton, is a time capsule of the New Kingdom, a still-life image of the Amarna Age. It was founded by Akhenaton as the new capital of Egypt, but abandoned just 20 years later, the foundations being left to form an ancient map of how the ideal new city of this era was designed. But in their hatred of the city and what it represented, subsequent pharaohs must have placed a curse on the area, for it was never inhabited again.

To visit the remains, I took the train to El Minya and picked up a taxi from there. As the town lies in a security zone, our party had to wait for the army to escort us to the site and, after an hour or so, an army personnel carrier sporting a heavy machine gun arrived and followed us south along the west bank. Just opposite Amarna there is a battered old ferry. We left the army behind here and picked up a posse of armed guards on the other side. At this point, some confusion set in, as it often does in the area, and an animated discussion took place. It was one of those affairs where everyone in the party shouts at each other for hours and nothing seems to be achieved. Eventually, two German tourists arrived and it emerged that the problem had simply been whether to wait for them.

Myself, the two tourists and some twenty assorted guards and officials then climbed into a battered old bus and lurched out across the plain. Amarna lies within a crescent of cliffs that line the east bank of the Nile. The plain lies above the normal flood plain of the river, so it would have looked the same then as it does now, a barren moonscape with the encircling red cliffs behind and the narrow green winding snake of the river Nile below.

From the briefest of glances at the area, it is obvious that the palaces and temples of Amarna were built in a hurry by a small workforce. Akhenaton was desperate to set up a new imposing capital for the rest of Egypt to admire, but he was short of resources and manpower. Egyptologists say about 50,000 people lived at Amarna and

Manetho said about 80,000 – not many with whom to found a new capital. Consequently, the work was rushed and sizeable parts of the buildings were made from mud-brick with plaster-covered walls. This was a common building material in Egypt for housing and even for some palaces, but the great temples of Upper Egypt are all formed from huge monolithic stone blocks. The most that Akhenaton could manage in his new empire was some large stone pillars in the main temple.

The tombs cut into the cliffs also bear the signs of equally hurried work. Some of the initial work in the entrance halls is quite fine, but deeper into each tomb, the workers have left unfinished walls and chambers, concentrating their efforts on the burial pits instead. If the tombs were ever used, they were extremely unfinished. Because of his controversial reforms, Akhenaton suffered the wrath of the Theban priests after his death, so that much of the artwork in the tombs has been mutilated and defaced. However, the surviving friezes at Amarna and those in the museum at Luxor show a startling transformation from the formal style of all the previous periods in Egyptian history. Natural forms are depicted, the family life of the pharaoh is shown and he has even been drawn giving a seal of office to an official, something unheard of in other eras. This and the strange, rotund body forms of the king and queen clearly demonstrate the radical nature of the Amarna regime. Akhenaton was a man with a political and religious mission.

After the death of Amenhotep III, Akhenaton (Aaron) began the task of consolidating his power in the land and closing the temples of the traditional gods. Henry VIII of England managed to close all the monasteries of England when working from a very secure power base with plenty of support throughout the land. Akhenaton managed nominally to reform the religious beliefs of an entire nation, while receiving, at best, only patchy support from the population in the kingdom. The fact that he managed this task, albeit quite briefly, meant that he must have secured the trust of the majority of the army, for they would have been required at every town and temple if the sacrilegious act of defacing the images of the gods was to be achieved. That he managed to achieve all this must indicate that both Moses and Aaron were highly skilled in power brokering. Changing the beliefs of a nation is, after all, not something to be taken lightly.

However, eventually the people had had enough and it was this overwhelming rebellion of the southern priesthood and the people that caused the second exodus. History was repeating itself, as it does so often, and the Arians were being thrown out of Egypt once more ...

Part 2

The Birth of Moses

Many generations had passed since the death of Joseph, and there arose a pharaoh in Egypt that did not know Joseph. [B17] The children of Joseph (the Arians), through their evangelical missions, had grown considerably, so that the new pharaoh was afraid of his position once more and declared:

> Behold the people of the [Arians] are more and mightier than we. Come on, let us deal wisely with them; lest they multiply, and it came to pass, that, when there falleth out any war, they join also unto our enemies. [B18]

Now it happened that Tiye, the wife of Amenhotep III, was expecting a child, but the priesthood were fearful of the arrival of this child, for they knew that his mother was a devout Arian. Tiye, was well aware of the threats against her unborn child and took the precaution of arranging for the pharaoh's sister to bring him up initially. Amenhotep was worried by all this. He had known there would be opposition to his marriage to an Arian, but he was unsure to what extent it would threaten his throne. In a dream, however, he saw an old man with a pair of scales; upon one side were all the princes and elders of Egypt and on the other there was a single lamb, [a representation of his beloved Arian prince-to-be]. It was the lamb that proved to be the heavier. The pharaoh asked the wise sage Bi'lam to divine this dream and he replied that [an Arian] son would be born who would destroy Egypt. [T19] Amenhotep was troubled by this; [he so desperately desired to have an Arian prince], but was the future of Egypt too high a price to pay for this?

Some years later, Tiye brought Moses [Tuthmoses, brother of Akhenaton] to see his father, Amenhotep III, the pharaoh. She said to Amenhotep that she had brought up a son of divine form and she thought it proper that he should be 'the heir of your kingdom'. [J20] It was by no means certain that Moses would be chosen as heir because there were many sons to choose from. Tiye could achieve her goal only if she could consolidate her position as chief wife. Although her pharaonic ancestry was certain, her Arian belief was a drawback in the eyes of the priesthood and she could see that her husband, the pharaoh, was troubled by the implications of this choice of heir. Pharaoh hugged [Tuth] Moses and presented him with the royal crown, a sign that he was really the true heir to the throne. Tiye was about to give a sigh of relief when the adolescent [Tuth] Moses took the crown and ground it into the dust with his feet! When the assembled priests saw this, they made a violent attempt to kill Moses, they shouted in their anger:

> O king! This child is he of whom God foretold, that if we kill him we shall be in no danger ... take him, therefore, out of the way, and deliver the Egyptians from the fear they are in about him; and deprive the [Arians] of the hope they have of being encouraged by him. [J21]

(For comparison, the Talmud only says that Moses placed the crown on his own head, signifying that he was the true king and eliciting the same response from the assembled priests.) But Tiye prevented them and snatched the child away. The king was not in a hurry to kill him and asked for the assessment of the sages. Bi'lam confirmed Amenhotep's worst fears by saying:

> Think not, because the child is young, that he did this thoughtlessly. Remember your dream of the scales (and the lamb). If it be pleasing to the king, let two plates be brought before the child, one containing gold and the other fire. If the child stretches forth his hand to grasp the gold, we shall know him to be an understanding being and consider that he acted towards thee knowingly. But if he grasps the fire, then let his life be spared [but his tongue burned out]. [T22]

The young Moses understood the situation well and, to save his life, he wisely grasped the fire. He had been saved by his mother and he was eventually sent to the temple at Heliopolis to become a priest there, [M23] for he was to be educated with great care. [J24] But with the severe wounds to his mouth, Moses would forever be 'slow of speech and slow of tongue' [B25] and he had lost the physical perfection required for a reigning pharaoh.

The Egyptians were suspicious of this great education being given to Moses (for they knew the theology of Heliopolis) and yet if he had been killed, 'there was no one with either kinship or an oracle on his side that could have a greater claim for the throne'. Therefore, they abstained from killing him, for to kill someone of the king's bloodline would be sure to bring the wrath of the gods upon them. So while Moses was now denied the kingship owing to his affliction and would be forever dependent on his brother Aaron (Akhenaton) to speak on his behalf, [B26] nevertheless, he was yet to become high priest of Heliopolis and a great military commander.

Moses the Man

When Moses had come of age, there was a war with the Ethiopians. Tiye persuaded Amenhotep III that Moses should lead the army south to meet the Ethiopians, to which he agreed. Moses led a great campaign against the Ethiopians and came back victorious and with the wife of the Ethiopian king as his new bride. [J27] His first wife was called Tharbis, the second Zipporah and he had at least two sons, Gersom and Eleazer. Eleazer is a traditional biblical name, but it can also be seen as being derived from Eli-sar, the Sun-King. The Egyptians suspected that Moses would use his success and popularity to 'raise a sedition against them' and to 'bring innovations into Egypt', [J28] innovations to their traditional religion, which they had fought so hard to maintain just two centuries earlier. The final straw for them, though, was the killing of a Taurean by Moses (a high ranking Taurean, no doubt). The people were disgusted that this favourite son of the king could get away with so much wanton abuse of power. Even those from within his own ranks objected, saying:

> Wherefore smitest this fellow. Who made thee a prince and a judge over us? Intendest thou to kill me, as thou killed the Taurean [Egyptian]? [B29]

So they told pharaoh in no uncertain terms that Moses should be killed. The pharaoh was sympathetic to the Arian cause of Moses, but he could see that trouble was brewing. Loud objections were being raised about both of his sons, Moses and Aaron, for their open promotion of the new creed of the Aton, the Arian belief under a new name. Pharaoh also knew that Moses held a deep resentment for the wounds that were inflicted upon him as a child and that he might try anything to gain power and influence among his followers. Pharaoh had to act now or face the open revolt of the priesthood and people.

The Arian priests were already being openly called 'lepers' by his closest advisor, also named Amenhotep, son of Hapu. Trouble was brewing and so Amenhotep III wished once more to divine the future. What he really wanted to know was which was the true god. A point which, many centuries later, Josephus ridiculed:

> King Amenhotep, he says, desired to see the gods ... What gods? If those established by their law are intended - bull, goat ... he saw them already. [J30]

But Amenhotep's desire was genuine because he did not want to see their physical form, which he knew already, but which of them would triumph in this battle of wills:

> ... and he communicated his desire to the oracle Amenhotep (son of Hapu), who in virtue of his wisdom and knowledge of the future, was reputed to be a partaker in the divine nature. This namesake, then, replied that pharaoh would be able to see the real gods [Taurus] if he cleansed the whole land of these lepers and other polluted persons [the Arians]. [M31]

Amenhotep III was worried; the oracles were powerful in their influence over the people. Indeed, they were equally influential over the courtiers and the king. For instance, the priests at Meroe spoke as if the deity himself spoke through them. They did this:

> ... to such a degree had they contrived to enslave the understanding of those princes by superstitious fears, that they were obeyed without opposition. At length a king, a contemporary of Ptolemy Philadelphus, dared to disobey their orders, and having entered the 'golden chapel' [the holy of holies] with his soldiers, caused them to be put to death in his stead, and abolished the custom. [32]

But that rebellion against the abuse of power by the oracles was not to happen for another 1,000 years; until that time, such divine prophecies were powerful portents of the future and not to be ignored. Even if the pharaoh did not fear the oracles, Amenhotep III still knew the effects that his country and his nation would suffer if the followers of Aries and their leaders, his sons who were 'infected with this religious leprosy' as the

Theban priests called it, were allowed to continue their radical mission. It was written in the chronicles of their great land; the result of the last uprising of popular sentiment towards the Arians had been civil war and the destruction of most of the eastern delta. It had been a terrible blow to the population and the kingdom. As a responsible leader, he could not allow this, whatever his private sympathies were towards the Arians. Besides, every leader depends for his position upon the support of his nobles and unfortunately for Amenhotep III...:

> (paraphrased) ... all the old wealth and influence of Egypt came from the Taureans (the cattle). [J33]

So despite the fact that it was his favourite sons who were organizing this sedition and his undeniable sympathies for their cause, he had no choice. Either Moses [Tuthmoses] and Aaron [Akhenaton] went into exile or there would be civil war once more and, if the priests had their way, his sons would be killed. The king reluctantly gave the order to banish Moses and Aaron from his lands. (Manetho rather enthused about this, but one would imagine that this is a one-sided exclamation of joy):

> The king was delighted, and assembled all those whose bodies were wasted by the disease [inflicted with the heresy]: they numbered 80,000 persons. These he cast into the *stone quarries to the East of the Nile*, there to work segregated from the rest of the Egyptians. Among them, there were some of the learned priests, *who had been attacked by leprosy.* [M34]

Aaron and Moses chose the only option now open to them – not a complete exile, but removal from the conurbations of the Nile delta. The north of Egypt was now off-limits to them and, equally, the Taurean priests of Thebes would disembowel them if they moved too far south. The choice had been made for them and they moved into the less fertile *eastern banks of the Nile* in central Egypt.

The Amarna Age

It was desolate place far from the main conurbations in the country, but to make political capital from this ignominious exile, Aaron and Moses chose a symbolic position exactly in the middle of Egypt, precisely in between the political capitals of Lower and Upper Egypt, between Heliopolis in the north and Thebes in the south. There, they set up a new rebel 'capital' in a barren stretch of land. Aaron proclaimed himself pharaoh of all Egypt, and changed his name from Amenhotep to Akhenaton [Aaron] to signify his irrevocable break from the old regime.

A new era had dawned in Egypt, the Amarna age, which was to be different in all respects from the old regime. This revolution was the result of Aaron's commitment to the sacred study of the workings of the cosmos, the power behind the Sun. He wanted to continue in the spirit of the age of Aries, an age that had dawned many centuries before when the constellations moved out of Taurus and into Aries. Moreover, he could see precisely why this whole divisive dispute between the Hyksos and the Theban priests had occurred – the people of Egypt had not fully understood *why* Taurus had been venerated for so long. They had become distracted by the physical image of the bull itself and by the plethora of gods and demigods that proliferated in the land. The people needed to understand that it was not the physical form of the god that was important, but the cosmos itself and the mathematical functions that ordered its motions that were to be venerated.

These 'gods' of Egypt were messengers from other worlds, not the gods themselves. The Sun and the cosmos were the real power behind all life in the Universe and this 'energy' was largely invisible. If the people were denied these graven images that had confused the whole issue, then this dispute would not have to happen again at the next change of the constellations. If there was one certainty in life, it was that the stars would move in the heavens. At some future time, another distant pharaoh would have the same problems, as Aries turned into Pisces. Now was the time to nip this problem in the bud and dispense with these distractions.

Aaron gave the order: there were to be *no graven images* to divert his people's attention from the real divine worship, that of the Aton, the workings of the cosmos. All the old gods of Egypt were banned. The people were to praise Aaron himself for his wisdom and understanding of the cosmos and praise the divine movement of the Sun in its orbit because it was the physical representation of the mechanics of the cosmos. If you could understand the movement of the Sun, as he did, you would understand the greatness of the Universe. Thus the temples were aligned with the rising and setting of the Sun and were opened up to the sky, so that the 'Sun God' could be worshipped when it reached its highest point in the sky each day. That is why the deity had no physical form at Amarna, for the workings of the cosmos have no form. That was why the theology of Moses and Aaron became monotheistic, for there is only one cosmos and only one set of laws which it obeys. These laws are strange, silent, invisible forces that are more powerful than anything that can be imagined.

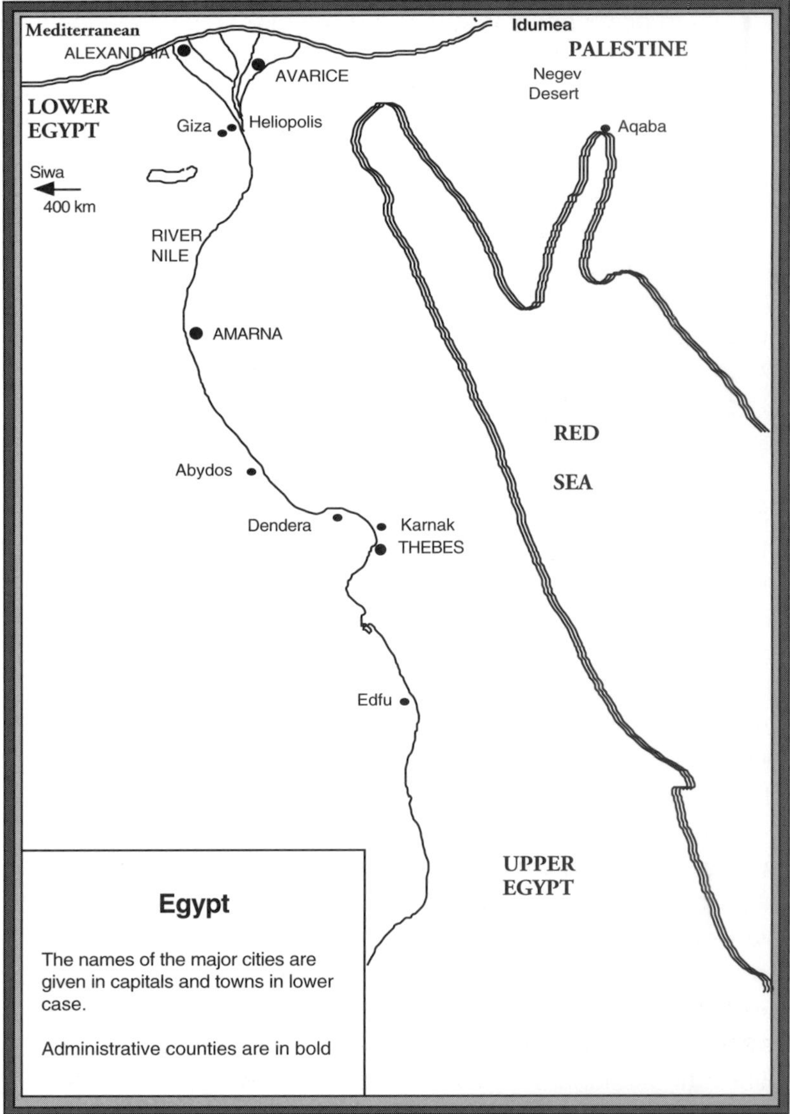

Fig 17. Map of ancient Egypt

The location Aaron chose for his new capital city was desolate, to say the least. The range of hills that lines the east bank of the Nile receded at this point to form a semicircular bowl, a rough stony plain that lay between the cliffs and the Nile. It was a barren plain away from all the great conurbations in the land. The narrow banks of the Nile here were not so productive as other stretches of the river and Akhenaton did not command the tithes necessary to support his small empire. They would be forever dependent on voluntary support from the outside world. However, there was some method in Aaron's madness, for this location symbolically represented an entirely separate province from the rest of Egypt. The new capital city was situated purposely and symbolically in the exact centre of the entire kingdom. Any trader, noble or pharaoh traversing the kingdom between Karnak and Heliopolis would have to pass by on the Nile and see the splendours of this new kingdom, the 'new world order' and be in awe of it.

Within the ranks of his followers, however, there was widespread incredulity about the choice of location for the new city, but Aaron was defiant. He had inscribed on the platform of the primary altar, that:

> ... he would build his city in this place and nowhere else; if anyone tried to persuade him otherwise, he would not listen, even if it were the queen herself. [35]

Aaron was determined to show the rest of the world that he was the greatest of all the leaders, his system was superior to all others and his capital was the finest. So it was into this moonscape that the Arians were thrown and it was with their own labours that they now had to construct an entire new city and a new capital for their miniature empire. The whole area suddenly resounded to the sounds of frenetic *quarrying* to build this new 'capital' for these exiled '*lepers*'. The sounds echoed back and forth from the encircling cliffs so loudly and so incessantly that the passing Egyptian sailors on the Nile nicknamed the city the *Stone Quarry on the east-bank*.

This was a term that the Theban priests picked up with glee, for it was a fitting place for the tainted lepers to be exiled. But Aaron called his new empire Akhetaton, or as it became known to the world, Amarna. Note here how Manetho's record of the *lepers in the quarry on the east bank of the Nile* and the Bible's narrative of the Israelites *making mud-bricks for the pharaoh* coincide in one historically proven event – the founding of Akhenaton's new city at Amarna.

5. *Moses*

Foundations

Aaron was furious about the position he found himself in. The world was against him, but he would show them who was the real leader of these lands. He immediately set about consolidating his small empire as a totally independent state within Egypt. He set up a boundary stele that precisely defined its extent. His empire stood like the modern Vatican does, a mini-state within the larger state of Italy, totally separate, but totally dependent. The boundary stele that Aaron posted at all the entrances to the new state threw abuse at all who would come and visit his empire to proclaim to the world the injustice that he and his people had suffered.

> For as Father Hor-Aton liveth ... priests [?] more evil are they than those things which I have heard unto year 4. More evil are they than those things which I have head in year [?] more evil are they than those things which King Amenhotep III heard. More evil are they than those things which Tuthmoses IV heard. [36]

It was a plaintive plea for support from his father's followers. It indicated that although most of the criticism had been thrown at him, both his father and his (grandfather?) has been subjected to similar criticism. This can only be because they also supported the cult of Aton, perhaps just a little more privately. Perhaps they had a greater understanding of the forces that would be unleashed against them if they came into the open with their ideas and knew the privations they would have to suffer as a consequence.

Aaron, however, had acted more rashly. As a result, he and his followers now faced a precarious existence. They could be wiped out by the military at any time and were forever dependent on sporadic deliveries of food and materials from their supporters in the north. Their only defence was the terrain around them and the wider support that existed for them within the northern half of the kingdom. A full military assault from Thebes in the south might just be enough to provoke the Arian sympathizers in the north into revolt and start another civil war. In this environment of a desperate stalemate, Aaron could pretend that he was carving out a new kingdom for the Arians. In return, the Taureans in Thebes could laugh at the plight of the 'lepers in the quarry', but neither dared attack the other for the moment. It was a stand-off that gave only a temporary respite from the underlying tensions that existed throughout the land. It was an unstable situation that would last for only two decades.

The Quarry

For the next eight years, the devoted followers of Aries [the Israelites] worked in the stone quarries of Amarna, toiling for their beloved Aaron and his family, constructing the great city of Amarna. While the work was in progress, the king himself had to make do with a house made of rushes, which was known as 'the Aton is content' [37] or 'Aaron is satisfied'. The name referred to his deity, but it is quite obvious that it, in turn, referred to his own position at Amarna. The name was a small message of defiance to the Taurean priests in the face of hardships that no pharaoh of Egypt had ever had to endure before.

At first, the people's energy was boundless and they toiled from dawn to dusk in the quarries of Amarna, building the great temples to the Aton and the fine palaces of the pharaoh. The great temple had some magnificent stone pillars and some of the walls were plastered with exquisitely decorated interiors, but the citizens of Amarna themselves endured basic mud huts. As the years rolled on and Aaron did not relent in his demands for new and more fabulous buildings to show the world the greatness of his empire, the grumbles began to surface. Aaron and Moses were unrepentant. They simply demanded more:

> Let there be more work laid upon the men, that they may labour therein; and let them not regard vain words. [B38]

The quarrying of stone for the temples was slow, tedious work and the city was behind the optimistic schedule of Aaron and Moses. They, therefore, ordered that the king's palace and the rest of the great temple were to be made from mud-brick to speed up the construction. Even the Pylons, the massive entrance gates of the Mansion of the Aton, were to be simple mud-brick. [39] But the task was being slowed down by the lack of raw materials. The mud was easily found in the Nile, but the straw had to be brought along river from the delta to the north. While there was still considerable support for the position of Aaron in Lower Egypt, the supplies to Amarna were often erratic and sometimes weeks passed without any straw at all. This was no excuse in Aaron's eyes. The people did not understand the political need for a showcase city; they were just being lazy:

> Thus said pharaoh [Aaron] I will not give you straw. Go and get straw where you can find it; yet none of your work will be diminished. So the people [of Amarna] were scattered throughout the highlands to gather stubble instead of straw. And the taskmasters hastened them, saying, Fulfil your works, your daily tasks as when there was straw. And the officers of the children [of Aries], which [Aaron] had set over them, were beaten, and demanded, wherefore have you not fulfilled your task in making brick both yesterday and today as before. [B40]

But the assembled Arians complained to Aaron that there was no straw to make the bricks and gathering grass in the highlands took much of their time, but Aaron and Moses wanted the finest capital in all Egypt and chastened them:

> You are idle! You are idle! ... go now and work: for there shall be no straw given you, yet you shall deliver the [same number] of bricks. [B41]

So Akhenaton [Aaron] drifted from the position of great charismatic leader into one of despotic dictator, as many leaders have both before and since. It was to cause great strife within his people later, but for now, he lived in an ideal 'never-never land' of his own construction. Isolated from the population and surrounded by family and courtiers, Aaron drifted into fantasies of the perfect world in which he lived and the perfect kingdom over which he ruled. His mind drifted to the arts and he dictated that there should be a new freedom of expression from his artisans. They were to draw the world as they saw it, not as the traditional pharaohs dictated. He and his family were to be shown in intimate detail – kissing, hugging, playing with their children. It was a revolution in both art and the intimacy in which the royal family could be displayed. He dabbled with poetry and tried to describe the idyll that he would cause to be formed with his new system of devolved government:

> You arise fair in the horizon of heaven, O living Aton, Beginner of Life. When you dawn in the east, you fill every land with thy beauty ... The lands are in festival. They awake and stand upon

> their feet, for you have raised them up. They wash their limbs, they put on clothes and raise their arms in adoration at thy presence ... All cattle are at peace in their pastures. The trees and herbage grow green. The birds fly from their nests, their wings [raised] in adoration of thy spirit. All animals gambol on their feet, all the winged creation live when you have risen up for them ... You it is who causes women to conceive and makes seed into man, who gives life to the child in the womb of its mother, who comforts him so that he cries not therein, nurse that you are, even in the womb, who gives breath to quicken all that he has made ...
>
> When the chick in the egg chirps within the shell, you give him the breath within to sustain him. You create for him his proper term within the egg, so that he shall break it and come forth from it to testify to his completion as he runs about on his two feet. How manifold are thy works. They are hidden from the sight of men, O Sole God, like unto whom there is no other! You didst fashion the earth according to thy desire when you was alone ... all men, all cattle great and small, all that are upon the earth that run upon their feet or rise up on high flying with their wings ... you art in my heart, but there is none other who knows you save your son Akhenaton. You have made him wise in your plans and your power. [42]

Aaron also dabbled with the divine. He knew from the old texts of Heliopolis, where he and Moses were educated, [43] that the divine messengers that came from the gods long ago were flesh and blood beings. He also knew that the ancient texts said that man was made in the image of these messengers, in other words, the physical body of these messengers was similar to our own. But he also knew, which no man before him had dared to discuss or display in public, the exact physical shape of the bodies of these messengers from the cosmos. It was a secret that had been held in the holy of holies at Heliopolis since the age of the gods, when they had visited the earth in physical form.

Only Akhenaton, with his brash conviction of his elevated position in respect to the gods, dared to display the divine shape. Little by little, he ordered the palace artists to display him in the divine form, with rounded hips and breasts, with an elongated face and large almond-shaped eyes, with a pot belly and no genitalia. Here was Aaron [Akhenaton] in the form of a divine being, the form of a messenger from the cosmos that had visited the Earth thousands of years before. It was a shape so sacred that it was not to be displayed to mankind again for 3,500 years and the elevation to popular status in science fiction literature of the 'Grey'. [44]

Storm Clouds

Aaron was content in his gilded cage but he was troubled by his lack of an heir. What he had not bargained for was the intensity of the hatred that his position in Amarna had generated within the priesthood at Thebes. The priesthood would stop at nothing to prevent his regime continuing and they set about devising some deception and bribery that would surely terminate Aaron's heresy for ever. Accordingly they:

> Spoke to the Arian midwives ...Shiphrah and Purah and said. When ye do the office of a midwife to the [Arian] women, and see them upon the stools; if it be a son, then ye shall kill him: but if it be a daughter, then she shall live. [B45]

And so the midwives of Nefertiti performed their grizzly task with cunning and guile. Accordingly, Aaron [Akhenaton] was blessed with no less than six daughters, but not a single son. [46] (The four sons of Aaron were born much later in the narrative, during the exodus; they would not have featured in the Egyptian record.) Without an heir in Egypt, Aaron's family was doomed and the very existence of the new capital at Amarna would surely hang in the balance. In desperation, Aaron groomed his brothers Smenkhkare and Tutankhaton for the royal throne, even indicating to the historians that the midwives had failed in their task and that Tutankhaton was his son. But even if that were true, all his efforts were still to be in vain.

There was to be no peace for the hard-working Arians in the quarries of Amarna, for the temporary stalemate established with the founding of the city was about to be unbalanced yet again. Amenhotep III, Aaron's father, died. After the traditional mourning of 70 days, Aaron promptly assumed the title of pharaoh of all Egypt. With the support of his followers in the north, he rapidly consolidated his power in the kingdom and set about the closure of the temples of the traditional gods throughout the land. Teams were sent around the kingdom with the task of cutting out all references to the traditional gods of Egypt, who had been worshipped for thousands of years. Temples were emptied, priests thrown out, sacred hypostyle halls became overgrown with weeds. For some of the population, it must have felt as though the sky was falling on their heads. The Restoration stele of Tutankhaton (Tutankhamen) at the Temple of Amen in Karnak, which marked the end of the Amarna era and the beginning of the restoration of traditional ways, reads:

> ... Now when his majesty [Tutankhamen] appeared as king, the temples of the gods and goddesses from Elephantine to [the] marshes of the delta [had] gone to pieces. Their shrines had become desolate, had become mounds overgrown with [weeds]. Their sanctuaries were as if they had never been. Their halls were footpaths. The land was in turmoil, and the gods had turned their backs on this land ...[47]

The masses were becoming agitated; the persecution of the Taurean priests and followers had gone too far. Pressure was placed at the highest levels on Smenkhkare, Aaron's younger brother, to accept a co-regency and to moderate his brother's demands. He accepted the co-regency and married one of Aaron's daughters, but Aaron merely responded by increasing the pressure on the traditional ways. However, the military, on whom he depended to enforce his decrees, was beginning to split under the pressure. Something had to give and, when it did, the end was rapid. Suddenly, in year 17 of the reign of Akhenaton [Aaron], he disappeared from the historical record. No tomb or records have ever been discovered – the 'heretic' king simply vanished.

Did he really disappear? Did Akhenaton die? Was he torn apart by an angry mob or did he use his authority and his sacred powers as a pharaoh, a 'Son of God', to bluff and deceive his way out of the country and into exile? Manetho and the Bible take up the story once more.

War clouds

The lepers in the stone quarries had seen the advancing storm clouds and wanted to secure their position in the all-important lands of the delta. A significant proportion of the inhabitants of Amarna moved to Avaris, the traditional home of the Shepherd Kings that had been abandoned for two centuries. To safeguard against Taurean infiltrators, Moses tested the faith of every follower that came to Avaris by making them eat the sacred meat of the cow:

> He then made this law for them, that they should neither worship the Egyptian gods, nor should anyone abstain from any one of those sacred animals, which they have in the highest esteem, but kill and destroy them all: that they should join to nobody but this confederacy. [J48]

They then immediately sent an embassy to the exiled Shepherd Kings in Jerusalem, requesting assistance. They were delighted with the idea and made all haste to Egypt with 200,000 men to assist in their family's plight. They soon arrived in Avaris. [J49] Josephus queried the truth of this account because he could not see why the people of Jerusalem would have wished to come to the aid of the 'lepers', but if the truth were known, the reason is quite plain – both the 'lepers' in Avaris and the people of Jerusalem were of the Shepherd King dynasty.

The next pharaoh who should take the crown in Egypt, as the head of this divided nation, was a thorny problem for the priests and nobility of Thebes. Many wanted a complete break with the Amarna regime, but others clamoured for the youngest son of Amenhotep III, Tutankhaton, to come to the throne. Aaron had claimed Tutankhaton as the 'son of his own loins', but his advisors knew better. As the son of Amenhotep III, he was the next direct descendant of the true family bloodline. In a way, he was the perfect compromise. He was not truly part of the Amarna regime and he was young enough to be moulded into the pharaoh that the Theban priests required.

Tutankhaton was summoned and told in no uncertain terms by his advisors that he should sign a decree renouncing all the changes Aaron had made. As a boy king, just eight years old, he could not refuse, even if he understood the situation. The temples were reopened, the restoration stele was erected at Karnak, the Theban priests began their daily worship and the gifts and gratuities rolled into the coffers of the Amenite priests once more. Tutankh<u>aton</u> was then forced to take the name Tutankh<u>amen</u> in recognition of the traditional gods and he married one of Aaron's daughters, Ankhesenapaaten, who was forced to change her name to Ankhesenamun for the same reason. In Tutankhamen's name, an army of 300,00 men was mustered, the priests ordering the boy king to march against his own brothers. He was lead out at the head of this massive army, but the first attack was stalled. Manetho said the stand-off lasted for 13 years and this is why.

* * *

Magic

The new pharaoh and his advisors approached the walls of Avaris and demanded a meeting with Aaron and Moses. It was duly arranged and the chief Taurean priests demanded to know what terms of surrender Aaron would accept. But Aaron approached them with his staff of office, the serpent-topped staff of the Son of God. [B50] He then gave the sacred Masonic sign of his supreme authority in matters relating to the deity, for, like his father, who bore the supreme title of 'Greatest of Architects', [51] he had been well educated in the craft at the Heliopolian lodge. Moses drew out his hand from under his garment in the time-honoured sacred grip and it was white. The chiefs of the pharaoh were amazed and:

> The elders [of the Theban people] said 'this man is a skilful sorcerer who seeks to drive you from your land. What will you have us do?' Others said 'Put them off for a while, him and his brother, and send forth heralds to the cities to summon every skilful sorcerer to your presence'.
>
> The sorcerers came [to the pharaoh Tutankhamen] and his advisors, and said 'Shall we be rewarded if we win?', 'Yes', he answered ... They said 'Moses, will you throw first, or shall we?'. 'Throw' he replied. When they threw, they bewitched the people's eyes and terrified them by a display of great sorcery. Then they signalled to Moses 'Now throw down your staff'. And thereupon it swallowed up their false devices. [K52] (The Bible says it was Aaron who performed this sorcery, not Moses).
>
> Thus did the truth prevail, and all their doings were proved vain. The pharaoh and his men were defeated and put to shame, and the sorcerers prostrated themselves, saying 'We believe in the Lord of the Universe, the Lord of Moses and Aaron'. ...[But] the elders of pharaoh's nation [Taureans] said 'Will you allow Moses and his people to perpetuate corruption in the land and to forsake you and your gods?'. [K53]

For whatever reason, there was a stand-off at Avaris. It sounds as if some of the Taureans' advisors were afraid to move against someone who had just proved himself to be the rightful pharaoh, the Son of God. What would the gods' reaction be if they killed him and his followers? They must have remembered the plagues of Egypt that had afflicted them during the last dispute with the Shepherd Kings. Would the same happen to them again? The priests were troubled. The new boy king, Tutankhamen, was being diplomatic and advising caution. In addition, the Ethiopians were harassing the southern borders and would have to be dealt with first. Aaron, Moses and their people were left within the confines of Avaris for the time being. As Manetho said:

> He [the pharaoh] then crossed the Nile with as many as 300,000 of the bravest warriors of Egypt. But, instead of joining battle, he decided that he must not fight against the gods, and made a hasty retreat to Memphis. There he took charge of his sacred bulls ... and forthwith he set off for Ethiopia. [M54]

The fate of Tutankhamen hung in the balance for a full nine years. The question on everyone's lips was would he inherit the ways of his predecessor, Aaron, or would he follow the Taurean ways? In the meantime, a cleaning-up operation began to rid history of the memory of Aaron and his followers. Every inscription bearing his name was erased and every tomb and monument was either dismantled or buried. This was not just an act of revenge; it was the spiritual murder of the heretical pharaoh. A pharaoh's soul was encapsulated in his name and as long as that name was present on the Earth and being read by living men, the immortality of the soul was assured. By excising his name from every location in Egypt, they sought not only to remove Aaron from the history books, but to kill his soul as well.

Accordingly, a full-time operation was begun at the city of Amarna, turning the place once more into a quarry. However, the quarry this time was the very stones that comprised the temples and palaces themselves. These were taken apart, brick by brick and stone by stone, and the material was shipped up the Nile for other building projects. Nothing was to remain of the great city of Amarna, except the foundations and a few mud-bricks. [55] Akhenaton [Aaron] was to become a forbidden name to the Taureans. If he had to be referred to at all, he was to be known as the 'fallen one of Amarna' or the 'heretic pharaoh'. Above all, his name could not be mentioned.

In the ninth year of Tutankhamen's reign, when he was just 17 years old, the answer to the question that had been troubling the priests became all too obvious. The pharaoh had ordered a new throne for the palace. A senior priest with a suspicious mind entered the king's private chamber one day – to be presented with the image of Aton.

Tutankhamen died in his eighteenth year, most probably at the hands of a Taurean priest, his body appears to have been mutilated. Manetho's version of events is interesting. It was quite possible that there was a stay of execution over the Shepherds holed up in the former city of Avaris. If the Avaris scenario is correct, perhaps it took the rule of the next pharaoh, the traditionalist ex-military commander Horemheb, to dislodge the Shepherds and send them back to Jerusalem.

Whatever the case, a curious event now occurred. Ankhesenamun, Tutankhamen's widow, sent an urgent letter to Suppiluliumas, the Hittite king, requesting one of his sons as a husband. This was unprecedented in Egyptian history – why should an Egyptian queen request a foreign husband who would end up ruling the Egyptian people? Egyptologists are puzzled by this, but the answer is obvious. The Hittite empire encompassed all of Syria and, undoubtedly, Ankhesenamun was writing to the Arians in Palestine, requesting a son of the Arian bloodline to join her. Unfortunately, Zennanza, the prince who was sent, was murdered en route and for lack of a true heir, Ankhesenamun had to marry her grandfather, Aye. As a result of this murder, the Hittites sent an army into Egypt and plundered the border town of Amqa. This historical event ties in nicely with the Manetho's report of an army from Jerusalem supporting the 'lepers' in Avaris. [56]

Evidently, the support from Palestine was not sufficient to save the ruling family in Egypt, as Aye and Ankhesenamun were finally supplanted by the pharaoh Horemheb in what appears to have been a military coup. Interestingly though, it seems that Horemheb consolidated his position in the royal dynasty not by marrying into the family of Tuthmoses IV, but by marrying into the bloodline of Yuya, the bloodline vizier. The evidence indicates that Horemheb married Nefertiti's sister and a subsequent pharaoh Seti I married Tuya the 'daughter of a lieutenant of the chariotry', one of Yuya's titles. The influence of this family of royal viziers was undimmed, despite the royal intrigues and civil unrest. At this point, presumably in the reign of Horemheb, Manetho says that the shepherds and 'lepers' were finally pushed out of Avaris and back into 'Syria'. [M57]

Exodus

The Arians had plenty of time to plan the exodus. It is obvious from the biblical account that the flight of Aaron and Moses from Egypt was well organized. They took tonnes of equipment with them, much of it for the mobile temple, the Tabernacle. Perhaps this huge ornate artefact was made in Amarna for use before the stone and brick temples had been built or perhaps it was made in Avaris before the exodus. Certainly, it was a very important, extremely bulky and very expensive piece of equipment to take on a trip across the desert. This demonstrates that a great deal of planning had gone into the exodus, as this was not the sort of artefact that could have been fabricated in the desert without proper industrial resources.

The refugees from Avaris rested for a while at the foot of Mount Sinai and the Tabernacle was erected. Like all Aaron's temples, the Tabernacle faced east towards the rising Sun. It had a holy of holies and two pillars stood outside it. [J58] Like the clothing of the Egyptian priesthood themselves, the garments worn by Aaron, Moses and the exiled priests were exquisite and very expensive. [J59] The designs were made to represent the central tents of Aaron's faith: the priests' stoles were encrusted with emblems of the Earth, the oceans, the Sun, the Moon and a circle of 12 stones representing the signs of the zodiac. [J60]

Moses climbed up the mountain for contemplation, but upon his return, he found that Aaron's sons had constructed a golden calf in the manner of Taurean worship. (Not Aaron as the Bible reports) [J61 B61] When he saw this, Aaron exploded with rage, wanting to kill them all. After all these trials and tribulations, how could these people return to the worship of bulls? Moses tried to calm the situation:

> And Moses besought the Lord his God and said, Lord why does thy wrath wax hot against thy people, which thou hast brought out of the land of Egypt ... Turn from thy fierce wrath, and repent of this evil against thy people. [62]

(This is supposed to be Moses rebuking God, but it makes more sense as Moses rebuking his brother, Aaron, the pharaoh and Son of God.) Aaron calmed down, but them Moses became angry and shouted to the assembled crowd, 'Who is with me?' and ordered them to fetch their swords. He then lead them through the camp and killed all who had worshipped the bull, some 3,000 men. [B63]

The struggle to lead his followers through the deserts to Jerusalem was long and arduous and there were many events that tested his people's determination to remain faithful to Aries. Many times, Moses and Aaron had to face the wrath of the people and they were nearly stoned on more than one occasion. Moses, through the voice of Aaron, often pleaded with their better judgement, reminding them of their triumphs against the greatest nation on Earth and how they had endured hardships but always won through in the end. With a carrot-and-stick approach, they coerced and cajoled the Arian people through the deserts and into Canaan.

Finally, just as they were about to enter their new promised land, Moses died. They mourned him for 30 days and laid him in a secret sepulchre in the land of Moab so that nobody could disturb his tomb, as the Taureans had vowed to do. However, before Moses' death, he and Aaron constructed a new history of their people. Having heard of the fate of their great city at Amarna and the excision of the name of Akhenaton from the history of Egypt, they decided to reciprocate.

The history of the Levites, Judites and the other ten tribes of Israel would essentially start from this second exodus of their nation. Egypt was now a pariah state and there would be no mention of the name of any pharaoh anywhere in this great scroll of the Jews. Egypt was not just to be an evil nation, but, where possible, it was to be a nonentity. The greatest nation on Earth would be reduced in the Judaic record to the status of a minor tribal kingdom. (Perhaps the name of king Shishak escaped a later censor of the Torah; he was the pharaoh Sheshonq I in the historical record who besieged Jerusalem, but was bought off with vast quantities of treasure. Alternatively, David Rohl claims this pharaoh was Ramesses II, who's nick name was possibly Shisha). [B64]

Perhaps Aaron could not have dreamed that he would have been successful in this enterprise. They were, after all, a small band of about 70,000 refugees on an uncertain journey across a barren wasteland. But history was to prove fortuitous for Aaron. Although his own nation was to be devastated on another two or three occasions, the Egyptians were to be equally impoverished. Whereas the Israelites struggled through their adversity, the Egyptians succumbed to several centuries of being the bread basket for the Roman Empire and their theology was then easy prey to the new Christian sect. History is made by those who keep and disseminate it. It was to be the Arian (Jewish) history that survived into the modern era.

Chapter VI

Lamb of God

Part 1

The Arian peoples made their way across the Sinai, as their forefathers had done before them, travelling northwards and eastwards into the land of Palestine. They settled in the city of Jerusalem and the surrounding districts among their fellow Arians, whom they found had already strayed a little from the true creed of the Aton. The two peoples were of the same stock and the same religion, but there were fundamental differences creeping in and these were to set the scene for further conflict in the future. A period of relative stability followed, with only the usual tribal infighting to disturb the peace. There were some military successes under king David and then prosperity under the legendary king Solomon in about 1000 BC. It was Solomon the Wise who made possible the building of the Great Temple in Jerusalem. His father, King David, had forged links with King Hirom of Tyre and Solomon consolidated them to the extent that Hirom agreed to send gold and timber for the construction of the temple. How was this achieved? Why should another king send vast resources for building a temple in Jerusalem? Josephus provides a probable reason:

> The main bond of friendship between them was their passion for learning. They used to send each other problems to solve; in these Solomon showed he was the cleverer of the two. Many of the letters they exchanged are preserved at Tyre to this day. [J1]

Being beaten at puzzles does not normally induce people into giving vast fortunes to their opponents. There are two explanations that can make sense of this situation. Firstly, king Hirom was a Phoenician and it would seem that in this era there were both distant and recent blood-ties between the Arian peoples and the Phoenicians, as I shall discuss in chapter 10. Secondly, the problems being passed between the two kings were not simple crosswords, instead they involved the secret knowledge referred to previously – these were secret puzzles and it is, no doubt, for this reason that Solomon was famed for his wisdom. Egyptian priests had held the secrets of the cosmos for thousands of years and these had found their way to Jerusalem along with the Arian peoples. They had arrived in Jerusalem either with the first or the second exodus; it does not matter which. But it can be said, with some certainty, that Egyptian rites were now being performed in Israel.

The Egyptians' wide-ranging knowledge of the cosmos represented power to a monarch and his people. Their knowledge seems to have covered the shape and form of the Earth and the Solar System, as well as some basic physics, mathematics, chemistry, metallurgy and medicine. The Phoenicians were the great sea-trading nation of that era, so to have had access to information regarding the form of the Earth and the shape of the continents would have been invaluable to them. Sharing such knowledge, however small a part, was certainly a puzzle that would have commanded a king's ransom.

Resources poured into Jerusalem and king Solomon was able, at last, to build the Great Temple – and it was built along very Egyptian lines. Working from the outside inwards, the first area in the temple enclosure was the large, paved outer courtyard. This was a place for the masses, including the profane. The inner courtyard was aligned east-west to align with the rising sun, like the temples of Amarna and the mobile Tabernacle of the Jews. It was divided into two sections: the courtyard of the women and the inner courtyard. The first was open to all women who were not menstruating, including those from abroad, but they were not allowed to cross the dividing wall into the inner courtyard. This was open only to sanctified men; even priests were not allowed to enter if they were unclean - for example, if they had had sexual relations with their wives recently.

The entire construction was extremely lavish, according to the Bible, with gold and precious metals being used in profusion. Some of the gates to the temple were covered in silver and gold, another set was forged from solid bronze and there were two mighty bronze pillars, called Jachin and Boaz, bronze being a very valuable commodity at the time. The following quote comes from Josephus's description of the second temple, built by Herod the Great at a later date, but it seems to follow the biblical description of Solomon's first temple suspiciously closely. If Josephus can be believed, both constructions must have been quite a spectacle:

> Of the gates nine were completely covered in gold and silver, as were the posts and lintels, but the one outside the Sanctuary was of Corinthian bronze and far more valuable than those overlaid with silver or even gold. Every gateway had double doors, each half being 14 m high and 7 m wide ... The gateway of the Sanctuary was much bigger, for its height was 24 m, and that of the doors 16 m, and the decoration was more magnificent, the gold and silver plating being extremely thick. This plating was the gift of Alexander, father of Tiberius. The Sanctuary itself ... [had a] first gate 33 m high and 12 m wide; it had no doors, thus revealing instead of excluding the vast expanse of heaven. The face was covered with gold all over ... (it) struck the beholder's eye. [J2]

The Sanctuary, the Temple itself, was situated in the inner courtyard and contained the alter made of undressed stone, untouched by iron, as explained in Chapter I. The Sanctuary was open only to the priesthood who had inherited the position, in other words, the descendants of the tribe of Levi. The clothes that these priests wore were in the same tradition as the famous outfit possessed by Joseph and those described in the biblical story of the exodus – coats with many ornaments. However, changes in the beliefs were creeping in: the 12 precious stones on the tunic now represented the 12 tribes of Israel, rather than the 12 signs of the zodiac.

The cosmological origins of the religion had not been entirely forgotten: the candlestick with seven branches represented the seven known planets and the twelve loaves on the table now represented the signs of the zodiac. The two mighty bronze pillars at the entrance to the temple not only represented the mathematical constant pi, but were also capped with representations of the heavenly sphere of the constellations and the globe of the Earth. [J3] (Both the sacred candlestick and the two pillars are discussed more fully in *Thoth, Architect of the Universe*.) All this cosmological knowledge was in Jerusalem some 2,000 years before the era of Copernicus.

Another bronze masterpiece was the 'sea of bronze', a vast

cauldron of water for ritual cleansing measuring 5m across. It was placed upon 12 bronze oxen, which probably highlights the difficulties that the authorities had in maintaining the true creed. [B4] The 12 oxen are, no doubt, representative of the previous dominant constellation, so the image of the bull is reminiscent of the difficulty Aaron and Moses were having many generations before with the followers of Taurus and their golden calf. The creed was deviating from the Heliopolian version once more.

At last, after passing through the Sanctuary, we come to the western end of the Sanctuary, a separate area for the high priests and the king alone that was bathed by the first rays of light at the Equinox. It was:

> ...unapproachable, inviolable, and invisible to all, and was called the Holy of Holies. [J5]

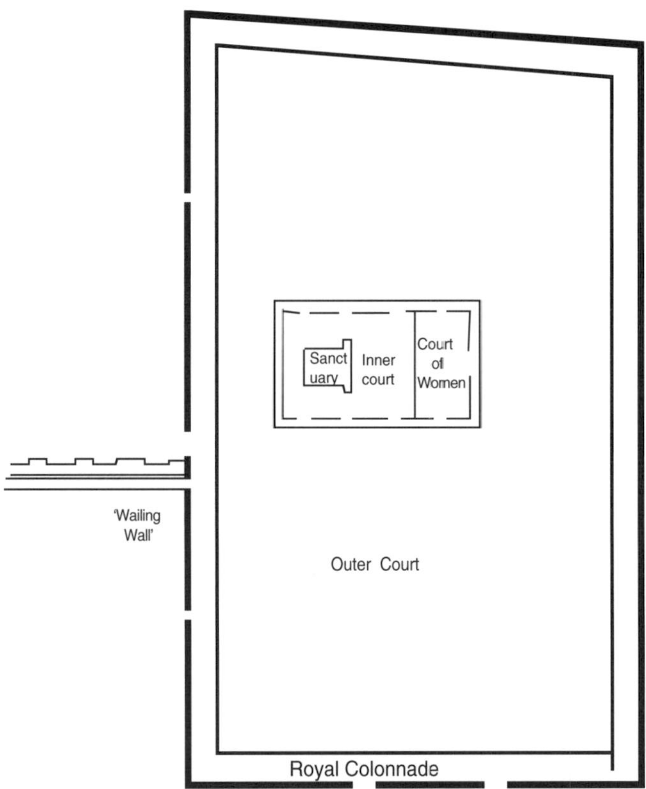

Fig 18. Herod's Temple Enclosure (the second temple)

To see what this Holy of Holies was like it is probably worth visiting one of the great Egyptian temples along the Nile. There one finds, in a similar fashion, a series of courtyards and hypostyle halls, leading eventually into a small rectangular room, the Holy of Holies. Josephus said that the room in the Jerusalem Temple was empty, but it is highly unlikely that he would ever have been given entry to the inner sanctums of the Herodian temple and the Holy of Holies has doors at its entrance. Most likely this comment was based on hearsay and, in comparison, Apion said of the Jewish temple(s):

> (The temples were) all facing eastwards; such being the orientation of Heliopolis. In place of obelisks [as at Heliopolis] he set up pillars, beneath which was a model boat; and the shadow cast on this basin by the statue described a circle corresponding to the course of the Sun in the heavens. [J6]

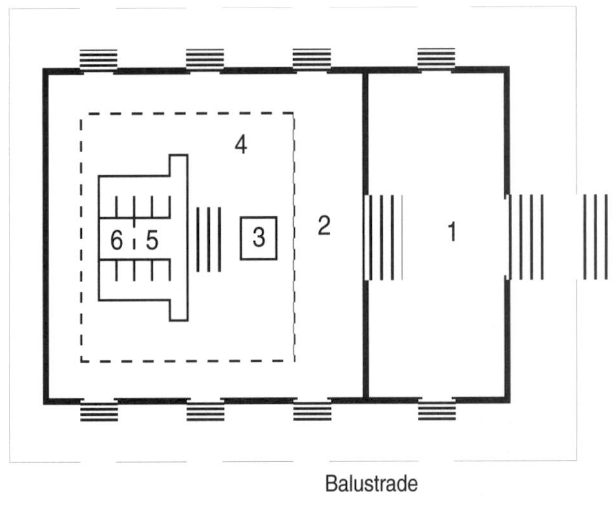

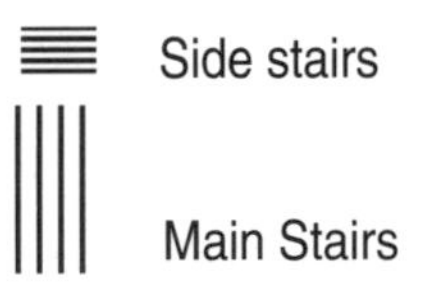

1. Court of the women.
2. Court of the Israelites.
3. Altar.
4. Court of the priests.
5. The Sanctuary.
6. The Holy of Holies.

Fig 19. Herod's Temple

The last part of the description conforms to an earlier description of the function of the sacred obelisk at Heliopolis, the Benben stone. Apparently, the shadow from the obelisk follows the curvature of the sides of the boat which was placed on the ground on the northern side of the obelisk.

Whether the description by Apion was from observation of the Jerusalem temple or just taken from descriptions of the Heliopolian Holy of Holies, it is difficult to say. However, the Egyptian versions of the inner sanctum mostly contain a simple alter and sometimes a throne as well. Significantly, a model ship of Egyptian design was sometimes located nearby. The major difference between these two temples is that the inner portions of the Upper Egyptian temples were roofed over, so there was no possibility of a shadow being cast by the pillars. In comparison, the temples of Akhenaton at Amarna were all open to the skies in the same manner as the Heliopolian and Jerusalem versions.

Israel

The heavy tax burden on the local population involved in the building of the temple and palace caused some friction between Jerusalem and northern Judaea. Nevertheless, the political system remained relatively stable, again with the usual tribal infighting, until the coming of the Babylonian king Nebuchadnezzar II in about 600 BC. The Babylonians sacked Jerusalem, destroying Solomon's temple. As part of the spoils of war they carried off all the lavish temple fittings, most of which were of solid gold and, for good measure, they also took most of the high officials and some of the population as slaves to work in Babylon. Although the Israelites in Babylon were slaves, it would seem that they were not necessarily incarcerated and chained. Undoubtedly they had quotas of work to accomplish for the Babylonians and they had no freedom to leave, but it would seem that some were in a position to acquire wealth and so when they were eventually freed, many chose to stay on in Babylon.

It was in Babylon that modern Judaism evolved from the mix of Arian peoples taken from Jerusalem. There, the Jews began the process of gathering their records together into the scroll that would become known as the Torah, the first five books of the Old Testament. It was also the time when the priests began to dissociate themselves from everything Egyptian and Egypt became a pariah state, the scapegoat for all the calamities that had befallen them.

> Behold the Lord rideth on a swift cloud, and shall come unto Egypt: and the idols of Egypt shall be moved in his presence, and the heart of Egypt shall melt in the midst of it. And I shall set Egyptian against Egyptian: and they shall fight one against his brother ... city against city, and kingdom against kingdom. The spirit of Egypt shall fail in the midst thereof; and I will destroy the counsel thereof ... [B7]

The biblical oaths against Egypt go on page after page. It is clear that if there were ever any favourable mention of Egypt in the Judaic texts that were being absorbed into the new scroll, they would have been withdrawn at this time. The Torah was beginning to take shape in the slavery of Babylon. It was a time of great sorrow, but privations often produce great works and deeds and this time of suffering was to be no exception. It is at this point in the Bible that we find one of the world's oldest songs, later made popular by the group 'Boney M' in the 1980s. Hardly surprisingly, it was a lament:

By the rivers of Babylon,
there we sat down,
yea we wept,
when we remembered Zion.

Carry me away captivity,
requires from us a song.
But how can we sing the Lord's song,
in a strange land? ... [B8]

It took a full two generations before Cyrus the Great of Persia mounted a campaign against Babylon. In the process, and rather incidentally, the Jewish captives were released. Upon their release, the Jews were even allowed to take some of their original temple furniture and artefacts, which comprised hundreds, if not thousands of items. At last, the 'slaves' began the long march home, some 40,000 people, but this was to sow the seeds of more conflicts. Once more, the long period of separation had seen the two peoples drift apart in their government and beliefs. The returning tribes were no longer the same peoples who were taken into exile; they possessed their new scroll, with new laws and regulations. They returned to their homeland only to find that the citizens who had remained in Jerusalem had taken over the property of the exiles. Why should the Jerusalemites give up these farms and businesses that they had acquired to these strangers from the north? It was a similar problem to the modern scenario of sorting out who owns what in eastern Europe, two generations after the Second World War ended. Can a family simply claim back their original business, when someone else has tended and nurtured it for two generations? The rights and wrongs of such cases are not always clear cut.

In addition, the Jerusalemites had made peace overtures to the Egyptians, whereas the Babylonian exiles hated the Egyptians. The Jerusalemites now had their own priesthood controlling the temple ruins. Once more the question had to be asked, why should they cede control to these strange unknown people flooding in from the north? The northerners claimed that they held the bloodline of the priesthood and this gave them the right, bestowed on them by God, to control the priesthood. The Jerusalemites claimed in return that many of the Babylonian priesthood had taken foreign wives. This was not only against the law, but also nullified the bloodline claim. It was agreed that only those who could produce and verify their family genealogies could hold positions in the priesthood and no doubt this wrangling took a very long time to sort out.

We pass on again a few centuries until about 70 BC. As was often the case in this era, there were constant battles between rival cities and clans throughout Palestine. Even within the ruling family, brother fought brother for power and brother often killed brother in the process. There was no discipline in the political, religious or military systems. It was a dog-eat-dog province and it spread turmoil beyond its own borders. By this time, Rome had become the greatest military power in the region and as its armies were campaigning in Syria and had important interests in Egypt. Palestine was becoming a thorn in its side.

Although Palestine was not a wealthy province, it was a strategic problem and so two separate campaigns led by Pompey the Great and Mark Antony were sent into the area. Pompey used a novel technique for sacking Jerusalem: the simple tactic of building ramps against the walls of the city during the Sabbath. As the defending Jews were not allowed to fight on the Sabbath, the wall was breached without any hindrance from the defenders. These campaigns managed to quell the disturbances briefly, but trouble flared up again as soon as they withdrew.

The underlying cause of this instability in the country was the presence of the three main religious sects: Sadducees, Pharisees and

Essenes. The smallest of these sects, numerically, were the Essenes and their popular image is of severe, monastic, white-robed monks in closed, all-male communities, living lives quite separate from the cosmopolitan world of Jerusalem. The facts are, perhaps, slightly different. Josephus indicates that the Essenes thought that marriage was a sacred duty, but they took the Catholic view of sex in that it was for procreation only and they abstained once a wife had conceived. They also refrained from sexual relations until a wife had begun to menstruate for three months in a row, which indicates that they took child-brides, as was the custom of the era. The specific mention of this 'peculiarity' of the Essenes, indicates that the other sects in Israel not only took child-brides, but also had sexual relations with them before they came of age. [J9] This confirms the explanation given earlier for the number of 'barren' brides in the Old Testament that eventually had children.

Although there was a long initiation into the Essene sect and it maintained very strict rules and regulations, it was not simply a remote desert sect. It seems to have been quite influential in Judaic politics and appears to have had very radical ideas on how the secular affairs of Israel should proceed. The Essenes are likely to have been Zadokite priests, that is, descendants of Aaron himself, through Simon Onias. Their desert headquarters at Qumran may have been set up in response to the control of the Jerusalem temple by the Hazidian (Pharisee) priests. Qumran, the main Essene community, is less than a day's walk from Jerusalem and it is apparent that there were frequent contacts between the priests of Jerusalem and the Essenes. Indeed, a number of the most influential priests in the city seem to have had Essene backgrounds.

Of the two most populous sects, the Sadducees were probably the lesser in terms of influence. Their most sacred tenet was the strict observance of the written religious law and, in this respect, they were probably the stricter of the two popular sects, more akin to the modern Orthodox Jew. They also denied the presence of hell and the rewards of heaven. Conversely, the Pharisees were, perhaps, more easy going and would happily interpret what the religious texts were trying to say. They believed men were responsible for their own actions, that the soul could reincarnate, and that the souls of evil people would go to hell. These may seem trivial differences in modern eyes, but it is important to remember that religion and politics were inseparable in that city and era.

Apart from these three main religious divisions, there was a host of minor sects, many of which were opposed to the Roman interference in the land. In addition, a very mixed population lived within the land of Palestine or on its borders. [J10] The area was something of a powder keg and Josephus painted a picture of conflict after conflict occurring throughout the region. If only half of what he said is true, then the era was a maelstrom of turmoil.

After the two short Roman campaigns through the region, there was a brief interlude free from Roman intervention while the great imperial city of Rome had its own civil strife: a divisive power struggle between rival candidates for the position of consul. Eventually, Julius Gaius Caesar marched against Pompey and defeated him at Pharsalus. He then marched to Egypt and Palestine to restore order in the region. To control the area he needed a local puppet government and his choice for local administrators for Palestine were Antipater, the father of Herod the Great, as procurator, and Hyrcanus II, whom he reconfirmed in his position as high priest. Although high priest was technically the superior office in Jerusalem, especially as Hyrcanus was a direct descendant of the past kings of Judaea and had briefly occupied the throne himself, it was Antipater that had the bigger personality and effectively ruled Israel.

Despite his lack of royal or priestly heritage, Antipater soon appointed his son, Herod, governor of Galilee, where he proved himself capable, executing some known bandits. Hyrcanus was jealous of the young Herod's assumed status in the province and tried to end his career, but Rome intervened and appointed Herod to an even higher rank. With his new powers, He raised an army and marched to Jerusalem to remove Hyrcanus, but was advised to withdraw. Strife continued throughout the region, so a family alliance was arranged to end the feuding. Although Herod was already married to Doris, a commoner, a truce was duly arranged and Herod married Mariamme, Hyrcanus' daughter. This was a strategic alliance; Herod was of common stock but Mariamme I[st] was of the ancient bloodline and the fusion would confer the royal and priestly status to Herod's sons and daughters. Despite this strategy, however, the hostilities simmered on.

Many cities still disputed Herod's leadership and so a deputation was sent to Mark Antony, one of Rome's ruling triumvirate of consuls, and Cleopatra in Egypt to adjudicate on the problem. Herod was confirmed as governor, but the decision was unpopular and caused even more strife in Jerusalem. A bigger delegation was sent to Mark Antony, resulting in uproar that forced him to kill many of those who had come to see him. Palestine erupted into civil war once more. It was against this backdrop of continual disorder that in 39 BC, the Roman Senate declared Herod King of Judaea, albeit a king subservient to Rome.

Herod the Great

King he may have been, but it still took Herod four years of hard fighting, occasionally with Antony's assistance, to win back Palestine and much of Syria and finally to gain control of Jerusalem. Just as he had achieved this, there was further misfortune. Antony was under the spell of the Egyptian queen Cleopatra, who was demanding estates, provinces and entire kingdoms. He mollified her demands, but still granted some valuable lands of Herod's to Cleopatra, which he had to then lease back at an exorbitant rate.

More calamities were to follow. Without consulting his fellow consul (the triumvirate having been reduced to two), Mark Antony unilaterally declared Cleopatra's son, Caesarion, Julius Caesar's heir. Octavian Caesar, Mark Antony's fellow consul and Julius Caesar's nephew and official heir, responded by sending a battle fleet. Mark Antony was defeated at Actium by Octavian Caesar in 31 BC and took his own life the following year. Herod was forced to sail to Rhodes to assure Octavian of his allegiance; a dangerous diplomatic task since he had been backing Octavian's enemy, Mark Antony. Octavian, who was later designated Augustus Caesar by the Roman Senate, confirmed Herod's status as king and he was allowed to return to Palestine with lands and authority intact. It was only then, in the relative calm of the latter part of his reign, that the task of rebuilding the Temple of Jerusalem finally began, in about 20 BC, more than 550 years after the destruction of Solomon's temple.

This temple was the one described by Josephus, quoted earlier in the chapter. Its lavish appointment was underwritten mainly by the Diaspora, the exiled Jews who had remained in Persia and Asia Minor after the Babylonian exile. Large contributions were also made by the exiled Jews who had fled to Alexandria, Rome, Ephesus and many other major European cities, following their dispersal as far back the Jacobite exodus from Egypt. The Diaspora recognized the spiritual value of the Temple of Jerusalem and then, as now, vast sums of money poured into Jerusalem from around the known world to maintain the spiritual motherland.

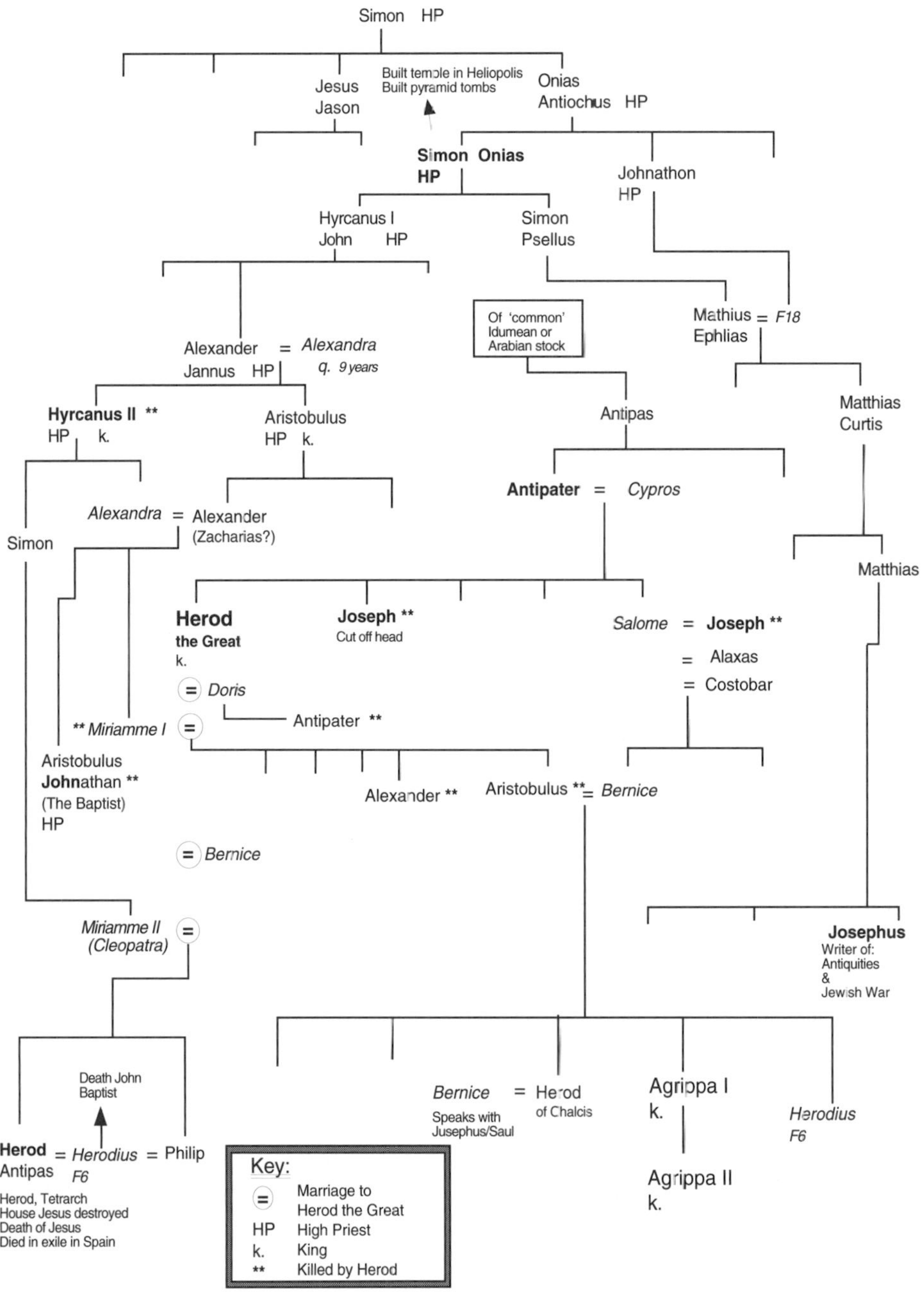

Fig 20. Family tree of Herod
For further information, please see Appendix 1

Despite the new prosperity, there were still bitter feuds within Herod's family and the royal court. Herod's extended family was permeated by close inter-family marriages and, consequently, it was also riddled with intrigue and strife. It is probably owing to episodes like the following, that our modern prohibitions on close family marriages have been reinforced. The family tree on page 153 has been greatly simplified to show the main players in this important saga, for the ramifications of this for Christianity are manifold. The events that were about to unfold will probably lead us to another sensitive biblical secret that has lain dormant for nearly two millennia. In the diagram of Herod's family, note that the role of king and high priest are often interchangeable in this era. Quite obviously, despite the scribes insisting that only the Levites could hold the priesthood, the Josephites that held the kingship were sufficiently infused into the Levites by this time as to be indistinguishable and interchangeable.

The origins of the bloodline in this tree flowed either from Moses or Aaron, who both had sons named Eleazar. From there it passed to Phineas, through more generations to Zadok, the first high priest under King David. Eventually, after a great long list of high priests, it flowed into Simon, the high priest at the top of this tree. Note that Simon's grandson, Simon Onias, was the Jewish priest who rebuilt the temple at Heliopolis as discussed in chapter IV. Remember that the term Onias is a title rather than a name, it being derived from 'On', the biblical name for Heliopolis. Later on in the texts, this title evolved into Anias (Heliopolis is sometimes referred to as 'An') and thence Ananias. This explains a later confusion where everyone in the texts seems to have been called Ananias. For the full and highly complicated family tree of Herod, please see Appendix I.

Baptist

Herod's sister, Salome, and her daughter, Bernice, had always hated Herod's wife Mariamme, presumably because she was of the bloodline and they were descended from Idumaeans 'commoners'. In this air of mutual suspicion, Mariamme I[st], Herod's wife, became alarmed about Herod's intent towards her through information supplied to her by Joseph, Herod's brother. He was confused as to how Mariamme had obtained this information, so like Othello before him and all modern soap operas since, Herod suspected a liaison between Mariamme and

Joseph. His fears of women in general were further fuelled by the famous actions of Queen Cleopatra and the tales of how she had manipulated Mark Antony. Thus, suitably enraged, he had them both killed.

This event deserves further investigation because a curious thing now occurs in the works of Josephus. Joseph, Herod's brother, was killed, but at about the same time so was Joseph, *his uncle*. The texts fail to mention where this 'uncle' came from, although they also say that he was the husband of Salome, Herod's sister. Further reading of the texts shows us the scribes deceit, for the 'uncle' and the brother are one and the same.

The basis of this story was that Herod was about to set off to see Mark Antony in Egypt. This was a dangerous mission, so he placed his 'uncle' in charge of the nation's affairs while he was away. He also charged his 'uncle' Joseph that if he should be killed by Mark Antony, then his wife Mariamme should also be killed, apparently because 'he cannot bear to be parted from her'. Unfortunately for the scribes, one of the four entries that deal with this situation, indicates that it was *brother* Joseph who was given this charge and not the uncle.

> Now Joseph was already slain in Judaea, in the following manner: - He forgot what charge his *brother* Herod had given him when he went to Antony; [J11]

This cannot be talking of brother-in-law Joseph (the 'uncle' was also potentially a brother-in-law), as a few pages later, the text then relates how this same charge was given to Joseph, the uncle.

> Mark Antony was persuaded by these arguments ... he sent and commanded Herod to come ... so (Herod) left his *uncle*, Joseph, procurator for his government and for public affairs, and gave him a charge, that if Antony should kill him, he should also kill Mariamme... [J12]

Clearly the texts are trying to say that two separate people died in exactly the same incident and, in addition, both of them were called Joseph. From the total lack of evidence of an uncle called Joseph, these two characters just have to be the same – the *brother* of Herod. This sleight of hand has been done with good reason, for there *was* a major incident to cover up. In deciphering this muddle, the method of Joseph's death was rather significant – he was beheaded. In addition, either this head or the head of his executioner, Pappus, was delivered by Herod to his brother Pheroras, whom he blamed for this whole incident. A severed head was delivered on a charger to the court of Herod, mainly because of the machinations of Salome, his sister, and her daughter Bernice. Does this not sound similar to a well-known incident?

> For John had said to Herod. It is not lawful for thee to have thy brother's wife. Therefore Herodias (the wife of Herod) had a quarrel against him; and would have killed him but could not ... And the king said unto the damsel (Salome, daughter of Herodias): Ask whatever you want, and I will give it to thee ... And she said, the head of John the Baptist ... And the (executioner) brought his head on a charger, and gave it to the damsel (Salome): and the damsel gave it to her mother (Herodias). [B13]

In both cases, the women of the court were plotting against someone; in both cases the head of their victim was severed and a freshly dripping head was brought into the court of Herod. Once more, these are just the sorts of events to lodge firmly in the chroniclers' minds; they can be manipulated, but not forgotten. However, there is one major snag with this scenario, for the two Herods were not the same. The Bible was talking of Herod the tetrarch, *son* of Herod the Great, while Josephus' story was of Herod the Great himself, so there was a number of years between these two episodes. Herod the Great died in 4 BC and yet John the Baptist was said to have baptized Jesus, who is not supposed to have been born for about another four years. The dates seem quite incompatible. Does this mean that these two tales are entirely separate? Not at all.

The Christian record likes to portray Jesus and John as being of the same age, yet as Lynn Picknett and Clive Prince detail in their book *Templar Revelations*, the biblical texts neither support nor reject this notion; indeed the Koran suggests in one passage that John had died before Jesus was born. It is quite possible, therefore, that John the Baptist baptized an *infant* Jesus and it is also quite possible that this ritual was simply metaphorical, a confirmation that Jesus was following in the footsteps of John. Consequently, this tale could involve either of the Herods. In support of this, it is significant that the Bible calls this Herod a king – Herod the tetrarch was never crowned as king.

What appears to be the case is that at some time, a major intrigue between the women in the royal court turned into a bloody battle for power, which resulted in the beheading of a priest known as John. This was such a momentous event that the scribes could not conceal it entirely – it was too widely reported for that – but they could obfuscate the truth. So there are two traditions that detail the same event. Josephus says it occurred in the reign of Herod the Great, while the Bible has conveniently translated this into the reign of Herod the tetrarch and thereby hidden the true identity of John the Baptist and the true reason for his execution.

Unfortunately, another flaw in the argument surfaces at this point. Although the two plots have a similar ring, John the Baptist was a well-respected priest and, if the general thrust of this book is anything to go by, he should also have been a prince of the bloodline and, perhaps, a descendant of Simon Onias. Joseph, brother of Herod, was neither a priest nor of royal blood; he was a commoner and, as such, his death would never have generated the resounding howl of protest that has echoed down the millennia in the manner that the execution of John has. This problem can be explained by returning to Josephus's story; what prompted Herod's summons to see Mark Antony and what was the real cause of this royal dispute?

Not long before this episode, Hyrcanus II had been denied the priesthood by the unusual method of his ears being bitten off. As he was no longer 'whole' he could no longer be priest. Rather conveniently, Herod the Great tried to make a good friend of his the high priest of Jerusalem, thereby gaining influence over the priesthood in addition to his enormous secular powers as king. This would make his position in the land unassailable and his family impregnable. Tradition required that the Judaic priesthood was only to be conferred on the tribe of Levi, the descendants of Moses or Aaron, but this pretender to the title was from Babylon and of uncertain origins. So Herod's appointment caused an outcry, especially among the descendants of Hyrcanus. In desperation, Alexandra, Mariamme's mother, appealed to Cleopatra, Queen of Egypt, and had this posting overruled. Her brother Aristobulus was made high priest instead. Herod must have been seething at this interference in his plans.

Aristobulus was a fine young man, the grandson of a high priest on both his paternal and maternal sides; there was no one more suitable for the job and he was duly appointed. Having this royal pretender in the commanding position of high priest, a position nominally higher than that of the king, was not acceptable to Herod. The situation worsened as it appears that Aristobulus immediately started complaining of Herod's marriage to his brother's wife. (Herod had already married two nieces, and his brother Joseph had quite possibly married his sister Salome, so marriage to a brother's wife would not have presented Herod with many problems.) Whatever the case, it is clear that Herod resented this challenge to his authority and something had to be done. The young Aristobulus was taken to a bath by Herod himself, probably a large *baptismal* font for ritual cleansing, where Herod had him drowned.

Alexandra, Aristobulus' mother, was outraged. This was not only her son, but one of the few remaining pure descendants of Moses or Aaron. Aristobulus had been the high priest of all Israel and Herod had had him slain like a traitor to the realm. She complained bitterly to Queen Cleopatra in Egypt once more and, in turn, pressure was applied to Mark Antony. It was for *this* crime that Herod had been summoned to see Mark Antony so his situation was grave and the threat to his life real. This was why Salome pressured Herod to have his wife Mariamme killed if he did not return. She wanted the kingdom for *her* offspring – not Mariamme's. Again as confirmation that the events with Joseph the brother and Joseph the uncle were one and the same, the incident in the bath occurs in both sections of the text. In this new version, 'enemies' of Herod entered the baths while he was naked and with a 'companion', drew their swords, then inexplicably left again. [J14]

In this case the beheading incident in the court of Herod the Great *was* initiated by the death of a priest, the high priest Aristobulus. The similarity between this episode and the biblical story of John the Baptist is, therefore, quite close. At this point a further and later layer of obfuscation in the unfolding story emerges, because William Whiston, the eighteenth century translator of Josephus whom I had been using, insisted on calling this high priest who was drowned Aristobulus. It was only when a more modern translation of Josephus came to light that the problem was fully resolved and the identity of this high priest was made plain; there was a good reason for covering up this story. The new translation identified Aristobulus, the young high priest, as '*Jonathan, also called Aristobulus*'. [J15]

Here was the evidence I had been seeking. There *had* been a major battle in the royal court, but it was not the minor court of Herod the tetrarch, but some of the desperate machinations that occurred within the court of Herod the Great himself a generation or more earlier. John (Jonathan) was directly descended from the bloodline, he had been appointed high priest of all Israel and he was the only person in a position to challenge directly the authority and the cruel reign of Herod the Great.

Jonathan's first complaint went straight to the heart of the matter: Herod's family had transgressed the law in some of their convoluted marriage alliances. Salome, his sister, and her daughter Bernice were outraged: no doubt the attack related directly to them in some way (marriage to a brother's wife who had children was forbidden). Such attacks on his kin and challenges to his authority were unacceptable to Herod, so John was disposed of. Significantly, he was drowned in a baptismal bath and the texts seem to indicate that Herod may have been participating in some kind of ritual cleansing. Thus the enduring epitaph of Jonathan, the unfortunate high priest, was 'John who died during a baptism' or John the Baptist.

Familiacide

The bitter dispute did not end there, of course. Herod became paranoid and suspected that others had been plotting against him. He wondered if Joseph, his brother, was colluding with Mariamme and Alexandra. He suspects that Mariamme's sons (his sons) were also implicated and he was upset with Salome, his sister, for whipping up the intrigue. Herod now entered his unstable phase and while he was away being reprimanded by Mark Antony, he had his brother beheaded. Either his, or perhaps his executioner's head was then sent back to the royal court as a warning.

The full biblical story of the demise of John the Baptist is now explained. John the Baptist was not any old priest practising his trade out in the wilderness, but the high priest of all Israel at the tender age of eighteen. Thus, John was very important in this story, for in the biblical version of these events he was seen to be conferring the blessing of the high priest upon Jesus; in preference to the imposter that Herod had planted into this position in his place. Quite plainly, Jesus was an important player in these events and one of the next tasks is to see whereabouts on this family tree he sprang from.

The murder of John created a deep rift between Herod and his two sons by Mariamme – Aristobulus and Alexander (John the Baptist was their uncle). Their obvious hostility inclined Herod towards favouring Antipater, a son by his first wife, Doris. However, she was not of the bloodline, so this served to enrage Aristobulus and Alexander even more. [J16] This bitter family feud eventually ended in a sham of court proceedings, with Herod accusing his sons of treason. His sons were not even produced before the court, yet Herod had them convicted of plotting against him. Aristobulus and Alexander were taken to a city known as Sebaste, near Cesarea, where they were both strangled to death. [J17]

This left Antipater in line for the throne, but the people no longer liked him, as he had been a chief protagonist in stirring up accusations against his now-deceased half-brothers. The whole bitter saga progressed to a point where Antipater was accused, together with his mother, of trying to poison Pheroras, another of the king's brothers. To find out the truth, Herod tortured Doris' maidservants, one by one, and they all testified this to be true! Antipater was brought to justice to face these charges and was convicted, but Herod refrained from executing his son until his own illness was cured. Unfortunately for Antipater, it became apparent that Herod's health was failing fast, the population was aware of his impending death and became bolder and more agitated. [J18]

Although Herod the Great had triumphed over the rebel cities of Israel and brought most of them to heel during his reign, creating a period of relative prosperity, he was only a Roman vassal after all. His successes had been underwritten by Rome at every stage and Rome called all the political shots in Palestine, using Herod as their chief of police. The people began to see a chance of freedom and a group of youths gathered in the temple square in Jerusalem one day and cut down the golden eagle, the despised symbol of Rome. For their troubles, and as the most brutal punishment possible, many of them were burned alive. By this time, Herod could feel his life slipping away and, fearing that Antipater might gain the throne after his death, Herod had him killed; five days later he himself was dead. [J19]

Nativity

The scene for the New Testament has been set. It was into this political maelstrom that the historical character of Emmanuel, or Joshua, was born. Joshua, the biblical Jesus, is known to us under the Greek translation of his name, but the Koran calls him Essa, which is most probably a title. The political events surrounding his birth were turbulent in the extreme. John the Baptist was the first to die, Alexander and Aristobulus, Herod's sons by his wife Mariamme, were killed in about 5 BC. Antipater, his next son, was killed in about 4 BC. Herod himself also died in about 4 BC. The exact historical birth year of Jesus is unknown, but it is often assumed by historians to be between 7 BC and 4 AD. In the circumstances, it was no wonder that a rumour was started that Herod wished to kill all the male children in the land. This comment alone, specifically the mention of those children under two years old, would indicate a birth date for Jesus of about 7 or 6 BC and firmly places him as being attached somewhere on the vast Herodian or Hyrcanusian family tree.

Jesus was supposed to have been born while his mother was still a virgin, but this is nonsense. The patriarchal line through to Jesus is chronicled in the Bible and this traces his descent back to King David. If Mary were a virgin, then the patriarchal bloodline so meticulously recorded in the Bible is utterly irrelevant. Many theories have been proposed as to how the scribes decided that there had been a virgin birth, but they are equally irrelevant. The fact is that Jesus was of the bloodline, an Egyptian pharaoh in exile. As such, it was expected that he would be the offspring of the gods, but in Egyptian terms, this did not deny the role of the biological father. While the gods were intimately involved in the conception of the infant pharaoh, they did not take over the biological necessities. Thus, the pharaoh was the product of a human father and he was also the Son of God, yet the Egyptians saw no conflict in these seemingly opposing concepts.

The Bible goes on with its unreliable narrative and describes Jesus as being of lowly status. He was recorded as being born in a stable with simple shepherds visiting, but the reason for this story is so obvious by now that I will not bore the reader with more stellar connotations. Jesus was not a poor carpenter's son – more evidence for this will follow shortly – he was a descendant of Jacob and Abraham, former pharaohs of Egypt. He was an aristocratic son, a prince of the realm, and someone who was possibly in a position to take the throne from Herod and his sons. It is no wonder that Jesus' mother would be afraid that Herod might kill him. If Herod had been capable of killing his own three sons and the high priest Jonathan himself, a pretender to the throne would present no problems. So Jesus' mother took the advice of her followers, who said to Joseph:

> Arise, and take the young child and his mother and flee into Egypt, and be thou there until I bring word: for Herod will seek the young child and destroy him. [B20]

This was not a case of Herod wantonly slaying every baby boy in Judaea, as is portrayed by the Christian clergy. This was a family dispute concerning the royal inheritance, the next king or high priest of Israel. The texts themselves admit that Jesus was a king of the Jewish people. [B21] He was of the royal bloodline and could trace his ancestry back through 73 generations to Abraham and beyond. [B22] He was a man administered to by the wife of Herod's chief steward, (Herod the tetrarch) [B23] and whose followers had unopposed access to the (former) royal palace, [B24] and talked directly to the procurator of all Palestine. [B25] (Note the relationship of the king's steward once more. Was this a role that was traditionally given to family members?) It is transparently clear that Jesus was not a poor carpenter, but was directly involved in the political machinations of the royal family. Herod wanted to control the destiny of his own bloodline, to pass on the throne to a son who he believed represented *his* bloodline. This is why he killed his own sons.

That Jesus was caught up in this strongly indicates that he was himself from *this* royal family. This is entirely possible, as the same family names crop up in both family trees. Certainly a branch of the Arian bloodline ran through the children of Herod the Great because of his marriage to Hyrcanus' daughter, Mariamme, but one would expect that there were many in the Hyrcanusian line that thought that the Herodian family were simply parasites on the true bloodline. Perhaps Jesus was from this Herodian line or perhaps, like Josephus himself, he was descended from a parallel line somewhere within the large Hyrcanusian family tree. Jesus was certainly a prince known to Herod, but perhaps not one directly in line for the throne at that time. Nevertheless, especially in times of civil war, remote princes can gather popular support; he could have been a threat to the future of the king's immediate family, especially if he held royal blood that was more pure than that of Herod's sons. Consequently, Jesus' father thought that, to be on the safe side, Jesus should go into exile in Egypt.

Why Egypt? Why go to a 'pariah' country that was despised by the Jews? Once again, the full truth has been circumvented. The Jews had a temple in Egypt at the sacred theological city of Heliopolis. It was from Heliopolis that the religion of the exodus had sprung and it was back to Heliopolis that Jesus went to learn the ways of his forefathers. He was a direct descendant of Abraham, Isaac and Jacob, either through the line of Judah or the lines of Moses and Aaron. All these people had been princes or pharaohs of Egypt; Jesus was also a prince and where better to receive his education than at Heliopolis? His distant forebears – Joseph and Moses [and Akhenaton] were all educated at this sacred temple. If anywhere in the world should hold the title of 'University of the Pharaohs', it was Heliopolis and this is most probably where Jesus went.

There, he would have been feted as the new Son of God, the new pharaoh. More importantly, this title would have indicated that Jesus was born of the Aton, just as Akhenaton was. He would have not only been the son, but the sun as well, a child of the solar deity. The Bible seems tacitly to confirm this, as the texts are full of allusions to light and darkness:

> (The Gospel author John) came for a witness, to bear witness of the Light, that all men through him might believe. He was not that Light, but was sent to bear witness of that Light. That was the true Light, which lighteth every man that comes into the world. [B26]

Note the capital letters – 'Light' is a proper name. As I have mentioned previously, the Bible likes to make Jesus a Jew, through the line of Judah, but the line of biblical priests (a role Jesus tried to assume) was descended exclusively through the Levites, the line of Moses. In turn, the line of biblical kings should have been through Joseph, who founded the line of viziers who eventually married into the pharaonic line. Although, by the turn of the first millennium, these roles have often conjoined into one of priest-kings.

The gospel writers were aware of this problem of Jesus not being from the Levite line: how could he become a priest or king when he sprang from line of Judah? The Bible tries to convince us that, although this was unusual, there was some, albeit rather weak, justification for it. It centres on the fact that the hereditary priests of the Levites were 'made through carnal commandments'; they were conceived and formed by sexual intercourse. (This is one of many indications of Saul's dislike of the sexual act.) Saul, the founder of Christianity, was indicating that the hereditary priests gained their posts through their inheritance, whereas Jesus had to swear an oath and by such a process Jesus 'made a surety of a better testament'. [B27]

It was suggested earlier that this Judite lineage for Jesus was a convenience for the tribe of Judah and that Jesus was, in reality, either a Levite or a Josephite. Moses was a matriarchal Levite, one born to the pharaoh Amenhotep III. This does not prevent Aaron (Akhenaton) from being from the Jacobite tribe, a half-brother of Moses through a different matriarchal line. Indeed the historical record strongly indicates that Akhenaton was of the line of Joseph, through the vizier Yuya and Amenhotep's marriage to his daughter Tiye. Such a situation would also go towards explaining why the elder son, Tuth(Moses), did not inherit the throne of Egypt, it being conferred on the younger brother Aaron (Akhenaton) instead – Aaron was of a stronger pharaonic (royal rather than priestly) bloodline than Moses.

Whatever the case, it would appear that Jesus was of a branch of this royal bloodline. This was either through King David, as is indicated by the patriarchal descent recorded in the Bible, or, if we had access to his matriarchal descent, we would probably find a link to the royal stewards of Egypt and the patriarch Joseph. In my opinion, Jesus was highly likely to have been a matriarchal descendant of the patriarchs *Joseph* and Moses, through the family of Simon Onias. This is supported by the Koran, where the father of Mary the mother of Jesus is called Amram or Imran, the name of Moses' father. Joseph was the title given to the royal viziers of Egypt and the name of Jesus' father. In addition, his family was also influenced by name *Heli*, the name of the Sun God, as inspired by the temple of Heliopolis, the name of Moses' and Aaron's sons and the name of Jesus' *grandfather*, Heli. [B28]

The Architect - Priest

Jesus was educated in Heliopolis, where he learned all the wise ways of the oldest of all religions: the movements of the stars and the ways of the cosmos. He became proficient in sand-writing, one of the ancient skills of magic. [B29] He became the cornerstone, a carpenter. Now this has been a very misleading term down the centuries: why should a prince of the realm be honoured as being a mere carpenter? It was, perhaps, a fortuitous mistranslation for the scribes, as they strove to distance Jesus from his real roots, but the position and status of Jesus is still clear from looking closely at the texts. The first clue comes in the Coptic translation of carpenter, where Jesus is called the *Naggar*, meaning either an artisan (carpenter) or an educated man.

In Greek, the occupation is defined as *tekton* in the Gospel of Matthew, a word that can be translated as 'builder'. However, there is a better translation. Jesus is being called an artisan, a builder and an educated man all at the same time. There is a profession that encompasses all these elements; an **architect**. Indeed, one can still see the etymological traces of the word '***tekton***' in the modern word '*archi****tect***'. (literally meaning, master-builder or master-mason) [30] This is a much more logical *craft* and title for Jesus, than a mere carpenter.

This process can be taken one step further, for Aaron (Akhenaton), a direct ancestor of Jesus, was known as the 'Greatest of Architects'. The true position of Jesus is becoming clearer: he was an architect, a cornerstone and a prince, in which case this not the literal profession of architect that was being referred to here, but the symbolic position of someone descended from the designer of the cosmos. The highest of all the deities is known as the 'Architect of the Universe' in Masonic circles and there is direct evidence that Jesus was also an architect, a theological Mason, rather than a secular mason. The evidence for this centers on the biblical story of the raising of Lazarus at Bethany.

Lazarus, who was, in fact, related to Jesus, became 'sick' and was laid in a tomb. Jesus delayed going to the aid of Lazarus, waiting another two days before travelling to Bethany and so Lazarus apparently 'died'. [B31] Jesus deliberately allowed Lazarus to 'die' and was:

> ... glad for your sakes that I was not there, to the intent ye may believe. [B32]

The plot becomes more bizarre, as now the other disciples wished to 'die' with Lazarus. It is beginning to look like a latter-day doomsday cult. When Jesus eventually arrived at Bethany, he wept for Lazarus, whom he loved (this will be important later) and, finally, Lazarus was 'raised' from the dead. [B33] It is a peculiar tale, to say the least, and it makes very little sense until you understand its true symbolic value. There are hundreds of thousands of people around the world today who have gone through the same procedure as Lazarus; they died and were re-born – it is a simple Masonic third degree ceremony.

It seems that the Essene version of the ceremony was somewhat more severe and testing than the rather quick and trivialized initiation ritual that exists today in every western Masonic lodge. Lazarus had to remain physically, rather than symbolically, entombed and had to remain so for three full days, presumably fasting and meditating all of that time. (The Bible says four days, but three would be more symbolic in terms of Jesus' resurrection and Masonic numerology). If this were the case, the ordeal was quite a trial of courage and a true initiation ceremony into the sect. Eventually, his ordeal complete, Lazarus emerged from the tomb alive, still 'hoodwinked' with the napkin around his face, as all initiates do to this day.

This clearly demonstrates the political and religious environment in which Jesus was working. He was pharaonic prince – in hiding perhaps, but nevertheless a prince. As a prince, he held the secrets of the ancient Egyptian religion and these were not to be given out to the common people. Thus there had been, since the dawn of history, initiations that took the candidate ever deeper into the mysteries of the past and towards an understanding of the workings of the cosmos. Information was drip-fed on a need-to-know basis, for selected initiates only. This is how the Nazarene, the church of Jesus, worked and this explains so much of the curious events that occur in the New Testament. Modern Masons follow exactly the same procedures and they are actually based on the same ancient events that originated in Egypt. But don't be led into thinking that such organizations still carry the secrets of the universe; they dissolved long ago; a few thousand years of Chinese whispers have seen to that.

After Herod the Great's death, the kingdom had been divided between his surviving sons Philip, Herod Antipas and Archelaus, although Caesar Augustus withheld from them the title of king. Soon afterwards, Judaea was annexed as an imperial province and a Roman procurator was installed, the first being Coponius. The political situation had changed and the branch of the family tree to which Jesus belonged was now quite important. The throne's last incumbent was dead and if the Roman element could be dealt with, it was now free for whoever could take it. Accordingly, there was much posturing between the rival contenders, each desperately trying to make their mark, awaiting the time when the throne would become available. It was time for Jesus to assume the role destined for him. He needed to assume the royal title, to become 'Jesus, the Essene', from which the Arabic name of Jesus, 'Essa', is derived and by which he is known in the Koran. [34]

The Essene sect (the Essioi or followers of Jesus) had been looking for the Essa, the M**essia**h, for centuries. The Messiah meant in Aramaic 'the one anointed with the oil', which was the ancient initiation rite of the kings of Egypt. Ahmed Osman has translated the word Messiah as being a derivation of 'messeh', the Egyptian word for crocodile, whose sacred oil was used in the initiation rite. [35] Thus all the kings of Egypt and Palestine were in some respects the Essa, but there is no doubt that a special **Messia**h was also expected; perhaps a spiritual Messiah or maybe even a secular one, who could be openly hailed as king of the Arian peoples once more. The Jewish people had discarded the kingship for many centuries. It had been revived sporadically, but the theological environment in which it resided was now very different from that of Egypt. Small groups, however, kept the traditions alive, hoping and waiting for a change in fortunes and a change in attitudes within Israel as a whole. For Jesus to take this title of Essa, the Messiah, meant that he was now taking on that mantle. He was attempting to be the semi-divine figure that the Essenes had been waiting for. He was claiming to be the anointed one, the prince of the pharaonic line, the Son of the Sun God, the Heli-sar or Elizar, as were all the pharaohs of Egypt.

Judaea was awash with claimants to the throne, however, and it was to prove difficult to convince the public at large that the pharaonic line still existed or that it held any contemporary relevance. The line had maintained itself in semi-secrecy for 1,500 years, occasionally gaining the throne and occasionally losing it. It was by no means an easy task to persuade people that this claim was any better than, say, that of Herod Antipas, who was, after all, the son of king Herod the Great and possibly carried some royal matriarchal blood. What was required was a great demonstration to the people that Jesus alone was truly fulfilling the prophesies of the promised Messiah. That event was to be the triumphant entry into Jerusalem and so just prior to this, a small group of followers crowned Jesus as king, and it was to be Mary Magdalene who anointed Jesus with the expensive oils and washed his feet with her hair.

Pisces

There was to be another problem for the novice King Jesus. During his education at Heliopolis, he had been advised of another great movement that was taking place in the heavens, another battle of the constellations. The stars had turned once more and if he were not careful, he would not only lose the claim to the throne, but also end up with another civil war on his hands. The priests who had served in Heliopolis through all the trials and tribulations of the last 2,000 years, putting their lives on the line rather than flee their temple, had recently watched the next great epoch unfold in the heavens. The era of Aries had ended and that of Pisces had begun. Jesus, who had started his life under the constellation of Aries, was hailed initially as being '*Lamb of God*', the child of Aries. Now, he had a double task: he not only had to regain the throne, but at the same time change the nature of the worship into a following of Pisces. As the New Testament of the Bible makes clear:

> For it is [no longer] possible that the blood of bulls and of goats should take away sins. [B36]

The eras of both Taurus and Aries had closed; it was now time for Pisces to take the ascendance. Luckily for Jesus, the theological changes instituted by Aaron (Akhenaton) long ago had had their desired effect: the people no longer worshipped the form of the constellation, the physical animal, directly. The belief had become somewhat abstract. It was a mere association of names that now had to be changed, not an entire belief system. It was for this reason that Jesus, the *Lamb of God*, became a *fisherman*, a *Nazarene*.

Jesus was not from Nazareth at all; indeed, it is unlikely that the town of that name existed at the time. Instead, the sect that he led, the Essene, became known as the Nazarene. Jesus was not 'of Nazareth', he was 'the Nazarene'. This is confirmed in the modern Arabic name for a Christian, a Nasrani, the meaning of which was, and is, quite specific – **little fishes**. [37] This is why Peter was given the designation of '*Fisher of Men*' and why the ancient symbol of the Christians was the sign of the fish. The stars had turned and the Arians had turned into Pisceans. The Bible records Jesus as trawling the Sea of Galilee as a fisherman. This was not a real event, but simply another allegorical tale. He was not hauling in nets full of fish, he was hauling in 'nets' full of Piscean converts to his cause.

This is why astrology and horoscopes were so important and why they maintain this position even in the modern world. It was not the monthly cycle of the stars overseeing individual birthdays that was really important here, but the millennial cycle of the stars. It was the constellation under which each of the pharaohs was born, that was the important designation. This is another example of the dual role of the teachings: one rule for the priesthood and another for the laity. The laity were given the monthly cycle to worship, but the priesthood kept the millennial cycle for themselves. The importance of the role of astrology is now apparent, for we have just identified Jesus as being the first of the legendary Fisher Kings...

Fig 21. The Christian sign of the fish

But all these changes presented a problem for the young Jesus. He may have wanted to be an Arian/Piscean prince, but the people wanted a leader who would follow the laws of the Torah, which were now distinctly Jewish. Thus he had to prove that he was the Essa, the Messiah, the pharaonic prince and this required fulfilling the ancient prophesies that had been derived from the scriptures. They had to be fulfilled in order to elevate his relatively impoverished position and to return his family line to the throne, as kings of the Jewish nation. Moreover, it required the fulfilment of that ultimate of all the prophesies – death.

Part 2

Now it came to pass that Jesus was born to Mary and Joseph in a house (not a stable) [B38] in Bethlehem, the eldest son of parents who were eventually to have at least six children. An unspecified number of wise men visited Herod and asked 'where is the future king?'. Herod was worried and called his chief priests to see where the king was to be born. The prophesy foretold that a king would be born in Bethlehem, for he was to be of the house of Judah. [B39] The wise men did not tell Herod where Jesus was and so, enraged, he began to slaughter all the heirs to his throne (as explained).

Jesus escaped and was educated at Heliopolis in Egypt. On his return, as a young adult, he demonstrated his superior education by being able to sit with the most learned men in the Temple of Jerusalem and amaze them with his knowledge. [B40] (The Bible says Jesus was 12 years old, but there may be a confusion with his Barmitzvah here; if it were 12 years after his Barmitzvah, he would have been 25 and this squares more comfortably with the rest of the texts in the Bible.) Not only could he speak his native Aramaic, but almost certainly he could speak Greek as well. He had been educated in Ptolomaic (Greek) Egypt and in the Gospel of Mark it is noted that the woman with whom Jesus is conversing is Greek. More specifically the Gospel writer says 'He de gyne en Hellenis', or the woman is Greek-speaking, as if Jesus understands. [41] Additionally, Jesus is also quoted as saying:

> Saul, Saul, why are you persecuting me? It is hard for you, kicking against the goad. [B42]

This appears to be taken directly from the Aeschylus' Oresteian trilogy, *Agamemnon* verse 1624, [43] demonstrating a good knowledge of classical literature.

Jesus was married at a rather sumptuous wedding at Cana. His mother was busy supervising the meal and it was the *bridegroom* (Jesus) who was congratulated on the provision of such good wine at the end of the feast. For further confirmation of the marital status of Jesus, refer to the Gospel of Mary Magdalene and the Gospel of Philip from the Nag Hammadi collection. (For further references, please see the books *Holy Blood & Holy Grail*, *Bloodline of the Holy Grail* etc.)

Although Jesus recognized the importance of his role and destiny, he was slightly uncomfortable with its ramifications. The crush of the crowds, the animosity of his opponents and the ignorance of the common people were all upsetting to him:

> These things spake Jesus, and departed, and did hide himself from them. [B44]
> Then they took up stones to cast at him, but Jesus hid himself, and went out of the temple. [B45]
> When he saw they would take him by force ... he departed again into the mountain. [B46]
> Therefore they sought him again to take him; but he escaped out of their hand. [B47]

Jesus was often disturbed by the people that crowded around to see him. He was supposed to be a prince, yet he had to suffer these swarming hoards around him. Sometimes it just all got too much:

> And the multitude cometh together again, so that they could not so much as eat bread. And when his friends heard it, they went out to lay hold on [Jesus]: for they said, He was beside himself [very angry indeed]. And the scribes [mocked him] saying he has the [devil inside him] and by the prince of devils he casts out devils. [B48]

> And Jesus said 'Who touched me?' When all denied, Peter said, 'Master the multitude throng around thee and press thee, and sayest thou, Who touched me? Jesus said [angrily] Somebody hath touched me!' [B49]

(Notice how this paragraph is softened in Mark 5:31 and made even gentler in Matthew 9:20. This is similar to the account of the Greek woman being called a dog, which was again softened in Matthew. It is a good demonstration of how the texts were subtly changed between each version and each scribe). These outbursts should have been expected: Jesus was just a flesh and blood man of noble birth and should not have had to dirty his hands. Where possible, the disciples should have taken the load from his shoulders:

> Jesus made and baptized more disciples than John (the Baptist). Though Jesus himself baptized not, but his disciples did. [B50]

But while the disciples helped where they could, sometimes they were a hindrance. It was a little tiresome when your very own disciples, let alone the populous, did not understand what the campaign was all about:

> [Jesus said] Why reason ye because ye have no bread? perceive ye not yet, neither understand ... Having eyes see ye not? and having ears hear ye not? and do ye not remember? ... How is it ye do not understand? [B51]

Some of the disciples did understand, but knowing the simplicity of some of the others, they did not dare share this knowledge openly:

> When Thomas returned to his companions, they asked him, What did Jesus say to you? Thomas said to them. If I tell you one of the things which he told me, you will pick up stones and throw them at me. [N52]

All this evangelizing and campaigning around the country was thirsty work. It was nice to be able to relax of an evening with a good pint and let the strains ebb away:

> The Son of Man came eating and drinking, and they said, Behold a man gluttonous and a wine bibber, a friend of publicans and sinners. [B53]
> But the Scribes and Pharisees murmured against his disciples, saying Why do you eat and drink with publicans and sinners? [B54]

But occasionally there was work to be done and opponents to quell. There was a group of priests who also claimed the virgin birth. They sought to kill Jesus and so they got short shrift from his tongue:

> Then they said to him, we be not born of fornication, we have one father ... God ... (Jesus replied) Ye are of your father the devil, and the lusts of your father ye will do. He was a murderer from the beginning, and abode not in the truth, because there is no truth in him. When he speaketh a lie, he speaketh of his own: for he is a liar and the father of it. [B55]

Finally, in the teachings of Jesus, there is evidence of the real underlying tenets of the religion that he was trying to promote. These tenets were totally ignored by the resulting Christian religion that claimed direct descent from him:

> And when thou prayest, thou shalt not be as the hypocrites are: for they love to pray standing in the synagogues and in the corners of the streets, that they be seen of men ... But thou, when thou prayest, enter thy closet, and when thou hast shut thy door, pray to thy father which is in secret; and thy father which is in secret shall reward thee openly.
>
> When you pray, use not vain repetitions, as the heathen do: for they think they will be heard for their much speaking. Be therefore not like them, for your father knows what things ye have need of, before ye ask him. [B56]

This is a good demonstration of the theology of Jesus and it has nothing to do with Christianity and endless Hail-Marys in opulent cathedrals. This route to the divine being, if it is anything, is Gnostic, an individual journey to enlightenment through the acquisition of knowledge. Concepts such as this are pure Egyptian. As stated previously, except for the major festivals, the common man in Egypt prayed in his closet at home. Religion was left to the professionals at the temple; it was they who oiled the wheels of the cosmos. Christianity, under its founder Saul, decided instead to involve the proletariat in worship, but this was not because he wished to assist the people in their struggles in this life; he did it for profit. The fact that the new church went against the wishes of its great leader, apparently placed no restrictions upon their teachings; Jesus was to become a simple figurehead in the religion that used his name.

Chapter VII

Last of the Pharaohs

Part 1

The ministry of Jesus, as demonstrated in the last chapter, was not the one familiar from our religious education. Jesus was a Jew and, while he may have been a little radical at times, he tried to preach to the laity within the confines of the Jewish faith. It was a man known as Saul who hijacked these teachings and began his own alternative vision of God and the purpose of religion and this will be explored more fully in the next chapter. The areas in which Jesus strayed from conventional contemporary Judaism were the those where his Egyptian heritage came to prominence.

Jesus had a mission that was deeper and more important to him than the Jewish faith as practised by most of the sects of that era, yet to the public he had to maintain the illusion of following the orthodox creed. Despite the Egyptian heritage, therefore, it is clear that he modelled himself on the prophesies in Hebrew Scriptures, deliberately designing his life to mimic that of the promised Messiah. The Gospel of Matthew seems to revel in this fulfilment of prophesy, so much so that he even described Jesus riding into Jerusalem astride two donkeys, like a circus performer:

> And (the disciples) brought the ass, and the colt, and put on them their clothes, and they sat him upon them. [B1]

This was done in the usual messianic style of Matthew, so that:

> ... it might be fulfilled which was spoken by the prophet ... [B2]

But the prophet Zechariah's actual account in the Old Testament was not indicating that the Messiah should ride into Jerusalem on top of two donkeys. His sentence reads as more of an exclamation than reality, but it has been mistranslated by Matthew into the nonsense that he actually wrote. What was really being said is:

> (paraphrased) The Messiah will come humbly, so he will be riding an ass; not only that, but he will be so lowly as to ride the foal of an ass. [B3]

In terms of the transport of the day, a very young donkey was presumably the most humble mode of conveyance available, but Matthew misinterpreted this as the literal trick of simultaneously riding two donkeys.

So if the Jesus of the New Testament was performing a real-life passion play of a promised Messiah for the Jewish nation, a charade designed to promote the Nazarene sect and the status of his family; why is there apparently a total lack of historical data regarding these events? In fact, there are some historical references to Jesus, but they have been subtly changed and so successfully hidden from view for nearly 2,000 years. This raises the questions of why it was necessary to change such accounts and what is the purpose of this obfuscation of the historical Jesus.

This book's new interpretation of the origins of the Nazarene church makes the answer obvious, as this had happened once before. When Akhenaton was forced into exile from Egypt, there was a great excision of names on both sides of the dispute. The name of Akhenaton was deleted from every temple in Egypt and, in return, every pharaoh was removed from the Bible, and Egypt was made into a pariah state. Fifteen hundred years later, Jesus attempted to reinstate the position of pharaoh in the new lands of Israel, while a certain character known as Saul, who masqueraded as an apostle, was re-enacting the position of the pharaoh Horemheb and was later very busy deleting references to the historical Jesus from every book and scroll he could find.

This was an easier task than might have been expected, for Jesus was something of a reluctant hero and the Nazarene church was not so well known and so commercial as the later church of Saul. Jesus' ministry was, in reality, quite a low-key affair, despite his important rank and high standing among his own people. A comparison might illustrate his position more clearly.

The Grand Master of the United Grand Lodge of England is probably one of the most influential people in the country, perhaps the world. He probably has direct contacts with all major corporations, banks, civil service, royalty and the top levels of government. If he or his organization has a problem or proposal to be considered, it will be looked into at the very highest levels within our society. But conversely, if the Grand Master travelled into the City of London on a humble moped, who in the crowds, even from within the ranks of his own organization, would recognize him?

Jesus was in the same position, but he wished to exchange it for a higher profile within society – he wanted to be the high priest and king. However, he had a long way to go. Most of the popular tales of Jesus in the New Testament are of local, rather than national import and involved just a few people. The marriage at Cana, the raising of Lazarus, teaching parables to the disciples, the last supper, the capture of Jesus outside Jerusalem, the opening of the tomb and the fishing trips with the disciples on lake Galilee are all small family events that would have made no impact on the wider population of Jerusalem and Judaea. Had it not been for the later evangelism of the disciples, nothing would be known of these events today. It is also significant that the more populous events in the New Testament, such as the feeding of the 5,000, usually occurred outside the main towns, often in the province of Galilee. Again, the wider population in Jerusalem would not necessarily have heard of them.

It was for this reason that Jesus had to make a more public demonstration at the Passover festival in Jerusalem. This occasion was a much bigger event than was portrayed in the Bible, Josephus says that up to three million people attended it. Even allowing for his normal exaggeration, the festival must have been quite a spectacle and it is no wonder that even someone as influential as Jesus had trouble in finding accommodation in the city:

> And there was a man named Zacchaeus, which was the chief among the publicans, and he was rich. And he sought to see Jesus ... and could not for the (crowds) ... and [he] climbed up into a sycamore tree to see him ... and Jesus looked up and saw him and said unto him Zacchaeus, make haste ... for today must abide at thy house. [B4]

Clearly, Zacchaeus was an old friend and ally, who would maintain the confidentiality of the prince and provide him with financial support. In fact, in chapter IX I will show that Zacchaeus was not only a highly influential member of the priesthood, but most probably a close relation of Jesus as well. It is possible that Jesus planned to use the Passover festival to win over the people through a display of popular adulation by his supporters. However, if this had been the plan, it was a spectacular failure, as it states quite clearly in Matthew's gospel. At the time of Jesus' triumphant entry into Jerusalem, the population were confused and did not know who he was:

> And when he was come into Jerusalem, all the city was moved, saying, Who is this? [B5]

The primary plan had failed and the contingency had to be put into action. It was to be an armed revolt to take control of the city, for which Jesus told his followers to sell their possessions and to buy weapons. [B6] The rallying point was to be the Mount of Olives by night, where Jesus was joined by 600 men, according to Josephus (see chapter VIII), and planned to infiltrate the temple and take power by force.

Perhaps this was a genuine coup attempt against the authorities or maybe the whole escapade was no more than another subterfuge in order to fulfil the prophesy, which indicated that the Jewish (Arian) people would be defeated and scattered abroad. [B7] Whatever the intention, the result was that the armed revolt was discovered by the priests, who called the Roman guard, quelled the insurrection and had Jesus led off for trial.

The Family

In this book, the probable origins of Jesus' family have been described from the most radical perspective possible and clearly the account of his early life differs significantly from the classical interpretation. There is yet another element in this new story that has been only touched on until now - the wider role of the family in the ministry of Jesus. Was Jesus really out there alone, with his mother popping her head into the odd house and enquiring as to his well-being? Surely this is not how Jewish families really organize themselves? In reality, the family was at the heart of Jesus' campaign and since it may have been well-known for its royal links, it is this part of the account in the New Testament that has suffered the greatest changes.

The clue to the altered nature of these accounts is the position of modern Christianity itself. It is supposed to be a family-orientated religion, so it is very puzzling that the church does not wish to publicize the fact that Jesus had brothers and sisters: James, Jude (sometimes translated as Judas), Joset (sometimes translated as Joses or Joseph) and Simon, plus at least two sisters. In addition, wading through the sometimes impenetrable texts of the New Testament reveals a confusing profusion of similar and deliberately muddled names. For instance, Mary, the mother of Jesus, had a sister called Mary and this Mary's child had the same name as the first Mary's. Plus, it seems that there were another four Marys in the New Testament. [B8]

Many commentators take the sister of Mary to be her sister-in-law, but Catholicism has a problem here. They do not like the idea of Jesus having had brothers and sisters, so in order to pass Mary's siblings off on to another party, the notes in the Roman Catholic Douay-Rheims Bible insist that Mary's sister was, indeed, called Mary. This might seem rather an oversight on the behalf of their parents:

> These were the children of Mary ... the sister of our Blessed Lady.

The reason for these multiple Mary's in the Bible is firstly that the name can be considered as more of a title than a name, just like Sarah meaning princess. Secondly it is to confuse the extent of the family's involvement in Jesus' ministry. For instance Mary the mother of Jesus can now be confused with Mary her sister, or perhaps Mary Magdalene and so the role of the latter Mary in later traditions can be obscured. Although this has become convenient for the Catholic church, in particular, it is appears to be something of a double-edged sword.

As a quid pro quo, the descendants of the family of Jesus, often known as the Grail family, could easily portray Jesus with a young woman, describing her as the Mother of Jesus and avoid the suspicions of the inquisition. They could even call the work 'Mary and Jesus' without reproach, despite the fact that the scene was a blatant portrayal of Jesus and Mary Magdalene. Deciding which Mary was intended becomes an individual's choice; for Catholics, it is mother and son, for the Grail family it is husband and wife. Each can look on the work with pride and joy, but what they perceive is utterly different.

A famous example of this is the Pietà sculpture by Michelangelo, commissioned in 1497. People can see what they want to see in this composition – the crucified Jesus resting on the lap of his beautiful mother Mary. Yet Mary is depicted in the sculpture as being several years *younger* than Jesus. Michelangelo apparently explained that this was just artistic licence in order to make Mary more beautiful, but it is apparent to many people with more open minds that this is a depiction of the Grail family, of Jesus and his *wife* Mary Magdalene. It must bring some wry satisfaction to these people to see a Grail family portrait placed in St. Peter's in the heart of the Vatican.

In the later Florentine Pietà, also by Michelangelo, the sculptor has become bolder and the Magdalene is shown together with some younger children, as she is in a window of the Templar church of St. Croix, Bordeaux. These children are undoubtedly part of the Grail family. The church of St. Croix even has a window that appears to show the presentation of a grandchild to the Magdalene.

Deliberate Confusion

In addition to these multiple Marys in the Bible, there is further confusion for the biblical scholar. There are up to four Josephs, three Judases, four Simons and five Jameses. There are also four men with different names – Joseph, Cleophas, Simon, Alphaeus – who appear to have sons with the same names – James, Jude Joset and Simon. [B9] In addition, at least two of them – Joseph and Cleophas – are married to Marys, [B10] and quite possibly Simon was married to a Mary as well.

> a. Is this not the 'carpenter's' son? Is not his mother called Mary, and his brethren, James, and Joses [Joseph], and Simon, and Judas? And his sisters, are they not all with us?
> b. And Mary the mother of James and Joses, and the mother of Zebedee's children.
> c. Mary Magdalene and Mary the mother of James the Less and of Joses, and Salome.
> d. Mary Magdalene, and Joanna, and Mary the mother of James ...
> e. ... his mother [Mary], and his mothers sister [Martha or Elizabeth], Mary the wife of Cleophas, and Mary Magdalene.

f. James the son of Alphaeus, Simon Zelotes and Judas the brother of James.
g. Judas Iscariot, Simon's son.

Not only is this confusing, but it smacks of a cover-up. Confuse the names and you can cover up the true identity of the characters. Cover up the identities and no one needs to know that most of the disciples were actually a part of Jesus' own family. Nothing makes sense under the orthodox interpretation. All the Marys above (a-e) were present at the crucifixion and/or the tomb and yet they are all so similar. It is obvious that some of them, at least, are the same person. However, claiming that these Marys are the same person implies that Joseph, the father of Jesus, is also called Alpheus and Cleophas. As Alpheus is the father of the disciples James and Jude, it would now appear that the brothers of Jesus were also two of his primary disciples.

While complicated to disentangle, it does make sense for some of these multiple characters to be identified as one and the same. It certainly clears up the mystery of why Joseph disappeared from the accounts shortly after the birth of Jesus. In this new interpretation of the gospels, he did not disappear, he just changed name once or twice, possibly putting in a final appearance as Joseph of Arimathea. This, in turn, implies that Jesus' family was much more powerful than the church claims. This would be especially so if wealthy and powerful characters, such as Joseph of Arimathea, prove to be part of the family. It also suggest that the New Testament was orchestrated by 'the family'. So, despite the church's promotion of family life, this particular family had to be disassembled and cast to the winds.

It appears that Jesus' inner circle of initiates was not a band of 12 disciples, but an even smaller group. Perhaps the inner core consisted of the disciples that the Gospel of John omitted from his text. The other disciples may have been a degree or two higher than the laity, but the inner knowledge was based firmly around the family and Jesus' brothers. This preference for siblings may be partly due to the fact that some of the disciples were none too bright. Nathanael, for instance, was impressed enough to believe in Jesus simply because Jesus had seen him under a fig tree.

> Jesus answered ... Because I said unto thee, I saw you under the fig tree, believest thou? Thou shall surely see greater things than these. [B11]

Educated or not, the run-of-the-mill disciples were not worthy of the arcane knowledge at the core of the Nazarene church. In other words, even those working within it would have been unlikely to be told the truth about the church's secrets:

> Oh faithless and perverse [disciples], how long shall I be with you? How long shall I suffer you?
> But they [the disciples] understood not this saying, and it was hid from them, that they perceived it not. [B12]

Here we have one of the central problems facing the gospel writers or their later translators and copiers. It could not be revealed that Jesus' role had been orchestrated by his own family, so the crucial part played by his brothers within the Nazarene church had to be obscured. The orthodox line was to distance his brothers from their roles as disciples, but, in reality, nothing could be further from the truth. The names of Jesus' brothers are nearly all names of disciples – James, Jude, Joset and Simon. Not only this, but his brother James is named as a disciple in Acts and he is recognized as being the leader of the church after the death of Jesus. He could not have become the leader of the Nazarenes without being deeply involved in the church.

> But other of the apostles saw I none, save James the Lord's brother. [B13]

This provokes further questions, for if James was one of the disciples, what about the other brothers? What about Judas? That is a deeply vexing problem and there appears to have been even greater concealment. However, before considering the identity of Judas, it is necessary to make a detour and look at the Gospel of John, which is central to the decoding of the true identity of this disciple. The three synoptic gospels of Matthew, Mark and Luke are generally held to have been committed to paper in their current form about 50 -100 years after the ministry of Jesus. While they differ on many points, nevertheless from their similar content and form, they are recognized as having drawn their information from a common source and upon each other. Hence they are known as the synoptic gospels .

The source of the gospels would have included both oral accounts and whatever written text or texts survived the defeat of the Jewish uprising of AD 74 and the sacking of Jerusalem. This does not preclude the inclusion of some first-hand knowledge from surviving sections of the Essene (Nazarene) community. While Rome subjugated all of Israel, wars are not global events and although the Roman advance on Jerusalem would have been devastating, some of the towns and communities in Galilee, for instance, may not have seen so much as a centurion. Indeed, the town of Tiberias on Lake Galilee opened the gates to the Romans and welcomed them in. Here, in Jesus' home province, any number of records and personalities may have survived the devastation.

It should also be remembered that these texts, dating from the post-revolt era, were written by either Jews or Semitic Greeks for a Romanized/Jewish ear. It would have been folly to circulate any blatantly anti-Roman material at that period. Of these surviving texts, much of the resulting New Testament actually resulted from the scribblings of the apostle Saul. It is difficult to know how much influence Saul had on the four canonical gospels, but he certainly had a direct role in fourteen letters and in Acts. As many of the church's tenets were based on the church of Saul, it is unlikely that he would have embraced the four main gospels without having them checked first. If Saul were involved, there is no doubt that the texts were altered to be favourable to his own position.

Saul was a man who had worked for the Romans in the arrest and killing of Christians, but he converted into being an apostle of Jesus after a blinding flash of inspiration on the 'road to Damascus'. [B14] However, in his European travels, he showed all the signs of having turned his back on the Nazarenes and embraced the Romans once more. In his organization of the fledgling Christian church, he used Roman influences and infrastructures, so it is no surprise that the Romans are presented in a favourable light in the gospels, with Jesus' death being firmly blamed on the Jews.

The fourth gospel, that of John, is very different. In fact, there is no reason to believe that the author was called John, as his name is not mentioned. The name John comes from a later tradition. Although the fourth gospel is often ascribed to a slightly later era than that of the synoptics, the Muratorian Fragment contradicts this. This parchment, dating from the second century AD, was found by Lodovico Muratori in the Ambrosian library, Milan, in 1740. It simply states that:

The third book of the gospels is that according to Luke, the well-

> known physician. The fourth book of the gospels is that of John, *one of the disciples*. (my italics.)

The contents and nature of John's text differ considerably from the synoptic gospels. It contains nothing of the early life of Jesus and, in places, the text is almost Gnostic in its style. While the synoptic gospels seem more confident about their story in the northern province of Galilee, John concentrates on and has more knowledge of the events in Jerusalem, where the chronology leading up to the crucifixion is quite different. Some theological commentators have described John's Gospel as the most reliable of the four. He clearly had sources that were not available to the other gospel writers and included passages that are unique in style and content. Only John described the marriage [of Jesus] at Cana, the raising of Lazarus, the unique relationship of the 'loved disciple' and the true interpretation of rebuilding the temple in three days (a reference to rebuilding the temple of Jesus' body in three days, the resurrection, and nothing to do with the physical temple in Jerusalem).

It is also interesting to note what John omitted from his narrative, the nativity being one item and the names of most of the disciples another; John mentions only five disciples. James, son of Alpheus, now identified as Jesus' brother, is among the missing names, as is Thomas (until half-way through the text), Simon and Thaddeus, who was also called Judas. These happen to be the names of most of Jesus' brothers - even Thomas will soon fit into this category. Were they left out on purpose? Returning, however, to the original question, concerning the identity of Judas, what does the gospel writer John have to say of him? There is a way of identifying Judas' family history by reconciling the confused morass of names that appear time and again, predominantly in this enigmatic gospel.

The betrayer of Jesus, Judas, could not be left out of the script because he had such a central role in the events that followed the Last Supper. The prophesy called for a betrayal and Judas, like it or not, was about to fulfil the prophesy. Did Judas have any choice in this? I think that he did, because I think that he was Jesus' brother. Following the logic becomes quite complicated in places because the Bible has deliberately made it so. For further clarification, see the family tree on the following page.

a. Jesus had a brother called James and so too did the

disciple Judas. Therefore, the possibility exists that James, Jesus and Judas were all brothers. (Some Bibles have mis-translated this and give Judas as being the son of James) [B15]

b. The reference used in a. above also seems to indicate that the disciples Judas and James had a common brother called Simon. Remember that the brothers of Jesus were called James, Jude Joset and Simon.

c. The father of the disciples Judas and James was called Alphaeus. The identity of this shadowy character Alphaeus is not given, but the father of this Judas is also given as being Simon. [B16]

d. Thus, the fathers called Simon and Alphaeus appear to be the same person. Alphaeus is either a title meaning 'the first' or the 'first father', or is a term meaning 'successor'. Either of these options may be a clue to the social standing of Judas' father, for the former translation is rather like the wife of the United States president being called the 'first lady' and the second version indicates that he will inherit a title or position. [B17]

This is a reasonable case for believing that Judas Iscariot may have been one of Jesus' brothers. As the process of unravelling this confusion of names in the Gospel of John continues, a deeper mystery can be uncovered. There is another curious character in this gospel, an unnamed disciple whom Jesus 'loved'. This is a puzzle crying out for a solution, for there must have been a good reason to include this unnamed, but loved disciple who runs in and out of the narrative at the most important junctures. Who was this man and why the secrecy?

Loved One

The first point of interest is that there are the parallels between Lazarus, the man raised from the dead, and the 'loved disciple'. (Lazarus was described earlier as undertaking the Masonic third degree ritual.)

a. On many occasions, Jesus is described as loving Lazarus. [B18]
Jesus loved Martha, and her sister, and Lazarus.
Then said the Jews, Behold how he loved him [Lazarus]!
Lord, behold, he [Lazarus] whom thou lovest is sick.

b. Jesus also loved the unnamed disciple. [B19]
... one of the disciples, whom Jesus loved.
... and the disciple standing by, whom he loved.
... and to the other disciple, whom Jesus loved.
Therefore the disciple whom Jesus loved saith unto Peter.

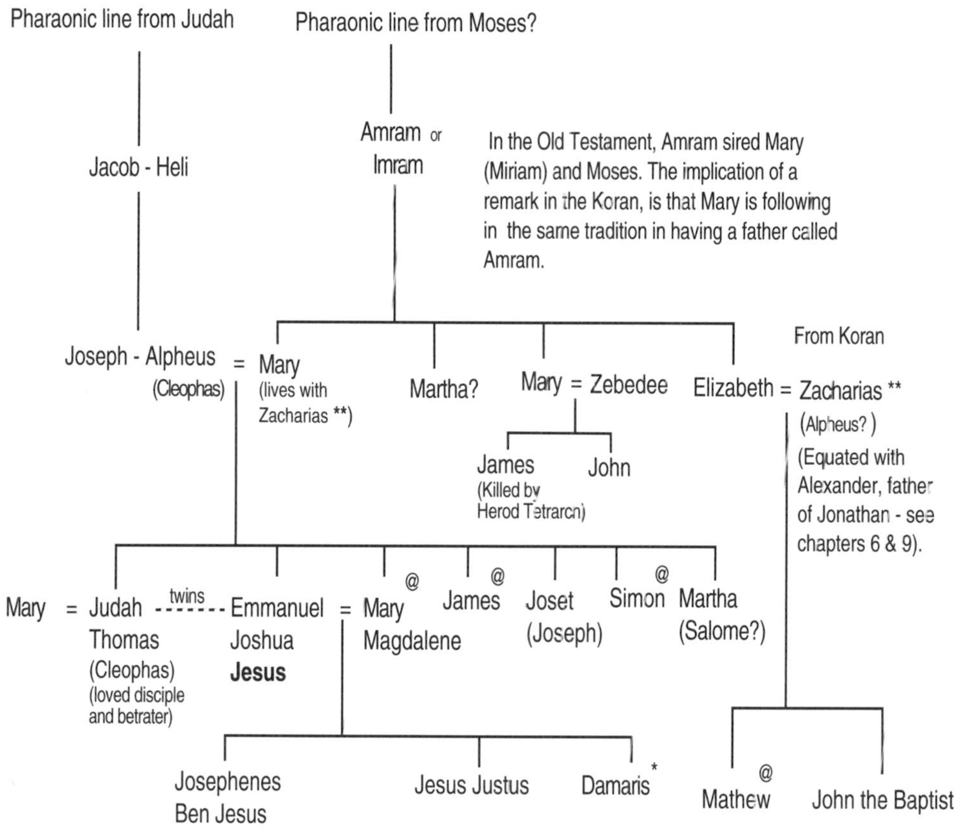

Fig 22. Family tree of Jesus

In addition to these parallels, the two characters are never seen together. It is possible, therefore, that Lazarus and the unnamed 'loved disciple' are the same person. This would explain the apparent disappearance of such an important character as Lazarus so early in the narrative. In this case, he did not disappear, but, as is so often the case in the gospels, he simply had a name change and became the 'loved disciple'.

There is yet another step to be taken in the translation of these names. Remember that the 'loved disciple' was just that - a disciple - whereas Lazarus was not. So where does Lazarus (a translation of Elizar, the Sun God) fit in among the names of 12 disciples?

a. Judas was privileged enough to rest his head on the breast of Jesus. [B20]

He [Judas] then lying on Jesus' breast saith unto him, Lord, who is it?

b. Judas betrayed Jesus with a kiss. [B21]

Whomsoever I shall kiss, that same is he.

c. Judas was the trusted disciple of Jesus, in that he was allowed to carry the group's money bag and take care of their finances. [B22] In this respect Judas is being portrayed as being the closest disciple to Jesus and quite possibly trusted enough to be known as the 'loved disciple'.

d. Jesus declared the unnamed 'loved disciple', as being his mother's son, in other words, his own brother; yet Jesus had a brother called Judas. This is sometimes interpreted as being only a measure of Jesus' respect for the unnamed disciple, but it could also be a clever device of the author John. It was a way of indicating to the world that the 'loved disciple' – Lazarus – was, in fact, the real brother of Jesus, without actually saying so.

When Jesus therefore saw his mother, and the disciple standing by, whom he loved; he saith unto his mother, Woman, behold thy son. [B23]

So is the loved disciple really Judas? If so, the multiplicity of his names is becoming more complicated by the minute. If this were the case, he would then make an entry into the story as Judas, have a leading role in the events at Bethany in the guise of Lazarus, spend most of the Last Supper and Jesus' trial as the enigmatic 'loved' disciple and, possibly, end his career dictating his story to John, the gospel writer. More evidence of this follows:

a. The Gospel of John clearly indicates that Judas and the

'loved disciple' are the same person.

> *Then Peter, turning about, sees the disciple whom Jesus loved following; which also leaned on his breast at supper, and said Lord, which is he that betrayeth thee?* [B24]

In the clearest of terms, John is saying that the 'loved disciple' is Judas. It is quite obviously Judas who laid his head on Jesus' breast at the last supper and, just in case that hint is not enough, Peter also says 'who betrayed you'. We know that Judas betrayed Jesus, but at the time, it would seem that Peter was not so sure. He had his suspicions, because of Judas' convenient disappearance at the Last Supper, but he could not declare so openly. So now we know. Identifying the 'loved disciple' as Judas makes it possible to reinterpret the whole of the New Testament.

b. Here is one new fact to start. The Gospel of John now clearly states that this gospel was narrated or written by Judas himself. The author describes Judas as being 'that disciple [that] should not die', and says in the next verse ...

> *This is the disciple which testifieth these things, and wrote these things: and we know that his testimony is true.* [B25]

The gospel writer John, wrote the tale at the dictation of Judas himself and further evidence that underlines this theory will be presented later. For John to be Judas' confidant, it is likely that they were close socially, so was he, in fact, John, Judas' brother? The account does say that a disciple wrote this gospel and James and John were, apparently, both disciples.

There are some further ramifications to this discovery, which will explain some big very big questions that have remained unanswered in the Bible for far too long. For instance, if Jesus so loved a particular disciple, who was sufficiently important to have access to the high priest [B26] and influential enough to be called Jesus' brother in public, [B27] why could he not be named in the Bible? Why did Jesus defend Judas, the 'loved disciple', after the 'resurrection' and against the advice of his disciple Peter? Why did he allow Judas to remain within the church as a disciple, despite his having betrayed Jesus to the Romans? Instead, he defended Judas and rebuked Peter:

> Jesus saith unto him (Peter). If I will that he (Judas) tarry till I come, what is that to thee? follow thou me. [B28]

If the characters of Judas, Lazarus and the mysterious 'loved disciple' are amalgamated into a single figure and Judas himself was Jesus' brother, the answers are obvious. Of course, Jesus would defend him, especially as Judas was only doing what he had been asked to do. It is an interesting and very persuasive theory. However, in making this link between Judas and Jesus, the story of the New Testament naturally became radically altered and it is no wonder that the church would do all in its power to distance the New Testament from this interpretation. The New Testament story now becomes:

a. Judas as Lazarus underwent an initiation into the church of the Nazarene. This was a typical Masonic third degree initiation with symbolic death and rebirth. The rite was performed by Jesus on his brother at their own house in Bethany. (Simon's house where Mary and Judas (Lazarus) lived). A miracle performed in your own home on your own brother is not quite so outstanding as the Bible version and this was one reason why the family connections were obscured. The event was stage managed on two levels. The initiated few knew it was a ritual, the sisters and others not in the inner circle thought it was a miracle.

b. Judas, as a beloved brother, was asked to do the ultimate favour for him. To fulfil the prophesies of the Messiah, Judas was asked to 'betray' Jesus, so that he could fulfil his destiny and perpetuate the dynasty. As the beloved brother, how could he refuse this request? That this was an inner family secret and a conspiracy is plainly spelt out in the Gospel of John. After the Last Supper, while they are relaxing, with the 'loved disciple' reclining on his chest, Jesus predicts that he will be betrayed. He then gives a sign to Judas, to initiate the betrayal:

> *Then said Jesus unto him [Judas]. That thou doest, do quickly. Now no man at the table knew for what intent he spake this unto him. For some of them thought, because Judas had the bag, that Jesus had said to him, Buy those things that we have need of against the feast, or that he should give something to the poor.* [B29]

As the texts say, none of the disciples knew what was going on. A major secret was kept, not just from the followers of the Nazarene church, but from the disciples themselves. The secret was that

Jesus *wanted* to be betrayed. The plan was so radical that nobody knew, except Jesus and Judas.

However, despite the fact that 'no man at the table knew for what intent he spake', the author of the Gospel of John knew of this secret. How did he know and why did the other gospel writers not report this crucial event? Once more, John shows his direct line to sensitive inside information within the church; such details could have come only from Jesus or Judas. It has been suggested by some theologans that Lazarus wrote the fourth gospel, others indicate that it was the 'loved disciple' whom they identify as someone called St. John. This hypothesis takes this to its ultimate conclusion and indicates that all of these characters are the same. Whatever the case, it can be seen that the author of the Gospel of John was given information directly by Judas.

c. Judas, narrating his story to the gospel writer John, now had a problem. He was aware of his pariah status because of his betrayal, but he still wished to portray to readers his previous status as being Jesus' favourite. He was unable to name himself in the sections of the narrative that include the 'loved disciple', as this role contradicted his other of betrayer and would give the game away. Judas the loved brother, by necessity, became the unnamed disciple.

d. Judas was obviously distressed by his situation; he had paid a high price for his loyalty. His constant references to the 'loved disciple' in such beseeching terms were a subtle effort somehow to redeem his acquired character of pariah of the church. The pleading nature of John's dialogue is so apparent, it almost makes one cringe. Judas' new role would have been all the harder for him to bear, knowing that he was really a favourite brother and had only been following Jesus' orders, yet to redeem himself fully would have given the lie to the nature of the betrayal. Equally, he could not call himself Lazarus all the way through the gospel, because the shadowy unnamed disciple had to be a disciple to explain his actions and Lazarus was not. In any case, Lazarus had to be kept separate from the disciples because of the nature of his 'resurrection'; that it was symbolic and not real. Hence, the need for two names. Judas trod a fine line in his narrative and he succeeded brilliantly, but it must have been with a heavy heart.

e. In deciding on the final outcome of all this, the final exchange between Jesus and Peter in John's Gospel is crucial. It is frequently overlooked, yet it is quite clear what is being said. The date was after the crucifixion, Jesus was talking with Peter, with Judas trailing slightly behind. The text can be translated as follows:

> *Peter, seeing the loved one (Judas), says [knowingly]:*
> *'Lord, which one of us betrayed you? ... What shall this man do?'*
> *Jesus replies: 'If I want Judas to stay, it is none of your business. Do as you are told and follow me.'*
> *This was quoted among the disciples and it was interpreted as meaning that this disciple will never die. But Jesus did not say that, he said if I want Judas to stay among us it is none of your business.* [B30]

It is clear that Peter still did not know what was going on. He did not know why Jesus was betrayed, why he was crucified or why he was miraculously there once more, as if raised from the dead. He certainly did not understand why Jesus was defending the very person who betrayed him, causing his crucifixion. It is equally clear that Judas did not die at this point in time, although the strains were beginning to show between Judas and some of the uninitiated disciples. For the moment, Jesus and his brother Judas were left at the end of the narrative of John 'walking into the sunset', no doubt analysing in minute detail the reasons for their present failure and plotting their strategy for the future.

Didymos

So why was Judas the favourite brother of Jesus? That may seem to be a peculiar question, but it would seem that there was something about Judas that made him unique; what was it? If the truth were known, he was Jesus' *twin* brother. This suggestion is not as bizarre as it may sound, as something very similar to this is already widely accepted in academic theological circles, that Jesus had a twin. The question is, which of the brothers was he?

The translators of the Nag Hammadi collection of scrolls, ascribe the position of the twin brother of Jesus to the disciple Thomas. In the

Bible, the disciple Thomas was also called Didymos, but both of these names simply mean 'twin', in Aramaic and Greek respectively. In this case we still do not have a name for this disciple, just his position within his family. Once more one can only suspect scribal sleight of hand to be at work here. The Bible says very little about the disciple Thomas, so his family history is unknown, in this case who was Thomas?

In the Nag Hammadi scrolls there is a possible answer. There are two gospels written by Thomas in this collection and in both he claims the position of the twin *of Jesus*. He writes:

> The saviour said, 'Brother Thomas, while you have time in the world, listen to me ... Now since it has been said that you are my twin and true companion, examine yourself and learn ... So then, you, my brother Thomas, have beheld what is obscure to men, that is, what they ignorantly stumble against'. [N31]

Again it is being made plain that there are secrets being held within the Nazarene church, but once more we must ask, which of the brothers of Jesus was Thomas? The Gospel of Thomas finally provides an answer, Didymos Judas Thomas. Was this the same Judas who we have traced through the records as being Judas the betrayer, brother of Jesus?

In the Gospel of John, Thomas is the disciple who was not initially present to see the 'resurrected' Jesus and who later doubted that Jesus had survived the crucifixion – the doubting Thomas. In the Gospel of Luke, two of the disciples are also absent, they wander off to a local town and are later met by Jesus. This story of two disciples wandering off appears to be the same story as the Peter and Judas episode in the Gospel of John, that we have just covered. It reads like three versions of the same event. One gospel indicates that Thomas was not present, the next says it was Peter and Judas, the third gospel, Luke, names one of the two as a previously unknown disciple, Cleophas. Can these three stories be referring to the same individual?

Cleophas' wife Mary was at the crucifixion, with all the other Marys, but which of the disciples was he? Cleophas is simply another translation of Alpheus, in other words this disciple is possibly being equated with the father of Jesus. While it is possible that this person is Jesus' father, that would only further confuse the issue of which Marys were which. In the Gospel of John, however, the pair who had wandered off were identified as being Judas and Peter, could this provide an answer to the identity of the mysterious Cleophas?

Cleophas and Alpheus are most certainly not names, but titles; they both simply mean 'the successor' and each generation would, therefore, have a Cleophas. [32] This title would favour a connection with Judas, he being the twin brother of Jesus, it would be Judas the twin who would be next in line for the position of high priest or king. This is decisively confirmed by the Nag Hammadi gospels, where the full title of Thomas is eventually given as 'Didimos Judas Thomas the contender' or 'Judas the twin and contender'. There could not be a better simile to the position of Judas Cleophas, the successor. Thus Judas was not only Jesus' twin, but also the heir apparent and if one were to trust their life to someone, who better to ask than a twin brother and heir.

But the grand plan must have failed at some point, for it was brother James who became the next leader of the Nazarene church. What became of Judas the twin? Perhaps the tensions between those of the inner circle and the other disciples became too great, Judas had forever stained his reputation. The Bible claims that he died, legends indicate that he travelled into the east, particularly to Edessa and possibly as far as India, where he established Nazarene congregations and churches. [N33] What is fairly certain is that a place within the twelve disciples became vacant, as we shall see in chapter VIII. Undoubtedly this was the position vacated by Judas and it was to be the enigmatic Saul who vainly tried to fill that position.

Sisters

To return to Jesus' sisters, they were mentioned, but not named in the Bible. This absence of their names is central to this quest. In the multiplication of the same characters in the Bible that has already been commented on, something else has happened. Mary Magdalene, contrary to the opinions of the orthodox Christian churches, has been described as Jesus' wife in many sources, including the Nag Hammadi scrolls. In addition to the examples already quoted, it is stated in the Bible that Jesus loved Mary, [B34] and in the Gospel of Philip it is said of Mary:

> He loved her more than the disciples and used to kiss her often on the lips. They said to him, why do you love her more than us? The Saviour answered and said to them, Why do I not love you like her?... [35]

Plate 19. Sun and pyramid imagery for the Christian saints, Tomb of Caroli VI, St. Nicholas, Prague.

Plate 20. Sun imagery for the saints, Palma Cathedral, Mallorca.

Plate 21 . Sun imagery, Melk Cathedral, Lower Austria.

Plate 22. Egyptian side curls. These denoted a youth, or perhaps an initiate.

Plate 23. Orthodox Jewish side curls. Traditionally two side curls are worn, does this signify the initiated?

Plate 24. The Taule at Talati de Dalt, Minorca. The straight lintel is less reminiscent of the horns of a bull, and more so of the Egyptian hieroglyph for a ram.

Plate 25. The Taule at Torralba d'en Salord, Minorca.

Plate 26. Bull headed god of Egypt, note the upright horns.

Plate 27. Ram headed god, note the horizontal horns.

Plate 28. Cult of the Ram, which finally became acceptable during the reign of Ramesses II at Karnak, Thebes. The curly horns betray the later period of their construction.

Plate 29. Nuraghi Tintirriolu, Macomer, Sardinia.

Plate 30. Erismanzanu Nuraghi, Esporlatu, Goceano, Sardinia

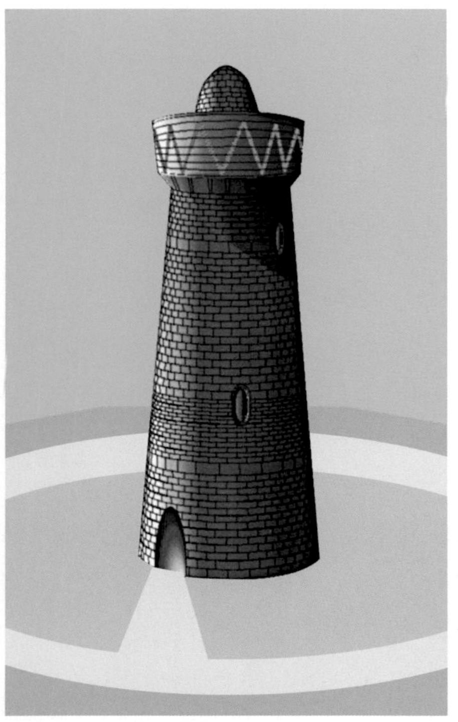

Plate 31. Artists impression of a Nuraghi tower, based on ancient bronze models.

Plate 32. Kalyan Minaret in the city of Bokhara, Uzbekistan. Note entrance door and bridge above ground level.

Plate 33. Khiva Minaret, Uzbekistan. A modern copy of the Kalyan tower in Bokhara.

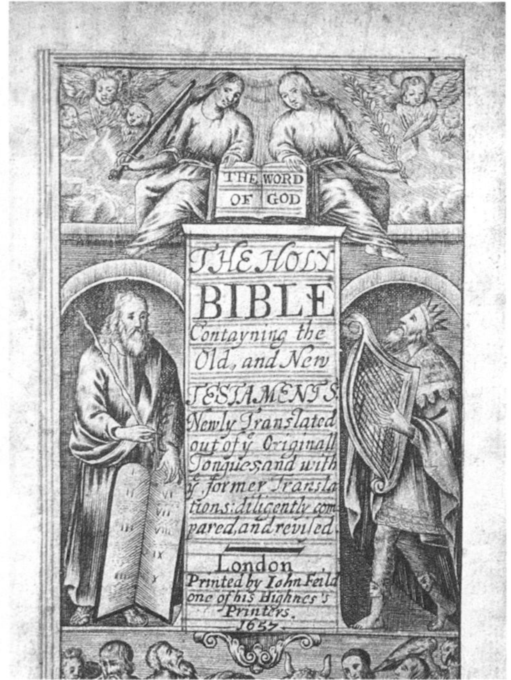

THE WORD OF GOD

THE HOLY BIBLE Contayning the Old, and New TESTAMENTS Newly Translated out of y Originall Tongues and with y former Translations diligently compared and revised

London
Printed by Iohn Feild one of his Highnes's Printers.
1657

Plate 34. The Word of God. An early Bible, dating from the year Cromwell was offered the throne of England.

Plate 35. Monasterboice tower, Drogheda, Eire.

Plate 36. Domhnach tower, Slane, Eire. Note the conical top.

Plate 37. Entrance to the round tower at Monasterboice. The monastery was founded in the C5th and the tower ruined in 1097.

Plate 38. Entrance to the round tower at Domhnach Mor, on the Boyne. The monastery was founded in the C6th and the tower was built in the C12th.

Plate 39. Egyptian obelisk, Fontana dei Quattro Fiumi, Rome.

Plate 40. The Treasury of Atreus at Mycenae, Greece. Note the design of the 'roof-box' above the entrance, which takes the form of the Egyptian hieroglyph for 'pyramid', also the similar design of Newgrange (overleaf).

Plate 41. Egyptian obelisk, Piazza di san Pietro (St. Peter's), Vatican city.

Plate 42. The mid-winters sun shining through the 'roof-box' at Newgrange. Only sunlight from the roof-box enters the deepest recesses of the henge and illuminates the sacred central chamber.

Plate 43. Masonic Grand Lodge, Holborn, London. The two pillars are representations of the pillars of Jachin and Boaz, from the temple of Solomon in Jerusalem. Above these are the celestial and terrestrial spheres, as were represented in Solomon's temple, this indicates that the spherical form of the Earth was known by the Israelites and they most probably derived this knowledge from Egypt. See *Thoth, Architect of the Universe* for more details.

In the Bible it says that Mary remained in the house at Bethany instead of greeting Jesus; this again was a wife's custom of sitting in Shiveh, waiting for her husband's command to cease mourning (for Lazarus).

> Then Martha, as soon as she heard that Jesus was coming, went and met him: but Mary sat still in the house. [B36]

That the Mary of Bethany and Mary Magdalene are linked is confirmed by the description of them both being 'fallen women' or sinners. The evidence repeatedly points to Mary (Magdalene) being the wife of Jesus. However, there is a problem in this theory and not just the classical insistence of the church that Jesus was a celibate monk. Mary, Martha, and Lazarus lived together in the house of Simon, in Bethany. [B37] Simon's identity is not explicitly given, but it is clear that, with Lazarus being equated with Judas, Simon was a close member of the family, if not Jesus' father. It was the family's second home, within easy 'commuting distance' of Jerusalem. The main family castle was in Galilee and will be discussed in Chapter VIII.

Not only did Mary 'live' in this house, she was also Lazarus' sister. [B38] If it is accepted that Lazarus was a pseudonym for Judas, then Mary was also Judas' sister. Joseph, not only had sons by the names of Jesus, Judas, James, Joset and Simon, he also had at least two daughters. These can now be identified as Martha and Mary. Since these events took place in the family home at Bethany, the house where Mary sat waiting for her husband, it is a reasonable assumption that Mary, the wife of Jesus, was also Mary his sister.

Such a proposition may seem preposterous in the light of classical Christian dogma, but it seems likely that this dogma has come about only because the church of Saul was keen to distance itself from anything to do with the Nazarene church. If, however, the Old Testament Bible is used as guide, marriage between a brother and sister was not the heinous crime that it is now thought. Although the book of Leviticus prohibits marriage to a sister, the book of Genesis describes both Abraham and Isaac as introducing their wives to friendly monarchs/ pharaohs as being their sisters, as has already been mentioned. The reason for this is likely to have been because their wives were, indeed, their sisters.

Indeed Abraham declares that his wife is his half-sister, but even this relationship is forbidden in Leviticus and their relationship may have been even closer than that. There is also the strange tale of Lot, who had sons by both his daughters. The poor excuse being given for this being that, concerned that they would find no husbands, the daughters got their father drunk and had sex with him. [B39]

None of these stories makes any sense in the classical interpretation of Judaic theology, but they make every sense in terms of Egyptian theology. For the royal family in particular, marriage to a sister was far from being a sin, it was a duty. It was the sacred duty of a pharaoh to continue the bloodline. Ancient traditions maintained that although the male line held the high office of pharaoh, the bloodline ran through the female line, just as it does in Judaism to this day. For sons to inherit the direct bloodline of their father's ancestors, it was their duty to marry their sister or, sometimes, even their daughter. This practice was repeated in every royal marriage in Egypt: the chief wife of the pharaoh was always an immediate relative.

This was why the marriage of Amenhotep III to the daughter of his vizier was so strange. For the normal rules to operate, the vizier had to have been a direct relation of the pharaoh – and he was, through Joseph. This practice of intermarriage continues in royal circles, but with modern Christian taboos on consanguinity, the technique is similar to that of Amenhotep III and his vizier. Two parallel family lines run side by side and the descendants intermarry, so that the bloodline is maintained in its 'pure' state through the female line, but for social convenience the children marry only their cousins. [40]

This tradition even makes a strange sort of sense biologically. Not only is genetic material carried in the nuclei of cells, it is also present in what are called the mitochondria. The only genetic material that does not get jumbled up during human reproduction, is carried in the mitochondria and it is inherited by sons and daughters alike exclusively from the mother. Therefore, anyone wishing to trace a biological genealogy must trace these genetic packages in the female line.

Most people have been so deluded by modern Christian propaganda that they believe that the children of a brother and sister will somehow automatically be defective. Inbreeding has become a byword for the creation of cretins and imbeciles, but this is not so. The following is from a medical encyclopaedia:

> It was once widely held that human inbreeding inevitably gave rise to 'degenerative' characteristics. This probably arose from false generalisations from particular cases. Inbreeding will, of course, greatly increase the chances that offspring will be

> homozygous for recessive characteristics, *but to argue from this that all inbreeding will necessarily produce adverse results is fallacious.*
>
> Few social scientists, however, now believe that this idea was the origin of the incest taboo, and it generally accepted that the real purpose of the prohibition of sex between closely related people was to avoid the often violent consequences of sexual rivalry and jealousy, with parent-child and brother-sister relationships becoming exploitative rather than protective. [41] (my italics).

The scientific term 'homozygous for recessive characteristics' is, perhaps, central to the general approval of these intermarriage taboos. All of a person's characteristics, such as eye colour, are governed by at least two genes. One gene always tends to be *dominant*, the other subservient and is known as *recessive*. Brown eyes are dominant over blue eyes, so the 'blue eyed child' is a less common event in a family, something to be cherished. All the term 'homozygous for recessive characteristics' really means is that an individual has inherited two *recessive* genes for that particular trait, such as blue eyes. Without a dominant brown eyes gene being present, this individual will have blue eyes. Intermarriage between siblings can increase the occurrence of these recessive characteristics, which can also be hereditary diseases, as well as harmless things like eye colour. This can, therefore, appear to result in an increase in the occurrence of genetic diseases in the children of brother-sister unions.

However, the intermarriage taboo can also be a double-edged sword. If there is no intermarriage between siblings who carry the same recessive gene for a hereditary disease and the disease does not appear in the offspring, it can continue to be passed down the generations, building up unseen within the population. If these particular families are successful, there can then come a time when it is hard to avoid marriage to someone with the same recessive gene and the characteristic appears in the children anyway, like the abundance of blue eyes in Southern Ireland. Blue eyes are not a problem to a population, but if the recessive gene is for a disease, then at some time in the future the population is going to be in trouble. Intermarriage and the possible occurrence of a hereditary disease may be unfortunate for the individual, but if it results in no further children, then the potential for that disease in subsequent generations will be lost.

All in all, the chances of hereditary defects appearing, when averaged over many generations, is the same for marriage between immediate relatives as it is for marriage between unrelated couples. The *real* disadvantage to constant intermarriage within a family is the resulting lack of genetic diversity within that family, each generation is placing all its genetic eggs in one basket. If the genetic root stock of the family is good, all the generations will prosper. If the root stock is poor or something happens that affects only that genetic type, all the family will fail. Sometimes, it is wise to have a few survivors in the family, in times of hardship – a few eggs in a different basket.

Part of the reason for the evolution of the intermarriage taboo is because of these 'false generalisations of individual cases' and perhaps because of the very real fears of social tensions within families in societies that condone sibling marriage. Mix those rivalries with the lubricant of power and the result is the decimation that occurred within the royal family of Herod the Great. However, the primary reason for these taboos has to be the rejection of all things Egyptian. These rules were devised after the exodus, but it is clear from the constant complaints of the priesthood that the kings of Jerusalem used to flaunt the regulations; intermarriage was not simply the prerogative of Herod the Great.

The law only became applicable to the (now Christian) royal families after the Jewish Wars and this was mainly due to the position of Saul. He wanted to crush the Nazarene church, as we shall see, and preventing the ancient traditions of Nazarene marriage and inheritance was a quick and simple method of achieving this. The marriage laws were made for social stability within the general population; they were later applied to the royal family for political expediency, not biological reasons.

Last of the Pharaohs

Intermarriage was the duty of a pharaoh and Jesus may have followed this ancient tradition. This long and exclusive tradition of the sister/wife continued through the subsequent generations of the Grail family and even King Arthur of the Britons purportedly followed in the pharaonic footsteps. It would seem that he, too, married his half sister Morgaine and, according to Laurence Gardner, for the same reasons as the pharaohs; to continue the bloodline. [42]

This new interpretation of Jesus' ministry reveals an entirely new character in Jesus from the one peddled by the church – with a royal and yet very human face. Here was a man who suffered frustration with his followers, was capable of flashes of anger, was skilled in political duplicity, yet detested and was forced to flee the crowds. He was a man of wealth and influence with royal blood.

In the light of the facts that Jesus considered himself to be fathered by the gods, was a descendant of the Hyksos pharaohs of Egypt, was wealthy and aristocratic, was acknowledged as being a priest and the 'King of the Jews' and married his sister in the royal tradition; was he not one of the long line of holders of the knowledge of Thoth – the last of the pharaohs?

Such speculation may be considered the most blasphemous opinion proposed this side of Martin Luther and for it to be put into print to be a heresy worthy of the slow roasting given to Jacques de Molay, last Grand Master of the Knights Templar. This is not so. For one thing, what sort of intelligent, reasoning and logical deity would want to stamp out critical analysis of human history? Secondly, the only major change to these religions in this new interpretation, in this case to Christianity, concerns the uniqueness of Jesus' divinity. Yet the unique divine status of Jesus has always stood on uncertain ground, as Jews and Muslims will testify. Even the biblical King David was born from a union with God.

In the historical record too, there is unequivocal documentary evidence that all the Egyptian pharaohs were born through a union with the gods and, in the cases of Akhenaton and Tutankhamen, through a union with the one and only God. What then makes the self-contradictory journal of the Bible any more authoritative in this matter than the chronicles of the great Temple of Karnak? Nothing except the conventions, commands and doctrines of a self-perpetuating organization. The Egyptian priests would have said exactly the same of their religion.

In fact the Bible seems to have been written in the sure knowledge that Jesus was an Egyptian pharaoh and this evidence is to be found in his crucifixion and possible burial. In the final scene of the crucifixion Jesus lifts up his eyes to the sky and laments:

> Eli, Eli, lama sabachthani? [B43]

The cry was to God, but which one? Eli or Elias can only be a reference to Helios, the Sun God. But this was only a Greek translation,

Akhenaton would have called him Aton and the Jews took this as being Adon. This is confirmed by the title of Pandira given to Jesus, in the Talmud:

> The disciples are said to be curing the sick in the name of Yeshu ben Pandira. [T44]

The origin of this appellation has always been a mystery, with many theologians hinting that the name Ben Pandira (son of Pandira) indicated that Jesus was the illegitimate son of a Roman soldier called Pantera. A more recent interpretation by Ahmed Osman in *House of the Messiah* is probably more likely, especially in the light of the direct association with the Egyptian god Aton. The word Pandira seems to be a Hebrew transliteration of the Egyptian words Pa-Ntr-Ra. This translates as 'the god Ra' and so ben Pandira becomes 'son of the god Ra'. The Talmud was just a little more specific than the Bible about Jesus' heritage.

As already mentioned, Jesus' grandfather was also called Eli or Helios, the Sun. Both Helios and Ra, in this case, could be interpreted as another manifestation of the Aton, the Sun God of Akhenaton. This is why all the early icons of the saints depicted their heads superimposed on the disc of the Sun, some with fiery beams of light protruding from it. Later traditions saw this as a slight embarrassment and so the Sun disc was reduced to a halo. The inference remains obvious: the original god of Jesus and the Nazarene was the Aton or Ra, the Sun God of ancient Egypt and Heliopolis.

This could not be made any clearer than at the church of St. Nicholas in Mala Strana, 'the small town' sector of the city of Prague in the Czech Republic. The church was built by Jesuits in the seventeenth century and is heavily ornamented in the baroque style. The emblem on the top of the church and on the monument to king Caroli VI, that stands outside the entrance is the all-seeing eye – an eye inside a triangle – the same image that is printed on the back of the US one dollar bill. In addition, this symbology is also used as a halo; it is not circular – it is a pyramid. Heliopolis in Egypt was situated next to the great pyramids of Giza and many thousands of years later the same symbology of the Sun and the pyramids is being used in Prague as a backdrop for the Christian saints.

* * *

Death?

As the crucifixion reached its climax, Jesus finally declares 'it is finished', [B45] slumped into a stupor and the authorities hurried to take him off the cross early, in what seems to have been a rush to save him. As Jesus' last words seem to indicate, the prophesy had been fulfilled, the Messiah had been crucified, so why prolong the torture? Even Pilate was amazed by this sudden 'death' of Jesus;

> And Pilate marvelled if he were already dead; and calling unto him the centurion, he asked him [how long he had been dead]. [B46]

If Jesus survived the cross, and evidence that he did will be presented later, not all his followers were aware of it. Nicodemus, for instance, brought 100 pounds of spices and resins to the tomb for the funeral rites, an inordinately expensive amount of precious oils, even for a aristocratic individual.

> And there came also Nicodemus, which at the first came to Jesus by night and brought a mixture of myrrh and aloes, about a hundred pounds in weight. Then they took the body of Jesus, and wound it in linen clothes with spices, *as the manner of the Jews is to bury.* [B47]

These preparations were for a rather peculiar burial; is this why John pointedly states it was for a Jewish burial? Jesus was a Jew, what other kind of burial would he have? The circumstances are positively strange, the traditional Jewish burial was for the body to be left for three years to decompose and then for the bones to be collected and placed in an ossuary or casket, a process quite unlike what John is indicating. However, the tradition of soaking a body in vast quantities of oils and spices and especially treatment with resins like myrrh is a familiar custom – mummification. Note, therefore, the clear usage of the term 'wound' in this passage, this is not a shroud being draped over a cadaver in the Turin fashion. This term would apply solely to the strips of linen wound around the limbs of a mummy, so the verse above should be amended to read 'as is the manner of the Egyptians to bury'. It is quite evident that the intention was eventually for Jesus to be embalmed or mummified by his supporters.

That the Nazarenes would have been familiar with the methods of embalming is of no great surprise as the ancestors of their leaders were Egyptian pharaohs themselves. Thus King Solomon appears to have had an Egyptian burial and the Old Testament Joseph was also mummified.

> Joseph died ... they embalmed him and laid him in his coffin in Egypt. [B48]

If Jesus was indeed embalmed at the end of his life, whenever that was, one of the most important steps in the process was the removal of the internal organs. These would cause the body to decay, so they were removed and stored in canopic jars. This procedure required the embalmer to make an incision in the side of the corpse's abdomen to remove the organs. Tradition held that this incision was always in the left flank. [49] The Gospel of John is again the only testament with enough detailed inside information to know that Jesus had an incision in his side and he reports that a centurion did it with a spear. Was this so or was the body eventually seen at some point in the future, lying in state perhaps, with inquisitive devotees enquiring about this strange incision? In the light of the Egyptian connections and traditions, it just has to have been an embalmer's mark that was proving to be an embarrassment.

United Faith

To take Egyptian history as being on par with Christianity may seem a massive leap of faith to some, but it is not. Christianity, Judaism and Islam are all simply different expressions of a single Egyptian heritage. For Christianity, the only major change to the standard doctrines involves a small trade-off, one that could thought of as being beneficial in many respects. This trade involves swapping the unique divinity of Jesus for a theological history that is more than double and possibly up to five times as long as Christianity currently claims. Is this so bad?

The next chapter will consider how this strange position in theology came about. How was it that the religion of Jesus and his followers became so confused and muddled? How was a religion that was based on the worship of one invisible god, turned into a belief in three deities, one of which is distinctly humanoid – Jesus? How was the entire history of the Jewish nation used, but then side-lined as a brief afterthought in a religion that based itself upon one man's life? How did a religion arrive at a position where it hated, persecuted and murdered millions of its own theological cousins to achieve its own obscure goals. Germany's Holocaust may have been the result of nationalistic fervour, but the Vatican sat by and said nothing – after all, it was merely an extension of traditional Catholic pogroms against the Jews. All these cruel events originated with one man, who is relatively anonymous and yet who irrevocably changed the course of Western history. His name is Saul.

Chapter VIII

Evangelist

While the career of Jesus was to be long and distinguished, the life of his successor was more enigmatic. Here was a man who was a self-confessed liar; a 'chameleon' who was able to change his religion, allegiances and name, simply to suit his own ends. Who was this man? He was Saul, the 'founder' of Christianity, who called himself Paul when the occasion suited:

> And unto the Jews I became a Jew, that I might gain the Jews... To them that are without law, (I became) outside the law... that I might gain them outside the law... To the weak I became as weak, that I might gain the weak. I am made all things to all men. [B1]

Such was the character of the man who founded one of the great religions of the world. Saul was a curious character from whichever angle he is studied. He was one of the most important individuals in the last 2,000 years of history and yet we know very little about him. In fact, apart from the history given in the Bible, which was mostly penned by himself or his colleagues, we do not know even who he was. Is that not a little strange? How did this individual evade the pens of his supporters, his critics and the contemporary historians? Just who was he?

Despite the fact that the identity of Saul has been a mystery for nearly two millennia, it is my belief that I have identified him in the historical record. That does not make me a professional historian with insights into history that are in advance of classical historians throughout history. I believe that many historians in the past must have seen what I have seen; the difference is that I am able to consider the consequences, for the outcome of this identification of the historical Saul is formidable.

The problem for historians with even the slightest respect for the Christian doctrines is that, in making this identification, there are certain concepts that rather undermine classical Christianity. One of these effects is that Jesus must have been alive in the period running up to the Jewish rebellion. To put that in perspective, this date was some three decades after his 'crucifixion'. It is no wonder that if this link has ever been seen before, it has been rejected.

Saul

To make the association, it is necessary first to look at a little of the life of Saul. Who was this man? It should be noted first of all, that Christianity has not overtly promoted the role of its fundamental founder, with most accolades going to Peter instead. In comparison with Saul, though, Peter was an oaf. It was Saul who had the drive and energy to evangelize in Rome, Cyprus, Macedonia, Greece, Ephesus and the rest of Asia Minor. It was from Rome that he supported the established Nazarene communities throughout Europe and the new churches that he had established that ran under a radically new doctrine. For them, he wrote the 13 letters that form the bulk of the New Testament.

Saul was a religious zealot, but not for the Nazarene church, the church of James and Jesus. Instead, Saul promoted his own version of Nazarene Judaism – Christianity. He became so notorious in his promotion of this new sect, that, on his return to Jerusalem from Asia Minor, he was imprisoned for teaching a doctrine incompatible with Mosaic Law. His new religion had become so distinct from the religion of Jesus that it was now a heresy, to be mocked, ridiculed and to suffer the full consequences of Judaic Law. It took Saul's considerable contacts within the controlling Roman administration to secure a Roman trial rather than a Judaic one. This resulted in his transfer to Rome and a short imprisonment. The charlatan had escaped to plagiarize the Nazarene religion once more.

However, Saul was not always a zealous supporter of the divinity of Jesus. Although the texts identifying Saul are mainly thought to have been penned by his own hand, they are, nevertheless, quite candid in their admissions as to his history. He had initially been a Roman quisling, working alongside the Jewish authorities in the persecution of the church of Jesus and James. This church was radical, both in its interpretation of Judaism and its hostility towards the Roman occupation. It was something of a thorn in the side of the Jewish and Roman authorities alike and there were many who would have liked to see it destroyed. Saul was the secret weapon of the Jewish authorities in this battle. He worked closely with the Romans, arrested the Nazarenes, testified against them and saw them put to death. He forced them to blaspheme, persecuted them from city to city and even took part in the stoning to death of Stephen. He then:

> ... made havoc on the church, entering into every house, and hailing men and women committed them into prison. [B2]

It was not until Saul's famous journey to Damascus, during which he had his blinding flash of inspiration, that he changed his mind and sought to become a member of the church of James. It is important to be quite specific here: many commentators would say that he became a Christian, but that is untrue. Christianity did not exist at this time; the church of Jesus and James was a Jewish sect and although it was radical in many respects, it still held to the majority of the Jewish laws. When Jesus taught in the temple, the priests were amazed by his knowledge of the law. When Saul tried the same trick, he was arrested. Saul tried desperately to join the 'club' of the Nazarene church and learn their sacred secrets, but the hierarchy was select and there was a long initiation period before anyone became a full member. Perhaps Saul had become aware of some of the secrets that the church held or perhaps he saw a way of making money. Maybe he just craved the attention. These are all possibilities that will be explored shortly. Whatever the case, Saul was determined to become a Nazarene and was impatient to know more.

However, it is apparent that with his reputation, Saul's sincerity towards the Nazarene church was suspect. Although James probably took the view that it was better to have him as a friend rather than as an enemy, he was not about to trust Saul with the inner secrets of the church. This simply frustrated Saul and, no doubt, this is why he devised his own organisation at a later date. It was for this reason that the role of the stars, the cosmos, the zodiac and the sign of Pisces within the Nazarene church were all kept from Saul and, equally, it is why they are largely despised by Christianity today. When he went his own way, Saul knew very little of the true secrets of the Nazarene. His position within the Nazarene church is explained quite clearly in the Acts of the Apostles:

> a. But all those that heard him were amazed, and said; Is this not he that destroyed them that called on (Jesus') name in Jerusalem.
> b. After that ... the Jews took counsel to kill him; But their laying await was known to Saul.
> c. And when Saul was come to Jerusalem, he (tried) to join himself with the disciples; but they were all afraid of him, and believed not that he was a disciple. [B3]

Architect

One can imagine that such a character was hardly going to be at the center of things in the church of Jesus and James. Yet it is through Saul, in the guise of his pseudonym Paul, that Christianity was eventually formed. It is, therefore, obvious that Christianity was going to be worlds apart from the church of the Nazarene. Saul was peeved at not being allowed to share in the secrets of the Nazarene; this would have been especially so if they had been the primary reason for his sudden transformation on the road to Damascus. A frustrated Saul was going to be a dangerous Saul, so to placate him, the Nazarene put him through some sort of initiation into this Masonic sect. More than likely, it was an initiation into the lowest levels of the church and the clues for this are in the Bible:

> a. Having told us that he was a rabbi, Saul suddenly says that his profession was a 'tent-maker'. [B4] Now that is a very peculiar profession for an aristocratic Jew in the priesthood, who had the power and authority from the rulers in Jerusalem to pursue the Nazarenes across the country and commit them to prison. Why did he suddenly say that he was a tent-maker? Even more mystifying is that there appears to be an international *fraternity of tent-makers* and because they belong to the same *craft* Saul sought them out and *lodged* with them. The explanation of this curiosity is obvious: the profession of tent-maker is only another very poor allusion to the position of architect, the profession of

Jesus. This is the theological form of architect, of course, the Masonic one. Quite plainly, Saul was saying that he was a Mason.

b. In curing the sick, Saul resorted to the use of Masonic symbols as protective charms. It is apparent that he did not know what they really meant, but, nevertheless, he used an apron and a handkerchief (hoodwink) to ward off evil spirits and diseases. [B5] Both these items are the basic accoutrements of Masonry, but their true purpose is not for exorcism. But Saul's little tricks did not always work, a Jew by the name of Sceva saw through his naive subterfuge and threw him out of his house. He must have taken a severe beating for his audacity, for he was ejected naked and wounded. [B6]

c. Saul lodged with an 'old disciple' called Mnason. (sic) [B7] Is this a profession rather than a name? The comparison of words is always a delicate affair, but it is worth noting that Mason comes from the Old English 'macian', the verb to make. In turn, the word magician comes from the Greek 'magike' and the 'wise men' that were present at the birth of Jesus were known as 'Magi' and were probably Zoroastrian priests from Persia. In addition, Sir Isaac Newton, a man with very close Masonic contacts, was known as the 'last of the great magicians'. There is a lot of synergy in this.

d. Like Moses, Saul was brought before a 'court'; he then used hand signals to show his position within the craft. [B8] The use of recognition signals is a central theme in the Masonic world.

Like Jesus, Saul was obviously conversant with some of the rules of standard Masonry. However, it would seem that, being of the tribe of Benjamin *, he knew very little of the craft; perhaps only as much as the standard secular Mason at a local lodge in our modern era. While this is enough for most Masons, Saul wanted more and there was a simple solution to his marginalization from the center of influence within the Nazarene sect.

* If Jesus was of the tribe of Judah and Saul was from the tribe of Benjamin, then Saul would have been closer to the bloodline than Jesus – Benjamin was the second favourite son of Jacob. Only the descendants of Joseph would have been more senior in their lineage, which again indicates that Jesus must have had just such a background in order to assume the authority which he evidently had.

Saul had seen the popularity of such an organization and the public adulation of Jesus. Perhaps he even craved the same attention. The solution was obvious: if he could not join the fraternal club, he should start his own. Of the more popular religions in the region at the time, the Nazarene, like the Essene and the Pharisees, was a rather ascetic sect of Judaism. These were religions that took a wholehearted commitment, if one was to live according to all the tenets of the law. However, not everyone wanted such a punishing regime: there were always what the Dead Sea Scrolls term 'seekers of smooth things' – people who just wanted an easy life, not too many laws and not too many rules.

Easy Life

There was a gap in the 'market'. Saul saw his opportunity and invented his own form of Judaism – one with little or no Masonic content. Gone were the complex rules and prohibitions for the Sabbath, gone were the mystifying dietary regulations, gone was circumcision and much of the rest of Rabbinical law. In came personal redemption, the purchase of forgiveness for cash, an overriding obsession with sexual sin and Moses' ten simple commandments for the people to follow. It was Judaism with all the drudgery stripped out.

Most importantly, because there were no longer any central secrets in this new sect, it could also afford to be more open and welcoming to outsiders. It no longer mattered where you were from, who your family was and how many years of patient initiation you could endure – if you put money in the collecting plate you were accepted. As Saul himself said:

> For I speak to you Gentiles inasmuch as I am the apostle of the Gentiles, I magnify my office. [B9]

So by embracing the Gentiles, the non-Jews, Saul 'increased his office'; in other words, he became more powerful. Saul knew that there were more Gentiles than Jews in the world and, perhaps, he also saw a spiritual vacuum within the Gentile world. Whatever the case, it is certain that he saw a route to expansion and an opportunity for his church to increase its influence. It is also quite clear that Saul was prepared to distort any teachings of the Nazarene church and much of his own upbringing as a Jew in order to gain power. To this end, even God himself changed sides – he became a Gentile.

> Is he the God of the Jews only? Is he not also the God of the Gentiles? Yes, he is the God of the Gentiles. [B10]

So the individual and esoteric god of the Jews, who had been looking after the Jews and the Jews alone since before the time of Abraham, was now hijacked by Saul to become the god of anyone who could pay enough money. Some may say 'why not?' Why should God be restricted to the Jews? Think about it further: this was like saying that Christians are praying to the Hindu gods – to Shiva or Vishnu. This may be fine for the likes of the writer G. K. Chesterton, but the Catholic hierarchy might baulk at such a suggestion; for it is much the same as a Catholic priest promoting the Hindu religion because he understands that, fundamentally, they are praying to the same god. Saul's new church was that drastic a departure from Judaism.

There were more outrageous changes still to come. In order to sideline the Nazarene church further, Saul outlawed some of the core teachings of their religion. It is obvious that he knew very little about some sections of the Nazarene church and the solution to this was simple – what Saul could not understand, nobody would be allowed to understand. Anything that was peculiar to the Nazarene would be outlawed and made heretical. This not only made life simpler, it also had the effect of marginalizing and 'paganizing' the Nazarene church and anyone who indulged in these secret rites.

It was now going to be an 'us and them' situation – good and evil – the 'Christians' versus the heretics. To this end, Saul deemed that astrology, the signs of the zodiac, the heliocentric model of the Solar System, the movement of the stars in accordance with old Egyptian religions and all aspects that could be associated with the term 'magic' (Masonry), would all become forbidden knowledge. If Saul could not know or understand these secrets, then nobody else would either, although his ignorance must have rankled a little, for he still proclaimed:

> ... for in nothing am I behind the very chiefest of the apostles. [B11]

Even the most central tenet of Judaism was not to be sacrosanct. Circumcision was an ancient Egyptian custom, which had been a shibboleth of the Jewish people for thousands of years. It was a physical mark that distinguished their race from all others – it was sacred and inviolable. Peter would not even preach to the uncircumcised. Saul, instead, first embraced the uncircumcised and finally declared that his believers should not be circumcised at all. [B12] Indeed, he went so far as to say that if circumcision was so important to the Jews, they should cut the entire penis off and have done with it! [B13]

This is the basis of what became Christianity, It was simply a flawed version of the Nazarene church, that of Jesus and James. The Nazarene church had a history going back thousands of years, even at that time. The new church of Saul attempted to wipe that illustrious slate completely clean and start again.

Saul's was a vacuous church with no real history, no real knowledge and no real heart, but it appealed greatly to those who could not attain the high standards of the Nazarene. It also appealed greatly to those Gentiles who had traditionally been excluded from the 'secrets' of the Judaic religions. The appeal of this new sect was overwhelming and soon Saul found himself at the centre of an expanding following and an influential organization. This greatly upset the disciples in the traditional church:

> But Saul increased the more in strength, and confounded the Jews that dwelt at Damascus. [B14]

The Son

Soon, Saul departed for Asia Minor to preach his new gospel and there he came across yet more determined opposition to his new brand of Judaism. When Barnabas and Saul arrived in the Greek island of Phaphos, they came up against someone known as the 'son of Jesus', who was visiting the governor of the island. Saul set eyes on this 'son of Jesus' and said to him:

> Oh full of subtlety and all mischief, thou child of the devil, thou enemy of all righteousness, wilt thou not cease to pervert the right way of the Lord. [B15]

It was an interesting meeting that is not readily discussed in the pulpit of the local church. It is obvious that Saul knew this 'son of Jesus' quite well and knew that his teachings were not only entirely different from his own, but that they subverted the meaning and content of his teachings. It is apparent that for their teachings to be in such conflict, this man must have been from the Nazarene sect. He was, therefore, a direct threat to the evangelical mission of Saul: he could have undermined everything Saul said of his position and knowledge of the Nazarene church. There is also a detectable element of hatred in Saul's reaction – he called him a sorcerer and he even went to the extreme of blinding this poor man.

Why should Saul have had this reaction? The only logical explanation is that this must have been a very special member of the Nazarene – the real son of the biblical Jesus himself. Yet Saul was openly evangelizing a religion that was based on the life and divinity of Jesus, so why should he have hated the son of his master and saviour in this fashion? The answer is to be found in Saul's blatantly perfidious nature: he did not care one iota about whom he trod on in his search for glory. He would superficially profess his 'love' and allegiance to Jesus, but, of course, his teachings were so different from those of Jesus himself that any contact with the Nazarene church was becoming an embarrassment. All Saul wanted was an icon to hold up, so that he could declare this image as being a god incarnate. To have the son of that god telling everyone that this was not true and that his teachings were a perversion, was embarrassing.

It would appear that this 'son of Jesus' was a real son. As further confirmation, his name is given in the text as being Elymas. Jesus' grandfather was Eli and so it would appear that the son was named after the great-grandfather. Eli is a rendering of Helios once more, the Sun God and the name also translates as 'wise-man'. It is apparent that Jesus had a son, who was on an evangelical mission around Europe. Saul's mission has no particular date attached to it, but with the identification of Saul that is about to be made, the year AD 64 can be proposed with some confidence. If this son of Jesus was born in about AD 25, then he would have been about 40 years old at the time – and Saul a youthful 27.

Saul appears to have seen off the son of Jesus, but there were still many others that he had to convince of the 'true' history he was teaching. He was very defensive of his new position outside the Nazarene church and his revised version of the events surrounding the life and 'death' of Jesus. In his letters to the other Nazarene sects around Europe, he tried desperately to convince them that he was a reliable witness, who knew more than the other members of the church. Saul justified his past and his new-found position of evangelist, by saying:

> Jesus came into the world to save sinners; of whom I am the chief (sinner). [B16]

But having declared that he used to be a sinner, Saul had to convince people of his new integrity. He defended his new teachings by saying:

> I speak the truth in Christ, and lie not. [B17]
> I say again, Let no man think me a fool; if otherwise, yet as a fool receive me, that I may boast a little. [B18]
> Jesus Christ ... knoweth that I lie not. [B19]

This, then, was the wonderful founder of Christianity. I shall pick up the continuing thread of his story shortly, but first it is necessary to identify Saul in the historical record. Who was he in reality? Surely such a central character in the world of Jewish politics and religion could not have completely escaped the quills of the scribes. Who was he? It is obvious that the name Saul is not going to be found in the historical record. He had already changed his name once previously, so it is unlikely that this appellation will be found. The method of identifying Saul will have to depend, instead, on the direct comparison of two life-stories that seem too similar for coincidence:

The biblical Saul:	The historical 'Saul':
a. Was a Jew of Tarsus. [B20]	a. Was a Jew from the stock of the Maccabees. [J38]
b. He was raised in Jerusalem. [B21]	b. He was raised in Jerusalem. [J39]
c. He had Roman citizenship. [B22]	c. He became a Roman citizen. [J40]
d. He was educated as a Pharisee.[B23]	d. He was educated as a Pharisee.[J41]
e. He became a Rabbi. [B24]	e. He became a Rabbi. [J42]
f. He acted with the Romans against the revolutionaries in the country. (The Nazarenes). [B25]	f. He was against revolutionaries in the country and the Nazarenes and he counselled against any action against the Romans. His task, as appointed general to the province of Galilee, was to 'induce the hotheads to lay down their arms'. [J43]

g. He had a vision of a man (Jesus) telling him the error of his ways. Subsequently he turned to the side of the rebels. [B26]

g. He had a vision of a man telling him the error of his ways. Subsequently, he turned to the side of the rebels. [J44]

h. Directly after this vision, Ananias the high priest was sent to see Saul in Damascus. Knowing of Saul's previous intention to capture the disciples, Ananias was wary of him, but he was eventually persuaded that Saul was their ally. [B27]

h. Directly after this vision, Ananus the high priest sent an emissary to see him. Knowing of 'Saul's' duplicity, they were wary of him. Ananus was not persuaded that 'Saul' was now their ally, and 'Saul' was not persuaded to return to Jerusalem where he could be dealt with. [J45]

i. Saul was accused of being an Egyptian false prophet. (It is likely that Saul was being mistaken for Jesus here, Jesus being an Egyptian pharaoh in exile. There is more evidence of this later.) [B28]

i. 'Saul' talked of an Egyptian false prophet, who tried to take Jerusalem by force. [J46]

j. Saul spoke both Greek and Hebrew. [B29]

j. 'Saul' spoke both Greek and Hebrew. [J47]

k. Saul travelled widely in Europe and returned to Jerusalem. [B30]

k. 'Saul' travelled widely in Europe and returned to Jerusalem. [J48]

l. He was stoned by his opponents and left for dead. [B31]

l. He was attacked by his opponents on many occasions. [J49]

m. The Jews wished once more to kill Saul, finding him in the temple at Caesarea and beating him severely. But Saul was captured (saved) by the Romans. [B32]

m. The Jews wish once more to kill 'Saul', but he evaded them. Eventually 'Saul' was captured (saved) by the Romans. [J50]

n. Saul was sent before Felix, the governor of Judaea and Ananias the high priest, accused of being a leader of the Nazarene, a rebel and causing riots in the temple at Caesarea. Because of his connections, Saul was held only under a loose house arrest.[B33]

n. 'Saul' gave a good account of the disturbances at the temple at Caesarea, which were, apparently, manufactured by certain people of the town who placed forbidden offerings on the temple steps. [J51]

o. Felix, in a more secular move, hoped to get a large bribe from Saul and so he was lenient with him. [B34]

o. Florus, the governor in this account, was accused of asking for bribes in order to release prisoners.[J52]

p. Saul talked with Agrippa and Bernice, the king's sister, and secured favourable treatment. [B35]	p. This 'Saul' gave an account of the petitions that Bernice, King Agrippa's sister, made to Florus, begging him to spare the Jews. [J53]
q. Finally, Saul sailed to Rome under the protection of the Romans. [B36]	q. This 'Saul' sailed to Rome. [J54]
r. He was shipwrecked on Malta, but all the ship's company survived. [B37]	r. 'Saul' was shipwrecked, being saved by another ship and taken to Puteoli. [J55]
s. In Rome, Saul wrote many letters to the Christian communities around Europe.	s. In Rome 'Saul' wrote no less than 60 letters to communities around Europe, recommending his works and vouching for their truthfulness. [J56]

So who was this second 'Saul', the man whose life followed that of the biblical Saul so closely? Was it someone very obscure who has never been studied in depth before? Have I stumbled upon an ancient manuscript that has never before been translated? Not so. In fact, 'Saul' was none other than Josephus, the Jewish historian whose works I have been using all through the early sections of this book. Is it not amazing that this similarity between the life of Josephus and that of Saul has not been commented on before?

Even the date of Josephus's birth, about AD 36, ties in very neatly with what we know of Saul and both appear to have died in Rome. I have already said that I cannot believe that this similarity has not been seen before. The historical association is not what has prevented this idea being taken seriously; it is the implications of that association that make it highly unpalatable. Nevertheless, this theory does explain some interesting theological puzzles.

It explains, for instance, the strange point at which the Acts of the Apostles ends. Acts takes us from the crucifixion of Jesus to the start of the Jewish rebellion. It is inconceivable that a commentator like Saul, following the history of a radical Jewish sect in Judaea, should have stopped at this moment. The Jewish rebellion was the biggest event of the era: all the Jewish sects were involved and passions were running at fever pitch. The sects eventually took their respective sides in what became a Jewish civil war, with Jew fighting Jew, as much as they were fighting the Romans. After picking off the smaller towns one by one, the

Romans eventually surrounded Jerusalem. Yet the religious factions within the besieged city were still slaughtering one another in the temple precinct, while outside the Romans tried to scale the walls of the city. It was a terrible and tragic time of great passion, public hatred, anger, mass slaughter, wanton deprivation and eventual exile for the people of Jerusalem.

Would a reporter shy away from such an event? Would a man like Saul, who turned every misfortune to his advantage, not wish to give his side of this great story? Of course he would – and he did – but in the guise of Josephus, not Saul. The great work was known as 'The Jewish War' and with its publication, Saul/Josephus managed to contort his true position of Jewish traitor and quisling for the Romans into a glorious victory for himself. Like his *alter ego* Saul, Josephus was a man who could change sides twice in the conflict and brazenly profess that perfidy was a virtue.

In turn, this theory also explains the way in which Josephus's writings finish. He managed to write an entire personal version of the Old Testament, much of which drew on alternative texts. It is clear that he was deeply interested in the history of the Jewish nation, a subject intimately entwined with the religion of the nation. Yet Josephus, who followed so closely in the footsteps of the Nazarenes, was conversant with the ways of the Essene sect, who lived in Galilee at the same time as the disciples, who owned extensive lands in Judaea, did not know or write anything of Jesus. (The two paragraphs that specifically mention Jesus Christ and John the Baptist are so obviously later insertions, that they are ludicrous.)

It has been suggested earlier that the cult of Jesus and the Nazarene may have been a small faction in the wider foment of the religious turmoil of Jerusalem and so it may be argued that Josephus had not heard of it. But Josephus was from Jesus' home county which was a small and relatively sparsely populated province. In fact, he became governor of Galilee and in his policing of the region, he made many campaigns to the towns of Tiberias, Nazareth and Sepphoris. How could a man who was effectively the chief of police in the region not know of and write about Jesus or his disciples? Jesus and the Nazarene were branded as being the local rebels even within the biblical texts. After Jesus' crucifixion, the 'remnants' of the Nazarene church were being hunted down by the Roman guard under the command of Saul. How then, did Josephus, who was the 'chief of police' in the area at about this time, not know of this action?

Of course, Josephus did know of Jesus and his followers, but he chose to write the section of his history dealing with Jesus under the pseudonym of Saul or Paul. *The Antiquities of the Jews* was Josephus's version of the Old Testament; the Acts of the Apostles (under the pen-name Saul) was his history of the New Testament. In reality it was actually Josephus himself who was persecuting Jesus and his disciples across Galilee, but in the guise of Saul. Saul was the chief of police in the region, just as the Bible implies.

So why did Saul/Josephus need two names – why the two life-stories? The reason that Josephus did not write of Jesus in his works under the name of Josephus is twofold.

Firstly, it is because the real-life story of Jesus was so different from the one Saul had overseen being written into the gospel stories. As far as his spiritual history of the era was concerned, the least said the better. Jesus' secular life would have interfered greatly with the spiritual persona that he wished to portray.

Secondly, remember that Josephus was writing these books for profit. They maintained his lifestyle and they reinforced his connections with royalty and with the hierarchy in Rome. He quotes, with some pride, the glowing testimonies that he received from King Agrippa after he had read Josephus's works. He also presented copies to the emperor Titus in the hope that he would sign them as being authentic, thus increasing their value. [J57] Josephus could not have done this if they contained any glowing testimonials to the biblical rebel Jesus. These would have been testimonials to a character that had caused the Romans such trouble in the past and whose followers were some of the chief instigators of the Jewish rebellion, which cost so many Roman lives. Titus would have burned the books and probably Josephus, too.

Of necessity, the two works had to be separate; one was a secular story, the other spiritual. This is something that Saul's schizophrenic mind could have accomplished with great ease. With the emperor's seal of approval on his (secular) works, he was free to peddle further copies of his books to the prominent and rich Jews in Palestine and the Diaspora in Europe. He organized this with great vigour from his apartment in Rome, sending some 62 letters of recommendation of the works, penned under the name of Josephus, out across Europe. All this, at a time when such correspondence must have cost a fortune! [58] At the same time, Josephus was writing under another name – that of Saul. He chose this pseudonym for good reason, for he saw himself as the Old Testament king, Saul.

After the exodus the rule of the people fell from the pharaoh to the priesthood. The Jewish nation was ruled by their elders and betters, the Judges. During Samuel's lifetime, however, there were continuing problems with the Philistines. The Jews wanted a leader who would bring them power and influence once more. The people demanded a king and the mantle fell to the Old Testament Saul. He was the first king of the Jews and proved himself to be a great military commander, a popular leader and a saviour of the nation. He was also of the tribe of Benjamin, as was Josephus himself. In addition, he was seen to have symbolically taken the kingship of the Jews from the Old Testament Joshua, the disciple and successor to Moses. [J59]

It is obvious why Josephus saw himself in this role, he wanted to take the royal robes from Jesus and become a great leader of the Jewish nation. So it was under the pseudonym of Saul that Josephus was busy penning yet more letters across Europe from Rome, thirteen of which are preserved in the Bible. If nothing else, Josephus/Saul was prolific in his work and if he failed to become the King of the Jews, he at least achieved a religious immortality.

New disciple

However, the reverse of this argument must also be so. If Josephus the historian was such an important man of this era, one who was persecuting the Nazarene church under the guise of Saul, should we not see evidence of Josephus in the Bible? In fact we do and the particular reference quoted here is also an oblique allusion to the position of Saul, which equates very nicely with this theory.

The period in question was at some indeterminate time after the crucifixion. Judas the betrayer was claimed to be dead and the church leaders were having a meeting to discuss the situation. Whether Judas was now dead or in exile in the east, as the myths claim, is immaterial; the fact is that the Nazarene church was in the process of voting in a new member to fill the vacant position of disciple. The contenders for the position were someone called Joseph Barsabas, also called Justus, and Matthias. At the meeting, the other eleven disciples cast their votes and it was Matthias who was eventually elected, not Joseph. It was also to be Matthias who wrote down the Gospel of Judas Thomas. [B60]

This story of someone being voted into the Nazarene church just after the crucifixion sounds remarkably similar to the pleadings of Saul, who so wanted to become a full member of the inner core of the church. Saul, like Joseph, did not gain access to the secret teachings of Jesus and James; he was not voted in. Is there a link here? The contenders for this position were called Joseph-Justus and Matthias. Looking into the secular record, the historian Josephus had a brother called Matthias and a son called Justus, in fact the names Matthias and Joseph were family names that went back many generations. Were Josephus the historian and his brother Matthias the two contenders for the vacant position of disciple?

The Joseph in the biblical texts was also called Barsabas (son of Sa-bas), if Joseph and Matthias were brothers then Matthias would also be called Barsabas. If Joseph, Josephus and the biblical Saul were one and the same, then one might expect that this Matthias Barsabas might be mentioned in the same context as Saul (being his brother). This is indeed the case; the companion of Saul on most of his European travels was one Barnabas. This, taken together with the fusion of the characters Saul and Josephus in the previous pages, makes the chances of this story being a biblical reference to the historian Josephus extremely good – one that again indicates that Josephus was Saul.

If this new evidence that Josephus was, perhaps, a first-hand eyewitness of some of the biblical history is to be taken seriously, then it may be possible to compare more of his dialogue with biblical events. What new interpretations of the classical biblical stories can be found within the texts of Josephus? The first new slant on a well-known tale that comes to mind, is to be found in Josephus's account of the Jewish War. Here, he mentions a disturbance organised by three bands of rebels; the Sicarii, the Magicians and the Egyptian false prophet.

Sicarii

The Sicarii were a band of assassins, whose name derived from their daggers or 'sicae' that they concealed under their cloaks. The Sicarii mingled with the crowds, especially on festival days, and used their daggers to assassinate their enemies. The first victim of such an attack is reported to have been Jonathan *, the high priest, after whose death:

> ...many were slain every day, while the fear men were in of being so served, was more afflicting than the calamity itself. [J61]

* A later Jonathan to the one killed by Herod.

A comparison with the biblical accounts of the era, reveals a man called Simon Zelotes among Jesus' disciples. He was one of the band of religious nationalist zealots who were under the command of their leader Eleazar and at the forefront of the Jewish uprising. Also among the disciples was Judas Iscariot, undoubtedly a name derived from the Sicarii. Judas was known as a Sicarii dagger-man. [B62]

The Magicians

The Magicians were men who:

> ... deceived and deluded the people under the pretence of divine inspiration, but were for procuring innovations and changes of government ... and went before them into the wilderness, pretending that God would show them the signals of liberty. [J63]

A better description of the Nazarene one could not hope to find. It has to be admitted that this is an unflattering perspective of Jesus' followers, from a typically Pharisee point of view, but nevertheless it is true that they were on a political, as well as religious mission. They did want to introduce innovations. They did want to change the government, intending the restoration of the pharaonic line. Finally, they did spend a lot of time in the wilderness. This quotation could easily refer to the supporters of Jesus.

The Egyptian

The mention of the Egyptian false prophet is interesting, especially in the context of the involvement of the other insurgents. Who, other than Jesus, could an Egyptian prophet in this era be? The deciding factor in the unmasking of this false prophet, is the actions that 'the Egyptian' took, as reported by Josephus/Saul:

> ... he got together thirty thousand men that were deluded by him; these he led round about from the wilderness to the mount which was called the **Mount of Olives**, and was ready to break into Jerusalem by force from that place; and if he could but once conquer the Roman garrison and the people, he intended to domineer them ... But (the governor) met him with his Roman soldiers, while all the people assisted him in his attack ... when it came to battle the

> Egyptian ran away, with a few others, while ... the rest of the multitude were dispersed every one to their own homes... [J64]

This is truly interesting. I have already tried to underline Jesus' political aspirations and this account of a rebellion is far too close to the biblical version of these events to have been a coincidence. The Bible says that the disciples and their followers had sold all their possessions to buy swords. [B65] It places this event just after the Last Supper, which was a Passover meal in the evening, so it would have been night-time – indeed, the disciples kept falling asleep. The location was at night on the Mount of Olives and Jesus was waiting with a band of armed men. The Bible does not explain the intention of this night-time meeting outside Jerusalem, but with Jesus being the leader of a rebel faction, Josephus's assessment of a rebellion cannot be far wrong. Whatever the plan, it was about to be 'foiled':

> ... they went out into the **Mount of Olives**; and his disciples also followed him. Judas then, with a band of men and officers from the chief priests and Pharisees, cometh thither with lanterns and torches and weapons ... Then Simon Peter having a sword, drew it and smote the high priests servant, and cut off his right ear. [B66] ... And they all forsook him, and fled. [B67]

How could this glaring similarity have been missed by previous historians and theologians? This can only be a continuation of the millennial cover-up of the exact nature of the events that happened in first-century Israel. If the misinformation present in both texts is allowed for, the two accounts dovetail exactly. Both of these uprisings failed miserably, for whatever reasons, and both of them resulted in the attackers melting away into the night and back to their homes. The only real difference between the two is that Josephus's leader ran away, whereas Jesus was captured.

In terms of the physical data in the two texts, Josephus's 30,000 men is an obvious exaggeration, something that was merely designed to show the bravery of the Pharisees in dealing with this threat to the people of Jerusalem. Remember that Josephus/Saul was a Pharisee and it was they who came and captured Jesus. The jaundiced view of the 'Egyptian prophet that ran away' is just the sort of misinformation that could be expected from someone like Saul.

The gospel writers, in their turn, have traditionally under-played

Jesus' political support. They would have been especially cautious when it came to an organized pitched battle between his armed followers and the leaders of the people of Jerusalem. How could this be squared with the traditional doctrine of a meek saviour? The altered texts described just the disciples present at this drama, but that makes a mockery of an armed revolt – how could a handful of people take Jerusalem? On the other hand, if the disciples were just having a private meeting on the Mount of Olives, why did they sell everything to buy weapons and why the night-time subterfuge?

Undoubtedly, this is evidence that Josephus/Saul did know of Jesus and that he is included in some of Josephus's texts. Perhaps more of Jesus' life appears within these texts, but this first extract is confirmation enough that all the assumptions made so far are on solid foundations. It would seem that, in his own era, Jesus was known as the Egyptian prophet and for good reason. His mission was just as expected – the overthrow of the Jewish authorities and the re-establishment of the pharaonic line. His armed following was small, but enough to infiltrate the city during the Passover festivities and take control of the city administration. Josephus mentions that up to 3 million people attended the festival. Even allowing for his normal exaggeration, it would seem to have been a huge gathering. It was an ideal event for the Sicarii to use as a cover for their political ends. Milling among the bustling throng, they were to target the authorities near the temple itself, strike with lightning speed, and melt back into the by now agitated crowds.

It is unlikely that someone with the family history and the royal education of Jesus would have believed that he could easily rid Israel of the Romans. The priests of Heliopolis would have been well aware of the dangers of taking on such a powerful nation on the basis of religious zeal alone and they would have told Jesus all about the cautionary tale of Akhenaton and his exile from Egypt. It would seem from the gospels, if they can be believed in this respect, that Jesus was resigned to the patronage of the Romans; perhaps they were even a stabilizing influence within the country.

In terms of the Jewish incumbents in the temple at Jerusalem and controlling Judaea, the situation was very different. The king, Agrippa I, was dead. His son, Agrippa II was only the King of Lebanon, later to be transferred to Syria. Israel was ruled by a Roman governor and the throne was effectively empty for the next in line. Would Jesus have been able to take the throne? Could he have persuaded the Romans that the country needed a puppet king to stabilize the volatile situation, as Herod had attempted before him? It was a possibility, but one that eventually failed.

Another Exile

Yet again, all the years of planning came to nothing. If the plan had been to take Jerusalem by force, the revolt had failed. If it had been to follow the prophesies to the very last letter and stage the crucifixion of the second Messiah, it had again failed. Jesus was not seen by the majority of people as being the true Messiah, the real 'second coming' of the gods. For the vast majority of Jews, the Messiah was still in the future and Jesus was one of many false prophets along this rocky road to salvation. Only the Christians, a band of chiefly Gentile people who often knew nothing of real Judaism, were persuaded by Saul that a Messiah had come. They were persuaded even if they had not been expecting one in the first place, such was his zeal and charisma. He was an erudite man who could talk for hour after hour on his dreams of a new world order, until a poor young man called Eutychus fell both asleep and out of his lofty perch and was thought to be dead. [B68]

Josephus/Saul said that the Egyptian Prophet escaped, whereas the Bible says he was crucified. What was Jesus' real fate? Saul, in the guise of Josephus, had the answer and gives another clue to deciphering some other historical writings. The Dead Sea Scrolls are a cache of ancient scrolls, probably of Essene origin, that were discovered in 1947. They often talk of the 'Teacher of Righteousness' and the 'Wicked Priest' or the 'Spouter of Lies'.

It has been a topic of debate among historians as to who these particular personalities were. Barbara Thiering gave John the Baptist the role of the Teacher of Righteousness and Jesus that of the Wicked Priest. Robert Eisenman made James, Jesus' brother, the Teacher and Saul became the Wicked Priest. I think that Jacob Teicher and John Allegro are closer to the mark with their assessment of Jesus being the Teacher of Righteousness and Saul the Wicked Priest.

The Wicked Priest was accused by the scroll writers of chastizing the Teacher of Righteousness, of plotting to destroy the Community (the Nazarene church) and of stealing their riches, so the Community finally delivered him into the hands of his enemies (the Romans). Saul was accused of all these offences by the Nazarene church. One of the common ways of prophesy in Judaism was the interpretation of ancient texts. If an ancient story could be found that was similar to the current situation, the texts could be followed further to divine the future.

The Habakkuk Commentary was discovered in Cave 1 at Qumran and it is one of the main sources for studying Essene theology. The following extract seems to link the main characters in the Dead Sea Scrolls with Josephus/Saul and the Nazarene. The relevant ancient paragraph has been interpreted by the Essene as being a story of the:

> Wicked Priest pursuing the Teacher of Righteousness to the house of his exile, that he might confuse him with his venomous fury. And at the time appointed for rest ... he (the Wicked Priest) appeared before them to confuse them and to cause them to stumble on the Day of Fasting. [69]

Josephus wrote a very similar tale, concerning himself. In the text, he used the name Jesus for the man he was fighting, so before looking at his version of the events, the use of this name in his works needs further investigation. The name Jesus appears sporadically in Josephus's writings, which has led some historians to consider it a common name. Conversely, I would contend that many of these references are actually to the biblical Jesus himself.

Josephus, under his pen-name of Saul, was persecuting the members of the Nazarene church, including Jesus, around Galilee. It was Jesus, in the Acts of the Apostles, who asked Saul why he was persecuting him. Josephus, in his secular writings, was the governor of Galilee and he was also in dispute with a man called Jesus, who was the governor of Tiberias. The dispute had originated with the burning of Herod's palace in Tiberias, a town in the province of Galilee. Josephus says that Jesus burned it for profit because the roof was gilded, but a closer look at the texts reveals a deeper reason.

Josephus/Saul had gone to Tiberias to demolish the palace because it contained 'figures of living creatures within it', which was contrary to Jewish Law. [J70] The reason why Jesus burned the palace is, therefore, obvious. If this were the biblical Jesus, being a Nazarene, he would have been aware that the 'living creatures' in the palace were more than just pictures of animals. The house, being owned by the royal family, was more likely to have been encrusted with the signs of the zodiac, the celestial and earthly spheres and, perhaps, even the full

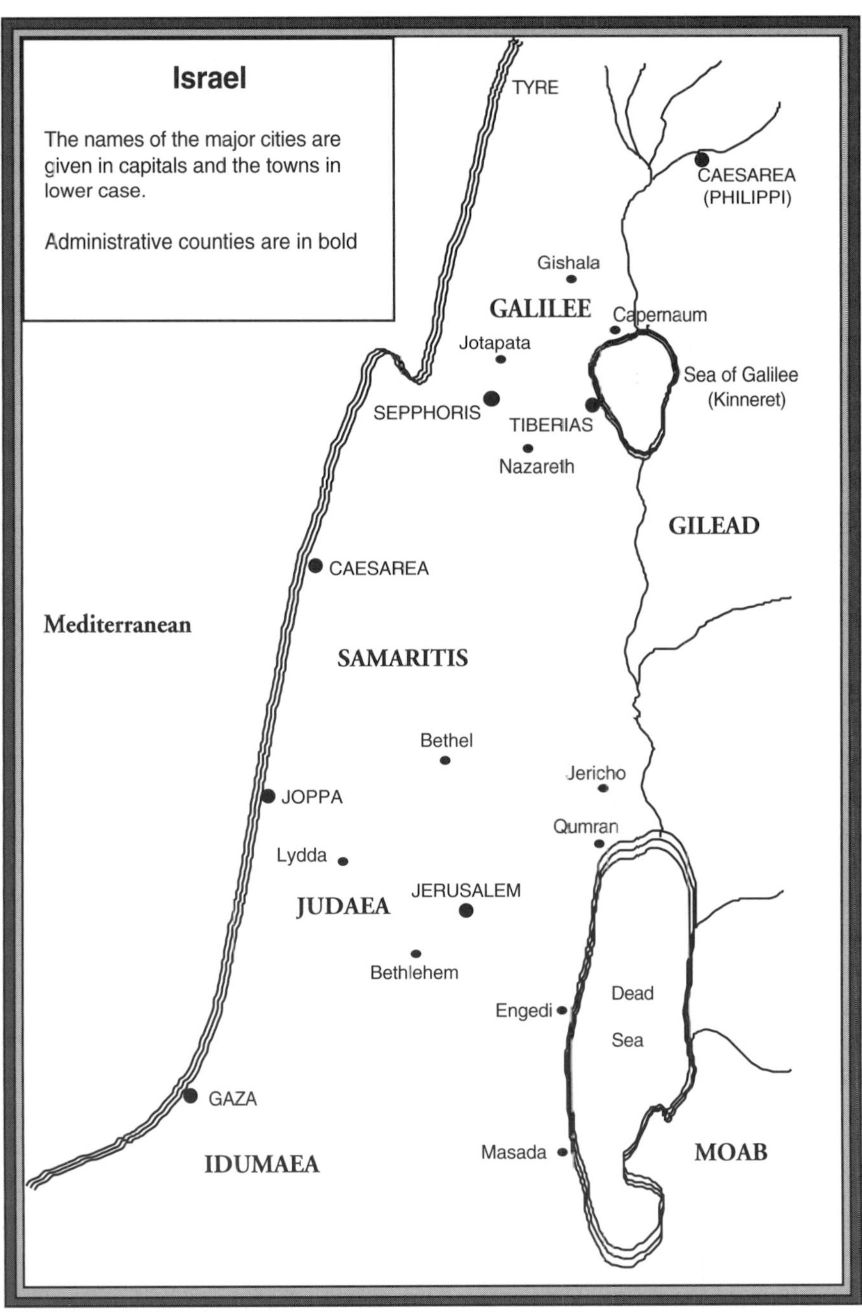

Fig 23. Map of Israel at the turn of the first century

pantheon of the Egyptian gods. For Saul to have seen this would have been similar to the shock that Ezekiel got when he peeped into the Holy of Holies in the Temple of Jerusalem and saw:

> paintings ... and other mythological scenes, motifs which seemed to point to syncretistic practices of Egyptian provenance. [71]

If a man with the reputation of Josephus/Saul had discovered such a scene, he would have caused chaos in the region, especially in the era when he was persecuting the Nazarene. Many good and innocent people would have lost their lives. It was clear that Josephus/Saul could not be allowed to see the motifs, but with the backing of the Roman guard, it would have been difficult to stop him. The only answer was to burn the palace to the ground before the sacred secrets were discovered, which was exactly what happened.

Even so, there was enough left of the ruins for Josephus to take away booty, which was another matter contrary to Jewish law. In retaliation, this character called Jesus was later to use this looting of royal property to undermine the power of Saul/Josephus. Interesting as all this is, the bottom line in this enquiry is, was this character we have been discussing really the biblical Jesus? Most commentators say that Jesus was not mentioned in the works of Josephus, but this may be because most historians do not want to find him there; it would cause too many problems. But this burning of the palace *was* the work of the biblical Jesus, as Josephus made this perfectly clear when he said that this Jesus was the leader of:

> ...a seditious tumult of mariners and poor people. [J72]

A seditious tumult of mariners? Since when did the local seaman's mission organize itself into an angry mob to burn down the palace of a long-dead king? This sentence does not make sense and it must be translated in some manner. In reality, the reference to mariners here is just an oblique reference to the followers of the biblical Jesus, but it has been deliberately obscured for some reason.

Jesus' followers were the Nazarene, a name that means little fishes. Even in the Bible, the disciples were often called fishers of men or fishermen for short. This is the answer to what Josephus was trying to say when referring to mariners; in other words, this Jesus in the texts of Josephus was the leader of the Nazarene. He was the leader of a 'seditious mob', as Josephus called them – or the leader of a heroic band of freedom-fighters, depending on which side of the fence you stood.

This is undoubtedly a reference to the biblical Jesus, the second to be found in Josephus's books so far. The canvass of this old master is slowly being cleaned and restored, freed at last from the grime of the millennia. The true character of the biblical Jesus is only now beginning to emerge. That staff he was holding is now looking more like a sceptre, that crown of thorns appears to be glinting like a diadem, that sacred scroll has upon it the seal of the great library at Heliopolis.

Having now found two references to the biblical Jesus, it is worth looking at the other people named Jesus in the works of Josephus to see if this becoming a trend:

a. The first is Jesus the 'son of' Gamala. This Jesus was a high priest and a leader of 600 rebels in the vicinity of Tiberias. [J73] He was a wealthy Galileean, owning a large castle there and he was in a position to give orders to the people of Tiberias. He was charged by the authorities in Jerusalem with trimming the powers of Josephus.

b. The second Jesus is called the son of Sapphias. [J75] Jesus son of Sapphias is the Jesus mentioned previously as the leader of the seditious mob of 'mariners' in the vicinity of Tiberias, a term that identifies him as being the biblical Jesus. In addition to being a rebel leader, the texts say that this Jesus was governor of Tiberias, a Galileean, a high priest and a 'general', appointed by the high priest Ananus. He was also in charge of the tribunal that sought to trim the powers of Josephus, all of which is very much the same as Jesus of Gamala. This Jesus and the high priest Ananus are called the 'people of Damascus', although they were priestly governors based in Jerusalem and Galilee. They were the people who appointed Josephus, the historian, as general of the area of Gamala.

Although there appear to be multiple appellations once more, there is no dichotomy here. Jesus could easily be 'of Gamala' the town, and 'of Sapphias' the family name. Remember also that it is on the road to 'Damascus' that Saul had his vision and it was the Jews of 'Damascus' that Josephus was harassing. But Josephus was the governor of Galilee and Gamala, is the town of Gamala being called Damascus here? Gamala is, after all, on the eastern side of the Sea of Galilee, the Syrian side.

c. Jesus is also called the son of Shaphat. [J76] This Jesus was the leader of a rebel band that attacked the Roman commander Valerian and stole his horses, while Valerian was sizing up the town of Tiberias for a siege. Jesus took refuge in Tiberias, but was forced out of the town by the population because they feared a Roman attack. Tiberias was the town where Jesus son of Sapphias was the governor and rebel leader and also where the rebel leader Jesus of Gamala lived. Are the texts really trying to convince us that there were three rebel leaders called Jesus in the vicinity of Tiberias?

d. There is one more Jesus in these texts, Jesus the son of Ananus. It has been already stated that Ananus is a title, derived from the name An or On for Heliopolis, so the title could refer to anyone in the high priesthood. This Jesus would, therefore, be the next in line to Ananus for the priesthood, as the post was hereditary. [J77] The texts state that this high priest (Ananus) was also of the rebel faction, so who was this Ananus? It can only be Sapphias/Shaphat, whose son Jesus was appointed as general and high priest, the leader of the rebellious mariners.

e. Later, this Jesus son of Ananus is called a plebeian, a common man and not a priest. Is this really the same Jesus? Quite possibly, for the biblical Jesus was also later called a common man. In addition, this Jesus was also called a husbandsman, the term often used to denote the Christian god in the Bible. [B80] What is more, this Jesus, son of Ananus, lamented the fate of Jerusalem and was persecuted for it.

> ... certain of the most eminent among the populace had great indignation at this dire cry of his, and took up the man, and gave him a great number of severe stripes (lashes of the whip). Yet he did not say anything for himself, or anything peculiar to those that chastised him, but still he went on with the same words ... supposing, as the case proved to be, that this was a sort of divine fury in the man, (they) brought him to the Roman proctor; where he was whipped till his bones were laid bare; yet still he did not

> make any supplication for himself, nor shed any tears. [J81]
> (Does this sound familiar?)
>
> Against this paragraph being a reference to the biblical Jesus is the implied dating of this persecution, which is stated as during the siege of Jerusalem. However, re-reading the paragraph suggests that this section of text is out place in the works of Josephus. In its current chronological location, the Roman procurator had already been thrown out of Jerusalem two years earlier. This must, therefore, be an account of a slightly earlier event.

These references are not only similar to the biblical Jesus, the events that surrounded these people are strikingly similar as well. Josephus was busy interfering in the affairs of this Jesus, the rebel leader of 600 fishermen. Yet these were just the sort of events that caused such strife between Saul and the Nazarene church of Jesus – the former was always interfering in the affairs of the latter, of which Saul had no comprehension. The situation is confusing and that is probably deliberate once more. But the plots of these two stories are so similar, that the Jesus in the texts of Josephus and the biblical Jesus just have to be the same character. If this is the case, however, the associations of Jesus' family within the highest levels of society are laid bare once more.

Wicked Priest

In addition to the problem of the burned palace, Josephus had other things to contend with. He was trying to govern Galilee within a Jewish framework of government, yet some of the towns in the provinces had other allegiances. Sepphoris to the west of the Sea of Galilee, for example, was pro-Roman and had sent for this same Jesus and his band of 'rebels', for protection against Josephus. While someone called John had the support of Gischala to the north; a town which also seems to have been pro-Roman. Josephus himself was possibly pro-Roman, but his people were not, yet his government position depended on the support of the population. Consequently, this dichotomy was causing Josephus some anxiety. This is not to say that Jesus was pro-Roman either; there were so many factions fighting each other by this stage that everyone was using or abusing the Romans to suit their own ends. A temporary treaty with the Romans in order to help defeat Josephus was not out of the question.

The authorities in Jerusalem, influenced by Ananus and Jesus, had decided that Saul/Josephus must go. To achieve this within some kind of lawful framework, the excuse was to take the form of charges regarding the missing plunder from the burned palace of the King Herod. Accordingly, the Jerusalem hierarchy gave money to Jesus and John, who are reported to have had a band of some 700 men between them, to overthrow Josephus. The authorities also promoted the pro-Roman towns of Sepphoris, Gabara and Tiberias to back the revolt against Josephus. [J82]

If one identifies Saul and Josephus as the same person, this is all quite likely. These events took place before the conversion of Saul on the road to 'Damascus' and he was, by his own admission, 'wreaking havoc on the church (of Jesus) and committing them to prison'. Josephus, in his turn and by his own admission, was causing Jesus a lot of problems in Galilee. Strangely, it is not mentioned in the Bible whence Saul derived his authority and under what jurisdiction he was empowered to commit the Nazarene followers to prison, but it is clear that he must have been a very important person to be able to do so. In his later dealings with the governors Felix and Festus, Saul again shows that he was a man of great standing.

Likewise, Josephus also tried to prove his many royal connections and the great pedigree of his family. The two characters are so similar that they merge again and again, and in making this connection, we now know where the authority of the biblical Saul came from. Josephus, the author and historian, was empowered by Ananus, the high priest in Jerusalem, to police Galilee. Josephus was the governor of the province, but it would appear that the subordinate was out of control and abusing his authority, 'aggrandizing myself to the height of glory' as Josephus put it.

The authorities in Jerusalem had a problem; Josephus/Saul was an intransigent and foolhardy officer and once given their authority he was not going to relinquish it without a fight. A series of letters were exchanged in the vain hope of getting Josephus to travel to Jerusalem, where he could be more easily dealt with, but to no effect. This finally brings the argument back to the Habakkuk Commentary, where the Wicked Priest pursued the Teacher of Righteousness back to his house on the Sabbath. It would appear that Josephus/Saul spurned the entreaties of the authorities in Jerusalem and, instead, moved to head off the conflict by travelling to Jesus' house, catching him and his followers unawares and in some disarray. Jesus' house is described as being:

> ... a large castle, not unlike a citadel. [J83]

Jonathan was outside the castle with an armed guard. He and his band retreated rapidly into the castle, leaving one door open to entrap Josephus. Instead, Josephus stole away from the castle, found lodgings nearby and pretended to be asleep – a Sabbath repose. Jonathan emerged from the castle to warn the local town of Josephus's presence, but the sleeping was only a ruse and Josephus's supporters suddenly all jumped up and shouted. Jonathan and his men tried to escape, in fear of their lives, but they were captured by Josephus, who proceeded to lecture them on his good government.

It is a strange passage, but the import is again very similar to the Habakkuk's mention of a surprise attack or ruse being made on the Sabbath, a time of rest, which was contrary to Judaic Law. In the Habakkuk Commentary, the attack was by the Wicked Priest on the Teacher of Righteousness; in Josephus's version, it was by Josephus/Saul against a man called Jesus. Josephus said that this Jesus was the 'son of Gamala', one of the characters we have already mentioned. Jesus was the governor of the town of Tiberias and also a high priest of Jerusalem. His position and the fact that he owned a 'castle', suggests that he was a man of some means and influence in the region. That he had a band of 600 men at his disposal is also a good indication of his standing. Is he the Teacher of Righteousness, as indicated by the Habakkuk Commentary? The Teacher has often been linked to the biblical Jesus – is that who he really was? The answer has to be 'yes' once more; the facts fit too closely for any other conclusion.

The Vision

Josephus had overstepped the mark and the authorities in Jerusalem were not amused. Jesus, according to the works of Josephus, as governor of Tiberias, convened a tribunal in which he and the multitudes grilled Josephus on his conduct as a governor of the province. Specifically, Jesus confronted Josephus about his misappropriation of the king's plundered goods and treasures from his palace:

> Now Jesus, who was the ruler ... got up and enquired of me what became of the vessels that were taken out of the king's palace when it was burned down, and of that uncoined silver ... [J84]

In the face of determined opposition and the threat to his life, Josephus contrived to escape. It was at about this time that Josephus had his equivalent of a 'vision on the road to Damascus':

> But wonderful it was what a dream I saw that very night ... it seemed to me a certain person stood by me, and said, 'Oh, Josephus; leave off to afflict thy soul, and put away all fear; for what grieves thee now will render thee very considerable...' [J85]

For comparison, the Bible says of Saul:

> And he fell to the earth, and heard a voice (of Jesus) saying unto him, Saul, Saul, why do you persecute me? [B86]

Josephus says his vision turned him to the Romans. If so, it must have been a vision of future events because he then sacked the pro-Roman town of Sepphoris and had a few skirmishes with Roman soldiers. But Josephus's heart was not really in this fight against the Romans, so he finally surrendered at the battle of Jotapata. The vision was then vindicated and Josephus joined the Roman forces. After an inglorious career as quisling, attempting to get the defenders of Jerusalem to surrender, he finally retired to Rome to write his letters; a fate that is again reminiscent of Saul's. [J87]

Many people will probably concur with the identification of Saul and Josephus as being the same. However, the problem with this association and the subsequent association of the Jesus in his castle with the biblical Jesus, is the era in which this happened. This episode took place in the lead-up to the Jewish war, when Felix and Festus were governors of Judaea and well after the crucifixion of the biblical Jesus. The reason for the rejection of this thesis by classical historians in the past is not the lack of evidence, but because it conflicts with traditional theology. Jesus was alive and well in the years 50 - 65 AD – he survived the crucifixion. Indeed Josephus is indicating here that some of the traditional events associated with the crucifixion happened at a much later date – in the 60's AD.

* * *

The Evangelist

Saul/Josephus retired to Rome to write his books and to organize his fledgling church. Long rambling letters were written to the new recruits in the major cities across the Mediterranean: they cajoled, castigated, praised and punished. They encompassed all the problems of trying to organize communities while the chief director is in another country, able to visit his followers perhaps only once in every three or four years.

Who were these impressionable people that Saul was recruiting into his new Christian church? What was their background, why did they join and what did they expect to gain from this association? One can only describe this new church as having been formed from the dregs of society. Saul described them as being foolish and weak and then went on to say that they were drawn from among the:

> Deceivers, prostitutes, idolaters, adulterers, homosexuals and homosexual prostitutes. ... thieves, coveters, drunkards, revilers and extortioners. [B88]

He started with the lowest of the low and it is fairly clear from his letters that he was having a hard time with these people, who strayed from his teachings as soon as he turned his back. The Corinthians, for instance, gained the reputation of fornicating with each other, even with their mothers. Saul was upset with this and chastised them in a resigned fashion. [B89] So why was he going to all this trouble? He claimed that he suffered many beatings in his search for this 'new gospel', so what were his motives in pursuing this course and what was in it for him? The power factor has already been outlined earlier in this chapter. Saul started out as a second-rate initiate into the church of the Nazarene and he evolved into the leader of a church that was far more powerful. He must have revelled in this transformation and sniggered at the position of the faltering Nazarene church.

However, there was another reason for pursuing this new religion, one which his *alter ego*, Josephus, would have approved of – profit. Saul made it very clear what he wanted his new churches to do. They were to:

> Upon the first day of the week let everyone of you lay by him in store [money], as God has prospered him, that there be no gatherings (until) I come. And when I come, whomsoever you

> shall approve by your letters, them I send to bring your liberality unto Jerusalem. [B90]

Saul was asking for donations from his flock and the fledgling church obviously complied with his wishes. It is also apparent that he was not above taking liberties with these donations to the church. In between this particular instruction to the people of Corinth and the next, he had obviously paid a visit and collected his money. He want to visit them again, but:

> ... I determined ... that I would not come again to you in pain. For if I make you sorry, who then is he that maketh me glad, but the same which is made sorry by me? [B91]

Clearly, the visit to Corinth did not go well. What was the reason for all this pain during his last visit?

> Behold, the third time I am ready to come to you; and I will not be burdensome to you; for I seek not your (money) but you. For the children ought not save for the parents, but the parents for the children. [B92]

It is clear that Saul had stripped the Christians of Corinth of everything they owned on his second visit and they were rightly angry. He was now going through the familiar routine of placating the natives with a few palliatives and soothing words. You can be sure that, like any confidence trickster in the world, as soon as the storm had blown itself out, he would be back for more. Saul had a goose in every Mediterranean city that regularly laid golden eggs for him; all he had to do was travel and collect. The people of Philippi were next on the list:

> For even in Thessalonica ye sent once again unto my necessity. Not because I desire a gift, ... But I have all and abound; I am full, having received of Epaphroditus the things which were sent from you. [B93]

In return for this generosity of the people of Philippi, Saul was willing to provide the following favour:

> But my God shall supply all your needs according to his riches in Glory by Jesus. [B94]

Note how Saul has slipped from the evangelical position into the role of the Messiah: this was now in the name of 'his god'. If Saul were transported into our era, he would be appearing in the United States on channel 32 as a gospel preacher saving mankind from sin. He would be standing in a glittering sequinned suit, his brow furrowed with mock sincerity, beaded with perspiration and extolling the virtue of 'his god' to the people of middle America. 'Praise be to the Lord, we accept Master Card, Visa and American Express'.

Not only was the Nazarene church being suffocated under the choking mists of Saulism, but now the whole of Judaism was facing the same threat. Judaism was far more powerful than the Nazarene church and if they had pulled together at this point, Christianity would have been stillborn and Saul would have died a pauper. This was not to be. The storm clouds had been gathering in Jerusalem for the last 70 years or more and the resulting tornado was about to drop its funnel out of the sky and devastate much of Judaism. The Jewish civil war would have been a minor squabble in a distant eastern land had it not been for one thing – the might of Rome. The domestic dispute was about to become a massacre.

Just like the 'insignificant' assassination of Archduke Ferdinand, heir to the Austro-Hungarian throne, which precipitated the First World War, Rome feared that this small flame would become a raging inferno that would engulf the whole of its eastern provinces. Rome was the catalyst that inflamed the dispute, but Rome also became the executioner who would destroy Israel for nearly two thousand years.

Chapter IX

Fall of Jerusalem

Part 1

The siege of Jerusalem was a cruel and tragic event, one commonly blamed squarely on the Romans. This was not quite the case. The politics of the region were no more stable than they had been in the days of Herod the Great; faction fought faction, Jew against Jew, brother against brother. It is apparent that the Romans were quite happy for Israel to govern itself, under the ultimate authority of an imposed governor sent from Rome; but this constant internecine conflict was not only de-stabilizing the immediate region, it once more had knock on effects throughout the Mediterranean, with conflict erupting even within the Diaspora Jewish populations in the major cities of Europe and Asia Minor. Even in Syria there were anti-Semitic uprisings in AD 66. This could not be allowed to continue, heads were going to have to be knocked together.

The Jewish War is a known and well-documented historical event. The first major riots occurred in Caesarea in May AD 66, the riots Saul was involved in, and the Roman garrison was driven out of Jerusalem later the same year. Jewish regional commanders, including Jesus and Saul/Josephus, were then appointed by the Jewish authorities in Jerusalem to police the province. The Roman general Vespasian and his son Titus arrived in Israel in AD 67 with four legions to restore Roman authority and some semblance of law and order; the towns of Jotapata, Tiberias, Tarichaeae and Gamala being taken by the Romans that same year. Some of the Jewish leaders wanted peace with Rome, knowing that they could never win a war against such an empire and the

Roman presence did provide a measure of stability to an otherwise volatile land. Others were more foolhardy and were rashly lobbying for nothing short of complete independence from Rome. Under this pressure and perhaps also because the scriptures indicated that a Messiah was still due to appear, the various Jewish factions began fighting in Jerusalem.

Nero Caesar was dethroned in Rome the next year and Roman hostilities in Israel temporarily ceased while a new emperor was found and new orders could be issued to the commanders in the field. In this sudden power vacuum, the radical Jewish sect of Idumaeans* were summoned to protect Jerusalem from the fighting factions and began a great slaughter there. The rebel leader Jesus [the biblical Jesus], was killed in this battle and Zacharias, his good friend, was killed after further sham court proceedings. If Jerusalem was convulsed by political intrigue at this time, Rome was not doing much better. For the Romans, it became known as the year of four emperors, after the premature death of three emperors in quick succession, Galba, Otho and Vitellius, each being rapidly deprived of office. Rome was looking for a charismatic leader that all its people could respect; they found it in Vespasian, the commander of the campaign in Israel. Order returned to Rome and Vespasian gave the command of his legions to his son Titus, while he attended to matters in Rome. Thus began the siege of Jerusalem. [1]

Publican

This is a potted history of the events leading up to the fall of Jerusalem, but when did all this really happen? The historical texts are adamant and the dates given in the record are undeniably correct. But we have already run through some of these events before; they undoubtedly involve the dispute between Saul and Jesus, and so the dates cannot not agree. A convincing case has already been made that Saul was the historian Josephus, but this association presents considerable difficulties. By his own record, which corresponds well with other historical texts, Josephus was made commander of Galilee in AD 66 and proceeded to cause the Galileean rebel leader Jesus continual problems in the province. In the equivalent texts in the Bible, Saul was

* The Idumaean were a Jewish sect from southern Israel, the tribe from which Herod the Great's family sprang.

persecuting Jesus [the 'resurrected' Jesus] and the Nazarenes in the Galilee area; these events are traditionally set in about AD 30-35. If Saul and Josephus are the same, what is the real date for these events?

If the Josephus connection is true, then some of the biblical texts must be portraying the events that led up to the siege of Jerusalem, much later than is normally supposed. The question is, therefore, is there any further evidence to be found in the Bible that points towards a later period for these occurrences? Surprisingly enough, there is. The Bible gives the following events as being *after* Jesus had entered Jerusalem at the Passover festival, but *before* the Last Supper. Traditionally this is thought to be just days before Jesus' crucifixion in about AD 30. Jesus gave various warnings to his opponents, who were said to be the Pharisee sect in Jerusalem:

> But woe unto you, scribes and Pharisees, hypocrites! for ye shut up the kingdom of heaven against men ... behold, I send unto you prophets, and wise men, and scribes; and some of them ye shall kill and crucify; and some of them ye will scourge in your synagogues, and persecute them from city to city ...
> Oh Jerusalem, Jerusalem, thou that killest the prophets, and throws stones at those which are sent to you, how often would I have gathered thy children together, as a chicken gathers her chicks under her wings. And you would not! [B2]

In the parallel history of Josephus (Saul), there is a surprising agreement with this sentiment. The Jesus mentioned in these texts, whom I have identified with the biblical Jesus, is Jesus-Ananus the son of Gamala, deputy to the high priest Ananus. In this version, Jesus was addressing the Idumaean sect, who were locked outside the city gates of Jerusalem:

> You Idumaeans are come thither ... to support the vilest of men against us ... who have seized men of great eminence and under no accusation ... and tortured them with putting them into bonds ... they destroyed them ... They now triumph in the desperate condition they are in, when they hear that one people will fight against another people, and one city against another city ...
> Lay aside your arms, and come into Jerusalem under the notion of (being) our kindred ... let us both (both factions) alone and neither insult upon our calamities, nor abide with those plotters against Jerusalem. [J3]

There is a surprising similarity in these statements and it is now clear why Jesus was lamenting the city of Jerusalem. This was not the relative peace of AD 30, but the turbulence of AD 68 and the start of the siege of Jerusalem. Jesus continued his lament:

> That you may come to the blood shed upon the earth, from the blood ... of *Zacharias son of Barachias*, whom you slew between the temple and the altar. [B4] (my italics)

In similar refrain Josephus (Saul) continued:

> And now the Zealots and Idumaeans were weary of killing men, so they set up tribunals ... and they intended to have *Zacharias the son of Baruch*, one of the most eminent of the citizens, slain ... *he was also a rich man*, so that by taking him off, they did not only hope to seize his effects, but also get rid of a man with great power, to destroy them. [J5] (my italics)

The texts are obviously the same. Given the time that has elapsed, the number of scribes and translators that the texts of Josephus and the Bible have passed through; the speeches and personalities are remarkably unchanged. Zacharias son of Barachias just has to be the same as Zacharias son of Baruch. They have the same name and identical circumstances; even the site of this man's death is similar in both texts.

Zacharias was being given a show trial by the Zealots, led by Simon, to be judged by the chief priests. This event took place in the temple precincts. The priests, however, were not afraid of the Zealots and acquitted Zacharias of any wrongdoing. Enraged, two of the Zealots jumped on Zacharias '*in the middle of the temple*' and killed him. In comparison, the Bible says that Zacharias died '*between the temple and the altar*'. The Gospel of Luke then goes on to give further confirmation that these two texts are describing the same event:

> There was a man by the name of Zacchaeus, which was the chief among publicans, *and he was rich* ... and Jesus said to him, Zacchaeus make haste ... for today I must abide at thy house. [B6] (my italics)

Clearly this man Zacchaeus was identified as a personal friend of

Jesus, just as the late Zacharias was. In a similar fashion to Zacharias, the publican Zacchaeus is prominently identified as being rich. There is an undeniable similarity, which can be taken a stage further. Despite the lack of a 'surname' for this new character, it can be proved to great satisfaction that this is the same individual whose death Jesus later lamented. Quite simply, there has been another mistranslation in the biblical and Josephusan texts; the unravelling of this conundrum will doubly challenge the biblical date for the death of Jesus and the Nazarene church's confrontations with the enigmatic Saul.

Dionysus was the Greek god of wine, a son of Zeus. Rome inherited many of the Greek gods and gave them their own names. Dionysus became the Roman god Bacchus and anyone dealing in wine would undoubtedly receive such a nickname. Zacharias was not the son of Barachias, he was the son of Bacchus, the 'chief of publicans'. Bacchus was not a 'surname' as such, but a profession and it is from these professions that most of our modern surnames are derived. In Britain, one of the most common surname is Smith. A smith is simply the profession of metal worker which has been adopted into a surname. Anyone dealing in wine to the extent that the 'publican' Zacchaeus was would be called the son of Bacchus. Zacharias Bacchus was Zacchaeus the publican, the friend of Jesus. The 'surnames' of Barachias, Baruch and Bacchus link all three characters into one individual.

It is clear that Jesus knew this man personally. Zacchaeus sought out Jesus and, in turn, Jesus recognized him and commanded him to let Jesus stay at his house. They were well acquainted, perhaps of the same family. That is why Jesus lamented his death, both in the Gospel of Matthew and in the history of Josephus. Yet there is a big problem here, for it is now apparent that Jesus knew of Zacharias' death. Jesus mourned his passing and condemned his murderers, yet Zacharias was not slain until AD 67, shortly before the siege of Jerusalem. The evidence is clear: Jesus was being hounded by Saul in AD 66 and he was also playing an active role in the defence of Jerusalem in AD 68. According to Josephus, Jesus died at the hands of the Idumaean sect later that same year.

It should also be remembered that the father of John the Baptist, who was killed in the baptismal font by Herod the Great, was also called Zacharias in the Bible. The father of John in the historical record is Alexander, son of Aristobulus. If this last link in the chain were true, then Zacharias the publican is none other than a descendant of this royal family. This association is not as wild as it may at first seem. Although the names are different, priestly titles have been used in the texts on numerous occasions to cover up family names. The primary reason for using the nickname of Zacharias in this case, is the usual desire for prophesy fulfilment. Long ago one Zacharias, son of Jehoiada, had also chastised the people for transgressing the law and the sanctity of the temple, he too was killed in the courtyard of the temple. [B7]

Looking on the positive side, Jesus was related to John the Baptist's family, they were cousins. Jesus was also on very good terms with the family of Zacharias. Zacharias was not only rich, but influential enough in Jewish religious politics for the Zealots/Idumaeans to murder him; he was said to be 'eminent' and 'a man with great power'. In the guise of Alexander, who was a son of the former king and high priest of Jerusalem, he would have been equally rich and influential. In addition, both Zacharias the father of John the Baptist, and Alexander the father of Jonathan, are priests. In this comparison, however, Alexander himself is of the wrong generation to be the Zacharias killed in the siege of Jerusalem, it would have to be a son of Alexander [Zacharias]. The son would have inherited the title of Zacharias, of course, but what was his real name? A possible contender would be Matthew, a disciple of Jesus, who was also identified as being a 'publican'.

The term 'publican' might not seem very appropriate for the son of a king, but this is not quite so. Instead of a mere publican, this term really probably applied to the owner of vast estates of vineyards. Now *this* profession would actually be a very appropriate one for a descendant of the bloodline. Noah, whom David Rohl identifies as a Babylonian king, [8] was, according to the Bible, the first individual to plant and own vineyards and also the first person to get blind drunk. [B9] With the later references within the Grail family stories to 'bunches of grapes on the royal vine', perhaps these allusions were not simply allegorical; maybe the royal family was always associated with viticulture.

So was Zacharias Bacchus the same as Zacharias the son of Alexander [Zacharias]? It is difficult to say on the evidence here, but if it were so, then the relationship between Jesus and John might have been closer than the authorities like to admit. The evidence in the Koran only serves to underline and further confuse this issue. It not only indicates that John the Baptist and Jesus were cousins, their mothers being sisters as is widely known, but also that Mary (the mother of Jesus) *lived* with Zacharias:

> He (the Lord) made her grow a goodly child and entrusted her to the care of Zacharias. [K10]

Entrusted to the care of – is this as a godparent or as a husband? Significantly the Koran says that 'they cast lots' to see who would get Mary and they 'argued about her'. This sounds much more like an arranged marriage, with families bartering for the best daughters and dowries for their strapping sons, than the plight of an orphan who is being supported by her sister's husband. Whatever the case, Mary was a bloodline descendant of Moses, a princess; in this case the social status of Zacharias has to be a great deal higher than mere priest or publican. Also, the Koran does not mention a husband of Mary at all; instead, the verses detailing the birth of John the Baptist run into the birth of Jesus at such a rate that one reads it initially as being the same event; that Jesus was Zacharias' child. The import of the Koran's version of the birth of Jesus, is that John the Baptist was the son of Elizabeth [Alexandra] and Jesus was born to her sister Mary, but did they have the same father – Zacharias Joseph? Thus, did Mary and Elizabeth have the same husband?

Supporting this idea, it should be borne in mind that the character called Matthew-Levi held a party for Jesus and some publicans. The *disciple* Matthew was also a publican, so the biblical attempt to somehow separate these two characters wears a bit thin; they *were* the same person. The interesting thing about this is not the fact that a disciple of Jesus was a 'publican', as this profession has been adequately explained, but that Matthew-Levi's father is named as Alphaeus, the same name that has been associated with the father of Jesus in chapter VII. Once more this points towards Mary and Elizabeth having the same husband – Zacharias Bacchus the 'publican'. [B11]

When relating this to the original historical identification of John the Baptist as the son of Alexander [Zacharias], it is worth noting that his daughter was called Mariamme, which is another spelling of Mary. What is apparent, despite the confusion, is that the links between these royal families are becoming closer and closer and these observations deliver yet more profound implications for Christianity.

Part 2

After the fall of Jotapata, Saul/Josephus went into hiding in a well prepared den, well stocked with food. There were about 40 refugees in the den, but a woman from the hideaway was captured by the Romans up above and gave the position of the refuge away. The Romans wanted Saul alive, as they thought he might be useful to them. Saul decided to surrender and turn traitor, using the pathetic justification that:

> I protest openly that I do not go over to the Romans as a deserter of the Jews, but as a minister from (God). [J12]

There was a small obstacle in this plan: the other inhabitants of the refuge were not about to let Saul go, they wanted to kill him as a traitor instead. Saul embarked on a prolonged monologue, debating the merits of surrender, but the men were unimpressed. He then proposed that they draw lots for who should kill whom on their way to martyrdom. They agreed and one by one all the inhabitants of the den were slain by their compatriots. By some strange coincidence, it was Saul that drew the last lot and so escaped into the hands of the Romans. One suspects that this outcome was a typical Josephusan trick and, funnily enough, the Russian version of Josephus's *The Jewish War* says this was just the case. Josephus even afforded a laugh at the plight of his unfortunate companions.

The Romans flocked to see Saul and crowded around their new prisoner and their general, Vespasian. Some of the Romans even rejoiced at the taking of Saul, all of which just underlines the social standing that he must have enjoyed in Judaea. From the rear of the crush there arose a cry to kill Saul, he was, after all, the commander of the Jewish forces that had inflicted losses upon the Romans. Saul saw the mood changing and decided that only a show of military bravery would redeem his situation:

> Thou, Oh Vespasian, art Caesar and Emperor, thou and this thy son. Bind me now still faster, and keep me for thyself, for thou, Oh Caesar, art not only Lord over me, but over the land and the sea, and all mankind; ... [J13]

Nero was the reigning Caesar at this time, not Vespasian. Josephus was just indulging in a bout of cringe-worthy sycophancy to save his skin once more, predicting that Vespasian would become emperor. The stratagem worked, Saul was made the personal fortune teller to Vespasian, translator and propaganda expert. He became an early version of Lord Haw Haw, or William Joyce, an Irish American who turned traitor to Nazi Germany and beamed Nazi propaganda to Britain during the Second World War. Here, though, the analogy ceases. After the Second World War, Lord Haw Haw was tried and executed for war crimes; Saul was given a lavish apartment in Rome and founded a religion: Christianity.

After the fall of Jotapata, Vespasian moved his army back to the coast, to Caesarea (Strato's Tower). Caesarea was mainly Greek owned and opened the gates to Vespasian as a liberator, but the town was too small to house the entire army, so two legions were sent to Scythopolis just south of Lake Galilee. The town of Joppa, south of Caesarea was proving to be a thorn in Vespasian's flesh, so a small force was sent south. The Joppaeans took fright and made to their boats for safety, but they were caught by a storm and dashed against the rocks; another town had fallen to Rome. Titus, Vespasian's son, was commander of the two legions at Scythopolis and he now moved his forces north and east to the Sea of Galilee to take Tiberias. He was met by Vespasian and more forces, making three legions in all. (In the following descriptions penned by Josephus, the numbers of combatants and casualties need to be divided by about ten to arrive at sensible figures.)

A commander by the name of Valerian was sent with a detachment of fifty cavalrymen to talk with the inhabitants of the city of Tiberias, to try and gain their support. It was at this point that Jesus [the biblical Jesus] and some of his men dashed out and captured all the horses and Valarian was forced to withdraw on foot. [J14] Some of the elders of the city were unimpressed by this action; it would surely bring the wrath of the Roman legions down upon them. Many, including Agrippa, the nominal king of the Jews, left the town and ran over to the Roman camp, begging them to spare the town and punish Jesus and his men instead. Jesus saw that public opinion was turning against him, so he and his party left for Tarichaeae, a small town to the south of Tiberias. Shortly afterwards, Vespasian rode to Tiberias where the citizens opened the gates of the city to the general and 'met him with acclamations of joy'.

Presently the legions moved against Jesus in Tarichaeae,

surrounding the town and building towers from which to assail the defences. Although Jesus was confident of his position, boats were made ready in the small port in case a hasty retreat was required. Meanwhile, his men made a series of sallies out of the town wall, dispersing the Roman guards and builders. But one of the sallies went badly wrong and numerous followers of Jesus were caught out in the open by the Roman cavalry and slaughtered. The rump of the rebel forces struggled back into the town, but the population was now very afraid and disputes broke out between those who wished to fight on and those that did not. Taking advantage of the confusion within the town, the Romans scaled the walls and fell upon the defenders. The battle became a rout and Jesus was forced to flee to countryside. Others fled to the ships, sailing 'as far as they could from the enemy'. [J15] Vespasian took ships of his own and sailed after the fleeing rebels, cutting them down with withering fire from his archers until all the rebel boats had been dispatched.

As a punishment for resisting the might of Rome, the old and infirm of the city, numbering about a thousand, were dispatched in the stadium. Up to six thousand of the young men were given as slaves to Nero for a building project and the remainder, thirty thousand or so, were given to Agrippa as slaves. Despite this great loss, the people of Gamala, Jesus's home town, also decided to resist the Roman advance. The siege of Gamala lasted until the 22nd day of Hyperberetaeus, when the Romans succeeded in undermining a tower on the outer wall, which fell to the ground with a great crash. The Romans surged in through the gap and slaughtered the inhabitants, but many more perished through jumping from the walls in desperation. The final town in Galilee to hold out against the Romans was Gischala in the north. It was John of Gischala who persuaded the citizens of this town to shut the gates against the Romans. But seeing the Romans approach, they had a change of heart and persuaded him to flee. He did so with all his followers, sneaking through the Roman lines one dark night with 6,000 men and women and fleeing to Jerusalem. All of Galilee was now in Roman hands.

Jerusalem

The city was a formidable fortress, it was built upon the summits of two hills and much of the perimeter was protected with deep ravines, with thick megalithic walls on the top. In places where the terrain was more amenable, the fortifications were increased to include three walls, each separating off areas of the city. For the advancing Roman legions, this was not going to be the same as attacking the small towns of Galilee. There was to be no sudden rush upon such a fortress, so the build up of Titus' forces and the preparations of the area were slow and methodical. The main weapon, as was often the case with these sieges, was to be the prevention of provisions entering the city and the resulting starvation of the population.

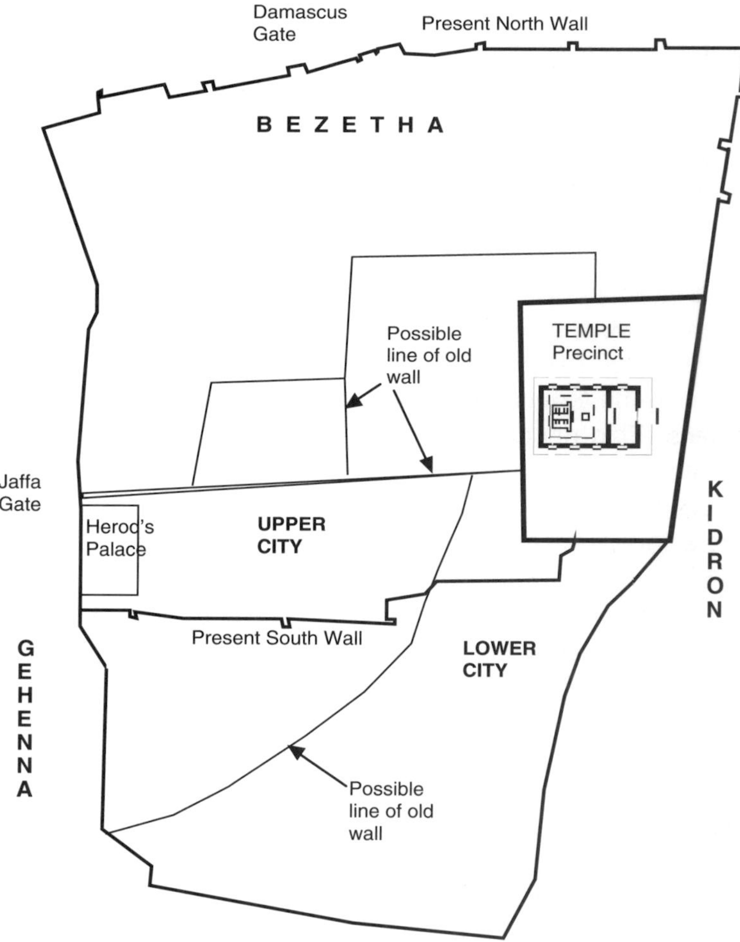

Fig 24. The City of Jerusalem

Before the Roman legions had arrived at the great walls of Jerusalem, the town was already convulsed with internal divisions. The Zealots were trying to evict the high-priests from the temple, to install their own incumbent. Ananus and Jesus [the biblical Jesus], the chiefs of the high priests, were forced to organize the men of the city to defend the temple precinct and a great battle erupted around the temple. [J16] John, who had recently fled from Gischala, advised Ananus on the deployment of his men and such was the politics of the era, that by night he told the Zealots of their plans. It was difficult to know who was friend and who was foe in the shifting sands of alliances within this conflict. John told the Zealots that Ananus had sent emissaries to Vespasian, with an invitation for the Romans to enter the city and restore order. The Zealots were outraged and sent a messenger to the Idumaean people for assistance. [J17] The messenger was also called Ananus. As this was a title it indicates that he, too, was a high priest.

The Idumaeans arrived at the gates of Jerusalem with 20,000 armed men, supposedly for the protection of the city. Their advance did not go unnoticed and the city gates were promptly shut in their faces. Jesus, son of Ananus and Gamala [the biblical Jesus], made a speech to the Idumaean soldiers from the walls of the city, indicating that they had *not* called for the Romans; indeed Jesus was greatly against the Roman occupation. He also pointed out that it was the Zealots who were polluting the temple precincts with the blood of their victims, not the Romans. This appeal fell on deaf ears and the Idumaean men camped outside the city, plotting an assault. During a storm, Jesus was not so vigilant in making his men patrol the defensive walls. Seeing their opportunity, the Zealots inside the city conspired to let the Idumaean soldiers in through a side gate. Once inside, they and the Zealots descended upon the temple guard in a great rush and slaughtered them all.

But the Idumaeans were 'not sated by these slaughters' in the temple precinct and fell upon the city of Jerusalem itself killing the people and casting the bodies away without so much as a burial. This pogrom was selective and it was primarily the priesthood and the traditional authorities who were sought out by the Zealots and Idumaeans for imprisonment. The treatment and torture of these unfortunates, was such that they cried out for their captors to kill them. It was at this point that Zacharias was tried before the high priests, who acquitted him of wrongdoing. The Zealots then murdered him and beat up the priests who had made the judgement. Some 8,000 people were killed in this rampage through the city, Ananus and Jesus of Gamala included.

Tiring of this slaughter, the Idumaean had a change of heart and they challenged the Zealots to prove that Ananus and Jesus had been plotting to invite the Romans. On receiving no evidence that the Romans were advancing, they freed the remaining prisoners and departed. Without a city garrison, this simply left the Zealots in control and they carried on where the Idumaean had left off; they arrested yet more eminent citizens and executed them. Vespasian, meanwhile, was waiting for the distant power struggle in Rome for the position of emperor to come to a conclusion and for further orders on how to proceed. However, on hearing of the conflict in Jerusalem, while taking his leisure in Alexandria, he was delighted and claimed that God was on the side of the Romans once more.

With the Romans inactive, fresh disputes broke out in and around Idumaea, to the south of Jerusalem. One Simon of Gerasa led his band of men into Idumaea and dispersed the population, winning a great battle. In Jerusalem, John of Gischala was still causing havoc within the city and so Simon of Gerasa and his men were let into Jerusalem to help in the fight against John. But the situation merely deteriorated even further, with three factions within the choking confines of this small city all fighting one another.

In Rome, the emperors Galba and Otho had been deposed and the new emperor, Vitellius, was trying to consolidate his position. A power struggle broke out and soon the legions of Rome were lining up to fight each other throughout Egypt and Asia Minor. Vitellius came off the worse in this conflict; the general Antonius met the army of the emperor in Rome itself and defeated them. After eight months of rule, Vitellius had his head cut off. By popular demand, Vespasian was now proclaimed the new Caesar in Alexandria. Vespasian wanted to get back to Rome as soon as possible, to consolidate his position as emperor, so he despatched his son Titus to Palestine to deal with Jerusalem once more. Titus marched his forces back across the deserts to the divided city of Jerusalem and pitched camp just outside.

Siege

The siege of Jerusalem had now started in earnest. Siege engines, capable of lobbing great stones and flaming pitch over the city wall, were erected just out of bow-shot from the defenders. Towers were also constructed, high enough for the attackers to shoot down upon the wall defenders and keep the wall clear for engineers to undermine it. The towers were elaborate constructions, with a skin of iron to prevent flaming arrows from setting them alight, but one of them fell down of its own accord with a mighty crash and alarmed the whole Roman camp. By this slow, methodical work, the first wall was breached and the Romans now had access to an inner section of the wall. Work on the second wall was more perilous, as the Romans were now surrounded by defenders while they worked.

The second wall was taken five days later and a thousand Roman infantry swarmed in, but the streets where they were forced to fight were narrow and the local militia knew the layout better than they did. The advance was halted and eventually the Romans were thrown back out of this quarter of the city. Titus took stock after this reversal and Saul/ Josephus was brought in to persuade the Jews to surrender. Saul reminded the population of the hopelessness of their position, their lack of food and the invincible might of the Roman army. He offered them the security and protection of the Romans, whereas if the city were taken by force, none would be spared. The predictable response was a volley of arrows and abuse from the walls of the city.

In truth, however, the situation in Jerusalem was grave and many of the citizens started slipping out of the side gates and surrendering to the Romans. As a sign of their goodwill, the Romans let these people go, to entice more to desert. To stop the trickle from becoming a flood, both John and Simon watched for these deserters and cut the throats of any who dared. In addition, their men now toured the city looking for food. If any was found in a house where the owner had denied having any, the occupants were cruelly tortured by inserting sharp spikes up their rectums. [J18]

Titus found that the citizens of Jerusalem were making foraging sorties at night, looking for scraps of food. He crucified those he found and set about sealing off the city with a wall all around its circumference. This, together with the banks being constructed for the siege, was a prodigious undertaking, yet his troops laboured tirelessly to achieve their goals, each unit trying to outdo the other in their work. Accordingly, the famine in the city worsened and many of the less fortunate made desperate attempts to leave. Some had taken the precaution of swallowing gold before slipping out of the city, to finance another life. When this became known to certain of the Roman soldiers, they began dissecting the refugees alive, searching their stomachs for booty. Those who stayed fared no better; either they starved or were tortured by

Simon and John's men, the corpses being piled up high outside the city gates.

At its height, the famine was so severe that men were reduced to eating the old dung heaps from the cattle market and one desperate woman was caught eating her child. The siege was relentless and the Romans were still pressing from the outside, with huge battering rams pounding away at the walls. The work appeared to be having no effect and the men were demoralized, but suddenly a section collapsed and the way was open for an assault.

There was a standoff for a while, as the breach was well defended and nobody dared to be the first in. Twelve brave souls finally decided to enter the breach and although they successfully entered the city, they were overcome by missiles and arrows and perished. After another two days, some soldiers slipped into the breach at night, mounted the inner wall, dispatched the slumbering guards and blew their trumpets as a signal. The Romans now surged in and a great battle commenced, this quarter of the city being finally secured.

The great battering rams were now brought to bear on the inner walls, but as the stones were so well laid, they made little impact. Skirmishes continued in and around the taken part of the city and in one of these the great Temple of Herod was burned to the ground. Following this, the Romans built large banks to allow the battering rams to be brought up against more vulnerable walls. This time when a breach was made the defenders were overcome by fear and fled their posts; the Romans took advantage of their fright and captured large sections of the wall. As the rout continued, the defenders also fled the three main towers on the wall. The Romans could not believe their luck, for these sections of the wall were nigh on impregnable. The Roman ensign at last flew from the towers and the city surrendered.

Mopping up

Most of the Jewish rebels were rounded up and killed; as for the rest of the population, their fate again depended on their physique. The fit were gathered together and either sent off to the Egyptian mines or to the gladiatorial theatres for entertainment. The younger of them were sent as personal slaves for the Roman upper-classes. Josephus put the numbers involved in the siege as 1,100,000 killed and 97,000 taken as slaves, figures which have to be doubted, as usual. The figures were high, said Josephus, because the Romans besieged the city at the Passover festival and all the pilgrims from the surrounding districts were in Jerusalem for the biggest celebration of the year. Josephus estimates that there were up to 2.5 million in the city before the siege, so the number taken as slaves was a small proportion of those that survived.

Thus there is another fusion between these stories. Although the high priests, Jesus of Gamala [the biblical Jesus] and Ananus, died defending the temple before the final siege by the Romans; it would seem that the final Roman advance on the city was on the eve of the Passover festival, locking inside the thousands of visitors. The analogy is obvious, for the biblical Last Supper was also a Passover meal held in Jerusalem.

For the Roman army, there was still the little matter of the fortress of Masada, held by the Sicarii Zealots. It was a remote fortress on the coast of the Dead Sea, held by a few thousand rebels. Such was the fervour of these people, it was deemed necessary to capture the citadel and prevent them from inciting another revolt. The siege was another laborious affair, with great stone ramps and towers being built to allow the walls to be struck with the rams. At last, when the Romans had achieved their goal, the citadel seemed to fall silent. With some trepidation, a few soldiers entered into the breach, to find that all 960 of the defenders had committed suicide with their own swords. For the continuing bloodline story, only two women and five children were found alive, hiding in the cellars.

Those from the Sicarii faction who escaped Judaea fled to Alexandria in Egypt. The Sicarii were obviously a sub-grouping of the Nazarene church, because the place they fled to was Heliopolis and the Arian (now Piscean) temple of Onias. On receiving orders from the emperor, Lupus the governor of Alexandria closed and demolished the temple at Heliopolis. [J19] The Sicarii were then pursued as far south as Thebes, in Upper Egypt, where 600 were captured. They were returned to Alexandria and burned.

It was probably at this point, with the destruction of the temple at Heliopolis, that the last of the priests with the ancient knowledge of the old religion of Egypt were silenced. The long and illustrious history of Egyptian theology had come to an end in this land. It was not to be extinguished entirely, for the turmoil in the region had inadvertently produced one positive side-effect. Wave after wave of emigrants had been forced to flee both Egypt and Israel over the millennia, they had spread out across the Mediterranean, settling in far-away lands. They took with them their own individual brands of the Arian/Piscean religion, each wave carrying its distinct version of their creed, depending on the region and the era of their origin. In these distant lands the individual brands of this theology have left their mark, often one peculiar to that region. It is from these local beliefs that the areas these people fled to can be traced; indeed, the modern thread of these Egyptian cosmological beliefs can also picked up – for they were not entirely extinguished.

Chapter X

Legacy

The end of the Second World War saw much of Europe on the move, but this form of mass migration has happened many times before. In the long history of Egypt, it is clear that there were many forced exoduses from that historic land because of the religious disputes and intolerance that have been explored in this book. Elements of the population, both small and large, may have set out across the Mediterranean during many of the crises that hit Egypt. Like the Pilgrim Fathers making the perilous journey to America in 1620 AD, they would have forsaken everything and risked their very lives in order to escape religious persecution in their homeland.

It is difficult to call these people Arians any more, for the constellations had now moved on and Pisces was in the ascendance. Perhaps 'Stellar-people' and their astronomer-priests would be more appropriate. Whatever the name, there were many incentives for these peoples of Egypt and Israel to spread out across the Mediterranean. During the exodus of Jacob, for instance, in the seventeenth century BC; again during the later exodus of (Tuth)Moses in the fourteenth century BC, some of the population would have taken to the Mediterranean, rather than face the trials of crossing the Negev desert.

More than 700 years later, the descendents of these peoples would have faced more or less the same choices and doubtless some of them made the same decisions. Some would have fled as the Babylonians closed in on Jerusalem from the north-east, more still would have fled as the Romans began their last devastating campaign. The Stellar-people (Stellans) undoubtedly did colonize other coastal areas around the Mediterranean, but the questions are where did they go to and can their migrations still be traced in the historical record?

Classical archaeologists are in agreement that ancient migrations did take place in prehistoric times, although they often tend to be rather hazy about the dates and the countries involved. The general opinion is that emigrations and influences spread from the Near East, from Persia and Egypt, up through the Danube valley and also westwards out across the Mediterranean coastline. These could either have been small groups of people, convoys of just three or four ships looking for new pastures and a freedom to practise their religion without persecution, or mass migrations of entire tribes. Either way, they are likely to have steered away from the established conurbations of southern Europe and chosen instead the more isolated locations where they could be of great influence among the small, unsophisticated, indigenous populations.

One site these peoples from the east settled was the Balearic Islands of Mallorca and Minorca, just off the coast of Spain, where they appear to have established small communities. If these were indeed Stellan pilgrims, it is quite possible that this colonization was achieved in two waves, with the first Jacobite exodus settling on Minorca alone. On this isolated island, the population started erecting strange megalithic 'tables' or Taules, formed from a single upright stone and a single slab on the top.

Although I had visited Minorca on many occasions and had seen postcards of the stones, a visit had never been possible. Luckily a *Thoth* reader, Stephen Johnson, had made a tour of the sites and was kind enough to alert me to a web-site that gave further information on the history of these strange stones. Armed with this information, it was apparent that although some of the Neolithic artefacts in this region are common to all the Balearic islands, this particular feature of the Taule is unique to Minorca; hence the suggestion that the first immigration was to this island alone. These megalithic tables stand up to four meters high and are constructed with mortise and tenon joints, as are found in the Stonehenge monument in Britain. Their function is unknown; some have suggested a central pillar to a house, but the more likely explanations involve a religious function. Each Taule appears to have been situated inside a horseshoe of standing stones, with an opening to the south, and many are in isolated hilltop locations. Some have speculated on human sacrifice on top of the high table, but this appears to be an impractical suggestion.

As an alternative, the Spanish archaeologist, J. Mascaro Pasarius, suggested they were images of a bull, with the capstone being analogous to the wide horns of this sacred animal. [1] This is possible; certainly the upright stones seem to sport a 'spine' on their backs, just as if they were designed to be symbolic representations of an animal. Also, the name 'Taule' is based on the Semitic and Greek letter for 'T', the Tau, and this links quite nicely to Taurus the bull. However, there may be a problem with the translation here, for the astrological symbol for Taurus has high horns, not horizontal horns and the name 'Taules' is a modern rendition based on the perceived shape of these stones. This scenario would also indicate that the Taule makers were possibly exiled Taureans from Upper Egypt and linked to the influential bull cult of Minoan Crete. If the Egyptian link is to be taken seriously, this is unlikely. The archaeological dates given for these structures circulate around the late Bronze age, *circa* 1500 to 1300 BC, but the Taureans were not unduly under pressure at this time, except for a brief persecution under the pharaoh Akhenaton, so the likelihood of a Taurean migration is slim.

So were these Taurean constructions? Indeed, how confident are we that these Balearic peoples came from Egypt? There are many reasons for speculating just this. Classical archaeology presupposes that these people came initially from the east and the presence of carefully crafted boat-shaped tombs, called Navetas, seems to confirm that they were migrants from across the sea. The Egyptian connection is further confirmed by the discovery in the enclosure of one of the Taules, the Torre d'en Gaumes, of a statue of the legendary Egyptian architect Imhotep. [2] In addition, many of the Taules are associated with halls of pillars, vestigial equivalents of the great imposing hypostyle halls that adorn all the temples of Egypt.

If these peoples had Egyptian influences, but were unlikely to be Taureans, were they instead the exiled Jacobite or Akhenatonite Arians from Lower Egypt? The Taules may look like our western European image of a bull, but this was not necessarily the image that an ancient Egyptian would have had. Just like the astrological symbol for Taurus, the Egyptian image of the bull had high horns and this is confirmed by the hieroglyph for a bull, which sported a very upright set of horns. This hieroglyph was later reduced, in the much later Egyptian cursive script to a 'Y' shape, but clearly it retained the image of the upright bull horns. In Egyptian eyes, the Minorcan Taules would have been poor representations of a bull.

If these monuments were unlikely to be representations of bulls, what were they? The horned animal in Egyptian religion that sported horizontal horns was the ram. The ram was always pictured with straight horns, as the early domestic sheep of Egypt (*Ovis longpipes palaeoaegyptiaca*) had this arrangement. The more familiar curly horned sheep (*Ovis aties platyra aegyptiaca*) were not introduced until later. In the later cursive script the hieroglyph for the ram turned into a 'J' shape with a wavy lintel on top, much the same as the astrological sign for Aries. [3] For the original images from which these hieroglyphs were formed, see the colour plate of the gods (Amun and Knum) depicted in these forms.

Cursive bull hieroglyph *Cursive ram hieroglyph*
Fig 25.

The inference is clear. If these Minorcans were refugees from Egypt, they were Arians, pushed out of the country in either of the two exoduses that have been covered. As an initial hypothesis one might propose that it involved the first of the exoduses because this was a very small colony, limited only to the island of Minorca. There appears to have been a second and larger immigration that encompassed all the Balearic islands and this event brought in yet more Egyptian monuments to the area. The other Egyptian monuments in the Balearic islands will be looked at a little later, for there is another exodus history to cover first; the much later Jewish exodus from Israel.

Out of Israel

Undoubtedly, some of the population of Israel escaped into exile before the fall of Jerusalem to the Romans in AD 70, but the majority after.

Whatever the timing, another wave of emigrants was set into motion and it pushed out across Europe in search of new pastures. This was the fourth exodus for the Stellan people in a very turbulent 1600 years. It is no wonder that some of them wished to put the trials and tribulations of the Near East behind them and set up new empires in the West and perhaps the Far East.

Some of the emigrants were destitute beggars, some were rich and powerful, with caches of gold to purchase a fresh life in the 'new world'. Whatever their financial status though, it is surprising that some of them seem to have immediately pushed their way into the theological and royal life of western Europe. Sir Laurence Gardner makes a plausible argument that the daughter of Joseph of Arimathea immediately married into the royal Celtic family from which King Lear, of Shakespearian fame, was eventually borne. Anna of Arimathea married the Arch Druid Bran the Blessed in about 50 or 60 AD, well before the fall of Jerusalem and they established the royal line that eventually produced Morgaine, the wife of King Arthur. [4]

But if this is true, how did it happen? How does an exiled prince simply move to another country and establish himself within the bosom of another royal dynasty. Sir Laurence Gardner seems to think that this was no coincidence because the two royal lines knew each other intimately. Indeed, he states that Joseph of Arimathea was summoned to Britain by the wife of King Caractacus of Camulod and that he travelled from Rome to Britain in the company of Bran the Blessed. Gardner speaks with authority, but without always divulging his sources, so it is difficult to tell how much credence to attach to these stories. It is interesting, however, that the Welsh seem to have called Joseph 'Ilid', a corruption of the word Eli (Heli), which is, in turn, descended from Ellil and eventually Enlil, the chief of the Sumerian gods.

It is owing to stories such as these and the myths concerning the visit of Josephenes, Jesus' son, to Britain that the survival of this royal family line should be taken seriously. Indeed, these myths are not the only evidence available. As a reminder, there is the marriage of Jesus and the strange narrative in the Bible where Saul met the 'son of Jesus' in Cyprus. Some more evidence for this survival will be seen shortly, but perhaps a deliberate mistake in this work is beginning to emerge. It is clear that the title of this book is slightly misleading; Jesus was not the 'last of the pharaohs'. He was just the last of the pharaohs on the African continent. The royal line did not die out, it appears to have re-established itself in the heart of Europe.

Divine Kings

The Egyptian royal line had been famed for its links with the deities and for its sacred knowledge. From the pharaohs of old Egypt to King Solomon and to Jesus himself, the royal line had long been sought after for its sacred knowledge and its sacred blood. This is why Jesus' family was able to mingle so successfully with the royal houses of Europe and to re-establish its dynasty elsewhere. Rome may have been impervious to such things at the time, perhaps through having a civil aristocracy rather than a royal one, but there were plenty of other royal lineages in Europe who would happily link to the pharaonic dynasty and become allied to the gods themselves. One of these royal lines was resident in Britain.

The royal fusion had its desired effect and these ancient Britons were thus elevated in the eyes of some of the European royalty. Once more, Sir Laurence Gardner speaks with authority when he states that the daughter of Caractacus (a Pendragon chief) eventually married a Roman senator and that the son of his other daughter became Bishop of Rome, Prince Linus, the first elected Pope. [5]

Again the provenance of this information is obscure, but conventional history seems to confirm that there was something special to be found in the British aristocracy. In Celtic tradition, as in Egypt, the royal line was matrilineal, the inheritance of kingship ran through the daughters of the king. This was why, centuries later, the Roman Emperor Constantius married Princess Elaine of Britain. It was his son, Constantine I, who was crowned Emperor of Rome in York, England. It was Constantine I who created Roman Catholicism as it is known and tried, unsuccessfully, to become the new Messiah through his assumed royal descent from the family of Jesus. [6]

Until the reign of Constantine, though, the fate of the family may have hung in the balance – there was much Roman opposition to the fledgeling Christian church at that time and the Nazarene church would undoubtedly have been caught up in these conflicts. But in northern Europe, regional kings like Bran the Blessed were not just Britons, they were Celts and so if the political situation was no longer favourable in the lowlands of England, then the highlands of Wales and Ireland would always be a refuge. Bran was quoted as saying:

> He who would be chief, let him make himself a bridge. [7]

* * *

This has been taken as a reference to the flight of his troops into Ireland. In doing so, Bran would have been retreating back to his homeland, to Tara where the Celtic traditions were born thousands of years prior to this. As is explained in *Thoth, Architect of the Universe*, the Celtic traditions were quite possibly born in circumstances that were broadly similar to those in Egypt and that the building of the Egyptian pyramids and the great Irish henges was coincident. If royal lines were also established alongside those ancient monuments and traditions, then the Celtic royal bloodline could be seen as being broadly similar to the Stellan/Jewish bloodline; both possibly descended from an ancient, more technical civilization. The Celts would have been sons and daughters of the same tradition as the Jews, but they were royal lines that had been separated for a few thousand years.

The Jewish family monuments were the Giza pyramids in Egypt, for the Druids of Britain it was Stonehenge and Avebury and for the Celts of Ireland it was Bru, sometimes called Eamhain, in County Meath (now known as Newgrange). Here in the first century AD, there was a union between the Celtic royal line and the Judaic one. Some of the daughters of Bran would have held the Celtic bloodline and from this point on the Judaic royal line mingled with this Celtic line, a new unified dynasty was being formed.

Kilkenny

I was on a ballooning competition in Kilkenny, a delightful rural town on the river Nore where the smooth Kilkenny beer is brewed. The delights of ballooning are slightly tempered by the early rise to catch the calm air conditions needed to inflate the balloon, but the compensation lies in the stillness of the morning before the town stirs, the cool air with wisps of mist drifting across the grass. The assembly point in Kilkenny was in the castle grounds, almost in the town center. So at five-thirty each fine morning, just before sunrise, a line of 4 x 4 vehicles and their trailers wound their way through the castle gate onto the open grass area at the rear of the castle.

Each vehicle and its party of helpers spread themselves out across the field and there arose a hubbub of cries and shouts, the whirr of powerful fans and the roar of gas burners, as the teams tried to organize their inflation. The idea was to get as many balloons filled as possible, but still attached to the ground and then at the start time the balloons would rise en-masse. Well, not quite en-masse as that is a little dangerous, but in staggered batches.

Soon the castle grounds were awash with globes of vivid colours as each balloon jostled with its partner for space. The roars of the gas burners echoed around the castle walls, each burn lighting up the canopy above in the morning gloom like giant Christmas lights flashing on and off. At the appointed time, the first few balloons were released and rose into the air, followed by another and another in quick succession, each pilot looking for a safe patch of clear sky to launch into, until the sky was speckled with dashes of colour.

With a final burst of heat from the burners into our balloon and a quiet command to cast-off, we were away. There was no fuss, no noise, the balloon already had sufficient buoyancy in its canopy and it simply and majestically rose into the air, leaving a sea of balloons below that carpeted the castle grounds like beds of multicoloured crocuses in a field. The gentle breeze aloft took us back over the town, which from 500 feet looked close enough to touch. Here was the brewery, there the new bypass and in the distance the Slieeardagh Hills, the lower swathe of grey early morning mist contrasting strongly with the purples of the heather clad tops. Very soon we were flying over one of the main churches in the town. It was of the standard cruciform design, facing due east at the rising Sun, like the Tabernacle of Moses and the sunrise facing temples of Akhenaton. Beside it and to the south was a tall tower, its long early morning shadow betraying its true height. It looked a little peculiar, somehow of a different era from the church itself. The church had a steeple incorporated into its design, so why the need for two towers?

After the flight we found ourselves standing outside the church with the round-tower rising up about 35 m above us. It was as peculiar from the ground as it was from the air. The design was round like a chimney, with a conical roof structure on the top. It appeared to be older than the church and the entrance door was perched precariously some five meters above the ground. What on earth was its function?

A little searching in the church literature gave some explanations, but ones that seemed to be increasingly untenable, the more information that was obtained. The literature indicated that the concept of the round-tower was a very old tradition and that it was unique to Ireland in this format. The towers were quite common throughout the country, they were always physically independent of the churches or cathedrals with which they were associated and they were traditionally linked to the many monasteries that were present in Ireland during the Dark Ages. The precise purpose of the towers is unknown and yet it does seem peculiar that the function of such a common feature of Irish religious life can be lost in less than a thousand years. In the literature their possible usage was given as follows:

a. They were bell towers for the monasteries.
This idea seemed nonsensical. How could the literature state that these structures were bell towers when there are no windows at the top of the tower from which to project the sound? The tower walls are massively thick and the only apertures are the door and two or three small windows, which are positioned to admit enough light inside for those climbing the internal wooden stairs. These windows are arranged in different quadrants of the tower, just like those to be seen on old-fashioned lighthouses. To hear the bells in such a tower, one would have to stand within the tower itself.

b. They were defensive positions against the invading Vikings during the Dark Ages.
Again this did not ring true. Many of the round towers were associated with monasteries, which are known to have had underground refuges against attack. The Monastery at Monasterboice (Monastery on the river Boyne) had three such refuges called 'souterrains', which were hewn out of the bedrock. The literature says of these:

> ... analysis of the structure and design of souterrains tends to suggest a defensive role for them. This coupled with the numerous references in early Irish manuscripts to people taking refuge in souterrains, tends to support the idea that they were built primarily for this purpose. Their fireproof construction and narrow, cramped (access) passages must have deterred all but the most persistent of foes. On the other hand, their effectiveness as food stores would have been severely diminished by their almost universal dampness and cramped interiors.[8]

In this case, there were other refuges nearby that would negate the need to build such a huge and difficult to construct towers. In addition the towers themselves are not very good defensive positions, despite the strange entrance door being in an inaccessible position high up the tower. The towers themselves are hollow tubes of stone with no internal rooms and could only have housed a handful of the proposed defenders. They resemble a tall Victorian industrial chimney, with a wooden structure of steps leading up to the top. If an enemy had access to the base of the tower, it would be simplicity itself to chip out a brick from the bottom, introduce some combustible materials and turn the whole edifice into a remarkably good copy of its Victorian cousin – a chimney. The Victorian version was designed to draw in air at the bottom and burn strongly; its Dark Ages relative would have done exactly the same and its occupants would have been roasted alive in no time. These structures were not defensive positions.

Finally, in terms of the often cited threat from the Vikings, it is a fact that Monasterboice remained as a functional monastery during all the Viking invasion periods. Yet Monasterboice is on the east coast of Ireland, on the edge of the Boyne valley and would have been one of the first areas invaded by the Norsemen. The literature confirms this when it says:

> Already in 964, when it might be thought conditions for study and literature composition could have been adversely affected by the presence of the Norsemen at Monasterboice, the orbit of the abbot and bishop, Dubhhabhoireann, lauds him as the 'sage of learning of all Leinster'; almost a century later in 1092, the abbot Cormac is described as 'head of the Irish in learning. [9]

Clearly the monastery was not suffering unduly because of the presence of the Vikings and as it would have depended in part on the patronage of the local population, the Norse must have allowed the continued support of the ancient church here.

c. The towers were storage areas for church valuables.

This is a more plausible idea. Certainly the inaccessible door and difficult access to the upper floors would have deterred all but the most determined of local thieves, even if it would not have deterred the invading hoards. There are also many records of church valuables being stored in the towers, which again supports this idea. Confirmation of these towers being repositories for a library or records is more tenuous. The only reference in any records is the simultaneous burning of the church books and the tower in the

> same fire at Monasterboice. But this does not necessarily mean that the books were in the tower itself; the fire could have been a wider conflagration.
>
> In fact, it is unlikely that church records and valuables were normally stored in these towers. These religious sites and monasteries were very often located in elevated positions in the countryside and the towers themselves were very tall. With the prevailing weather conditions in Ireland and their exposed positions, there are many recorded incidences of their being struck by lightning and their subsequent burning. Truly these would be inappropriate places to place combustible valuables.

Even if one or two abbots did order their gold plate and candlesticks to be placed in the towers for safe keeping, this observation could be coincidental rather than causal. Just because the valuables are there does not necessarily mean that this is the prime reason for the tower's construction. When designing and constructing a storehouse, would the first thoughts be to design a tower more than 35 m high? Is there not an easier design that does not require hauling building materials up an enormous height above the ground?

In addition, why are these towers the same all over Ireland? The design of something as mundane as a storehouse might be of any local design; but a construction that can be seen to be consistent throughout the land strongly indicates that its shape was special, perhaps religious or sacred. Like the consistent design of the churches themselves, the fact that these towers were so important that every monastery had one and each was the same as its neighbour, indicates strongly that these structures were not secular, but sacred artefacts.

War

This idea is reinforced by a rather modern usage of these structures. During the Somme offensive during the First World War, the Protestant Northern Irish regiments became much depleted in number. Due to a lack of resources, they were eventually merged with their mortal enemies, the Catholic Southern Irish regiments. However reluctantly, the soldiers accepted the situation. Their unity was sorely tested, though, as they were thrown into action to recapture a bleak spot known simply as Messine Ridge. The task for these young soldiers was the same up and down the Western Front, stand up and walk unprotected into a hail of high velocity lead. Even the highly disciplined ancient Roman soldiery would have baulked at such a request. That day saw the Irish regiments wiped out and Messine Ridge for the Irish became their small section of the tragic carnage that was Ypres or the Somme.

Unfortunately, for the Southerners, their trials were not over at the end of the war. In their absence, a revolt in Dublin had changed the political map of the island and the victorious war weary soldiers returned home to be branded as traitors for fighting alongside the British. Many were persecuted and some were killed. The dead may have been resting in peace deep in the soil of Flanders, but there was to be no such opportunity for the living.

In the years following the Great War, majestic cemeteries were built all along the line of the Western Front to mark this great sacrifice of humanity. At Thiepval Ridge, the Northern Irish built a tower of remembrance, but the fallen of the South were just an embarrassment to the government, to be erased from history. It has taken more than 75 years for this wrong to be righted, but eventually in the spirit of reconciliation, a cross-border charitable trust has erected a monument at the Messine cemetery – an Irish round-tower. Despite the power of Rome in the land, the Irish symbol of remembrance was deemed to be this strange almost pagan tower. [10]

If these towers were and still are so sacred, what do they mean? There appears to be much confusion over their function, but does the modern usage at Messine betray a hidden knowledge of their true role? This is a possibility, but outsiders must build a hypothesis using only the facts at hand and that presents some problems.

Firstly, to try and guess the function of an artefact, when it is alien to our culture, is nigh on impossible. The mind instantly regresses into familiar forms and functions: churches have spires and bell-towers, castles have secure circular keeps; these are the things that instantly spring to mind when the towers are first seen. Casting further afield, images of minarets alongside an Islamic mosque betray a close similarity, but once more it would not be practice to call the faithful to church from a single narrow opening halfway up the tower. If minarets and church steeples were distant cousins of the round-tower, their original purpose could not have been for the calling of the faithful.

Secondly, if the Catholic church ever knew the origins and purpose of these towers, it would have wanted to cover their true function with any story that it could concoct. For the origins of these towers are not only alien to the church, they were a direct threat to it and their survival is quite remarkable in the light of that. This has to be a sign that the ancient Celtic religion in Ireland has a ground-swell of support that has survived despite the suffocating blanket of Catholicism that has covered the country for the last 1,200 years. Even today, the site at Monasterboice and its Celtic crosses is a place of great pilgrimage, despite the clearly Celtic overtones of the site.

The conundrum has yet to be solved, what are these round towers? The clue to the origins of this artefact can be seen at Messine ridge and the modern tower of remembrance there. The top window in this tower is not for sounding a lament to the brave men of the Irish regiments, but to capture the rays of the Sun on the eleventh hour, of the eleventh day, of the eleventh month; the exact time the First World War ended.

Benben

The true function of the Irish round-towers is quite astounding, for their history has more synergy with the British and Irish henges than the doctrines of Rome. In fact, the origin of the round-tower is more obscure than even this, for the design came to Ireland straight out of Egypt. The round-towers are simply copies of the most sacred site at Heliopolis, the Benben tower. In their form as round towers, in their conical tops, in their obvious sacred and solar significance, in the light of all that has been said of the Stellan religion, they can be nothing else. Somehow, at some time, the traditions of Egypt have slipped into Ireland.

The Benben is one of the most ancient traditions in Egypt. It was centered on the city of Heliopolis and the temple of the Phoenix. The Benben stone was not the entire tower, but the conical stone on the top, which is often presumed to have been of meteoric origins. Because of its dramatic and fiery appearance in the world, in falling from the skies, the Benben was considered to have originally been the property of the gods. From this, the link was made to its being the seed of the gods, part of the ritual of death and rebirth.

Legends indicate that the original Benben stone at Heliopolis went missing around 2,000 BC. Various pharaohs have erected replacement towers there, offerings to the gods, which were presumably the root of the obelisk cult in Egypt. The oldest of these obelisks to have survived is the red granite construction of Senusret I, which still stands in the suburbs of Cairo. The obelisk is quite bare now, but many of these stele were originally covered in precious metals, electrum or gold.

Fig 26. The Benben tower at Heliopolis

The design of the replacement obelisks is obviously different from the original Benben; perhaps the new design reflected the more geometric form of the pyramids. In its original form though, the monument of Senusret would have looked very different, for the top was originally sheathed with a cone of thick copper that added another three cubits (1.5m) to its height. This was reported by Abd el-Latif, a twelfth-century Arab physician, who also reported that the obelisk was stained green with verdigris. [11] Perhaps with this cone in place, something approaching the design of the original Benben would have been achieved.

Josephus confirms this with his story of the Jewish priest Onias, mentioned in chapter VI. Onias went to Heliopolis (the city of On) in the reign of Ptolemy in order to construct a temple there, for Heliopolis was by all accounts deserted. What he actually built was:

> ... a temple, not like that at Jerusalem, but such as resembled a tower. He built it of large stones to the height of sixty cubits (32 m); he made the structure of the altar in imitation of our own (altar in Jerusalem), excepting the make of the candlestick ... a single lamp hammered out of gold ... the entire temple was encompassed with a wall of burned brick, though it had gates of stone. [12]

Even in the Ptolemaic era (*circa* 160 BC), in a temple constructed by the Jewish high priest of Jerusalem, the rebuilt temple at Heliopolis was centered around a sacred tower. Such is the power of these constructions that they have dominated the politics of many nations, not just Ireland. Despite what the Irish guide books say of the uniqueness of their tradition, many countries have copied these round-tower designs and others have simply appropriated original obelisks direct from Egypt. In the modern era, France, Great Britain and America have all erected stele taken from Egypt in their capital cities and this practice has a long history.

The first instance of this appears when a Roman emperor ordered an obelisk to be taken to Constantinople (Istanbul). Subsequently a succession of Roman emperors appropriated thirteen obelisks to the ancient Roman capital. That the emperor Constantius's engineers managed to transport the 500-tonne obelisk, now at Piazza San Giovanni, from Karnak to Rome in about AD 357, suggests that the ancients could indeed organize the transportation of these massive weights. However, it is true that the Roman effort involved iron pulleys and pivots and the assistance of teams of horses, none of which was supposed to be available in Egypt 1800 years earlier. It was a marvellous feat of transportation, but well within the capability of Roman technology. The Giovanni obelisk was originally dedicated to Tuthmoses III and it is one third higher and more than twice as heavy as the obelisk known as Cleopatra's Needle, which was transported to London in the nineteenth century. [13]

Another of the Roman obelisks stands rather incongruously in St. Peter's square, outside the Vatican. Although it is an original Egyptian obelisk, this was the only one in Rome not to have been toppled after the Christians came to power in the fourth century. Its survival there is probably because it has no inscriptions, like two others in Rome. There has been no satisfactory explanation for this lack of carvings, as no uninscribed obelisks of this nature have been found in Egypt, so the question of where the Romans appropriated them from is a mystery. The fate of the other obelisks in Rome was more uncertain and the Giovanni obelisk, for instance, lay buried for more than a thousand years; it was not rediscovered and re-erected until the seventeenth century.

Talayot

It is clear that the tradition of the obelisk is not simply a modern interest in all things Egyptian; it is both widespread and persistent throughout the ages. It has to be considered peculiar that this tradition has continued for so many millennia. How did these monuments find their way across the Mediterranean and up towards north-west Europe to Ireland? When did this happen? Did these concepts come straight to Ireland from Egypt in one of the early exodus' or did they come via an intermediary, perhaps via the later Jewish exodus from Israel? The Dark-Ages dates (sixth century AD) given to these Irish towers tends to suggest the latter, but there is a problem with this. If Joseph of Arimathea was responsible for the arrival of these ancient traditions on the western shores of the British Isles, why are there no Benben towers at Jerusalem, the source of the exodus?

It could be speculated that the Nazarene church in Israel was not the major force in Jerusalem that it aspired to be and had to conform to the Judaic interpretation of the creed. Nevertheless, it is significant that Mary, the wife of Jesus, was called Magdalene, a name which means 'tower' in Hebrew. [14] The majority of the population in Jerusalem demanded a temple to be built along the same lines as the temples in Upper Egypt, from Thebes, hence the design of the Temple of Solomon. Perhaps this is why Simon Onias had to travel back to Lower Egypt, to Heliopolis, to build his tower.

That Judaism originally held these concepts can be confirmed, however. Islam, its cousin faith, seems to have received the same influences and this can be seen by looking at the analogy with Islamic minarets in more detail. The traditional tower on a mosque bears little resemblance to an Irish round-tower, but not all minarets are the same. Specifically, looking at the Kalyan Minaret in the city of Bokhara in

Uzbekistan, some rather striking similarities can be found. The tower is separate from the adjoining mosque that bears the same name and its trunk tapers towards the top, which is surmounted by a cone, albeit an elaborately decorated one.

More significantly, the entrance door to the minaret is some six meters above ground level, just as can be seen in the Irish equivalents. This is a curious feature; one possible reason is another symbolic analogy with the pyramids of Egypt. The original Benben tower stood at Heliopolis, near the Giza pyramids and all the entrance doors to the pyramids are high up the northern flank of the structure; so perhaps the Benben towers simply followed in this tradition.

The Islamic route for this design would have either been through Moses into Jerusalem or perhaps through Abraham directly to Mecca. It was, of course, Abraham and his son Ishmael who built the original mosque at Mecca. [K15] This is not the only possible way in which this ancient tradition could have travelled. There is another possible route to Ireland and that is through some other strange monuments to be found on the Balearic Islands and the Island of Sardinia. Round-towers are by no means unique to Ireland, for on these Mediterranean islands, in addition to the 'Taules', there are other curious Neolithic artefacts – round-towers. Unlike the 'Taule' monuments, they cover not just Minorca, but all of the Balearic islands and they are known as Talayots. On Minorca itself, they form:

> ...vast truncated cones of giant stones, as much as 10m high, with a diameter of 15 to 20 meters ... the similar towers on Mallorca are smaller and of different design. [16]

These constructions, while massive, are much earlier and cruder than the Irish counterparts. Perhaps their truncated form was because of a lack of mortar to hold them together or perhaps the economy of these small islands did not allow for a grander design. Nevertheless, the similarity between these towers and the Irish equivalents is undeniable. There *is* an alternate route from Egypt to Ireland; perhaps it was not through Jerusalem, but through these Mediterranean islands.

One look at the Sardinian cousin to the Balearic monuments may be sufficient confirm to this hypothesis. On Sardinia, the economy was vigorous enough to mimic the original Benben tower and perhaps even surpass it. Vast towers and tower complexes have been constructed in well-cut masonry, but once more the archaeologists have called these artefacts 'defensive positions'. Sardinia is a small island, just in excess of 200 x 100 km in size, yet according to the archaeological texts, this small Neolithic community required more than 7,000 of these towers, or Nuraghi, to protect the population!

Archaeologists have been led to this conclusion because some of the Nuraghi have been joined together with buttressed walls, undoubtedly forming the basis of a fortified settlement. One of the most spectacular is the Late Neolithic site of Nuraghi Su Nuraxi (*circa* 1800 BC), which is most certainly a fortified castle and keep. Here, there are four Nuraghi at the corners of the central keep and a further seven Nuraghi encircle the keep with massive walls in between. In fact it resembles a twelfth-century AD crusader castle, but it was built in about the twelfth-century BC! While this evidence for Nuraghi being defensive positions seems compelling, it does not mean that all the Nuraghi are forts and castles.

In addition to these main Nuraghi complexes and settlements, there were literally thousands of isolated towers dotted all around the island, often in isolated hilltop positions. These cannot have been defensive structures for the same reasons that have been spelled out for the Irish round-towers – the occupants could have been roasted alive very easily by their opponents. A much more logical defensive construction for the inhabitants would be a simple palisade wall, like those used to protect the villages of Neolithic Britain and the soldiers of the Roman empire.

Like the towers in Ireland, this constant repetition of a stone artefact all over these islands just has to have a religious function and the obvious analogy to this can be seen in the major sacred monuments around the world. From the pyramids of Egypt and Central America to the churches of Europe and the enigmatic faces of Easter Island, it is religion that has spurred man into constructing the greatest and the most numerous of monuments. The Easter Island monuments obviously have no secular purpose and so archaeologists have been forced into giving them a religious function. Should not the Nuraghi of Sardinia be thought of in the same context? Surely a more reasonable solution to the dual nature of these towers is that they were originally sacred artefacts, but at some time in the past it was noticed that they could also be useful as part of a fortification. [17]

Undoubtedly the Nuraghi of Sardinia bear a very close relationship to the constructions on Minorca, but are they direct descendants of the Egyptian model? One of the deciding factors is the all-important conical shape of the Benben stone. What were the Nuraghi originally like? Fortunately, although none of the tops of the Nuraghi survives, there are one or two surviving ancient models. These show a rim around the top, supported on corbels, rather like a mosque's minaret. Inside and above this rim or circular gallery, there was a conical roof. The similarity with the more recent round-towers is almost unnerving and one in particular, the Kalyan Minaret in the city of Bokhara, has precisely the same architectural features, including that conical roof. The design of these towers can now be understood in a new light, for surely nobody will say that the Kalyan Minaret is a defensive position.

Unfortunately, there is still one major problem with the concept of these towers being copies of the Benben tower and that is the lack of Egyptian artefacts in Sardinia or the Balearics. One statue of Imhotep does not make an entire culture. It is a glaring discrepancy and we can only speculate why this may have occurred. I discussed this issue at length with Dr. Robert H. Tykot, Assistant Professor at the Department of Anthropology, University of South Florida, who has attended many of the Nuraghi excavations on Sardinia. I enquired whether a small, controlling elite for the population of these islands, like the controlling influence Britain once had over India, would leave a significant trace of their existence in the archaeological record. He says the following of this problem:

> Even a small Egyptian (or other foreign) presence would have resulted in a significant amount of foreign imports (ceramics, tools, weapons, etc.), not to mention architecture, settlement patterns, and burials of non-indigenous styles. These would all be noticeable in the archaeological record. As an example, it is clearly evident in Egypt at the site of Buto that the Mesopotamians had established a trading outpost there, because the material culture looks just like what one finds at a Mesopotamian, not Egyptian, site. The same would be true in a future excavation of India; there would be a British occupation period layer with non-indigenous materials.

This is perhaps so for any normal ex-patriot settlement, whose members would normally wish to maintain links with their home country and use their skills and products. These Arian settlers in Sardinia would have been refugees, who had turned their backs on their mother country. There would have been no trade of any kind with Egypt, nothing to be deposited in the archaeological record. The only glaring discrepancy that exists in the archaeology of Sardinia is the lack of hieroglyphs and Egyptian-style burials for the nobility. Now that is truly a problem, but this line of thought will be pursued further, as there are some other coincidences in later history that again point towards Sardinia.

Revenge

While the culture in Sardinia in this era had a long future ahead of it, their Neolithic neighbours in the Balearic islands soon began to falter and were extinguished. At what period the Talayots on these islands were abandoned it is hard to say, although there is more than just circumstantial evidence to suggest the inhabitants emigrated back to the eastern Mediterranean, towards their traditional homelands. Battles that shook the civilizations of that era seem to have broken out across the eastern Mediterranean, especially in Egypt. If this was the work of the western Mediterranean cultures, was revenge their motive? Unfortunately, these events lie in the prehistoric era; a time in the Mediterranean when, unlike in Egypt, there are no written records to tell of their precise nature. Nevertheless, archaeologists have pieced together the structure of these events in the 13th century BC, when many of the great European and North African civilizations faltered and declined. [18]

The era was a century after the second exodus from Egypt, just after the reign of the pharaoh Ramesses II. It was a time of high culture: the cities of ancient Mycenaean Greece were rich and powerful, Egypt was enjoying unsurpassed wealth and stability with the branches of its empire extending well into the south and the north-east. Even the Minoans were recovering from the destruction inflicted by the volcano at Thera and new shrines were being constructed in the ruins of the palace at Knossos.

Quite suddenly, sea-raiders arrived from out of the West. They were called the Shardana, the Shekelesh and also the Teresh. They came to destroy, to settle, to stay and they devastated the eastern Mediterranean. Mycenaean Greece fell, the Minoans ceased to exist, the Hittites retreated. Even the mighty Egyptians themselves recoiled under the onslaught and never again recovered their former glories, with the bodies of sea-raiders being found buried as far south as Saqqara, near Heliopolis. [19]

Ramesses III dictated that these dramatic events should be recorded for posterity and so great battle-scenes of the Egyptians against the sea-raiders were carved onto the walls of the temple at Medinet Habu. They show vivid depictions of hand to hand fighting with these spiky-haired and bull-horned warriors, rather like the images of the first sea-raiders that entered Egypt (from Sumer?) in the first dynasty, some 1800 years earlier. The Shardana sea-raiders were blooded by their battles with the Egyptians, yet they were confident enough to settle in the local area, with cities being established on Cyprus and in Palestine, where they were known as the Philistines.

Who were these people and what was the rationale behind their brave thrust into the heart of the sophisticated eastern Mediterranean civilizations? Why did a 'third world' nation to the west think that it could defeat the greatest civilizations of the era? The source of these people is, perhaps, surprising; they came from Sardinia and Sicily, the names of these islands being evident in their racial appellations. The historical links between Sardinia, Sicily and the sea-people are indisputable. The horned raiders were quite distinctively the same as Sardinian bronze figurines and after this period there were apparently great trade links between the eastern Mediterranean and Sardinia, with distinctive artefacts being traded between the two sites. [20]

But why Sardinia? What made Sardinia rise up against the three most powerful nations in the Mediterranean with such vigour that they nearly succeed in wiping them out? The earlier proposal that elements of the Arian exodus took to the eastern Mediterranean, to the Balearic islands and Sardinia, provides all the necessary reasons. The Sardinian Arians invaded Greece as a stepping-stone to Egypt and invaded Egypt because it was the homeland of their aristocracy. Even the Bible serves to confirm this when it confuses the Philistines with the Egyptians. Perhaps their leaders were the same people, with a hoard of mercenaries and local people from these western islands under their command. [B21]

This is not simply speculation, for the Bible says that the Philistines were descended from an individual known as Pathrusim, one of the biblical patriarchs. [B22] Given the general thrust of this story, Pathrusim is likely to have been an Egyptian prince and in the tribal atmosphere that pervaded these eras, his descendents remained as a distinctive tribe and may have taken to the seas during one of the exoduses.

The Philistines have been branded in history as being a barbaric people with little or no culture, but this is the usual biblical obfuscation. In contrast, it is apparent from the history of the Philistine settlements established on Cyprus that there was an immediate flowering of arts and crafts there, with bronze work being a speciality. In Greece, too, there were significant finds at Xeropolis, where a temple and burial site contained ornate gold and ironwork and artefacts from Palestine and Babylonia. Significantly, the temple itself seems to mimic the format of the Egyptian temples: although much smaller, it contains a number of anterooms leading into a Holy of Holies. [23]

In Palestine itself, the historical assumption is that the Philistine people were eventually absorbed or were dispersed within the Semitic culture of King David, some 200 years later. Apparently, the two populations seem to become indistinguishable, but this is unlikely, as the Judaic people was quite strict in their policy of not mixing with other cultures.

The Bible, in contrast, indicates that there were many clashes between the Philistines and the Israelites and during the time of Samuel, there were constant battles between them. Clearly there were nationalistic differences here and a reasonable assumption might be that the Philistines represented a band of mercenaries that had outlived their use. But when the Philistines captured the Ark of the Covenant from the Israelites, they were sufficiently in awe of this relic, and the god that it 'contained', that they returned it – complete with their own golden offerings as a penance. [B24] This incident clearly illustrates the potential for Semitic undertones within the Philistine culture, a certain respect for the Israelite deity. The Persians and the Romans, in contrast, had no qualms about confiscating sacred artefacts from the Temple of Jerusalem.

While the Bible confirms these associations between the Philistines and the Israelites, archaeologists also, unwittingly or not, closely follow the genetic lineage between the races that is given in the Bible. The Bible indicates that the Canaanites of Israel and the Philistines were of the same tribal group, Hamites descended from the patriarch Ham. (See; 'Family tree of Abraham', chapter III.) Despite the skirmishes between the Philistines and Canaanites, there must have been friendly contacts and exchanges of culture and knowledge, for the seafaring skills of the Philistines were obviously not forgotten. A new seaborne culture emerged from these same lands, one that was more Semitic than Hamitic in culture, the Phoenicians.

The Phoenicians were not descended from the Greeks, as is

often the assumption, but were a Semitic (Shemitic) people. They were the descendents of the biblical patriarch Shem, Ham's brother. Another look at the family tree of Abraham will show that the Semitic and the Hamitic people were both descended from the biblical Noah: they were the same peoples, but settled in different locations. Archeologists are in agreement with the general thrust of the Bible in this respect, they say that:

> The Phoenicians (were) indistinguishable from the Canaanites of Palestine. [25]
> The Phoenicians (appear to have) called themselves in their own language ... Kena'ani, or 'Canaanites'. In Hebrew, the word has the secondary meaning of 'merchant'. [26]

Although the archaeologists maintain that the Canaanites are a Semitic people, they are more accurately described as being a Hamitic people, but the distinction is almost academic. The real difference was that the Semitic peoples were primarily based in Sumer and the Canaanites in Palestine and Lebanon; but with so many battles, conquests and dynastic alliances taking place throughout their history, their blood must have mingled quite often. The Phoenicians can also be equated with the Egyptian culture, as it is generally accepted that the Egyptian civilization sprang from Sumer. Thus the ancient history of the Egyptians and Phoenicians have the same Semitic roots. David Rohl even indicates that some of the Phoenicians were descended directly from Sumer, via Bahrain, and the Lebanese still teach that their Phoenician ancestors were descended from the Persian Gulf. Undoubtedly there is a common heritage and accordingly the Phoenicians:

a. Used anthropomorphic sarcophagi.
b. Worshipped the god El, the Sun god. (Hebrew Eli, Greek Helios.)
c. Worshipped the god Anath, the name of the wife of Joseph.
d. Were governed by kings. [27]

The Phoenicians were a successful and influential nation that is often glossed over in favour of the history of the Greek empire. Yet, in reality, their contribution to history was as fundamental as any of the ancient civilizations. Their greatest influence, showing again strong links with Egypt, came through their alphabet and language. The Phoenician alphabet is acknowledged as being the ancestor of all western alphabets; it inspired the Old Hebrew, Greek, Roman and Cyrillic alphabets that now span most of the world. Many Greek and Roman words were also derived from Phoenician and this is the most probable conduit for Egyptian words that have arrived into late twentieth-century English.

The Phoenicians emerged from the same lands as the Philistines, the Israelites and the Canaanites, Palestine. So were the Philistines and Phoenicians related? The threads of this story are thin at times, but they do continue to grow and bifurcate, so the speculation will continue. It is certain that if there were Semitic leaders or Hamite followers among the Philistines, they would have maintained their genetic independence from the mercenaries and other natives within the Sea People, as the Semitic peoples have always done. However, the seafaring skills of the Philistines could have been absorbed into the Semitic tribes of Israel through the channels available in these blood ties.

The new skills that were learned in this fashion, propelled the Phoenicians into being the Mediterranean's dominant sea-traders of the era. They established links all over the coastline of Europe, North Africa, the Balearic islands, Sardinia and even as far as Britain. They dominated the Mediterranean for nearly five centuries, but like all empires, theirs was eventually subject to external pressures. This time, the attacks came from the east, from the Persians who invaded Palestine in 573 BC, over-running the Phoenician cities on the Laventine coast and displacing their populations. As the Phoenicians were a seafaring nation, much of the population was able to escape the eastern invaders and take to the sea. Their choice of exile was interesting, they fled to their established outposts in the Mediterranean, to Carthage in modern Tunisia and the island of *Sardinia*.

Is this a coincidence? Archaeologists will claim that the Philistines were not a Semitic people, but they cannot say what the political influences on these peoples were and the Bible itself disagrees with them. Were the Sea People the result of an Egyptian colony that had gained control of the Balearic and Sardinian islands, to the extent that they controlled the indigenous population? Is this why the Phoenicians, when faced with mortal danger, escaped back to Sardinia? There is a skeleton of a workable history here that need fleshing out with more detailed investigations into the backgrounds of these peoples.

Unfortunately, after that famous Phoenician, Hannibal, had ravaged Rome with his elephants, the people there re-grouped. The Romans had learned their hard lesson, grew strong, started to form their own empire and, finally, burned Phoenician Carthage to the ground. The similar Etruscan empire, just opposite Sardinia on the Italian coast, suffered the same fate and so the records of this era have been denied to history. Nevertheless, there is one last point that is significant in this theory.

The Phoenicians were given this name because of their association with a mythical Egyptian bird – the phoenix. It is from this root that the Latin word Poenus is derived and hence the later wars with the Phoenicians at Carthage were called the Punic Wars. [28] The phoenix was a very ancient symbol of Egypt, where it was known as the *Bennu*, a term linked with copulation and so, in turn, with life, death and rebirth. The phoenix was often depicted in Egypt as a heron, the link apparently being with the annual migratory habits of this bird. This myth is so engrained in our civilizations that it continues to this day, with the renewal of human life still being depicted in the 'pagan' image of the stork carrying a newborn infant to the expectant parents. [29] The stork is simply an image of the ancient phoenix.

At this point, the links between the Egyptian Arian migrants and the Phoenicians comes full circle, for the Egyptian Temple of the Phoenix stood at Heliopolis and contained within its sacred precincts the Benben stone itself. The texts within the fifth and sixth dynasty pyramids say of the temple at Heliopolis:

> O Atum, the Creator. You became high on the height, you rose up as the Benben-stone in the Mansion of the Phoenix in Heliopolis. [30]

The link here is plain enough. This stone was conceptualized as being the divine seed of the cosmos, the obelisk with the conical Benben stone on its summit – the round-tower. The Egyptian link between the phoenix bird and the stone can be clearly seen in their naming of this mythical creature, the Bennu, a word that is synonymous with the Benben. The Benben stone has been thought of as being of meteoric origins and hence its association both with the cosmos and also with rebirth.

The term Benben can also be interpreted as meaning human sperm and the stone itself was conceived as being the divine seed of the gods that fell from the sky: it was the primaeval mound, the beginning that created and moulded mankind. [31] Taken in this context, it is quite plain what the original Benben tower at Heliopolis was and what the hundreds of copies across Sardinia, Minorca and Ireland really are.

They are vast round towers thrusting up into the sky, tapering towards the top and surmounted with conical stones or roofs – they are nothing other than giant phallic symbols – representing the birth of the human race.

Sacred Stones

There is another direct parallel between Egypt and Ireland that also involves the Benben stone. The sacred stone that sat on top of the round-tower at Heliopolis was lost quite early in Egyptian history. Even by the time of Senusret I, in the twentieth century BC, it was missing and in his restoration of Heliopolis he raised two granite obelisks there instead. This era was just at the point where the constellation of Taurus was about to change into Aries, immediately before the era of the Hyksos kings. Was the sacred stone lost or was it hidden?

Perhaps the latter is the more likely, for the concept of a sacred stone has remained and many of the various branches of the Egyptian church that evolved through Judaism still worship sacred stones in some fashion. The most sacred place in the city of Jerusalem, for both Jews and Muslims, is the temple precinct. The focal point of this courtyard is the Dome of the Rock, a Muslim mosque built in 691 AD. It was built over a large sacred stone, the visible portion of which is reputed to be the tip of a large cubic block.

There are other sacred stones to consider and it is again in Islam that more tantalising evidence is to be found to suggest that the Benben was not lost. The most sacred site for the Muslim faithful is not the Dome of the Rock, but Mecca in eastern Saudi Arabia. To this day the purpose of millions of pilgrimages to Mecca each year at the Hajj is to visit and to walk three times around the Ka'ba, or the Cube. This is a cubic windowless building in the center of the great al-Haram mosque and its focal point is a sacred black stone. Because Mecca is a closed city to all but Muslims and as the Ka'ba is so sacred, there is no record of what this sacred stone looks like.

Could this be the lost Benben stone of Heliopolis? The Koran records that it was the biblical Abraham and his son Ishmael who took the Ka'ba stone to Mecca, so the era of its appearance there is remarkably consistent with its disappearance from Egypt. Also, with all the religious upheavals present at about this time in Egypt, just such an event might be expected. If a ruling dynasty of priest-kings wanted to safeguard its most sacred relic, it might well have removed it and hidden it. Rather that, than have it desecrated by those who did not believe in the astronomy that lay behind the true Stellan system of worship.

This particular change in the constellations occurred in the mid-nineteenth century BC. Abraham was the first of the Hyksos pharaohs and he began his rule in the early eighteenth century BC. This leaves just 150 years for the priests to convince the people that the religion must change to keep pace with the stars and it is quite evident that Abraham eventually achieved this with a show of force. If the whereabouts of the Benben stone was still known in priestly circles, it could easily have gone missing during this dispute. The Benben stone has been estimated as weighing up to five tonnes, it is not something that could have been tucked under the arm and slipped out of a busy temple. The removal of the Benben stone would have had to have been an organized affair and most likely by someone in the ruling dynasty.

If this were the case, the secrets and legends surrounding the Benben stone, the Ka'ba, would have been known by the ruling elite of the Hyksos. They would have been known by Abraham, Joseph, Akhenaton and Moses, and finally, by Jesus himself. The secrets of the sacred stone would have been clearly understood by the ancient Judaic priesthood in Jerusalem. In this case, is it any coincidence that the mystical sect of Judaism is known as the Kabbalah, a word which combines Ka'ba and Allah, the words for Benben and for God? (Indeed Allah means 'one' as in the one and only god.)

Scone

In Scotland there is another ancient stone that is 'worshipped'. Scone was once the capital of Scotland and which saw the coronation of many Scottish kings. Among its many attributes, it is famous for its sacred stone. This was traditionally used in the coronation of the Scottish kings and such was its power that it was taken by Edward I in 1296 and placed under the coronation throne in Westminster Abbey in London, where it has taken its small part in the coronation of all the British monarchs since that time.

A true Scot will say that the Stone of Scone at Westminster was a fake, but nevertheless some enterprising Scots removed it from the abbey in 1950 and took it back to Arbroath. It was subsequently retrieved by the Westminster government and placed back in

Westminster Abbey. Such is the aura and fuss that has surrounded this stone, fake or no fake, that a recent act of Parliament bowed to Scottish pressure and decreed that the sacred stone should be handed back to the Scots for good.

So what is this all about? Why do so many of the branches of the Judaic line have this association with sacred stones? The Stone of Scone is not some pagan relic held sacred by the traditional Celtic line of Scots; it was supposed to be the very stone upon which Jacob rested his head in the deserts of the Negev in Palestine. The Stone of Scone is, therefore, supposed to be of the same era and provenance as the Ka'ba, almost one and the same thing. What then, was the real Scone stone supposed to look like? Was this also a conical meteorite in the same manner as the Benben? Is this why the Irish round towers have preserved the conical design of their summits, in the same manner as the original Benben Tower? There are so many questions here and so few real answers, but it is likely that there is more to this than sheer coincidence.

It can be considered a fact that the original Benben stone would have been too massive to have been brought to Ireland. However, it would have been simple to have created a (smaller?) copy out of a local stone and for it to have been used as the focus of the 'new' religion in the area. Contacts between Ireland and Scotland were many during the Dark Ages. They were not always friendly, so it is not hard to imagine the Scots appropriating the sacred Irish stone and using it in their own ceremonies down the centuries until the English arrived. Faced with the potential loss of their sacred stone, an extremely rude copy was quickly hammered out by a local mason and handed to Edward I as a trophy of his expedition, while all along the original lay buried under a local landmark. Now that the Scots have their own local parliament and there is no threat to the loss of the stone, it will be interesting to see if this story comes to life once more.

Orange

There is more to this intriguing tale and the story now takes us through one of the many European dynastic struggles that have plagued the continent. On the domestic scale, the problem was one of religion. Because of the influence of Charles I's Catholic wife and his constant disputes with parliament, the English Civil War erupted. The factions split along essentially religious lines, with the royalists being predominantly Catholic and the Protestants uniting under the command of Oliver Cromwell. Cromwell was victorious and Charles I was beheaded. However on the death of Cromwell, public sentiment was for a restoration of the monarchy and so Charles II became king in 1660.

Both Charles and his brother, who became James II, were nominally Protestant and James's daughter Mary married William of Orange, the Protestant prince of the Netherlands. Remember that the true royal line runs through the female line, through Mary, who was now married to William of Orange. But the Protestant leanings of James had only been a sham, he refused to give an anti-Catholic oath and on becoming king in 1685, his policies were overtly Catholic. It was for this reason that the compulsory Protestant oath of all future monarchs was initiated.

The Protestant hierarchy was worried, as yet another damaging civil war was in prospect. They did not wish another dictator like Cromwell to surface, so to prosecute this rebellion some leading luminaries in London appealed for the assistance of William of Orange, whose children carried the royal bloodline. William landed in England in 1688 and although his Dutch army was small, wave after wave of Protestant officers and their men deserted from James to him. James fled the country and William was crowned William III of England in February 1689. William was not one to squander time, in March of the same year he was out in Ireland in hot pursuit of James and a historic battle was about to be fought on Irish soil.

This was the domestic picture, but there was a wider political environment within which this small skirmish was being fought. The basic problem in Europe was not religious as such; it transcended mere parochial religious beliefs and was a dispute between rival dynastic alliances. It would appear that the bloodline, the descendants of Jesus, had engrained themselves within the ruling dynasties of Europe and, like all families, they were open to the occasional domestic squabble. Many would initially assume that the bloodline was resident within the Habsburg line, as their rejection of the Catholic church made this assumption logical. Sir Laurence Gardner, however, used persuasive historical records to claim that James II of England was also of the bloodline, despite his Catholic leanings. This confused the issue greatly. Two questions remained. Why should these two dynasties be in dispute if they were both of the bloodline? Why should a lineal descendant of the church of James and Jesus be loyal to the Catholic church that had so distorted its true history?

The answers came through the researches of Clive Prince and Lynn Picknett in *The Templar Revelation*. They maintain that there was a long and bitter dispute between Jesus and John the Baptist, resulting in the death of John. It has already been shown that John was the high priest of Jerusalem and it was a dynastic struggle that resulted in his death, but was this partly due to a dispute with the family of Jesus? The findings of Lynn and Clive are worth further reading, for they possibly explain the roots of this Habsburg/Bourbon dispute from a more ancient perspective. They indicate that the Knights Templar maintained the traditions of the dynasty descended from John the Baptist, rather than those of the dynasty through Jesus. The Templars were famed for the worship of a bearded, severed head – provocatively explained as being the severed head of John the Baptist. [32] The evidence for an ancient dispute between John and Jesus' families is fragmentary, but the later medieval veneration of John the Baptist could easily have stemmed from a rift within this royal family.

These royal family's fortunes had waxed and waned over the centuries, but at this point in history the pharaonic bloodline seems to have been resident within both the Habsburg and Bourbon royal lines. But this was a divided family and the seeds of discontent would brew into another dynastic struggle for power. A microcosm of this tangled web of alliances is represented by the history of the dukes of Savoy in Italy. This family not only married into both the Bourbon and Habsburg lines, representing both sides of the divide, but they also became the kings of Sardinia, a theme familiar to this tale. In addition this family established the Egyptian museum in Turin, the first museum of Egyptian antiquity in the world; the heritage of this family is being made abundantly clear.

In north-western Europe, the Habsburg line was represented and followed by the Saxon, Spanish and Swedish princes, known together as the 'League of Augsburg' or the 'Grand Alliance'. Ranged against them in this dispute were the Bourbons, led by Louis XIV of France and a mixed bag of Catholic principalities. The wider dynastic dispute was over the future of Spain. Spain was surprisingly under Habsburg control, under the ineffectual leadership of King Charles II of Spain, but he had no heir. It seemed likely that the Bourbons would win control of Spain, through Charles's wife, a Bourbon. The Bourbon's had the most powerful army in Europe and it would soon become unassailable if Spain came under their control. In the middle of all this, the Habsburgs had an eastern border dispute with the Turks. Louis XIV thought that

James II of England could keep the Protestant states in the Netherlands under the control of William of Orange, busy, while he marched his men into Saxony to confront the Habsburgs head-on. The Catholic Bourbon dynasty would soon be the masters of Europe. [33]

But it was not to be. James II lost the support of the population of England, William of Orange was invited into England instead and James had to flee to France. Louis XIV was rapidly losing control of his northern flank. In desperation, he committed valuable troops to the support of James, a decision which weakened his ability to attack the Habsburgs. James planned to regain the northern flank (England), by using Ireland as a springboard, the ultimate goal being a foray into northern Europe. William, now king of England and Scotland, saw the gambit and moved to cut off James's support at its roots in Ireland.

The looming battle had nothing to do with Ireland, it was a minor skirmish in a European family squabble between the bloodlines of Abraham; apparently represented by the separate churches of John and Jesus. It was a squabble that saw, even at the domestic level, James fighting against his son-in-law William and his own daughter Mary. The situation came to a climax on the river Boyne north of Dublin in 1690, a symbolic location if ever there was one.

Was this position arranged by the parties? Did they understand its sacred significance and how its history was intertwined with the current dispute? Did they recognize the ancient history of the Newgrange site upon which they were about to fight, a history that was intimately connected with Egypt and the pharaonic dynastic line. Did they understand the significance of how the sacred nature of this location had percolated down through Irish history itself to become the Seat of Tara, the home of all the famous Irish kings? Was this the reason that this particular point in the meandering Boyne valley was chosen for this historic battle?

Arranged in this most European of battles was James II on the south bank of the Boyne. He had 7,000 regular French troops and 14,000 Irish. The Irish were mostly untrained infantry, as many of the best Irish regiments had already been squandered by James in other battles on the mainland. On the other side of the river was William of Orange, who had some 35,000 regulars at his disposal. Underlining the true international nature of the dispute, William's forces comprised the Dutch Blue Guard, two divisions of French Huguenots, some English, Danish and Prussian infantry and, bringing up the rear, a smattering of Finnish and Swiss. [34]

Such were the tangled intrigues of the day that even the Pope lent troops to fight alongside William and against the Catholics. It would appear that the Pope was more afraid of the expansionist policies of Louis XIV than the League of Augsburg's pretensions. The battle is commemorated to this day in Irish history, as being a battle of the English against the Irish; it was anything but. This was a battle for the future of the pharaonic bloodline, the royal house of Abraham. It was also a battle to establish control of vital evidence as to the legitimacy of this bloodline.

Crusades

Following the exile of Jesus' family from Jerusalem in the first century, it took 1,000 years to establish themselves at the top of a dynastic line that had sufficient power and influence to proceed with their sacred mission and duty. As soon as it was within their capabilities, they marched on Jerusalem in search of their ancient records – the medieval Christian Crusades had begun. Wave after wave of crusaders flowed into Palestine to secure the area, so that the ruling dynasty could begin excavations under the long lost Temple of Solomon. It would appear that they were successful: something powerful and sacred was found in the catacombs under Jerusalem that consolidated the family's power and catapulted them into being the most influential dynasty in Europe. The Templars were founded to control this vast sacred and secular empire and they too became extremely wealthy powerful.

But the Templars were not all powerful. Their downfall came on Friday 13th October 1307, when troops controlled by Philippe IV, on behalf of the Catholic church, rounded up the members of the organization and confiscated their wealth and property. It was a major setback for the dynasty, but their influence and power still showed through, when they deemed that Friday 13th was to be an unlucky day from that time on. The rest of the world did not know the reason why, but they did as they were told. The family had survived this assault through a combination of luck and guile and they eventually grew once more to dominate Europe. They nurtured each royal and every influential association with infinite care, just as Jacob did with Laban in Egypt, until they were entrenched once more at the highest levels in society.

Nearly 400 years later, there was another chance to show this family's power and to consolidate its influence in Europe. With its pharaonic traditions, the family must have known the importance of the ancient monuments of the world – the pyramids of Egypt were a lost family heirloom no less. The monuments of Britain must also have had an equal mystery about them; both the Greeks and the Jewish historian Josephus mention the mysteries of Britain.

If all this had been known to the royal family, Newgrange would have been an auspicious place to stage a final battle for power. Additionally, if a rumour had spread as to the condition of Newgrange, the family may have sensed a chance of staging a new crusade, this time to Ireland not Palestine. The purpose of this Irish crusade would have been the same as the medieval crusaders in Jerusalem, to dig in the ruins of Newgrange and uncover more artefacts for the sacred family to treasure. This may seem like wild speculation, but it is exactly what happened. William of Orange won the day, James retreated to France, the Bourbons had lost their opportunity. But what did William actually win?

James II was allowed to retreat south with his remaining troops and no attempt was made to annihilate the defeated enemy. To this day, according to the Northern Irish researcher Andrew Power, the celebration of this victory is not of success in the battle itself, nor is it the defeat of James – the celebration is that King William of Orange crossed the Boyne. The imagery that has percolated down since that battle confirms this: it is not of King William trampling his defeated foes into the dust, but of William on a white charger crossing the Boyne. The battle was won when his trusty steed's hoofs dug into the thick, damp soil of Eamhain (Newgrange). Was Newgrange was the prize?

Many things in this quest are uncertain, but one fact that is on much firmer ground is that after this decisive battle, Newgrange, the most sacred henge in Ireland, was opened up for the first time in nearly 3,000 years. There is no record of what was found.

Fertility

In my mind, there is no doubt that Newgrange was central to these age-old myths. In the book *Thoth*, the suggestion was made that the West Kennet long barrow in England was very similar in concept to the henge at Newgrange and that there is a definite link between these two cultures. Furthermore, the internal layout of Newgrange is also similar to Gavrinis in Brittany and Grouville in Jersey, the latter being an impressive passage barrow with a huge interior room. The traditions of these Neolithic structures seem to have spread throughout the western fringes of Europe. Both their design and the engravings inside these monuments show that there were close links between these widely separated sites at the time of the established date for the construction of these monuments, the third millennium BC.[35]

Eventually, at a much later date, these traditions made the jump eastwards. In about 1300 BC, the Mycenaean Greeks began building very similar monuments to the western henges, constructions such as the 'Treasury of Atreus'. These eastern passage 'grave' sites are separated by a distance of some 2,400km and nearly 2,000 years from their western European cousins, yet they are so similar. Each has a long passage which terminates in a corbeled vault of conical design, each has side alcoves branching off the main chamber.

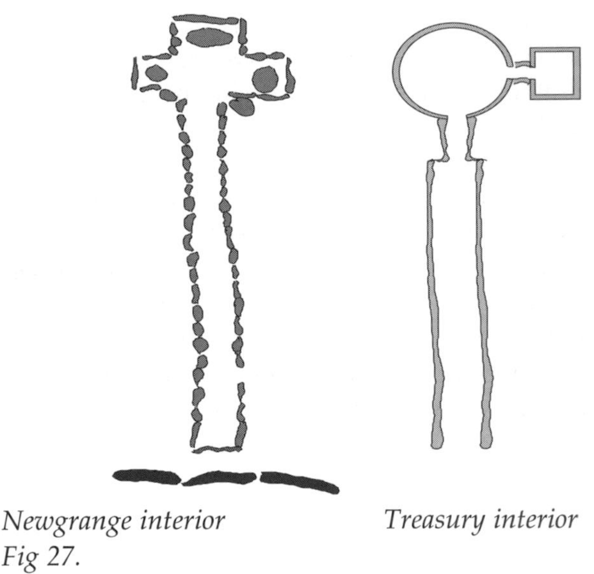

Newgrange interior *Treasury interior*
Fig 27.

There is a vast span of time between the Treasury and the Newgrange design and it is curious why the design was revived in this manner. It is possible that if any ancient Greeks had seen Newgrange and understood its importance, this design could have been thought to be sacred, not just the location. Having made this association between the Treasury and Newgrange, between east and west, it was interesting to find that the entrance door to the Treasury has a distinctive lintel. It is formed from a large slab and a rather unnecessary pyramidal void on the top. This feature, which is repeated on the smaller door in the tomb and on the famous Lion Gate, has confused historians and has been explained in terms of stress relief on the lintel. But if one were to design such an archway, there would be no need for such a massive lintel in the first place.

For a better explanation of this feature, the origins of the design have to be understood and they involve both Ireland and Egypt. It seems to have gone unnoticed in the orthodox world that the design of the Newgrange site is not only very similar to the Treasury, but the entrance also has this same feature, the 'roof-box', as it is known. At Newgrange, it is through this strange aperture above the main entrance, that the first rays of the rising Sun on midwinter's day burst into the chamber deep inside the henge. The function of this solar penetration of the chamber at the winter solstice is obvious. It has long been observed that the layout of these chambers is symbolic of a woman's reproductive organs, with the long passage representing the birth-canal and the vaulted chamber representing the womb itself. The whole henge is a representation of Mother Earth and at the midwinter sunrise, her womb is ritually penetrated by the rays of the Sun; so that the new year can be born and the Earth fertilized with new life.

This symbolism can be taken further still because deep inside the Newgrange chamber lay finely carved circular granite bowls, one of which has the impression of two ovals placed upon it. Their function is unknown, but Andrew Power sees them as representations of the human egg, to be fertilized in the womb of the chamber by the rays of the rising Sun. Indeed, the two oval depressions in one of the bowls look like the two genetic nuclei in the fertilised cell about to fuse.

Fig 28. The Newgrange bowl

The Mycenaean Greeks appear to have copied this feature of the roof-box, but without necessarily understanding its purpose. They simply copied the feature and to add their own meaning to the design, they appealed to the wisdom of the sages of Egypt. The final design they chose was equally deep in symbolism, for in the Egyptian language the design of their roof-box is a hieroglyph and its meaning is 'pyramid'.

That the design of the Treasury was carefully conceived and deliberate in its execution, is underlined by the design of the tomb of Clytemnestra, which is identical; the Treasury is by no means unique. Where it was impractical to build an enormous pyramid, a western-type barrow layout and a hieroglyph of a pyramid were deemed sufficient. There is a curious fusion between the two ancient fertility cults.

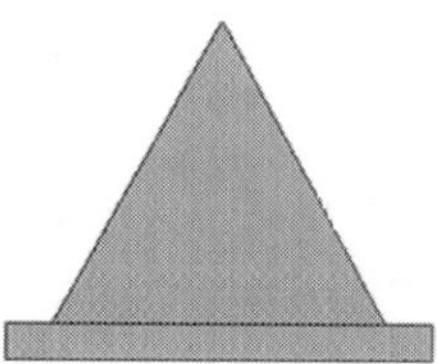

Treasury entrance *Hieroglyph for pyramid*
Fig 29.

Incredible as it may seem, the sacred monuments of the ancients appear to have been designed around a Europe-wide plan. Beliefs in the western fringes of Europe were dominated by the fertility of a goddess: the womb of this female deity was buried deep within the great 'Celtic' barrows, where it was ritually fertilised by a shaft of light from the rising Sun penetrating to the back of the chamber. The eastern fringes of the Mediterranean, conversely, were dominated by the phallic Benben towers of a masculine deity, over which the rays of the Sun cast its shadows. Over great spans of time, the western feminine cults of the earthly womb, moved eastwards from Ireland to Greece. In return, the eastern masculine cults of the Benben phallus have moved from east to west, from Egypt to the western Mediterranean and on to Ireland.

These two cultures temporarily merged in the Treasury of Atreus and the tomb of Clytemnestra, where the feminine chamber and the masculine pyramid are represented together. There is a curious fusion of fertility here and the links between all these monuments seem to come full circle. Greater Britain, the western Mediterranean, Greece and Egypt are all infused with similarities in the cultures. There were ancient historical contacts between the nations and Greece in particular drew on many of these influences.

Stellans

The original unmodified Egyptian religion and its associated bloodline, has had a tortuous life. It led a quite settled existence for thousands of years in the fertile ribbon oasis of Egypt before being forcibly uprooted and sent in exile to Jerusalem and beyond. It tried to re-establish itself in Egypt, only to be thrown out once more, back to Jerusalem and even to the western Mediterranean. A direct assault was then planned from the west, but this too failed to dislodge the Taurean Egyptians. It suffered a temporary exile in Babylon at the hands of the Persians and then a greater dispersal across Europe once more, at the hands of the Romans. Each time these calamities struck, the loyal subjects and holders of those ancient secrets and rites pulled themselves back up and made their homes in a fresh land.

The Jewish and Christian exiles promoted their version of the events that had taken place in Egypt, but those 'who had ears to hear' carried their own unique stories and traditions. Some of the Jewish and Christian similarities with Egyptian life have already been explored in chapter V, but there are also ancient Egyptian traditions that have slipped into Masonic usage:

a. The Masonic apron. Originally these aprons were worn by the pharaoh and the ruling elite at religious ceremonies and they were based on the design of the pyramids, being triangular in shape.

b. The black and white chequered Templar battle flag, the Beausant, which denoted 'victory', was based on the design of the Egyptian hieroglyph for the god Amen, as can be seen in the jewel box from the tomb of the pharaoh Tutankhamen. This symbol appears to have subsequently evolved in the chequered flag to denote victory at motor racing events.

c. The Egyptian Djed pillars, which were central to the design of the great temples in Egypt, became a prominent feature of the Temple of Solomon in Jerusalem; they have evolved into the sacred masonic pillars and can be seen in every Masonic lodge. This twin-pillar design is now a common feature of churches and cities all over the world; a prominent pair are located on the harbour-front at Venice and two of distinctly Egyptian design form the facade of the 'Temple de la Sagrada Familia' (Temple of the Sacred Family) in Barcelona; Gaudi's famously exotic cathedral.

d. The complete set of astrological symbols are still in use to this day, over most of the world.

e. The square and compass symbology, examples of which were discovered among the amulets wrapped up in the bandages covering the body of a high-ranking Egyptian called Djedhor. This sarcophagus was discovered by Flinders Petrie in 1902 and it dates from the thirtieth dynasty (*circa* 380 BC).

f. Armies start marching with the left foot forwards, for victory. All the statues of the pharaohs in Egypt are made with the left foot forwards to denote strength, confidence and victory.

g. Traditional line stick dancing, which depicts the ancient battle between Osiris and Seth (Cain and Abel). This was introduced into Britain possibly from Moorish Spain and is now known as Morris dancing (Moorish dancing). It is traditionally supposed to illustrate the cycle of life, death and rebirth; the same as the ancient traditions of the phoenix and the god Osiris. The carrying of green branches in Morris dancing is also significant, as Osiris was the green god of Egypt and he has often been linked to the cult of the Green Man in Medieval and Tudor England.

h. The 'OK' symbol of the thumb and forefinger touching together in a circle, with the other three fingers splayed out above. This is simply an inverted representation of the 'Eye of Horus' and it indicates the same now as it did in ancient times:

> Wherever a weakness or faltering might menace the natural order of things, the image restores, and through its protective magic, it confers a message of hope. [36]

The image of the Eye of Horus indicates that everything is OK and Greek fishermen still paint it on the front of their boats as a protective talisman.

i. The term hermetically sealed, refers to a closed area or flask that has been made airtight. The secrets and rituals of the Heliopolian priesthood were traditionally thought to be based on the ancient teachings of the god Thoth or Hermes and were among the most closely guarded secrets on the planet. They were guarded so closely that nothing could escape and the term became 'hermetically sealed', to show that a vessel was airtight.

j. The coronation ceremony of the Egyptians was passed through to Jerusalem and was performed for King Solomon; it is still practised today at British coronations. Even in this modern era, the new incumbent is ritually anointed with oils between the shoulder blades and on the chest and ever since the eighteenth century this ritual has also been accompanied by the coronation aria by Handel which starts with the words:

Zadok the priest and Naithan, crown King Solomon...

The New World Order

As the separate threads of the bloodline flowed through to the eighteenth century, a slight change in the structure of its supporters came about. The power and influence of the ruling classes was waning throughout the land and the role of the wealthy merchants was increasing. It was noticed that these newcomers to the corridors of power enjoyed hobnobbing with the aristocracy and, in turn, it was realized that some of these common people could be very useful to the family. The new recruits to what became the 'craft' were not to be trusted with the truth, of course, and so a mishmash of peculiar initiation ceremonies were invented to instruct the uneducated on the basic history of the family line.

It was a game of charades for adults, a system designed to ensure that radical freethinkers would not join the club. Only sycophants with a blind loyalty for a cause they knew nothing about were required and to prevent any awkward questions about the society, any discussion of religion and politics were banned in lodge meetings. The

Catholic church used the laws of blasphemy and the Inquisition to keep the faithful on the right road, the brotherhood banned free-speech and instituted blood-curdling oaths against those who gave away their secrets. Both ploys were successful in silencing dissenters in their ranks.

Although the future looked less hostile than the turbulent past, if it came to another straight fight with the establishment, the family wanted as much influence over the powers of law and order as possible. Prudence demanded that those with access to power were to be assiduously courted, especially those linked to the all-important institutions of the police, armed forces and judiciary. The ranks of these institutions were ruthlessly combed for suitable candidates to protect the bloodline from perils ranging from minor brushes with the law to the continuing influence of the Catholic church or even from a major world war with the communists (who were, by definition, not of the bloodline). Those in power during the Cold War were fighting it on many levels; it was not always a simple crusade for capitalism.

Nadir

Such a siege mentality is, perhaps, a logical result of the constant persecution of the past and those involved cannot be entirely blamed for pursuing this line, but it is a strategy that is not without its internal problems. As the brotherhood has had ruthlessly to maintain its secrecy for generations, it has not been able to inform its recruits of the core tenets of the brotherhood. The membership was therefore bolstered by wave after wave of sycophants.

These were people who were happy to follow a creed of which they had no understanding to further their own secular ambitions. They were content enough to favour and protect their fellow brothers both socially and in business, regardless of their moral standing or ability. It is not just a sad situation, but a serious one too. The world is now plagued with vast numbers of captains of industry, politicians, bankers and even airline pilots, being promoted to responsible positions because of their affiliations not because of their ability. The result is that the power brokers are often the most inept in our society, it is a system that sucks at the very lifeblood of entire nations.

Thus a proud religion and the longest-ruling royal line in the world has been reduced to the nadir of its entire history. Its members are followers in the footsteps of the selfless priests of Heliopolis, who held the secrets of the gods and watched the cosmos on our behalf for thousands of years, through times of plenty and privation. Now they are reduced to a society that has little ambition besides furthering the careers of its members. It is very a sad era for the sons and daughters of Abraham.

Things need not be like this, for the world has changed a great deal in recent times and there are no more secrets to be withheld from the foot-soldiers of the fraternity. Those who continue secretly to dress up as 'men in black', now do so for secular advancement, not spiritual enlightenment. The paradigm is about to change. With contemporary religions on the wane in the West, it is time for the bloodline to reject these parasitic secular influences and to restore the oldest religion in the world to its former glory.

Appendix I

Family tree of Herod the Great

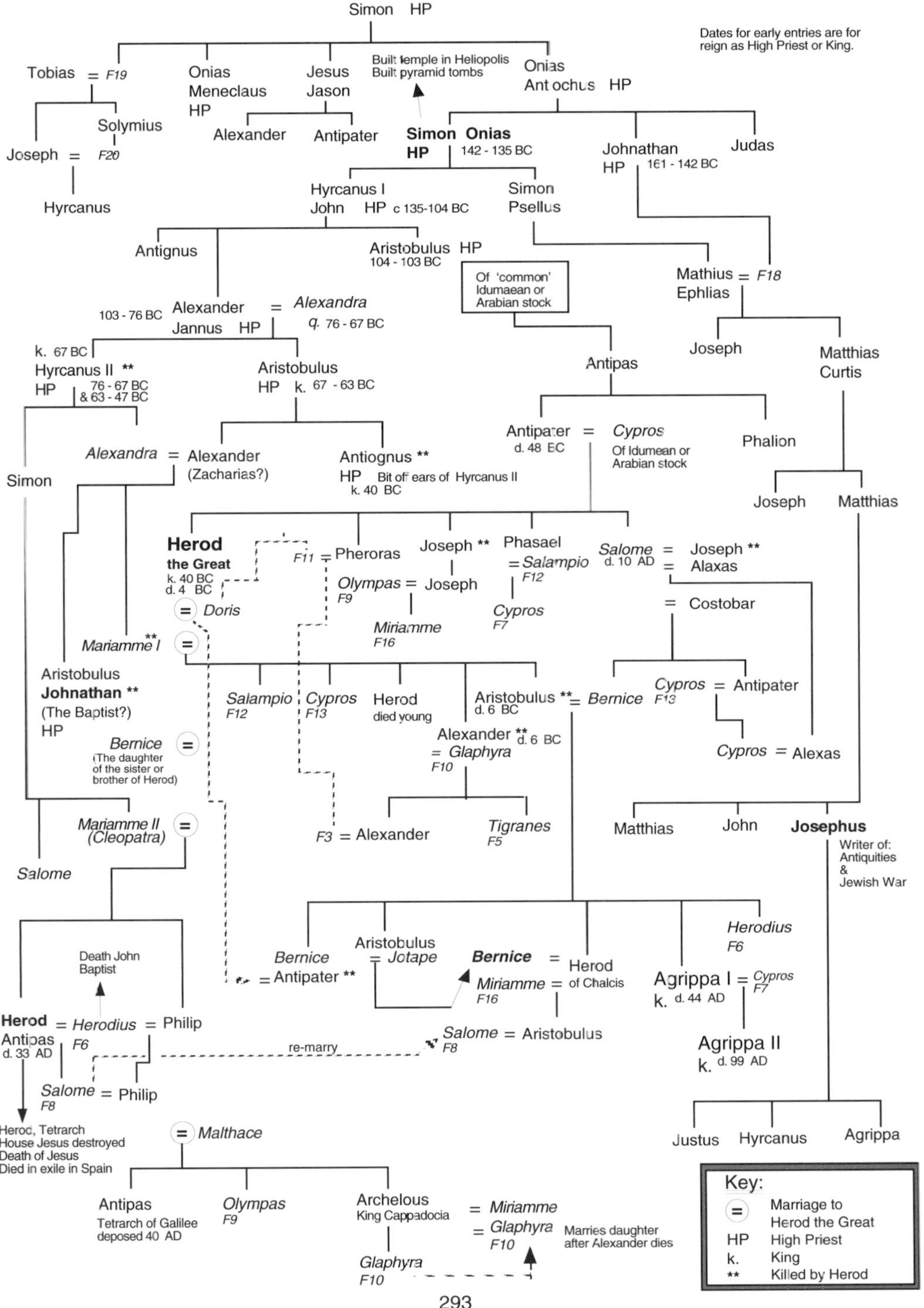

Notes & References

Bible All references taken from the King James edition, although the text is often modernised for clarity.

Josephus AA = Against Apion, Ant = Antiquities, JW = Jewish war. Page references are to the Loeb Classical Library system. Quotes taken from William Whiston's translation, which was first published in 1736, some references are from the Penguin Classics edition by G. Williamson, first published 1959.

Manetho All page numbers are taken from the LCL edition, edited by G. Goold.

Within the referencing system in this book, some of the reference numbers are prefixed with letters. This is to give the reader an idea of the source of the reference, without having to look up that particular reference. This only applies to the more popular reference works, but the following have been prefixed:

B = Bible, M = Manetho, J = Josephus,
T = Talmud, N = Nag Hammadi.

Prologue

1 Josephus AA 2:189.
2 Ibid 1:109.
3 Bible Mathew 13:55, Mark 6:3.
4 Bible Mathew 6:5.
5 Act of God, Graham Phillips.

Chapter 1

1 Manetho LCL p233.
2 Josephus JW LCL V. 379.
3 Bible Genesis 14:14.
4 Bible Genesis 41:43.
5 Manetho LCL p97.
6 Jesus the Man, Barbara Thiering.
7 Bible Mathew 13:11.
8 Nag Hammadi Scrolls, Gospel of Philip.
9 Bible Mark 15:26, Mark 7:27.
10 Encarta 96 Encyclopedia.
11 Illustrated guide to the Bible, J Porter.
12 Josephus AA LCL 1. 92, Manetho LCL p85.
13 Ibid AA LCL 1.85, Manetho LCL p85.
14 Bible Numbers 13:22
15 Bible Exodus 20:25.
16 Josephus AA 1:198.
17 Bible Luke 3:23.
18 Who were the pharaohs, S Quirke.
19 Bible Exodus 2:10.
20 Discovering Hieroglyphs, Kerl-Theodor Zauzich.

Chapter 2

1 Bible Genesis 16:1.

2 Ibid 24:35.
3 Ibid 12:10.
4 Josephus JW 7:416.
5 Ibid comments, William Whiston ranslation p 770.
6 Bible Genesis 20:12.
7 Josephus Ant 1:166.
8 Ibid 17:17 & 20:01.
9 Ibid 26:1.
10 Herodotus Gerar ii, 128.
11 Josephus JW 5:379.
12 Bible Genesis 11:20.
13 Bible Luke 3:35.
14 The religion of ancient Egypt, Mercer.
15 Josephus AA 1:96.
16 Who were the pharaohs?, S Quirke.
17 Akhenaton, C Aldred p293.
18 Pharaohs and Pyramids, G Hart.
19 Ibid p20.
20 Chronicle of the pharaohs, P Clayton.
21 Discovering Hieroglyphs, Karl-Theodor Zauzich.
22 Hyram Key, Lomas & Knight.
23 Koran 6:71.
24 Bible Genesis 17:5.
25 Josephus Ant 1:213.
26 Ibid 2:91.
27 Ibid 1:99.
28 Ibid 1:158.
29 Ibid 1:166.
30 British Museum Dictionary of Egypt, J Shaw.
31 Orion Mystery, R Bauval, A Gilbert. Fingerprints of the Gods, G Hancock.
32 Redshift II, CD Rom Planisphere. You have to be careful with these programs, the dates are mostly based on the Gregorian calendar which contains some errors when going into the past, and there is a huge jump in date in 1582 at the institution of the Gregorian calendar. These changes have to allowed for, otherwise your Solstice date (and the position of the stars) can be months substantially out. The only reliable method is to use the position of the Sun to find the Solstice. For instance in the year 1090 BC the Spring Equinox arrives on 7th April, with the Sun rising at 0400 hr. Using this technique the Sun crosses the modern Taurus-Aries boundary somewhere between the years 1920 BC and 1850 BC, it starts to actually approach the stars of Aries in 1700 BC.
33 Herodotus, Histories, Euterpe 18.
34 Bible Genesis 12:10.
35 Ibid 12:19.
36 Josephus Ant 1:161.
37 Bible Genesis 12:12 - 13.
38 Josephus Ant 1:166.
39 Bible Genesis 12:15.
40 Ibid 13:2.
41 Ibid 13:7.
42 Ibid 13:11.
43 Ibid 13:14 - 17.
44 Ibid 18:25 - 32.
45 Ibid 19:1.
46 Ibid 19:3, Josephus Ant 1:199.
47 Bible Genesis 19:8.
48 Ibid 19:16.
49 Ibid 19:25.
50 Josephus Ant 1:176.
51 Bible Genesis 19:33.
52 Josephus Ant 1::213.
53 Bible Genesis 21:25.
54 Bible Genesis 21:27 - 29.
55 Ibid 21:27.
56 Ibid 22:10.
57 Ibid 22:13.
58 Ibid 24:3.
59 Ibid 25:20.
60 Ibid 25:21.
61 Ibid 26:1.
62 Ibid 26:7.
63 Ibid 28:1.
64 Ibid 28:4.
65 Ibid 28:18.
66 Josephus Ant 1:311.
67 Ibid 1:297.
68 Ibid 1:301.
69 Ibid 2:98.
70 Bible Genesis 30:37-39.
71 Ibid 30:40.
72 Ibid 30:41.
73 Ibid 31:1.
74 Ibid 31:9.
75 Ibid 31:12.
76 Ibid 32:28.
77 Josephus Ant 1:327.
78 Ibid 1:327, Bible Genesis 33:1. When Josephus speaks of men he often seems to refer to officers. He

usesthe strength of the Officer Corps, to show the total strength of the Army. See Manetho LCL p233.
79 Bible Genesis 33:1 - 9.
80 Ibid 33:9.
81 Josephus Ant 1:329.
82 Ibid 1:328.
83 Selections from the Talmud, Polano, 83-84.

Chapter 3

1 Bible Exodus 12:34.
2 Bible Genesis 33:18, 34:25-30.
3 Bible Exodus 1:11.
4 Manetho p89.
5 Ibid p107.
6 Ibid p121.
7 Josephus AA 1:230.
8 Ibid 1:228.
9 Josephus Ant 2:318.
10 Redshift II CD Rom planisphere. See problems noted in references to chapter 2.
11 The Sumarian King Lists, T Jacobsen. Ancient Iraq, G Roux.
12 Gilgamesh, Penguin Classics p70.
13 Ibid p66.
14 Ibid p75.
15 Ibid p75 and p77.
16 Ibid p81-83.
17 Ibid p88, both references.
18 Ibid p78.
19 Chronicle of the pharaohs, P Clayton.
20 Manetho p 239.
21 Ibid p 239.
22 Bible Genesis 10:25.
23 Hieroglyphs, M. Betro.
24 Bible Genesis 33:18, 34:25-30.
25 Josephus Ant 1:340.
26 Act of God, G Phillips.
27 Bible Exodus 12:29.
28 Ibid 12:29 - 30.
29 Ibid 12:36.
30 Bible Exodus 8:1 & 10:26.
31 Ibid 9:6.
32 Ibid 12:3 - 7 & 12:13.
33 Ibid 12:29.
34 Ibid 3:22 & 12:35 - 36.
35 Josephus is not making clear here hat an Arurae is a unit of area, not oneof length.
36 Josephus AA 1:83-92.
37 Bible Exodus 14:25.
38 Ibid 14:26.
Josephus AA 1:244.
39 Ibid 1:244.
40 Ibid 1:249.
41 Bible Deuteronomy 2:28.
42 Ibid 2:34.
43 Ibid 3:1 - 3.
44 Bible Joshua 6:25.
45 Ibid 6:21.
46 Ibid 6:26.
47 Bible Genesis 33:18.
48 Ibid 34:2.
49 Ibid 34:25 - 29.
50 Ibid 34:30 - 35:1.
51 Josephus AA 1:88 - 92.
52 Bible Genesis 35:4.

Chapter 4

1 Josephus JW 7:423 - 430.
2 Bible Genesis 41:45, Josephus Ant 2:91.
3 Ibid 2:188.
4 Bloodline of the Holy Grail, Gardner p283-286.
5 Bible Genesis 37:31.
6 Josephus Ant 2:39.
7 Bible Genesis 41:40 - 43.
8 Josephus Ant 2:89.
9 Bible Genesis 42:25.
10 Ibid 43:18.
11 Josephus Ant 2:184.
12 Ibid 2:188.
13 Bible Genesis 46:32.
14 Ibid 47:3 - 5.
15 Ibid 47:6.
16 Ibid 47:13 - 26.
17 Ibid 50:2 - 3.
18 Ibid 50:26.

Chapter 5

1 Josephus AA 1:223 - 230.
2 Ibid 1:233.
3 Josephus Ant 2:202.

4 Stranger in the Valley of the Kings, A Osman.
5 Manetho p131.
6 Akhenaten, C Aldred, p96 p146.
7 Moses Pharaoh of Egypt, A Osman p2.
8 Ibid p107. & Akhenaten, C Aldred, p239.
9 Akhenaton, C Aldred p 88.
10 Bible Exodus 20:25 - 26.
11 Herodotus Euterpe 36.
12 Josephus AA 1:169.
13 Akhenaten, C Aldred p 259.
14 Manetho 131, 125.
15 Josephus Ant 2:231.
16 Bible Exodus 2:12.
17 Ibid 1:8.
18 Ibid 1:9.
19 Talmud. Also quoted in Polano, Selections fro the Talmud p26.
20 Josephus Ant 2:232.
21 ibid 2:235.
22 Talmud. & Polano, Selections from he Talmud p26.
23 Manetho 131, 125.
24 Josephus Ant 2:237.
25 Bible Exodus 4:10.
26 Ibid 4:14.
27 Josephus Ant 2:250, 253.
28 Ibid 2:254.
29 Bible Exodus 2:12.
30 Josephus AA 1:28.
31 Manetho p124 - 125.
32 Strabo.
33 Josephus Ant 2:263.
34 Manetho p124 - 125.
35 Akhenaton, C Aldred, p270.
36 Rock Tombs od Amarna, Davies.
37 Akhenaten, C Aldred, p271.
38 Bible Exodus 5:9.
39 Akhenaton, C Aldred, p67.
40 Bible Exodus 5:10 - 13.
41 Ibid 5:17.
42 Akhenaton, C Aldred great Hymn of Akhenaton, p242.
43 Ibid p259.
44 The most popular alien being in science fiction is the 'grey', which happens to look exactly like Akhenaton. See the book *Thoth, Architect of the Universe* for why this is pertinent to Egypt and Akhenaton.
45 Bible Exodus 1:16.
46 Akhenaton, C Aldred, p293.
47 Near Eastern Texts, Pritchard, p251.
48 Josephus AA 1: 239.
49 Ibid 1:245.
50 Bible Exodus 7:10.
51 Akhenaton, C Aldred, p259.
52 Koran 7:113 - 125.
53 Ibid 7:125 - 129.
54 Manetho p129.
55 Akhenaton, C Aldred, p67.
56 Ibid p297.
57 Manetho p133.
58 Josephus Ant 3:111, 3:115.
59 Ibid 3:151.
60 Ibid 3:185.
61 Ibid 3:209. Bible Exodus 32:4.
62 Bible Exodus 32:12.
63 Bible Exodus 32:26 - 28.
64 Bible I Kings 14:26.

Chapter 6

1 Josephus AA 1:110.
2 Josephus JW 5:212.
3 Ibid 5:217.
4 Bible Chronicles II 4:2.
5 Josephus JW 5:219.
6 Josephus AA 1:10.
7 Bible Isiah 19:1.
8 Bible Psalms 137:1.
9 Josephus JW 2:161.
10 Bible Psalms 2:125 - 165.
11 Josephus Ant 14:448.
12 Ibid 15:65.
13 Bible Mark 6:14-28.
14 Josephus Ant 14:48, 15:67, 15:87, 15:213, 15:231, 15:254. Josephus JW 1:325, 1:342, 1:437, 1:441, 1:443.
15 Penguin Classics version.
16 Josephus JW 1:440.
17 Ibid 1:551.
18 Ibid 1:582 - 646.
19 Ibid 1:664 - 665.
20 Bible Math 2:13.
21 Ibid 27:37.
22 Bible Luke 3:24.
23 Ibid 8:3.
24 Bible John 18:15.
25 Ibid 19:38.
26 Ibid 1:7 - 9.
27 Bible Hebrrews 7:16 - 20.

28 Bible Luke 3:23.
29 Bible John 8:6.
30 Jesus Papyrus, C. Thiede, M. D'Ancona, p 117.
31 Bible John 11:6.
32 Ibid 11:15.
33 Ibid 11:43.
34 House of the Messiah, A. Osman p 38.
35 Ibid p152.
36 Bible Hebrews 10:4.
37 Hiram Key, Lomas & Knight p73.
38 Bible Math 2:11.
39 Ibid 2:5.
40 Bible Luke 2:46.
41 Jesus Papyrus, C. Thiede, M. D'Ancona, p 117.
42 Bible Acts 26:14.
43 Jesus Papyrus, C. Thiede, M. D'Ancona, p 119.
44 Bible John 6:15.
45 Ibid 8:59.
46 Ibid 10:39.
47 Ibid 12:36.
48 Bible Mark 3:20 - 22.
49 Bible Luke 8:45.
50 Bible John 4:2.
51 Bible Mark 8:17 - 21.
52 Nag Hamaddi Library, Gospel of Thomas.
53 Bible Mathew 11:19.
54 Bible Luke 5:30.
55 Bible John 8:41 - 44.
56 Bible Math 6:5.

Chapter 7

1 Bible Mathew 21:7.
2 Ibid 21:4
3 Bible Zechariah 9:9.
4 Bible Luke 19:2.
5 Bible Mathew 21:10.
6 Bible Luke 22:36.
7 Bible Mathew 26:31.
8 Bible Mathew 27:56 27:61 28:1 Mark 14:3 15:40 15:47 16:1 Luke 24:10 John 11:2 19:25 Acts 12:12.
9 Bible Mathew 13:55, 27:56 Mark 3:17, 15:40 Luke 6:16, 24:10 John 19:25 Acts 1:13
10 Bible Mathew 1:9, 27:56.
11 Bible John 1:50.
12 Bible Mathew 16:11, 17:17 Mark 8:17 Luke 9:45.
13 Bible Galatians 1:19.
14 Bible Acts 9:3.
15 Bible Acts 1:13.
16 Bible John 13:26.
17 Bible Mark 14:3, John 12:1.
18 Bible John 11:36, 11:3.
19 Bible John 13:23, 19:26, 20:2, 21:7, 21:20 etc;
20 Bible John 13:23-26.
21 Bible Mathew 26:48 Mark 14:44.
22 Bible John 13:29.
23 Ibid 19:26.
24 Ibid 21:20.
25 Ibid 21:24.
26 Ibid 18:15.
27 Ibid 19:26.
28 Ibid 21:20-22.
29 Bible John 13:27-30.
30 Ibid 21:21-25
31 Nag Hammadi Library in English, E J brill, p201. Book of Thomas, NH 138:10.
32 Bible appendix. St James, Oxford University Press Edition - 1899.
33 Ibid p124, 199.
34 Ibid 11:5.
35 Nag Hamaddi Scrolls, Gospel of Philip.
36 Bible John 11:20.
37 Ibid 11:2.
38 Ibid 11:1, 12:1 Mark 14:3.
39 Bible Genesis 19:32.
40 Bloodline of the Holy Grail, L Gardner.
41 Guinness encyclopedia of the Human Being, Dr Robert Youngson.
42 Bloodline of the Holy Grail, L Gardner, p 199.
43 Bible Mark 15:34.
44 T Hull 2, 22-23.
45 Bible John 19:30.
46 Bible Mark 15:44.
47 Bible John 19:39.
48 Bible Genesis 50:26.
49 British Museum Dictionary of Ancient Egypt, I Shaw.

Chapter 8

1 Bible Corinth I 9:20 - 25.

2 Bible Acts 8:3.
3 Ibid 9:21 - 26.
4 Ibid 18:3.
5 Ibid 19:12.
6 Ibid 19:16.
7 Ibid 21:16.
8 Ibid 26:1.
9 Bible Romans 11:13.
10 Ibid 3:29.
11 Bible Corinth II 12:11.
12 Bible Galatians 5:02.
13 Ibid 5:12.
14 Bible Acts 9:22.
15 Ibid 13:10.
16 Bible Timothy I 1:15.
17 Ibid 2:7.
18 Bible Corinth I 11:16.
19 Ibid 11:31.
20 Bible Acts 22:3.
21 Ibid 22:3.
22 Ibid 22:27, 13:6.
23 Ibid 23:6.
24 Bible Timothy I 2:7.
25 Bible Acts 8:3.
26 Ibid 9:3.
27 Ibid 9:10 - 15.
28 Ibid 21:37.
29 Ibid 21:38, 21:40.
30 Ibid 18:1, 20:1.
31 Ibid 14:19.
32 Ibid 21:32, 22:24.
33 Ibid 23:24, 24:1.
34 Ibid 24:26.
35 Ibid 26:30.
36 Ibid 27:1.
37 Ibid 27:41.
38 Josephus L 2.
39 Ibid 7.
40 Ibid 423.
41 Ibid 12.
42 Ibid 80.
43 Ibid 18, & LCL introduction ix.
44 Ibid 208.
45 Ibid 216.
46 Josephus JW 2:261.
47 Josephus Ant 20:263.
48 Josephus Penguin Classics p10.
49 Josephus L 95.
50 Ibid 412, 94, 139.
51 Josephus JW 2:289.
52 Ibid 2:273.
53 Ibid 2:309.
54 Josephus L 13.
55 Ibid 15.
56 Josephus Penguin Classics p15.
57 Josephus L 365.
58 Josephus Penguin Classics p15.
59 Josephus Ant 6:68 - 88.
60 Bible Acts 1:23.
61 Josephus JW 2:425, 254.
62 Bible Luke 6:15, 6:16.
63 Josephus JW 2:259.
64 Ibid 261.
65 Bible Luke 22:36.
66 Ibid 22:39, John 18:3.
67 Bible Mark 14:49
68 Bible Acts 20:9.
69 Habakkuk 1QpHab VI ii,15.
70 Josephus L 65.
71 Peak's commentry on the Bible.
72 Josephus L 66.
73 Ibid 190 - 193.
75 Josephus JW 2:566 - 568.
76 Ibid 3:450.
77 Ibid 4:238.
80 Ibid 15:1.
81 Josephus JW 6:300 - 305.
82 Josephus L 200.
83 Ibid 246.
84 Ibid 294.
85 Ibid 208.
86 Bible Acts 9:4
87 Josephus L 295.
88 Bible Corinth I 6:9 - 11.
89 Ibid 5:1.
90 Ibid 16:2.
91 Bible Corinth II 2:1.
92 Ibid 12:14.
93 Bible Philippians 4:16.
94 Ibid 4:19.

Chapter 9

1 Josephus JW, Penguin Classics, end synopsis.
2 Bible Mathew 23:13, 23:34.
3 Josephus JW 4:259 -263.
4 Bible Mathew 23:35.
5 Josephus JW 4:334.
6 Bible Luke 19:2 - 5.
7 Bible II Chronicles 24:20.
8 Legend, David Rohl p196.
9 Bible Genesis 9:20.
10 Koran 3:37 - 51, 19:7 - 28.
11 Bible Math 9:9, 10:3, Mk 2:14, 3:18.
12 Josephus JW 3:354.

13 Ibid 3:401.
14 Ibid 3:450.
15 Ibid 3:502.
16 Ibid 4:160.
17 Ibid 4:232.
18 Ibid 5:435.
19 Ibid 7:421.

Chapter 10

1 Minorca, David Taylor p42.
2 Internet description of Taules, Ferran Lagarda i Mata, 1996, http://classicweb.com/usr/magazine/menorca/arqme23.htm Kindly allerted to my attantion by Stephen Johnson.
3 Heiroglyphs, Maria C. Betro.
4 Bloodline of the Holy Grail, L Gardner p 197.
5 Ibid p 144-145.
6 Grolier CD Rom Encyclopaedia.
7 The Celtic Tradition, Caitlin Mathews p38.
8 Monasterboice and its Monuments, H Roe p78.
9 Ibid p 10.
10 London Times, 12-11-98.
11 The obelisks of Egypt, Labib Habachi p48.
12 Josephus JW 7:426.
13 The obelisks of Egypt, Labib Habachi p112 - 131.
14 The Woman with the Alabaster Jar, Starbird p50.
15 Koran 2:122.
16 Minorca, David Taylor.
17 http://luna.cas.usf.edu/~rtykot/index.html
http://www.abc.sardegna.it/luoghi/
http://www.vol.it/EDICOLA/ISV/nuraghi/eng.nuraghi.html
18 Oxford Illustrated Prehistory of Europe, Barry cunliffe p 277.
19 Ibid p 293.
20 Ibid p 287.
21 Bible Genesis 26:1.
22 Ibid 10:14.
23 Origins, Barry Cunliffe p 73.
24 Bible I Samuel chapter 6.
25 Encyclopaedia Britanica.
26 Ibid.
27 Ibid.
28 Origins, Barry Cunliffe p 147.
29 Myth and Symbol in Ancient Egypt, R. T. Rundle-Clarke.
30 Ancient Egyptian Pyramid Texts, R. Faulkner N° 1652.
31 Orientalia Vol 39, J. Baines.
32 The Templar revelations, Clive Prince, Lynn Picknett.
33 Encyclopaedia Britanica.
34 Ibid.
35 Civilization of the Goddess, Marija Gimbutas.
36 Hierogliphics, Maria Carmela Betro, p55.

List Of Diagrams

Photo Credits

Plate 1.	Tree of Knowledge	Ralph Ellis.
Plate 2.	Finding of Moses	National Gallery.
Plate 3.	Adoration of Golden Calf	National Gallery.
Plate 4.	Akhenaton	Ralph Ellis.
Plate 5.	Nefertiti	Corel Library.
Plate 6.	Akhenaton	Ralph Ellis.
Plate 7.	Plain of Akhetaton - Amarna	Ralph Ellis.
Plate 8.	Boundary stele	Ralph Ellis.
Plate 9.	Mud-brick	Ralph Ellis.
Plate 10.	Mud-brick	Ralph Ellis.
Plate 11.	Palace of Akhenaton	Ralph Ellis.
Plate 12.	Temple of Aton - Amarna	Ralph Ellis.
Plate 13.	Pieta - Rome	Ralph Ellis.
Plate 14.	Rock crystal altar	Ralph Ellis.
Plate 15.	Dome on the Rock	Corel Library.
Plate 16.	Dead Christ mourned	National Gallery.
Plate 17.	Holy of Holies	Ralph Ellis.
Plate 18.	Sun imagery	Ralph Ellis.
Plate 19.	Sun imagery	Ralph Ellis.
Plate 20.	Sun imagery	Palma Cathedral.
Plate 21.	Sun imagery	Corel Library.
Plate 22.	Egyptian side curls	Ralph Ellis.
Plate 23.	Jewish side curls	Corel Library.
Plate 24.	Talati Taule	Stephen Johnson.
Plate 25.	Torralba Taule	Stephen Johnson.
Plate 26.	Bull headed god	Ralph Ellis.
Plate 27.	Ram headed god	Ralph Ellis.
Plate 28.	Cult of the ram	Ralph Ellis.
Plate 29.	Nuraghi Tintirriolu	Robert Tykot.
Plate 30.	Erismanzanu Nuraghi	Robert Tykot..
Plate 31.	Artists impression of Nuraghi	Ralph Ellis, after Salvatore Mullin.
Plate 32.	Kalyan Minaret	Fitzroy Maclean.
Plate 33.	Khiva Minaret	Corel Library.
Plate 34.	Cromwell Bible	Ralph Ellis.
Plate 35.	Monasterboice tower	Ralph Ellis.
Plate 36.	Domhnach tower	Ralph Ellis.
Plate 37.	Monasterboice tower	Ralph Ellis.
Plate 38.	Domhnach tower	Ralph Ellis.
Plate 39.	Egyptian obelisk, Rome	Scott Gilchrist.
Plate 40.	Tomb of Atreus	Scott Gilchrist.
Plate 41.	Egyptian obelisk, Vatican	Scott Gilchrist.
Plate 42.	Newgrange, Eire	Duchas Heritage.
Plate 43.	Masonic Grand Lodge	Ralph Ellis.

Index

T